American Bandstand

American Bandstand

Dick Clark and the Making of a Rock 'n' Roll Empire

John A. Jackson

Oxford University Press
New York · Oxford

Oxford University Press

Oxford   New York
Athens Auckland Bangkok Bogotá Buenos Aires Calcutta
Cape Town Chennai Dar es Salaam Delhi Florence Hong Kong Istanbul
Karachi Kuala Lumpur Madrid Melbourne Mexico City Mumbai
Nairobi Paris São Paulo Singapore Taipei Tokyo Toronto Warsaw

and associated companies in

Berlin   Ibadan

Copyright © 1997 by John A. Jackson

First published by Oxford University Press, Inc., 1997

First issued as an Oxford University Press paperback, 1999

Oxford is a registered trademark of Oxford University Press

Library of Congress Cataloging-in-Publication Data
Jackson, John A., 1943–
American Bandstand : Dick Clark and
the making of a rock 'n' roll empire / John A. Jackson
p. cm.   Includes bibliographical references and index.

ISBN: 978-0-19-513089-8
1. American Bandstand (television program)
2. Popular music—United States.
3. Rock music—United States.   I. Title.
ML 3477.J33 1997   791.45'72—dc21   96-53474

For my sister and brother,
Joanie and Bob

Contents

Preface

"I don't make culture, I sell it."
—DICK CLARK

Amerian pop culture, which exploded after the conclusion of World War II, was fueled by a cornucopia of consumer goods that included television—a window that provided visual context where none had existed.[1] Nationwide programming, whereby a single broadcast could be beamed into every American city and town, began when the East and West Coasts became linked by coaxiable cable in November 1951. It was this event that transformed television from a largely urban, eclectic phenomenon into an effective entertainment delivery system aimed at the widest possible audience, and it was from that moment on that television became the unstoppable financial and cultural force that it is today.

The advent of rock 'n' roll, a music drawn from the minority genres of blues, rhythm and blues, hillbilly, and country and western, was an integral part of America's pop-culture boom, which happened to coincide with the development of network television. The music was originally the stepchild of radio—which took to playing records as a cost-saving measure after network television siphoned off radio's most lucrative sponsors. But it was network television, and specifically the teenage dance show *American Bandstand* that, by beaming bowdlerized rock 'n' roll into America's living rooms, ultimately legitimized—some would say destroyed—what was viewed by most adults as vulgar, low-class music.

One man was responsible for making *American Bandstand* happen. On the surface, the bland, seemingly mild-mannered, white middle-American Dick

Clark may seem like an unlikely selection for that role, but a closer look indicates that a man of Clark's make-up and character was needed to pull off the feat he did.

One of network television's first indigenous personalities, Clark has logged more hours in front of the cameras than Johnny Carson. He is one of the medium's foremost celebrities (the first to have shows appear simultaneously on all three networks) and one of Hollywood's most successful independent producers. Yet Clark remains of interest primarily because of his association with the landmark network television show *American Bandstand*.

Given today's multicultural, one hundred–plus TV channel culture it is almost impossible to appreciate the impact *American Bandstand* had on popular music, the business of music, and on American society itself. Beginning in August 1957, Clark's afternoon show—an endless offering of popular recording stars, hit songs, dance crazes, and other fads—became a rallying point around which America's first teenage constituency was able to connect. *American Bandstand* also afforded Madison Avenue and its sponsor-clients their initial marketing assault on the leading edge of the country's teenage post–World War II baby boomer population and became the very heartbeat of a revived pop music industry in which Clark was heavily—albeit somewhat clandestinely—involved.

Ironically, during the mid-1950s, the concept of teenagers dancing to current hit songs was so anomalous that the television networks wanted no part of it. It is a credit to Clark's tenacity and persuasive manner that he singlehandedly convinced the then-struggling ABC network to give his show (which had already been a hit in the Philadelphia area for five years) a national tryout. *American Bandstand* proceeded to do nothing less than lead ABC into daytime television.

A good portion of the universal appeal of Clark's show stemmed from its likeable, low-key host. But few realized that behind his unostentatious, "aw shucks" mask there lurked a cunning business impresario who could stand toe-to-toe with the best of them when negotiating a deal. And just as there was more to Clark than his "good guy" persona, there was more to *American Bandstand* than met the eye. The surprise success of the show thrust Clark into the national spotlight, thereby affording him the opportunity to capitalize on his unique status as the country's only nationally televised disc jockey. Although Clark had originally entered broadcasting in pursuit of a career in television (as well as for financial gain—but not because of any interest in music), given his fortuitous circumstances, he decided to let music make money for him.

At the time, the record business was an unbridled industry in which it was possible for an entrepreneurial soul such as Clark to invest a few hundred dollars to make a phonograph record and come up with a million-seller. Virtually anyone could walk into a radio station with a freshly pressed record under his arm and fifty dollars folded neatly into the record sleeve and convince a disc jockey to play the song that very evening. Although Clark was never accused of partaking in that controversial practice, he did involve himself in every facet of the pop music business, utilizing his national TV podium to promote records that he owned, or in which he had a financial stake. Utilizing his choir-boy looks and a squeaky-clean image, Clark shrewdly melded the fledgling ABC television network and rock 'n' roll, making the music (and himself) safe for household consumption.

As the nation's top disc jockey, Clark enjoyed the best of both worlds. He had to convince no one but himself to play records in which he held some financial interest. "I was an entrepreneur," he explained. "I used every single opportunity I could to make money. I managed artists, I pressed records, I did tours, I owned labels, I did everything I could think to turn a dollar. . . ."[2]

Surprisingly, most of the recording artists who appeared on *American Bandstand*, and whose records Clark had an interest in, do not regret that the show's host profited from their efforts while they received nominal (if any) record-sales royalties and often had to kick back their *Bandstand* performance fees in order to appear on the show. Even though many of the singers were not aware of the wheeling and dealing that went on behind their backs at the time, most say that, had they known, they still would have approved of it, because they considered an appearance on Clark's show to be a coup.

Many of those performers feel fortunate just to have experienced a brief moment in the limelight. Some do believe they were cheated or used, but almost all agree that the backroom business deals that went down did not interest them in the least. All they wanted to do was perform, make records, and, if fortunate enough, make a living from doing so. Clark, on the other hand, wanted to make big money.

Initially, *American Bandstand* was an amalgamation of those disparate yet compatible desires, but the broadcasting payola scandal that erupted in 1959 —in which various disc jockeys were accused of taking bribes to play certain records on the air—upset the applecart and put the promising career of America's chief rock 'n' roll progenitor squarely on the line.

To Clark's credit, he not only survived the scandal, he emerged from it bigger than ever. But the violent social upheaval of the 1960s proceeded to knock *Bandstand* from its pop pedestal, and the show's popularity, as well as its impact within the pop music business, began to wane. *Bandstand* regained some of its popularity during the 1970s, but by then the show's reputation as a musical and social authority was eclipsed by its storied legacy.

For millions of fans today, *American Bandstand* remains a fond memory. And thanks to cable television rebroadcasts of episodes of the show from the seventies and eighties, Clark's dance show has become familiar to yet another generation. But even after nearly four decades of viewing, few really know what went on behind the cameras of the show that, for a time, shaped rock 'n' roll and teenage culture itself.

American Bandstand is the first comprehensive study of *American Bandstand* not authorized or orchestrated by Dick Clark. The book provides an impartial look at the influential television program and examines how Clark came to appropriate *Bandstand* and skillfully apply the show to further his own career. In doing so, *American Bandstand* considers facets of the *Bandstand* story heretofore unexplored: Why and how was the local *Bandstand* concept originally conceived? Why was a person with Clark's impeccably clean-cut image needed to rescue the show from a teenage sex scandal? How did Clark singlehandedly convince ABC to broadcast *Bandstand* nationally, and how did he use his unique position as America's only nationally televised disc jockey to fashion a financial empire from within the pop music industry?

American Bandstand also reveals just how close Clark came to being dismissed by ABC, why such a move would most likely have meant the demise of *American Bandstand* and how Clark not only survived the ordeal, but managed to bounce back bigger than ever. Also examined is the mutual relationship that existed between *American Bandstand* and ABC; how societal forces managed to overcome broadcasting's racist restrictions and ultimately cause *Bandstand* to embrace blacks and their music; and how the network's eventual success contributed to the show's decline. *American Bandstand* also reveals why Clark finally pulled the plug on his celebrated program just months short of it entering its fourth decade on television.

Until now, much of the *Bandstand* story has existed only in the memories of those who have lived it—music business and broadcasting executives, disc jockeys, recording artists, and Dick Clark himself. Many of those who had a hand in this tale had already passed on before I began the research for this book, and in the four years since, no less than four others have died, thereby injecting a sense of urgency into the task of completing this story. To an overwhelming degree, the persons I sought to interview for *American Bandstand* readily agreed, but I was told by several individuals, including one particularly close to Clark, that Clark would not take part in an unauthorized project such as this. (Clark has classified writers as "the lowest." He says, "I don't know anyone who has good feelings about people who write for a living. . . . Their overt jealousy of celebrities comes out in print. Their stories reek of sour grapes."[3]) Nevertheless, when I explained to Clark what I had in mind, he replied in his most congenial and businesslike manner: "Why don't you shoot me direct questions? I'll see what I can do to come up with the answers."

The recollections of those who were there, plus a substantial amount of additional research, have resulted in *American Bandstand*, which tells a story that, until now, few outside the show's inner circle have been aware of. Unless otherwise noted, all quotations in this book are taken from interviews which I conducted over the past sixteen years. See the bibliography for complete list of interviews and dates.

John A. Jackson
1996

Acknowledgments

Thanks to Lou Antonicello, Stan Barbato, Steve Bass, Vicki and Steve Blitenthal of Whirlin' Disc Records, Mark DelCostello, Peter Dorchak, Jim Gallagher, Marv Goldberg, William F. Griggs, Wayne Jones, Doug Lumpkin, Richard Nader, and George Nettleton for their assistance in this project. I also wish to remember the late "Krazy Greg" Milewski, whose help was appreciated. I miss Greg's friendship and his boundless enthusiasm for rock 'n' roll. Thanks also to all those who consented to be interviewed and extended their time and shared their recollections with me. A special thank you goes to R&B Records baron Val Shively for his generous and invaluable assistance, and to Val and his wife Patty for making me feel at home during the time I spent in Philadelphia.

I also wish to thank the staffs of the Copiague (N.Y.) Public Library; Temple University's Paley Library, particularly Margaret Jerrido and George Brightbill of the Urban Archives collection; the Philadelphia Public Library; and the New York Public Library at Lincoln Center, especially the staff of the Billy Rose Theatre Collection.

Thank you to Oxford University Press music editor Maribeth Payne for having faith in this project when it was little more than an outline; to my editor, Soo Mee Kwon; and to my literary agent, Nancy Love.

Finally, thanks to Dick Clark for making *American Bandstand* possible and for taking the time to be interviewed for this book.

—*John A. Jackson*

American Bandstand

If you're off to Philadelphia in the morning,

You mustn't take my stories for a guide.

There's little left, indeed, of the city you will read of . . .

— RUDYARD KIPLING, *Philadelphia*

CHAPTER 1

Genesis

After almost forty years *in show business and broadcasting Jack Steck, program director at WFIL-TV in Philadelphia, thought he had seen everything. Summoned to the office of general manager Roger W. Clipp one afternoon in 1952, Steck arrived in the boss's lair and was greeted by Clipp and "this good-looking kid."*

"I know this boy's father," said Clipp. "Audition him and tell me if we ought to hire him."[1]

It was not out of the ordinary for Steck to conduct a job audition at WFIL, so he barely gave a thought to Dick Clark as he escorted the twenty-two-year-old prospect into the program director's office and handed him the usual assortment of tongue-twisting material he used to audition would-be announcers. Steck then showed Clark into a studio and said, "Look them over, son. I'll come back in fifteen minutes to listen to you."

Clark, who was then employed by a small television station in upstate New York, said in 1994 that the WFIL position "was the biggest one" of the three job offers he had at the time, and was the one he wanted so badly that he literally had something up his sleeve to help land it. "God, if I could jump from Utica, New York to Philadelphia, that'll be amazing," he thought to himself.

Steck, who began his show business career on the vaudeville circuit ("some of my best friends said I helped kill it") as a dancer, comic, and an emcee, did not expect to hear anything out of the ordinary when he returned to give the dapper job applicant a listen.[2] *At that point, Dick Clark was just another pretty face to the veteran program director, who sat with arms folded and head down. "I didn't want to look at him," recalled Steck. "I needed a man for radio and I didn't want to be influenced by his appearance. I wanted a voice!"*

Steck had just begun to concentrate on Clark's delivery when he was inter-

rupted by the engineer on duty, who said, "Hey Stecky, look at this kid!" Steck raised his head and observed Clark standing in front of the microphone, "with no notes in his hands, no papers, doing the commercials word-for-word, introducing the music, the sports, doing the whole thing."

"How the hell's he doing this?" wondered the program director. "Has he got a photographic memory?"

What Clark had was "Elmer," a Webcor wire recorder that was hidden from Steck's view. In one of Clark's ears was a tiny earphone connected to the recorder by a wire concealed under his clothing. As he surreptitiously listened to the recording he had just made of Steck's audition material, the young announcer repeated it for the program director without so much as a glance at the script.

It did not take Steck long to discover Clark's wire recorder and earpiece, and when he did he was impressed, not so much by Clark's ingenuity, but by the fact that he was able to repeat the playback without a faraway concentrated look in his eye. "He had mastered that thing!" recalled Steck, who fired off a memo to Roger Clipp: "In spite of his university education, this is a smart kid. Let's hire him."

• • •

Whether Clark would have landed the WFIL announcer's position without the assistance of Elmer will never be known, although the subsequent course of his career indicates that to think otherwise would be foolhardy. In order to display greater broadcasting skill than he then possessed, Clark relied on his hidden tape recorder for assistance, making himself out to be something greater than he actually was. But after being hired by WFIL and embarking upon his quest to become a twenty-something millionaire, Clark adopted a new, self-effacing tack, portraying himself as something less than he actually was. Despite his introduction to America as a benign television host, when it came to advancing himself, Clark was more akin to a wolf in sheep's clothing—a sharply focused self-promoter and cunning businessman who went to great lengths to contrive his public image.

As Jack Steck observed that fateful day in 1952, there was more to Dick Clark than met the eye.

• • •

Richard Wagstaff Clark was born on November 30, 1929, the second son of Richard Augustus and Julia Barnard Clark, in the tiny village of Bronxville, a corporate executive haven of turn-of-the-century homes, located just north of New York City. Although Dick Clark was not born with the proverbial silver spoon in his mouth, his father's position as sales manager for a New York-based cosmetics firm ensured that young Dickie, as he was called, would enjoy a comfortable, if isolated, childhood.

In 1933 the Clarks moved to the affluent Westchester bedroom community of Mt. Vernon, just south of Bronxville, where they leased a garden apartment adjacent to spacious grounds where Dickie and his brother Bradley could romp freely. The younger Clark brother, a frenetic, contentious nail-biter of a child, idolized Brad, who was five years his elder, and in later years would describe him as a "quiet, very loving, wonderful guy . . . everything I wasn't."

Noted dancer Kathryn Murray was a neighbor of the Clarks and sometimes baby-sat for Dickie. Mrs. Murray remembered him as "the sassiest baby, always busy, always into something." But despite Dick's cantankerousness, the Clark brothers developed a tight bond. Brad "lugged Dick around everywhere and was so patient with him," Julia Clark told a reporter for the *New York Post* in 1958.[3]

By the time Dick became a teenager, the personable, good-looking, and star athlete Brad was a Big Man on Campus at Mt. Vernon's A.B. Davis High. Meanwhile, Dick, who envisioned himself as "peculiar looking and generally odd," was handicapped by a severe inferiority complex.[4] Not even his election as junior class president helped overcome any shortcoming Dick felt from being overshadowed by his revered older brother.

Brad graduated from Davis High in 1943, and, as World War II raged, he applied and was selected for a coveted spot in the army air corp' pilot training program. The realities of war were overshadowed by what Brad saw as a golden opportunity to learn to fly at the government's expense, and he elatedly shared his good fortune with his thirteen-year-old brother. But Dick did not share Brad's enthusiasm. "I sat on the bed in the room we shared and I sulked," wrote Clark in his autobiography, *Rock, Roll & Remember*. "It was like he was deliberately deserting me."[5]

By the time Dick entered Davis High in September 1943, Brad was flying P–47 fighter missions over Europe. Cowed by the school's labyrinth of corridors crowded with upperclassmen who appeared to be a million years older than they actually were, Dick Clark's greatest fear was about to be realized.

A few days after Christmas, 1944, the Clark family received the devastating news that Brad had been shot down and killed during the Battle of the Bulge in Germany. The death of the older brother he idolized has had a profound effect on Clark, who each year finds it more difficult to comprehend that Brad died before reaching the age of twenty-one. "My children are all older than this man I visualize as my big brother,"[6] he told Ralph Emery in 1992.

Debilitated by his grief, Clark embarked on a mad spree to become the equal of his dead brother. He headed for the football field where Brad had starred as a first-string tackle. But the 120-pound novice quickly discovered that aside from being a tackling dummy he was not much use to the team. He tried other sports at which Brad had excelled, but failed to make the swimming and track squads as well.

Frustrated by his athletic failure, Clark retreated to his bedroom, turned on the radio, and sought refuge in what he called "the disembodied fantasy world that came out of the speaker." He had recently discovered what he termed "the magic world of radio" when, at age thirteen, his parents took him to New York City to see a live broadcast of the Jimmy Durante–Garry Moore radio program. Captivated by the performances of the radio personalities as well as by the behind-the-scenes activity in the control room, Clark told his mother, "That's what I want to do."[7]

Clark was able to break the shackles of insecurity through his participation in the high school drama club, which his parents encouraged him to join. Clark's dramatics teacher recalled that because of his emotional performance in the senior class play, "there wasn't a dry eye in the house."[8] Clark gave serious thought to becoming an actor, but his father—who once harbored those same youthful aspirations—dissuaded his son from the pursuit of what he viewed as a capricious facet of show business.

By the time Clark was ready to graduate from high school, vestiges of his future were evident. He gave great consideration to the pursuit of a radio career, and was deemed by his premonitory peers to be "The Man Most Likely to Sell the Brooklyn Bridge."[9]

In the spring of 1947, just prior to Clark's graduation from high school, his family moved from Mt. Vernon to Utica, a small city located in the rolling hills of central upstate New York. Clark's uncle Bradley Barnard lived nearby in the city of Rome, where he owned the local *Sentinel* newspaper and the ABC-affiliated, Utica-based radio station WRUN. Aware of his brother-in-law's sales and promotion savvy, Barnard asked Dick Clark's father if he was interested in making a career change.

After twenty-six years, Richard Augustus Clark and his wife had had enough of the cosmetics business rat race and longed to return to their upstate roots. In addition, the elder Clark, who was aware of Dick's interest in a radio career, realized that a move to WRUN would enhance his son's broadcasting opportunities. So it was that when Barnard offered his brother-in-law the opportunity to become the station's first promotional manager, Richard Clark accepted.

When it came time for Dick Clark to apply to college his first choice was

Yale, but Clark's grades were not up to Ivy League snuff. Rejected by Yale, he opted for nearby Syracuse University, his father's alma mater.

With Bradley Barnard's approval, Richard Clark hired his son Dick as a summer replacement at WRUN, where the college-bound student worked in the mailroom, ran the office mimeograph machine, and longingly eyed the broadcasting microphone. Dick's initial broadcasting opportunity came when he was assigned to read hourly weather forecasts for a vacationing FM announcer. Although Clark admitted he was buried at WRUN, "about as deep as they could bury someone without experience," it was of little concern. He was on the air, and the following morning he rigged up a home antenna so his mother could hear his voice on the radio.[10]

Clark entered Syracuse University in the fall of 1947 as an advertising major with a minor in radio. Although he was required to concentrate on his major area of study, Clark was not deterred from seeking out WEAR-FM, the campus radio station known as Radio House. After auditioning for Radio House student manager Jerry Landay, Clark joined the WEAR staff as a disc jockey and newscaster. But the would-be announcer was already looking beyond the microphone. In 1987 Clark revealed that he "never fully intended to make radio announcing a lifetime pursuit," and that as early as his WEAR days he was eyeing the *business* aspects of broadcasting.[11]

Clark worked at the campus radio station during his four years at college, and in January 1951—during his last semester before graduation—he landed a weekend job at WOLF-AM (1490hz), a tiny 250-watt station in downtown Syracuse. In less than a month he was working a full forty-hour week at WOLF, in addition to completing his studies at Syracuse University. From WOLF's Onondaga Hotel studios Clark announced the news and hosted a show called *The WOLF Buckaroos*, on which he spun country records by the likes of Gene Autry, Eddie Arnold, and Roy Rogers. After graduating from Syracuse that May with a B.S. degree in business administration, Clark stayed on at WOLF, where he earned a dollar an hour.

It was the wish of Richard Clark, then the communications-sales manager at WRUN, that his son eventually succeed him in that position. That June, Dick Clark quit WOLF and returned to Utica and a summer replacement job at the station where his father worked, but the younger Clark, who had moved back in with his parents at their home, was no longer comfortable working in his father's shadow. It seemed that whatever he accomplished, someone stood ready to credit the feat to his father's influence. "I was working too hard to prove myself to get put down like that," said Clark.[12]

Determined to make his own mark, Clark left WRUN in the fall of 1951. To punctuate his emergence from his father's shadow, he changed his name to

"Dick Clay." Clark was certain the name change hurt both his parents, and he even confessed to his own dislike of the moniker. But he kept it.

With his new name, "Dick Clay" went looking for a new job. He auditioned for a newscasting position at Utica-Rome's WKTV, where he was hired by the general manager, who had come to know Clark's father. It was while Clark was employed at WKTV that he was taken aback by fellow newscaster Bob Earle, who, rather than rely on a hand-held script to deliver the news, stared directly into the camera and did the entire newscast—up to fifteen minutes at a stretch—as if he had it memorized. Unable to contain his curiosity, Clark asked Earle how he was able to manage the feat, and Earle shared with him the secret of "Elmer," his wire recorder.

As impressed as Clark was, he set out to one-up Bob Earle. After purchasing his own Webcor wire recorder Clark devised a system that incorporated a foot pedal, which enabled him to start and stop the tape whenever he chose and then move about freely in front of the TV cameras. When Clark was not working he spent many hours secreted away at WRUN's radio studio, where, out of sight of his WKTV colleagues, he practiced his tape-recorded delivery. WRUN's Al Cole recalled that after Clark began doing televised news commentary on WKTV, "Utica teenagers suddenly became very interested in current events."[13]

Clark's chores at WKTV also included playing Cactus Dick, the host of the television station's country and western music show, *Cactus Dick and the Santa Fe Riders*. Besides serving as the show's announcer, Clark did some singing. "Badly," he confessed to Ralph Emery in 1992. "They used to make fun of me."[14]

Clark, who now earned $52.50 a week and was the proud owner of a 1941 Oldsmobile sedan, began to be courted by Syracuse's WHEN-TV. WKTV general manager Michael Fusco promptly upped Cactus Dick's salary to $75 a week, which kept his budding star from jumping to WHEN, but, salary increase or not, after less than a year, "Dick Clay" had grown too big for Utica. When he told his father he was ready to move on to a larger city, Richard Clark, knowing exactly who to contact, telephoned a colleague in Philadelphia whom he had befriended through ABC's executive channels. (WRUN was an ABC affiliate.) It was that call to WFIL's Roger Clipp that led to Dick Clark's audition with Jack Steck.

After Clark was hired by WFIL Steck offered him a summer replacement slot on the station's FM band, but not before the veteran program director, who envisioned the coming age of television, admonished the young announcer that he was crazy to even consider returning to radio—particularly FM radio, which was then considered a broadcasting graveyard. After his TV experience in Utica, Clark was not at all certain he wanted to return to radio. A job offer he had recently received from a television station in Schenectady, New York only served to complicate matters. But Schenectady was no larger than Utica, while Philadelphia was a major city where Clark knew he would attract more attention. Philadelphia was also closer to New York, an important consideration for a young man on the move who still considered himself a New Yorker. "After all," said Philadelphia's newest announcer as he bid farewell to Utica, "WFIL has a TV station, too." [15]

Dick Clark may have glided into broadcasting on his father's coattails, but the innuendos that linked Clark's advancement to being the boss's son understandably rankled him. His initial broadcasting success was due at least as much to his considerable professional aplomb as it was to his father's broadcasting connections. Nevertheless, Clark was once again beholden to his father. But what mattered most to the young announcer was that he would now be heard in Philadelphia, a city whose three-and-one-half-million potential listeners—a far cry from Utica's one hundred thousand—made it the fourth-largest metropolitan area in the United States. Clark began work at WFIL on May 13, 1952.

One of the country's oldest commercial broadcasters, WFIL was founded as WFI in 1922, became an affiliate of the fledgling American Broadcasting Company in 1943, and was purchased in 1945 by Triangle Publications Inc., a blossoming communications empire owned by Walter Annenberg, the wealthy son of a publishing magnate. In 1947 Annenberg established WFIL-TV, which was Philadelphia's first commercial TV station. WFIL-TV not only became ABC-TV's initial affiliate, it quickly developed into that network's key TV outlet outside New York City.

Forty-eight-year-old Roger W. Clipp, who ran WFIL for Walter Annenberg, was the quintessence of the obdurate organization man, and then some. After earning a degree from the University of Pennsylvania's prestigious Wharton School of Business, Clipp had embarked upon a banking career cut short by the stock market crash of 1929. Clipp received his baptism into the backroom world of broadcasting via a stint as an NBC accountant before advancing to assistant manager of NBC's owned-and-operated stations. He became WFIL's business manager in 1935, after which he methodically climbed the station's executive ladder until he oversaw WFIL's entire operation as its general manager.

Clipp "was a very unreasonable, temperamental man . . . very cruel and pretty vicious," said Jack Steck, who recalled the time a young announcer committed a mispronunciation gaffe on the air just before Christmas and was summarily dismissed by Clipp. Many on the WFIL staff grudgingly characterized Clipp as "a son-of-a-bitch, but *our* son-of-a-bitch," which, thought Steck, "was a pretty good description." But despite Steck's animosity towards Clipp, whose antics were "carefully shielded" from Walter Annenberg, Steck conceded that the station's general manager was a "great administrator . . . [who] turned WFIL into a $210-million property for the boss."[16]

• • •

During the summer of 1952, WFIL combined its center-city radio facilities with the station's TV operations, already housed in a ware-house-type structure at 46th and Market Streets in West Philadelphia. No one had the slightest inkling that the beige brick building situated in the shadows of the Market Street elevated railway would spawn the longest-run-ning network television show in history and for a time enable Philadelphia to become the pop music capital of the world. By then, WFIL was one of over three hundred ABC-affiliated radio stations, but those numbers were illusory, for when the Federal Communications Commission (FCC) lifted its four-year ban on the establishment of new TV stations that summer, network sponsors abandoned radio in favor of television. Local radio affiliates such as WFIL were thus forced to develop and expand their own radio programming in order to generate local advertising revenue. Since the most economical form of programming available to a radio station was a disc jockey with a stack of records, WFIL became one of hundreds of radio stations across America to fire their costly resident studio orchestras and embrace such a for-mat. Due largely to such cost-cutting motives, the golden age of the disc jockey was about to begin.

As the summer drew to a close Roger Clipp and radio station manager George Koehler informed Dick Clark that WFIL was about to undergo a radical change in format and they wanted him to be a part of that change.

The decision was not surprising, considering that the hard-nosed execu-tive Clipp, who Clark described as "respected and hated" and a "very difficult man" to work for, had hit it off instantly with his hard-driving young employ-ee. "I found him to be intimidating," Clark revealed in 1994, "but I felt very close to him and he toward me." In fact, Clipp looked upon the recently hired Clark not as the son of a friend, but as the general manager's own son. "He took very good care of me and he didn't frighten me as badly as he frightened some of the other employees," explained Clark. Indeed, Clipp took such good care of Clark that he offered the young announcer a radio program of his own.

Dick Clark's Caravan of Music (weekdays from 1:45 to 6:00 P.M.) was added to WFIL's revamped radio line-up at a time when pop radio's biggest hits were sung by the likes of Patti Page, Perry Como, Rosemary Clooney, Jo Stafford, and South Philadelphia's own Eddie Fisher. But Clark was ordered to forgo even those insipid tunes (which were deemed too extreme for WFIL's conservative daytime format) in favor of easy listening standards.

At that point, it did not matter much to him what type of music he played on his new program. Clark was happy just to have the job, for he was now a married man. One month after joining WFIL's permanent staff he married his high school sweetheart, Barbara ("Bobbie") Mallery, a pretty, blue-eyed cheerleader at A.B. Davis High when she and Clark first met at a Halloween party. Although Barbara was dating Clark's best friend at the time, she soon realized that "Dick was the only boy for me." She and Clark quickly developed into a steady item, but Barbara's mother took a dim view of her fourteen-year-old daughter seeing only one boy. "She liked Dick," recalled Barbara, "but she insisted I was missing half my life, going with just one boy." Barbara and Dick actually broke up for a time, but after dating others they came to realize how much they truly cared for one another. In 1946—Dick's senior year in high school—the couple began to go steady again, and this time, recalled Clark, "we were sure of ourselves."[17]

When Barbara graduated from high school in 1948, the Mallerys moved to Salisbury, Maryland, and Clark began to date other girls at Syracuse. But he preferred seeing Barbara, who was then enrolled at Salisbury State Teachers' College, which necessitated what Clark described as seventeen-hour "sheer suicide" motor trips in his heaterless '34 Ford convertible in the dead of winter.[18]

After two years of this long-distance liaison Barbara transferred to Oswego (N.Y.) State Teachers' College—a mere thirty five-miles from Syracuse—for her junior year. The couple saw each other every weekend until June 28, 1952, when, shortly after Barbara's graduation, they married. After subletting a one-bedroom apartment in suburban Philadelphia, Barbara obtained a job teaching second grade in a nearby school and Clark set out to establish himself at WFIL. Clark would parlay this storybook romance into a vital component of the "All-American Boy" image he so deftly projected to his audience, but, unlike most storybook endings of that era, this one would not find the parties living together happily ever after.

• • •

In 1952, pop radio in Philadelphia was dominated by WPEN-AM (950) and WIP-AM (610), two stations that, not coincidentally, played a part in the genesis of *American Bandstand*. If any program can be designated the prototype for Dick Clark's legendary dance show, that distinction goes to WPEN's *950 Club*, named for the station's location on the AM dial. Originated in 1945 and hosted by the popular duo of Joe Grady and Ed Hurst, the *950 Club* was the first radio show on which a studio audience was invited to dance to records being broadcast over the air. The show, which saluted a different high school each day, quickly became the focus of the area's bobby-sox set, who, seeking admission, deluged WPEN with two to three thousand pieces of mail each week.

But the scores of teenagers drawn to the center city skyscraper that housed WPEN also stuffed mailboxes, rode the elevators, and "created a problem for the tenants of the building" as they ran wild, recalled Ed Hurst, who added that WPEN eventually "got kicked out of the building." The radio station found a new home in a nearby facility that contained a luncheonette in the front and a dance studio in the rear, an arrangement that pleased everyone. The *950 Club* crowd could now munch on hoagies and hot dogs as Grady and Hurst spun the top hits of the day, interviewed celebrity guests, and occasionally allowed the teenage dancers to introduce themselves on the air and mention the high schools they attended. By the early 1950s it was the number one afternoon radio show in Philadelphia and was recognized as a "must" stop by performers making promotional swings through the area. Hurst and Grady interviewed all the top names in the record business.

The big gun at WIP was local favorite Bob Horn. Born in 1916 (d. 1966) in Cherry Run, West Virginia and raised in Reading, Pennsylvania, Robert L. Horn attended the University of Michigan before beginning his broadcasting career in 1938 in Camden, New Jersey. He worked at WIP for a short time before venturing to California, where he put in a brief stint as a Hollywood newscaster. Horn returned to Philadelphia after World War II and landed a job at WPEN, where he developed an evening hour *Bandstand* show consisting of current top pop recordings. In 1951 Horn moved his highly popular *Bandstand* to rival WIP.

As Grady and Hurst cavorted over the airwaves with the Philadelphia area's teenage set, and Bob Horn drew large audiences to his radio *Bandstand*, WFIL radio remained a loser in the local ratings race. As such, the station began to eye Horn — considered about town to be the most knowledgable man on music of the day — to close the gap. "He had the highest rating," recalled Jack Steck, "and we decided to hire him."

Steck, who was then manager of programs and production for WFIL-TV, said Horn was "easy to get because he wanted to get out of radio and into television, and we were his opportunity." So fervently did the video fires burn within Horn that he jumped to WFIL even though there were no immediate television openings at the prestigious TV station. In joining WFIL, Horn reasoned that when such an opening did occur he would be there to grab it.

By far the hottest properties WFIL possessed, Horn and his radio *Bandstand* were assigned two shifts. But as he bided his time for a shot at TV, he was unaware that he had been snookered by his new employer. When the need for an afternoon TV show host arose at WFIL, Horn would be bypassed for none other than Joe Grady and Ed Hurst.

• • •

It was of no concern to Dick Clark that the music he was ordered to play on his WFIL radio program was not current and was certainly not aimed at Philadelphia's "950 Club" crowd. The music be damned. Besides hosting his daily radio program, Clark was afforded the opportunity to work as a commercial announcer on WFIL-TV. In addition to Clark's base pay as a disc jockey he received a fee for each TV commercial he read on the air. Radiating an aura of equanimity, the boyishly handsome Clark set out to do as many of them as humanly possible. "I was a great pitchman," he said. "I sold pots and pans, vacuum cleaners, diamond rings, Mrs. Smiths pies, the works. Eventually I landed the Schaefer Beer account. I did one hell of a beer spot."[19] Clark later revealed in his 1976 autobiography that, "It was the commercials that kept me on the air."[20]

Those close to Clark from childhood were not surprised at how quickly he recognized the lucrative financial opportunities commercial announcing afforded, for Clark had demonstrated a relentless proclivity for entrepreneurship as a youth. The motivation for the boy businessman apparently had had little, if anything, to do with the trappings that money could buy, however, and much to do with the inherent satisfaction of generating his own cash. Not content to draw freely from the family money dish Clark's mother kept in a bureau drawer, Dickie had opted to earn his own money.

As a boy, Clark did not have neighborhood friends so much as he had customers. His activities included publishing a neighborhood gossip sheet and peddling it for two cents an issue; running a "restaurant" in his family's home (when the family peanut butter supply ran out, Clark scoured the kitchen cabinets for old magazines and gum, which he proceded to sell); and operating a shoeshine stand where customers could have one shoe shined for three cents or both for a nickel.

Julia Clark said her son was also a compulsive collector who saved "everything not worth saving." She would periodically clean out his room only to find the same trash reappear, along with "whatever treasures the neighbors had thrown away." But what Clark's mother saw as trash her younger son viewed as valuable merchandise. He held a backyard carnival and used his cache of castoffs as prizes.

As Clark matured, his propensity to earn money grew stronger. One reporter wrote that Clark made himself "eminently hirable" while at Syracuse University, washing dishes in a hashhouse, husking corn, crating chickens, making frat house beds, and trying his hand as a door-to-door brush salesman. "He's always been that way," Julia Clark told a reporter in 1958. "He's always busy."[21]

Indeed, once Clark managed to gain a national television audience of millions and set out to create his own pop music empire, his seemingly innate entrepreneurial drive would serve him well.

• • •

Dick Clark and Bob Horn gave each other a wide berth at WFIL. The fact that Clark, with his fresh, photogenic face, had quickly become one of Philadelphia's busiest commercial announcers particularly rankled the veteran Horn, who coveted a television career of his own. Clark, on the other hand, was solely intent on blazing his own trail and paid Horn no mind.

One of the first commercials Clark did on WFIL-TV was for Barr's Jewelers, the sponsor of the station's early-afternoon movie. He also did a considerable amount of announcing on Paul Whiteman's *TV-Teen Club*, which, along with Grady and Hurst's *950 Club*, proved to be a crucible for WFIL-TV's afternoon dance show called *Bandstand*.

The first personality in Philadelphia to host a network TV show featuring local teenagers was the venerable bandleader-turned-disc jockey Paul Whiteman, the same figure who was dubbed the King of Jazz in the 1920s, but in fact was more "great white hype" than "king" (although he did display a talent for hiring great sidemen). Beginning in 1949, Whitemen invited local teens to a Saturday evening dance and talent show, Paul Whiteman's *TV-Teen Club*, which was televised by WFIL-TV. The show was also broadcast over the fledgling ABC-TV network, in part because Whiteman was vice president in charge of music for the struggling web, but mostly because the program's production expenses were footed by the financially independent Whiteman.

Tipping the scales at almost three hundred pounds, and clad in ornate shirts and loud sports jackets as he articulated hip teen phrases such as "Real gone!" the sixty-two-year-old "Pops" Whiteman seemed to enjoy a second childhood as he conducted his TV show, which was sponsored by Tootsie Roll candy. As the rotund host dispensed his sponsor's chocolate-flavored nuggets to his young guests, Dick Clark stood before the TV cameras and extolled the sugary treats to the viewers at home.

Although *TV-Teen Club* was the first television program to feature teenagers dancing, a more important circumstance of that show was the convergence of Dick Clark and musician/songwriter Bernie Lowe. Whiteman's TV show benefitted Clark in the short run by providing the young announcer with lucrative commercial opportunities, but, more significantly, for the long run it put Clark in good stead with Lowe, a man who in the not-too-distant future would command Philadelphia's leading rock 'n' roll record company.

After Lowe was named musical director of *TV-Teen Club* early in 1952, the show's teenage guests began to partake in what was described as "plain and fancy jitterbugging," to the sounds of his ten-piece band.[22] What is more, the show's weekly talent contest enabled several local teens—Charlie Gracie and Bobby Rydell included—to embark on recording careers that would blossom during the forthcoming *Bandstand* era.

All of the components necessary for the creation of WFIL's televised *Bandstand* were now at hand. Ironically, Dick Clark, who was to become synonymous with the show, was not one of them. For the moment anyway, Clark's vaunted status as a TV pitchman on the programs of others, and the ample income generated by that role, was more than satisfactory to him. The same could not be said for Bob Horn, who burned for his own TV show. While WFIL had the veteran announcer's marquee name and his considerable broadcasting experience at its service, the station had absolutely no reason to offer him a TV slot. But that situation was about to be altered.

CHAPTER 2

Bob Horn's *Bandstand*

While WFIL's radio station struggled to become competitive, WFIL-TV endured problems of its own. The television station's affiliation with the American Broadcasting Company was of dubious value in 1952, because the network had a mere fifteen affiliated TV stations, whereas rivals CBS and NBC commanded thirty-one and sixty-four, respectively. In cities able to support only one or two TV stations ABC was not seen at all. In addition, ABC offered scant evening programming to its affiliates and possessed no daytime schedule whatsoever. To fill its afternoon hours, WFIL-TV showed movies, but Hollywood viewed television as a rival and leased only its most outdated dogs to the upstart medium. It was no surprise, then, when station manager George Koehler informed Roger Clipp that WFIL's afternoon movies were a flop and had to be replaced.

Clipp, who passed the hoards of teenagers waiting to be admitted to WPEN's *950 Club* as he went to work each day, decided he would use WFIL's formidable television station as bait with which to lure Joe Grady and Ed Hurst away from WPEN. Clipp planned to simulcast Grady and Hurst's popular show on radio and television. "You start in two weeks," he told Hurst. "Name your figure."

Hurst, who described himself as being "young and naive" at the time, believed WPEN would grant their wish when he and Grady told the radio station they would "like out" of their contract. Grady, seven years older and apparently that much wiser than his radio sidekick, had his doubts.

Grady was right. It turned out that WPEN was owned by a prosperous pharmaceutical company that poured a million dollars a year in advertising into Walter Annenberg's *Philadelphia Inquirer*. The drug company threatened to pull its account from the *Inquirer* and give it to the rival *Bulletin* if Annenberg's broadcasting outlets continued to woo Grady and Hurst. "So that was the end of that," said Hurst. "[WFIL] called and told us, 'We find this is not the propitious time to bring you guys over here.'"

With the *950 Club* team effectively removed from the picture, WFIL needed something else to fill the slot left vacant by the cancellation of the station's afternoon movie. But what?

It so happened that Roger Clipp had recently (and uncharacteristically) let himself be hoodwinked into purchasing two collections of filmed musical performances—Snader and Official films—one worse than the other ("They were *terrible!*" recalled Jack Steck). Gathering dust in WFIL's archives, the dated musical clips were Clipp's personal skeleton in the closet. Recognizing an opportunity to redeem his folly, he suggested that WFIL begin televising the film shorts.

How to utilize the antiquated clips was George Koehler's problem. Seeking someone with show business acumen, Koehler offered Bob Horn, still marking time at WFIL radio, the TV opportunity for which Horn had been waiting. Laying aside whatever misgivings he may have had concerning the outdated films, Horn told Koehler he would give afternoon television a try.

Horn's new TV show, featuring interviews with whatever guests he could lure to the studio interspersed with Roger Clipp's filmed music shorts, made its debut on WFIL-TV in September 1952. But the host's broadcasting savvy notwithstanding, it was apparent from the start that the show, even as an afteroon timekiller, was dead in the water. While Horn's blend of studio guests and Clipp's outdated music films lacked the catalyst necessary to make the format gel, Horn remained determined that the combination of music and talk could click on TV.

"I'd like to do something else that I know the kids will like," he told WFIL management. "I think it'll guarantee us a great audience."[1] In a move somewhat less daring than Roger Clipp's raid on WPEN, Horn wanted to transfer his successful radio *Bandstand* to television, utilizing Grady and Hurst's highly popular *950 Club* format.

Still smarting from the rebuff by Grady and Hurst's employers, Clipp concurred. But a problem arose when George Koehler insisted that any show based on the popular radio duo's format would need cohosts. Horn, whose plans did not include sharing the television spotlight with anyone, objected strenuously until Koehler gave him the bottom line—no partner, no show.

Bob Horn had thrived in radio, but pitfalls loomed in his attempt to attract Philadelphia's teenage set via TV. Unlike the undiscerning radio microphone behind which Horn had become so popular, the television camera provided an unrelenting visual appraisal of the thirty-seven-year-old broadcasting veteran. Sporting slicked back hair and carrying a few too many pounds, Bob Horn looked more like a used car salesman than a teenager's Svengali.

To complicate matters, Horn's new designated partner, the diminutive, forty-one-year-old Lee Stewart, whose large nose was accentuated by eyeglasses, was himself no teenager's dreamboat. Koehler's plan—lifted straight from Grady and Hurst—called for Horn to play the straight man to funnyman Stewart, but there was one problem: Lee Stewart was not funny. Horn and Stewart were a mismatch if ever there was one.

To capitalize on Bob Horn's considerable local reputation, WFIL appropriated the name of his popular *Bandstand* radio program for the new TV show, which was to be produced by the station's talented jack-of-all-trades, Tony Mammarella. Born in Atlantic City, New Jersey in 1924 (d. 1977), Anthony Septembre Mammarella moved with his family to South Philadelphia when he was a young child. After graduating from South Philadelphia High in 1942, Mammarella, whose father was a revered local family physician, enrolled in a pre-med course at St. Joseph's College in Philadelphia, where he also indulged in his secret passion, stage acting. Mammarella appeared in several school productions, including Shakespeare's "Othello," for which he won an award still displayed at the college.

He was drafted into the Navy during World War II, and when the war ended he returned to St. Joe's needing but one course to complete his pre-med degree. But when the professor of that course died suddenly, Mammarella interpreted the death as a sign that he himself was not meant to be a doctor. He channeled his passion into his beloved acting, earned his B.S. from St. Joseph's in 1950, and set out to pursue a thespian career, uncertain as to what his next step would be.

It was then that fate, in the form of good friend and noted Philadelphia restaurateur Frank Palumbo, intervened on Mammarella's behalf. Roger Clipp happened to be a regular patron at Palumbo's establishment, and one day the owner asked him if he could find an opening at WFIL for an unemployed actor friend.

Clipp did have an opening at WFIL, and although it was not one Tony Mammarella would have chosen, a job was a job. He became WFIL's weekend telephone switchboard operator and, after serving for several months as the station's general handyman, interviewed with Walter Tillman for an opening in WFIL-TV's film department.

Tillman's secretary, taken aback by Mammarella's good looks and suave manner, called her coworker Agnes McGuire on the office intercom and told her to look out her door "and see what I have in my office!"

"Oh my god," thought McGuire as she peered down the hallway at Mammarella, "He's too good-looking to be nice!"

But Mammarella, who would marry McGuire in 1957, proved to be as nice as his dashing manner and looks. (Jack Steck characterized him as "one of the nicest, fairest people I've ever known.") Mammarella landed the film previewing job, but his creativity remained stifled as he poured through WFIL-TV's film library. Nine months into his new job, he quit. He was soon rehired as a stage manager, however, and then assigned to a television camera crew before finally being appointed to WFIL-TV's production staff.

In addition to Mammarella's production duties, the would-be thespian was afforded the opportunity to appear in front of the television cameras, where he made frequent appearances as a short-notice stand-in whenever regularly scheduled TV guests failed to show. As part of his regular assignment Mammarella donned a cowboy shirt and hosted WFIL's daily "Hopalong Cassidy" movie, and he and a local singer performed a musical interlude on camera at five P.M. each evening. Mammarella's widow said he "loved show business," recalling a time when the producer went so far as to get "dressed up in drag" to be interviewed. He "was on camera all day long," she explained, so "it was no big deal" to him when he was named *Bandstand*'s producer.

The good-natured Tony Mammarella was about to cross paths with the tempestuous Bob Horn. Although Horn possessed a "very strong personality . . . [that] kind of rubbed people the wrong way," the fact that he and his producer clicked as a team came as no great surprise to Mammarella's widow, because "Anthony got along fine with everybody."

As the producer of *Bandstand*, Mammarella described his function as "riding herd on the show," which he accomplished through a daily routine that included readying the set, deciding when it was time to bring the audience in, making certain the guest artists were present and were briefed before they appeared on camera, and acting as a liaison between the show's sponsors and Bob Horn. If a sponsor was unhappy, said Mammarella, "they would usually complain to me."[2]

Jack Steck, who became WFIL-TV's executive producer in 1952, recalled that Mammarella "had a great sense of everything that had to do with the business," whether acting as the show's producer, troubleshooter, cameraman, or stand-in guest.

Working on a modest budget, WFIL readied its new TV show, which it hoped would knock Grady and Hurst's radio program out of the afternoon ratings box. A canvas backdrop painted to simulate the inside of a record store was hung at one end of WFIL's Studio B, and a mock-up sales counter was placed on a small stage in front of the drop. Adjacent to the canvas hung a smaller drop, on which banners from neighborhood high schools were fastened. Horn and Stewart stood behind the counter, giving home viewers the illusion that the pair worked in WFIL's fantasy record store. To accommodate the studio audience, pine bleacher seats were installed on one side of the room, creating the ambience of a high school gymnasium.

Bandstand made its debut on Tuesday afternoon, October 7, 1952, during an era in which America was imbued by deep conservatism and an underlying paranoia (although that very same month another element of pop culture in the form of the irreverent humor comic book *Mad* appeared on newsstands). The Soviet Union had detonated its first atomic bomb less than a year earlier; the United States military was locked in a stalemate in Korea; and Wisconsin senator Joe McCarthy was about to initiate extensive government hearings and investigations into his secret list of alleged "card-carrying" communists. Within in a matter of weeks, the American people would overwhelmingly elect the popular World War II hero Gen. Dwight D. Eisenhower as their next president, and anticommunist senator Richard M. Nixon of California as their vice-president.

Although such uninjurious fare as the police drama *Dragnet*, the comedy *I Love Lucy*, and the comedy-variety *Your Show of Shows* were among the most popular programs on television, and radio was dominated by soap operas and bland white pop music, 1952 was also the year in which congress created the House Subcommittee on Legislative Oversight to investigate the morals of radio and television programs. If anything, *Bandstand*'s benignity ensured that if the new show did not become a roaring success it would at least slip unobtrusively into television's function as a bastion of stability.

Despite the fact that three area high schools—West Philadelphia High, West Catholic High for Girls, and West Catholic High for Boys—were located within walking distance of the TV studio, and WFIL had conducted a three-week on-the-air promotional campaign for its new show, station executives feared the humiliation of televising a near-empty studio to home viewers. But as it was, WFIL's fears of poor attendance for Bob Horn and Lee Stewart's new television program were uncalled for. The station's promotional campaign worked *too* well, as up to fifteen hundred teenagers appeared at 46th and Market that first day, hoping to be admitted to a studio that held only two hundred. "We were panicky at first," recalled Jack Steck, who dispatched Tony Mammarella to the sidewalk to divide the teenagers into groups that were then rotated into the studio every half-hour.

As they had done on Grady and Hurst's radio program and on Paul Whiteman's *TV-Teen Club* for years, teenagers danced as records were played.

Horn and Stewart were fearful that the home viewers might grow tired of watching televised dancing, but it did not take them long to discover that viewers could not get enough of Philadelphia's dancing teens. Dick Clark told *Rolling Stone* editor Ben Fong-Torres in 1973 that WFIL had been deluged by viewers who called to say they enjoyed watching the young dancers, and that after the first week, "the response was overwhelming."[3]

But *Bandstand* offered area viewers more than dancing teenagers who were also afforded the opportunity to identify themselves (à la Grady and Hurst) and tell which schools they represented. Bob Horn also introduced Rate-A-Record to the show—a weekly segment during which selected teenage guests offered numerical evaluations of new songs heard there (which inspired the hoary expression now inexorably linked to *American Bandstand*: "I'll give it a ninety-two because it's got a great beat and it's easy to dance to"). In addition, there were daily studio visits by recording artists, who were introduced by Horn bellowing, "*We've got company!*" after which they lip-synched (mimed) their latest records.

Broadcast in the Philadelphia area from 3:30 to 4:45 P.M. five days a week, *Bandstand* was "a sensation from the start," according to Jack Steck, who insisted "there was no period of build-up. It didn't need a build-up." In less than three months five thousand area high school students possessed membership cards entitling the bearers to admission to the new show on two specific afternoons of the week. *Bandstand*'s ratings were so impressive that rival WPTZ-TV instituted a Saturday morning dance show hosted by Grady and Hurst.[4]

As 1953 began, *Bandstand*'s daily airtime was increased to 105 minutes, proof, claimed local TV critics, that Horn and Stewart had solved the vexing problem of "transferring that radio staple, the disc jockey show, to TV."[5] What is more, there was talk in Philadelphia broadcasting circles of network interest in the show.

That spring, *Bandstand*'s airtime was advanced to 2:45 P.M. in order to coincide with the dismissal of the area's nearby high schools. Admission to the show became a major concern not only for area teenagers, but also for WFIL management, which discovered it could not hope to accommodate the crowds that flocked to the studio. Agnes Mammarella recalled seeing lines "double, quadruple all the way around the building," as neighborhood teenagers began to queue in the shadows of the Market Street el shortly after noon each day. In street scenes reminiscent of World Series baseball games, vendors hawked their wares as the area's youths gathered on the sidewalk.

Local high-schoolers were known to cut out of school early (some went so far as to quit altogether) in order to appear on *Bandstand*. Other young Philadelphians lost their jobs after being spotted dancing on the show by their bosses during hours when the teens should have been working. In order to accommodate the lines of disappointed adolescents lingering on the sidewalk after the show's initial audience was let in, the studio was emptied halfway through the proceedings and a new group of teenagers was admitted.

The *Bandstand* club membership soon approached 10,000, and a late-summer club picnic in 1953 drew 12,000 fans, many of them parents, to Philadelphia's Woodside Park. *Bandstand* annexes were established in fire-houses and other public buildings in outlying communities, where, said Bob Horn, teenagers gathered to "turn on their TV sets and dance to our music."[6]

The music that they danced to during the show's early years was sung primarily by white pop singers, as was the case on most television and radio programs during this era. Black rhythm and blues music had not yet become acceptable to mainstream white audiences and rock 'n' roll had not yet taken the nation by storm, and so it was that white popular stalwarts such as Joni James, Georgia Gibbs, Frankie Laine, and big band-era holdovers Connie Boswell and Helen O'Connell defined *Bandstand*'s initial guest list.

Given the number of regulars fighting to get into the studio, not to mention the thousands of fans who watched from their living rooms, it was no surprise that vocal groups and other pop acts would go to great lengths to appear on *Bandstand* to promote their songs. When Joni James—scheduled to lip-synch her latest release in 1952—missed her train to Philadelphia after giving a performance in Atlantic City, the songstress paid for a two-hour cab ride to *Bandstand* rather than forgo the opportunity. And the Detroit-based group the Three Chuckles drove all the way from the Motor City to Philadelphia to perform their hit "Runaround." Lead singer Teddy Randazzo explained that *Bandstand* was "a big show, it was just huge. That was the place to go!" Given a boost by hefty sales of the song in Philly, "Runaround"—which began as a local hit released on the tiny Detroit-based Boulevard label in 1953 and was later released nationally by RCA Victor—became a national best-seller in November 1954 and eventually sold a reputed million-plus copies.[7]

Bandstand may have been an important vehicle for pop music stars to promote their latest records, but Bob Horn and Lee Stewart's teenage regulars were more interested in dancing than in meeting performers out to promote records. From its earliest days, *Bandstand* spawned dance crazes, the first of which was inspired by Ray Anthony's "Bunny Hop," a bouncy novelty tune with a beat so accentuated that even someone with two left feet could follow the rhythm.

"Bunny Hop" was released about the same time that *Bandstand* went on the air. Since the animated dance proved visually entertaining to home viewers and was popular among *Bandstand*'s young dancers (because it required no partner), Horn and Stewart decided to use the song for a dance contest. Spurred largely by phonograph record sales in the Philadelphia area, "Bunny Hop" went on to become one of the country's biggest-selling hits, and three months after the dance was introduced on *Bandstand*, Stewart said that "the kids won't let us stop it."[8]

After the resounding success of "Bunny Hop" it became axiomatic that catchy, danceable tunes played on *Bandstand* could generate considerable local record sales. Furthermore, songs that flopped on a national basis often became *Bandstand* favorites and sold well in the Philadelphia area. It was not surprising then that local record distributors began to realize the promotional value of having their records aired on *Bandstand* and made it their business to cozy up to Bob Horn.

The *Bandstand* audience did not care about the business deals that influenced what songs were played. Whatever the music, TV's teens found a way to dance to it. In Detroit they called it "cat dancing," while in Chicago it was known as the "shuffle." In Philadelphia, the swing-era appellation "jitterbug" still applied. Although *Bandstand*'s teens performed their share of slow dances in front of the cameras, Bob Horn noted in 1953 that, "when all is said and done, they prefer the jit."[9]

Bandstand's resident "jit" master was Jerry Blavat, a talented and dynamic dancer who was noticed, not only by his peers, but by Tony Mammarella, who continually looked to recruit engaging, light-on-their feet males to counterbalance the preponderance of females in the show's studio audience.

Unfortunately, the show's hosts did not know that Blavat was underage (*Bandstand*'s minimum age for admittance was fourteen) and that, with the help of his older, streetwise South Philly buddies, he had managed to slip by "Big Jack" who stood guard at the door. By the time Horn realized his flashiest dancer was underage, Blavat (who in the early 1960s established himself as a popular radio and television personality known as "the Geator with the Heater") was already receiving copious amounts of fan mail. The savvy Horn dared not risk alienating his audience by banishing one of its local favorites, so Blavat remained on the show, where he quickly became so popular that Horn not only chose him to join *Bandstand*'s elite teenage committee of twelve, he asked Blavat to lead that influential cadre, with a "salary" of fifteen dollars a week.

Early on, *Bandstand* gave rise to a caste system that progressed from the level of periodic visitor, to studio regular, and ultimately on up to elite committee member. But to reach the highest status, one not only had to be good-looking and popular, he or she also had to be an excellent dancer. To be named to the "committee" was to enter *Bandstand*'s coveted inner circle, where the members' camaraderie extended beyond the show. Committee members hung out together on weekends and often organized committee parties of their own. "There were no rivalries," said Blavat. "We were all friends."

It was Tony Mammarella's firm belief that "when you were dressed right you behaved right," so, from the start, *Bandstand* imposed a dress code on its teenage guests. Boys were required to wear a jacket or a sweater and a tie, with dungarees or open shirts outlawed. Dresses or skirts were the order of the afternoon for girls, and any of them discovered wearing pedal pushers or other tight clothing were turned away at the door.

It was left to the committee to enforce the dress code and to maintain general order on the show. Blavat arrived at the studio before the doors opened and served as straw boss to *Bandstand*'s other regulars. He also determined who would appear on the show's weekly Rate-A-Record and he selected other teens to accompany Horn and him to local record hops (dances emceed by disc jockeys who played records and perhaps introduced one or more live acts) and other personal appearances. Blavat, whose parents divorced when he was quite young, spent an increasing amount of time with Horn's family, and Horn "almost became a second father" to the teenager.

· · ·

When it came to experiencing the white teenage epiphany of rhythm and blues, the Geator, who ran with an older crowd, had a leg up on most of his *Bandstand* cronies. A favorite late-night hangout was Pat's Luncheonette in South Philly, where Blavat prowled the pool table as his friends fed nickels into the R&B-gorged jukebox. It was on one such night out in 1954 that the teenager's world was turned upside down by the lusciously lascivious sound of the Midnighters' "Work With Me Annie," a tune so sexually blatant that it had to be rewritten as "Dance With Me Henry" before it was deemed acceptable for white audiences.

Like Blavat, more and more white teens discovered the music of black recording artists such as the Midnighters, the Crows, the Spaniels, and the Drifters. Coast to coast, hip white teenagers were in the process of discovering, either on distant "clear channel" fifty-thousand-watt megastations or on local low-wattage outlets situated at the far end of the AM radio dial, the exciting and sensuous sound of rhythm and blues music. But while rhythm and blues was becoming the preferred dance music of America's hippest teens, and R&B hits were beginning to appear regularly on the previously lily-white pop music charts, there was little exposure of that black-derived genre at the local television level, and even less on a national basis.

Most television programs of the early 1950s (such as Lucky Strike's *Your Hit Parade* or *The Alcoa Hour* drama anthology) were created and controlled not by the networks, but by New York advertising agencies who handled the accounts of the programs' sponsors. It was those sponsors who, in effect, ruled the TV roost, and most of them quaked at the prospect of their mainstream products becoming too closely identified with blacks. "It was mostly the advertisers [who exhibited racism], and they controlled what could sell in a white market," said Jerry Wexler, a producer with Atlantic Records, a leading rhythm and blues label during that era. "The ad agencies were Jim Crowing the business." [10] When black singers did make an infrequent appearance before the TV cameras, more often than not they were required to perform in a pop or jazz-oriented mode that was acceptable not only to white audiences, but to the sponsors whose products were being pitched to those white viewers.

When Roger Clipp named Horn director of recorded music at WFIL in 1952, as part of the package to lure him away WIP, he virtually granted the *Bandstand* host a license to play any records he desired. Utilizing this power to its utmost, Horn shrewdly catered to the preferences of the show's audience, which was initially drawn from the predominantly white neighboring high schools. But as the audiences taste in music began to change, Horn knew the show's programming would have to change too, over time.

The *Bandstand* breakthrough for rhythm and blues occurred during the summer of 1954, after a black group called the Chords recorded a jump tune entitled "Sh-Boom." Adhering to a standard practice of the broadcasting industry, pop radio stations across the country shunned the Chords' original version of "Sh-Boom" in favor of a watered-down white copy sung by the Crew Cuts. Bob Horn did likewise.

"Hey, that's not the version," protested the show's regulars, "the *real* version is by the Chords!" But Horn would not be swayed. As head of *Bandstand*'s teenage committee, Jerry Blavat also had input as to what records were heard on the show's weekly record review. He and seasoned Philadelphia promo man and long-time Horn crony Harry Finfer—who also was perplexed by his pal's intransigence—together convinced Horn to at least test the Chords' version of "Sh-Boom" on *Bandstand*'s Rate-A-Record. After the record received the highest score possible, "Bob Horn started to play [the original] 'Sh-Boom,'" recalled Blavat.

But although Horn then began to program rhythm and blues with increasing regularity, as 1954 drew to a close *Bandstand* remained predominantly a white pop music venue, with guest celebrities including singer Tony Martin and comedian Milton Berle continuing as the order of the day. Meanwhile, across the nation, rock 'n' roll was taking shape. The music produced its first real star in Bill Haley, who, with the Comets, had two top twenty smashes that year in "Shake Rattle and Roll" and "Dim, Dim the Lights" (while Elvis Presley's first two records on Sun went unnoticed). Then, rock 'n' roll was officially christened when disc jockey Alan Freed—who had recently moved from Cleveland to New York City—referred to the black recording stars of his upcoming "Rock and Roll Jubilee Ball" as "rock 'n' roll artists."[11]

To commemorate the second anniversary of *Bandstand*, what was then the hottest daytime TV show in Philadelphia was featured prominently in the Philadelphia edition of *TV Guide*. In the aptly titled paean, "Two Down and Eons to Go," the magazine wished Bob Horn's "mighty baby" a happy birthday, and hailed the surprising show as "the people's choice" for a 1954 *TV Guide* award.[12] What was not said was that *TV Guide*, a baby in its own right, had been established a year earlier by Walter Annenberg, who also happened to own *Bandstand*.

By the onset of 1955, over a quarter-million teenagers had passed through *Bandstand*'s hallowed portals. It was now policy for everyone but the show's "regulars" to send an advance letter to WFIL-TV stating the specific day they wished to attend the show, and only if there was room that particular day was a card of admission issued.

Nineteen-fifty-five also was the year in which Bob Horn finally shook loose of Lee Stewart. Jack Steck had watched Horn and Stewart squabble on a daily basis for the past two years, with Horn threatening to quit the show at least twice a week. "I'd soothe him down and Tony [Mammarella] would soothe him down," said Steck. But the rancor between Horn and Stewart continued to fester, and on the eve of a scheduled vacation, Horn refused to entrust *Bandstand* to Stewart, insisting that Mammarella stand in for him until he returned to the show. At that point, said Steck, Horn "had had it up to his neck" with Stewart.

Mammarella told George Koehler that a decision had to be made to retain either Horn or Stewart. "You can't have both. Horn will not continue as it is."[13]

As the man responsible for foisting Stewart upon Horn in the first place, Koehler defended Stewart's continued presence on the show. "But it was a 'no-go,'" said Steck. "By that time Horn was adamant, and so was Tony."

Koehler grudgingly removed Stewart from *Bandstand*, mollifying the TV pitchman by giving him a morning show of his own called *Lee Stewart's Coffeetime*. Designed along the lines of *Bandstand* but geared to an older audience, Stewart's new show "only lasted a couple of months before it went down the hopper," recalled Steck, who added that the cohost's removal from *Bandstand* made Bob Horn "very happy and he did a better job."

Meanwhile, Horn, who remained cognizant of his advanced age and his visual shortcomings, cunningly diverted the spotlight away from himself by fostering the celebrity status of the show's teenage regulars.

If there remained any doubt as to who the real stars of *Bandstand* were, that uncertainty was eliminated that summer when one newspaper in Philadelphia ran a feature story titled "Teen-Agers Outpull Name Guests on *Bandstand*." "We're not ready to start making stars from our youngsters, yet," cautioned Horn, who would not hesitate to chastise the *Bandstand* teens off-camera before he disappeared behind a curtain to puff on a cigarette.[14] But it was too late, the genie had escaped from the bottle; *Bandstand*'s regulars were already stars.

Committee members received fan mail almost from day one, as the wily Horn abetted its flow by distributing it on the air. The most popular members received hundreds of letters on certain days. Billy Cook (who died in 1993), one of the show's earliest regulars, received up to one or two shopping bags of mail each day, "and I wasn't even the most popular kid on the show."[15] But after many of the regulars proceeded to tuck their envelopes conspicuously in their pockets—all the better to be visible as they danced—Horn was forced to move the daily mail call to the end of the show. The relationship between the fans and the regular dancers "was so intense, I can't think of anything else to compare it with," recalled Cook. Indeed, some of the most popular committee members even had fan clubs of their own, and "when you walked down the street in your neighborhood, everybody knew you," attested Jerry Blavat.

Although the committee members came to be local celebrities, Bob Horn still held the hammer. If a member's head swelled to the point that he or she began to think *Bandstand* could not survive without that individual, Horn said he relieved the swelling "by taking away their membership cards for a while."[16]

• • •

As *Bandstand*'s popularity continued to grow in the Philadelphia area, other local TV stations across America tried telecasting similar popular radio disc jockeys in one format or another, but none met the same success that *Bandstand* did. A month prior to *Bandstand*'s inception, popular Minneapolis disc jockey Jack Thayer instituted a televised teenage pop music program of his own, utilizing a fictitious drug store setting, but the show did not become a national phenomenon, as *Bandstand* soon would.[17]

Although Dick Clark said in 1990 that *Bandstand* could have developed in any large city and that "it just happened to be in Philadelphia," there were crucial reasons why the show thrived as it did in Philadelphia and failed in other cities.[18] For one, the unique combination of the city's size — large enough to command the credibility necessary to establish a movement such as the *Bandstand* phenomenon, yet not so huge as to have the phenomenon overshadowed — and its location — situated on the doorstep of New York City, the media capital of the world — played a key role in ensuring national recognition.

In addition, as a "break-out" city where pop records were tested before being distributed nationally, Philadelphia already commanded the attention of pop music's movers and shakers and boasted its own thriving music industry. Writer, publisher, label-owner, and producer Lee Silver, who produced and recorded the Royal Teens during the *Bandstand* era and was based in New York at the time, said that whenever he promoted a record "we used to go directly to Philadelphia. Philadelphia was really the *pulse* of the business."

Indeed, it was. Talent booker and manager Ernie Martinelli explained how in those days the major promotional circuit for New York-based record companies consisted of Baltimore–Washington, Cleveland, Pittsburgh, and Philadelphia. "These were the areas where you paid your dues," he said. "Believe it or not, everything past that was almost unimportant." Philadelphia record promotion man, concert booker, and talent manager Irv Nahan claimed his city accounted for 5 to 7 percent of the total record market in those days, with only New York responsible for more.

Philadelphia's considerable size, its close proximity to New York City, and its status as a break-out city in the record market all contributed to the development of *Bandstand*. But it was the city's ethnic composition — a peculiar juxtaposition of blue-collar, working-class Italians and blacks — and their concomitant relationship to each other (as well as to the surrounding city) that were fundamental to the formation of *Bandstand*'s nature and to the changes in pop music and dance wrought by the show.

Popular styles originating within minority groups have a manner of working their way into the broader society. Although Philadelphia's blacks originally had minimal visible presence on the show itself, their songs and dances, which were appropriated and adulterated for mass (white) acceptance, heavily influenced *Bandstand* musicians and audiences and thus played a vital role in the *Bandstand* story. The city's Italians, who came to embody the very essence of *American Bandstand* through teen idols like Frankie Avalon and Fabian, resided in close quarters with the city's blacks at a time when most other whites had moved into the suburbs, and inevitably were influenced by black styles of music.[19] This influence was evident in the audience's eventual demand for music sung by original black artists and by the styles that the Italian and other white singers were beginning to adopt, although in watered down versions. It is this ethnic diversity and juxtaposition that allowed Philadelphia to become one of the first cities to embrace black-derived rhythm and blues and rock 'n' roll music, and thus put *Bandstand* in a unique position to stay on the cutting edge of the music scene and become as successful as it did.

Dick Clark also credited much of *Bandstand*'s early success to Bob Horn's keen awareness of what was happening with the show. "He knew he'd struck gold," said Clark, "and now he wanted to mine the vein."[20]

And mine it he did. To capitalize on the increasing popularity of rhythm and blues, Horn, Bernie Lowe, and attorney Nat Segal formed the Teen and Sound record labels, on which they employed local artists to record cover versions of national rhythm and blues hits. Afforded exposure on *Bandstand*, such records generally sold well in the Philadelphia area and provided a steady, if not spectacular, source of income for the labels' owners. Sound Records even managed to score a national hit when Gloria Mann's "Teen Age Prayer" cracked the charts in the winter of 1955–56.

By that time Bob Horn seemed to have it all. An apparent family man with a wife, children, and a comfortable income, Horn cruised Chesapeake Bay's waters on his yacht—which he christened the *Bandstand*—and he cruised Philadelphia's streets in his spanking-new 1955 green Cadillac Eldorado. And just like his committee members, Horn developed his own following and became one of the Delaware Valley's most recognized personalities. As for the records he programmed on *Bandstand*, Horn answered to no one, and it was said around town that the show's martinet was "courted night and day by pluggers hoping that he'll give their platters a spin."[21]

Although no one outside the pop music industry was aware of it, payments to Horn by local record distributors had increased steadily since 1953. Such payments were not necessarily illegal, and in many instances were carried on the record distributors' books as "promotional expenses." How they were subsequently listed on the recipients' income tax returns was a matter between them and the Internal Revenue Service. In Horn's case he simply never bothered to tell the government. The late Tom Donahue, a popular rock 'n' roll disc jockey at Philadelphia's WIBG radio in the 1950s, claimed Horn, "was making a *lot* of money" and was "the closest thing to a Roman Emperor" he had ever seen.[22]

While Horn indulged himself in a flamboyant lifestyle, Dick Clark, save for his TV commercials, toiled in virtual anonymity. WFIL radio went so far as to institute a ploy to boost Clark's anemic "Caravan of Music" ratings. In an attempt to take advantage of the popularity of Horn's TV program, the station programmed a show called *Bandstand* on the radio. Although WFIL insisted Clark adhere to his adult-oriented, pop-standard format ("what we called in later years middle-of-the-road music," he explained), that decision did not ruffle Clark nearly as much as did the second part of WFIL's scam.

"Bob would come in and open the show, spend five or ten minutes with me and then leave for the whole day," recalled Clark. It was only after Horn left the radio booth that Clark introduced himself to the listeners and suffered the abomination of having to reassure the remaining audience that Horn would return to close the radio program. After signing off from his popular TV *Bandstand*, Horn did return to radio, albeit for a mere "four or five minutes," according to Clark, "and the show would be over."

Clark was not alone in his displeasure with this arrangement. Wary of the young, personable, and good-looking announcer whose strengths served to magnify the veteran broadcaster's weaknesses, Horn feigned politeness to Clark on the air. But off the air Clark received little more than a "sour nod" from his ersatz partner.[23] In 1994, Clark summed up their relationship by saying he "never cared for [Horn], nor he for me, particularly. We were working associates. We were cordial to one another, but we weren't particularly close."

To make matters worse, Clark came under pressure from WFIL brass, who could not understand why the radio version of *Bandstand* did not match the popularity of Horn's TV show. Clark's explanation that the radio show's outdated musical format was to blame fell on deaf ears, and WFIL management ordered him to Pittsburgh to listen to one of that city's most popular deejays. The station also arranged for Clark to do remote *Bandstand* broadcasts from Philadelphia's Tower Theatre and invited local teens to stop by, but only the squarest of them bothered to do so. Eventually WFIL management was forced to relinquish the notion of linking its two *Bandstands*, and Clark's radio program was re-christened *Dick Clark's Caravan of Music*. Consigned by WFIL to his languid radio listeners, Clark occasionally stood in on TV for the vacationing Horn. It was after one such stint during the fall of 1955 that Clark realized he "could really progress" if he "could get out of radio and get a TV show like *Bandstand*."[24]

He also realized that the prospects of landing a *Bandstand*-type show at WFIL were nonexistent so long as Horn remained on the scene. Furthermore, Clark's option of jumping to a rival station—contractually problematic to begin with—was eradicated when Joe Grady and Ed Hurst began their own daily TV *Bandstand* show on Wilmington's WPFH in October 1955, setting the stage for what the local press described as " a big struggle for the teenage audience, with no holds barred." [25]

What Clark did not know was that within a year's time Horn would be banished from the show he had originated. If, indeed, *Bandstand*'s creator exhibited the demeanor of a Roman emperor, he did so in a rapacious manner. Like the emperor Nero, who, legend has it, fiddled while Rome burned, Horn, it began to be whispered about town, was engaged in his own fiddling—with some underage girls on his show. Slowly but surely, *Bandstand* became imperiled by a coming conflagration.

Dick Clark's *Bandstand*

Bob Horn was not happy to see sixteen-year-old Dolores Farmer appear at his table as he dined at his favorite Germantown cafe in north Philadelphia one evening in 1956.[1] Horn was at the restaurant on business, and so, apparently, was Miss Farmer (not her real name). Horn later claimed that Farmer asked him for $1,000, which she needed in order to extricate herself from some "unspecified trouble."[2]

Horn and Farmer had known each other for some two years, with the true nature of their relationship most likely positioned somewhere between the two widely divergent tales they would tell in 1957. A tiny brunette who looked older than her years, Farmer claimed to have been a member of Paul Whiteman's *TV-Teen Club* before she became a regular visitor to WFIL-TV's studios in 1952. She alleged that one week after she met Horn at WFIL's studios sometime during the summer of 1953, he drove her to a local apartment where the couple engaged in a "discussion" she would not elaborate on. The teenager further maintained that she and Horn, a married man with three young daughters and an adolescent stepson, began having sexual relations that November—when she was just thirteen years old—after which they saw each other once or twice a week until the end of 1955, having "improper relations on nearly every occasion."[3]

Bob Horn told a different story, claiming that although he had noticed Farmer lurking about WFIL's studios, the two did not speak until a time in 1954 when Farmer appeared at his office one evening, introduced herself, and told him she wanted to appear on *Bandstand*. Horn said he told Farmer her request "was not possible." But he also claimed that, "She isn't reluctant or shy. She just walks up and introduces herself," a quality that enabled her to eventually get "to know the same people" he knew.[4] Because of the similar social patterns brought about by Farmer's friendliness, Horn claimed he ultimately "got to know Miss Farmer real well."[5] But he denied ever having any sexual contact with her.

Unbeknownst to Horn and Farmer at the time of their restaurant encounter, Philadelphia District Attorney Victor Blanc had just ordered the undercover investigation of a suspected vice ring that police had reason to believe preyed on unsuspecting teenage girls in the area, using promises of modeling careers to lure them into pornographic photo sessions and orgies disguised as "social gatherings" at Hound Dog Hill, a country estate north of Philadelphia. Dolores Farmer was suspected of being involved with the ring.

Sometime during the wee hours of June 21, 1956, just one month after being confronted by Dolores Farmer, Horn's green Cadillac Eldorado careened through a red light in North Philadelphia, causing a police cruiser to veer sharply to avoid a collision. Never one to live the quiet life, Horn's late-night escapades had recently begun to escalate. Jerry Blavat told of witnessing the *Bandstand* host "hanging out at nighttime an awful lot, drinking an awful lot . . . [and doing] a lot of things that eventually had to catch up to him."[6] Indeed, Horn had been drinking that night, and after giving the police a hard time, the *Bandstand* host was taken to a nearby police station where he was issued a summons for running a red light, pronounced "drunk and not capable of operating a motor vehicle," and summarily arrested for drunken driving.[7]

At 5:30 that morning Jack Steck received a telephone call from George Koehler, informing him of Horn's arrest. "You know the magistrate," said Koehler. "See if you can do anything to calm this thing down so it doesn't get any more publicity than necessary."[8]

At the station house Steck conveyed to the sergeant on duty his desire to keep Horn's arrest quiet. "I think you're gonna have some trouble," replied the sergeant as he glanced across the room. "See that man over there with the brown hat? He's from the *Evening Bulletin* and he's here to cover this thing."

Steck, who realized that the presence of the *Philadelphia Evening Bulletin* (owned by Walter Annenberg's competitor, WCAU-TV), augured trouble, warily approached the reporter and asked him not to be "too tough on Horn." But when the scribe replied, "Look bud, you do your job and I'll do mine," Steck knew all too well "what was going to happen next."[9]

With the city's DWI (driving while intoxicated) arrests running double those of the previous year, the Philadelphia Police Department was in the midst of a month-long campaign to rid the city's streets of drunken motorists. Tycoon/philanthropist Annenberg championed the police department's efforts through a vigorous editorial campaign in his *Inquirer*, and to punctuate those editorials, the *Inquirer* each day listed under bold headlines the latest motorists arrested for drunken driving. The arrest of Horn proved to be a personal anathema to Annenberg.

Unable to ignore Horn's arrest, the *Inquirer* did the next best thing and buried his name deep within a page-six story. But the *Evening Bulletin* did not overlook the opportunity to tweak Annenberg's nose, and with nary a mention of the other arrestees, printed a two-column account of Horn's misfortune, topped by the boldface headline, "*Bandstand*'s Bob Horn Held for Driving While Drunk." [10] WFIL promptly suspended Horn from *Bandstand* and named Tony Mammarella temporary host of the show.

Horn's renowned status as *Bandstand*'s host, coupled with the *Bulletin's* relentless publicity, guaranteed that the details of his embarrassing arrest would not be constrained, but what began as merely an embarrassing situation for WFIL turned into a potentially lethal one. Jack Steck recalled that shortly after Horn's arrest somebody called Roger Clipp and told him that Horn "had been messing around with one of the [*Bandstand*] kids."

Rumors linking several local broadcasting personalities to Philadelphia's undercover vice probe had circulated about the city for weeks. Faced with the looming possibility of Horn being implicated in the growing scandal, WFIL executives realized that if they did not act swiftly, sponsor defection might cause the station to lose its golden daytime television franchise. In a foggy cloud of corporate jargon, WFIL announced that Horn had been replaced because of "embarrassment to the station." [11]

As far as outsiders were concerned, WFIL's statement referred to Horn's drunk driving arrest, but in actuality the station replaced him because it anticipated the imminent dropping of the other shoe. "We could have weathered the drunken driving [charge]," explained Steck, "but we couldn't stand the other, [so] we fired him."

To Tony Mammarella, Horn's sudden dismissal from *Bandstand* afforded him the opportunity he thought would never arise. The show's versatile and personable producer thought he had his best chance yet to become *Bandstand*'s permanent host, but what Mammarella did not know was that he had no shot at all at succeeding Bob Horn.

• • •

Knowing that Bandstand was in "substantial danger" of being cancelled after Horn's removal, WFIL management "decided that they'd better get somebody in there who had a chance to save it," according to Dick Clark. [12] Jack Steck, who had recommended Tony Mammarella as interim host of the show, thought the producer should continue to host *Bandstand* on a permanent basis. "Tony had been on the show since its inception," explained Steck, "and I thought he had a shot."

But Tony Mammarella declined Jack Steck's endorsement. Tony said he refused consideration for the position "because [George] Koehler hates my guts and would never let me have the job," but his widow, Agnes, suggested that it was because Tony was aware of prejudice toward Italian-Americans at the office.[13] She claimed "there were several people at the station that didn't particularly like people that were Italian." Rick Lewis, a black raised in Philadelphia who became the lead singer of the Silhouettes, agreed that in the 1950s "people looked down on you if you were Italian. If you were Italian, shit, you were almost a nigger!"[14] Lewis, who knew Mammarella well, said of the *Bandstand* producer's decision: "Tony knew [about the prejudice], so he found his niche [as producer] and he did what he could do."

It is uncertain whether the ethnic factor was of any concern to Roger Clipp, who, as the recently named general manager of Triangle Publications' new radio and television division, had the final say on who would become *Bandstand*'s new host. Clipp favored Dick Clark for the position. For some unspecified reason, however, the general manager wanted his choice to be proposed by someone other than himself.

Jack Steck recalled that, while Mammarella served as temporary host of *Bandstand*, Clipp continued to "fiddle on" without making a final decision about Horn's eventual successor. Then one day Clipp abruptly announced that a luncheon meeting of all WFIL department heads would be held. After the meal Clipp told his subordinates that he had summoned them there "to select a successor to Bob Horn." Then "he deliberately looked at each of us *contemptuously*, which wasn't unusual," said Steck. Clipp fixed his glare on production manager Roddy Rogers and asked, "Roddy, who should get the job?"

"Roddy unhesitatingly said, 'Dick Clark!'"

"That settles that," responded Clipp. "Let's get back to work!"[15]

"*Nobody's* recommendation meant a damn thing. . . . [Clipp] didn't want anybody's recommendation," recalled Steck, who nevertheless insisted that the luncheon meeting had not been a set-up between Clipp and Rogers. "I don't think Roddy would have worked that way."[16]

But although Rogers most likely was not involved in Clipp's machinations, Richard A. Clark—Dick's father and Clipp's close friend—may have been. Once it became public knowledge that Clark had the job (Johnny Carlton inherited Clark's afternoon *Caravan of Music* radio program), some people in

Philadelphia whispered that he had landed it primarily because his father was in a position to get it for him. "It was rumored that that was the reason," recalled singer Lee Andrews.

The rumor remains unsubstantiated, but Clark apparently did have designs on *Bandstand*. Ed Hurst, who was at a party with him just after Horn had been fired, claimed he heard him say, "I'm gonna have that show and that's all there is to it. That [show] will be mine!"

Hurst said he took Clark "at his word. I figured, 'He's gonna be there,' and he was! . . . He had the face, he had the line of shit, and he was perfect for the job. That was just what they were lookin' for."

Local songwriter/musician Artie Singer, who had been friends with Clark since they worked on Paul Whiteman's *TV-Teen Club* together, claimed he was in the WFIL studio chatting with Clark during the latter's radio program when "somebody stuck their head in the door and said, 'You got *Bandstand* starting as of tomorrow!'"

"Hoo, yeah," the twenty-six-year-old Clark allegedly replied when asked by George Koehler if he wanted the *Bandstand* position. "It was my dream." [17] Clark said he walked out of Koehler's office, "not a little astonished" at his good fortune. [18]

For his part, Clark said that *Bandstand*'s imminent cancellation was "probably one of the reasons" he was considered for the job, and that he "was the right age, looked the part, and was safe." He also maintained that while some luck was indeed involved in his selection as *Bandstand* host, he had spent nine years "working to be in the right place at the right time." [19]

True enough, but was it purely determination Clark evinced as he vowed he would "have" Bob Horn's old spot? Or did he know at the time he was a shoo-in for the job? After all, Richard A. Clark had already interceded once on his son's behalf when he called Roger Clipp four years earlier. And now Clipp expressed a desire for Clark to succeed Bob Horn, yet he was unwilling to go on record as saying so. What, if anything, took place between Clipp and the elder Clark will never be known, but the history of their personal and professional relationship indicates that it may have influenced Clipp's decision to name Dick Clark as the new *Bandstand* host.

Whatever was behind Roger Clipp's decision, Tony Mammarella thought that WFIL "was convinced that Dick was in time going to become perhaps the biggest personality in the city. They just weren't sure of the exact format his success was going to take." [20]

As for Mammarella, having missed the brass ring, he returned to the background as *Bandstand*'s producer, lamenting that such disappointments were "the story of my life at Channel 6." [21]

Although Bob Horn had been banished from the show he helped create, Jerry Blavat and most of his fellow committee members on *Bandstand* believed that as long as Mammarella remained as interim host of the show, Horn would eventually be reinstated. Once Dick Clark was named *Bandstand*'s new host, however, it became apparent to them that Horn's firing was meant to be permanent.

As he assumed leadership of *Bandstand*, Clark's immediate goal was to make sure that he was accepted as the show's host, which would secure his future in the business and increase his prospects for earning more money. But his acceptance as the new host of what many of the regulars still regarded as Bob Horn's show was anything but assured, and trouble brewed as Clark geared up to take over WFIL's popular afternoon program. Instigated by Blavat, *Bandstand*'s committee members constructed signs and organized picket lines in preparation for a protest calling for Bob Horn's return. The protest was not *against* Clark, but *for* Horn, he explains. "The kids did not know who Dick Clark was," says the Geator. Nor did they care. "They just wanted to dance. They wanted to be *stars*."

Seeking to retain as much continuity as possible for *Bandstand* during the Horn–Clark transition, Tony Mammarella, who was unaware of Blavat's complicity in the forthcoming protest, asked the teenager to continue to head the show's committee. "I can't do that," replied the Geator, whose upcoming attempt to show his dissatisfaction with the recent turn of events would be his final act on *Bandstand*.

On July 9, 1956, the first day of Clark's new assignment, the Blavat-led committee members marched around the outside of the WFIL-TV building, placards in hand, demanding that Horn be reinstated. Clark arrived at two o'clock that afternoon and brushed past the sidewalk protesters without giving them a second thought. But as *Bandstand*'s airtime approached and the show's committee members failed to appear, he grew concerned. Tony Mammarella assured the new host that there were already enough kids in the studio to do the show, but that was not good enough for Clark, who ventured outside to confront the sidewalk picketers.

In *Rock, Roll & Remember*, Clark says he introduced himself to the protesters, and, after being met with silent stares, explained to the recalcitrant teens that Horn's dismissal was a done deal that he, Clark, had had no part in. After inviting the protestors into the studio, Clark returned inside alone and minutes later "breathed a sigh of relief" as the protesters filed in.[22]

But there was more to Clark's defusing of Jerry Blavat's sidewalk rebellion than Clark's account revealed. Blavat insisted that, as the instigator of the protest, WFIL made certain the authorities "pinched" [arrested] him. "They were sharp enough to get me out of the way for a couple of hours [and] after they brought me in, Dick went out and spoke to the kids."

Blavat never returned to *Bandstand*, but he and Clark did develop a friend-ship, which began one Sunday morning, two years later, when they ended up on the same train back to Philadelphia. Blavat, then the road manager for a local recording group, felt compelled to broach the subject of his *Bandstand* protest, explaining that he had meant no disrespect to Clark. Clark told him that even though everyone else involved with the show "just came directly over to me, you were the only one that did not . . . [and] I respect your loyalty to Bob Horn."

"I realized that Dick Clark respected my position as a kid," said Blavat. "He did not have to be nice to me, because I was the kid that tried to stop those other kids going on *Bandstand*."

As part of *Bandstand*'s transition, Clark left intact the successful format developed by Bob Horn, but the committee's protest made it clear to the show's new host that one change *was* urgently needed. Whereas Horn had concentrated *Bandstand*'s power and prestige among a small group of privi-leged insiders over which he held a tight rein, Clark proceded to increase the committee's size to more than thirty—almost doubling it—thereby diluting that body's exclusivity and cliqueishness.

According to Joanne Montecarlo, a committee member during the Horn-Clark transition, Clark's shrewd move successfully democratized *Bandstand*'s administration. She thought Clark "never favored anyone over anybody else [and was] always nice and respectful to everyone on the show."

If not for Tony Mammarella, however, Joanne and her sister Carmen might never have had the opportunity to meet Clark. Joanne said that after Horn was fired, her father forbade his daughters from returning to the show, and relented only after receiving a call from Mammarella assuring him that *Bandstand*'s new host was a "clean-cut family man."[23]

But despite Dick Clark's equanimity, hard feelings persisted among those original committee members who remained loyal to Horn. Horn's personal shortcomings aside, Jack Steck thought the *Bandstand* originator possessed "an intuitive feeling about teenagers. They liked him and he liked them. They got along beautifully, and on the air it showed." Years later, Andrea Kamens, who was a committee member at the time of the Horn-Clark transition, defended Horn, saying that he had been "very nice . . . [and] very straight" with his young guests, and that there had never been "any mention of sex" from him.[24]

Due to the process of attrition among the show's teenage guests, however, Bob Horn gradually faded from the memory of *Bandstand*'s committee members. One by one his loyalists fell by the wayside, having succumbed to more adult pursuits or having been involuntarily "retired" by *Bandstand*'s age limit of seventeen. Dick Clark's expanded committee was soon dominated by grateful teens who, unlike many of its earlier members, had no loyalty whatsoever to the show's creator and original cohost.

Following a shaky transition month, Clark's professional demeanor permeated *Bandstand* from top to bottom and he swiftly established himself as the program's prime mover. But that is not to say that WFIL-TV's afternoon dance show was out of the woods yet. *Bandstand* continued to be the most widely viewed daytime TV show in the Philadelphia area, but even so, its ratings plateaued. And although Clark looked to have righted the *Bandstand* ship, he and the WFIL brass had cause to remain wary of viewers' attitudes towards the show once Bob Horn was publicly implicated in the vice probe.

Philadelphia's festering sex scandal broke wide open in October, 1956, when the police raided a local photography studio where pornographic photo sessions were alleged to have taken place. *Bandstand*'s moment of truth arrived three weeks later when warrants for the arrests of Horn and nine others were issued by Philadelphia District Attorney Victor Blanc's office. Horn's accuser on some twenty statutory rape offenses was Dolores Farmer.

The *Philadelphia Inquirer* may have buried Horn's name deep within its pages after his drunk driving arrest, but this time Walter Annenberg's newspaper hung the ex-*Bandstand* host out to dry, trumpeting the vice arrests and running a photograph of Horn being arraigned. In addition, Roger Clipp attempted to distance WFIL from Horn, reminding the public that the former *Bandstand* host was not "in any way" affiliated with Annenberg's radio or TV station.[25]

Meanwhile, Clark, who claimed to Henry Schipper in 1990 that, had *Bandstand* been "a snake pit of writhing bodies," it would have been "off the air in a week,"[26] could do nothing but ignore the scandal and have implicit faith in his choirboy image.

Forty years after the fact, it is difficult to appreciate the debilitating effect the lurid sex revelations (described by D.A. Blanc as "unspeakable" tales of vice and "sexual depravity") and highly-visible trials had on the public's perception of *Bandstand*.[27] "Like anything else involving sex," said retired Judge Paul Chalfin, who was second assistant D.A. to Blanc in 1956, "it had a lot of publicity. People were amazed that this happened where it did, and [that it] involved minors."

A string of sensational vice trials played to overflowing courtroom galleries that November, and although Bob Horn's trial was postponed several times, the *Philadelphia Bulletin* continued to place his name in boldface headlines at every opportunity. Horn, who had always been more popular with his listeners than among his peers, watched as the hangers-on abandoned his sinking ship. "That's when it all went downhill," said Jerry Blavat. "He couldn't get a job here."

Horn fled Philadelphia in disgrace. Calling himself "Bob Adams," he managed to land a job at KILT radio in Houston, Texas in 1956, but when his true identity was discovered Horn was bumped to KILT's sales department. "He was despondent," said Blavat, the product of a broken home who had grown so close to Horns' family that he accompanied them to Texas. "I saw him drink and drink and drink at night."

• • •

Having won over Bob Horn's resistant committee, Dick Clark tiptoed gingerly into uncharted territory, possessing what he termed "only a foggy notion of what the kids, music, and show were really about." The new host of *Bandstand*, who claimed he was terrified because of the vice allegations lodged against Horn, strove to establish what he described as "the most platonic of friendships with the kids" on the show.[28]

The *Bandstand* tenure of Clark and Tony Mammarella commenced on a tentative note as the easygoing, trusting producer—"Tony *Mootzarelle*" to his pals in the record business—displayed an uncharacteristic coolness towards his new partner. Clark, who understood that any animosity between himself and his producer "would spoil my chance of establishing myself on the show," called Mammarella to task.[29]

Mammarella explained that Horn had been his good friend, and that it would simply require time to make the adjustment. "I like you," he reassured Clark. "I know we can work together."[30]

And work together they did, out of a tiny office at WFIL shared by secretary Marlene Teti and several mail sorters and openers. To gain some semblance of privacy for Mammarella and himself, Clark erected wall panels to form a room about ten feet by six feet, into which was squeezed a double desk, a record player, and a single telephone. "It was *very* small," said Agnes Mammarella. "A cubby hole would describe it better."

Because of the potentially damaging sexual allegations levied against Bob Horn, WFIL made the projection of Dick Clark's wholesome image top priority. "The show was very influential," he explained, "and to keep it going was a hell of a lot more important than whether people liked what I was doing."

What Clark was doing was cultivating his "All-American boy" image for the viewers at home. "I wore a coat and tie," he said. "Everybody in that *Bandstand* studio who was male wore a coat and tie. The thinking behind that was if we looked presentable, normal, the way they think we oughta look, they'll leave us alone."[31] His squeaky-clean television image was "150 percent deliberate and well thought out," said Clark, who revealed that when he was off-camera he "smoked and drank and swore."[32]

His image may have been contrived, but not necessarily to protect the music he played on *Bandstand*. At that point, Clark had more important things on his mind than proselytizing rock 'n' roll. "I'm not gonna sit here and tell you I did this solely to keep the music alive," he revealed to Henry Schipper in 1990. His squeaky-clean image was projected "in order to perpetuate my own career, first and foremost, and *secondly* the music."[33] (Italics are author's.)

Although Clark considered the promotion of his own career paramount to the promotion of rock 'n' roll, that is not to say that the new music of the younger generation did not cause him some degree of consternation. The juxtaposition of the cursed rock 'n' roll with a personality as apparently virtuous as Clark had yet to be accomplished on a national basis, and no one could say that Clark would be successful at it.

With the exception of Bill Haley and the Comets (who had already performed numerous times on *Bandstand*), rock 'n' roll remained largely the domain of black artists. That is, until 1956, when a young white Southern singer with the name Elvis Presley altered the face of American popular music, if not society itself. When it came to assessing the gyrating, hip-swivelling "Elvis the Pelvis," there was no middle ground; one either loved him or loathed him. America's schizophrenic reaction to Presley's antics was evinced by the fact that as his first RCA Victor release, "Heartbreak Hotel," raced to the top of six *Billboard* sales charts, Presley's week-long Las Vegas engagement was something less than a smashing success.

The two most identifiable names in rock 'n' roll that year were Presley and Alan Freed—the outspoken New York disc jockey who had unabashedly dubbed himself the "king of rock 'n' roll." Both were regarded by the Establishment as pariahs more than as spokesmen for the new music, and both were excoriated mercilessly, Presley for carrying on during his performances as no white man before him had ever done, and Freed for zealously championing black artists and their rhythm and blues to white youngsters.

Despite Presley's staggering record sales (in 1956 he sold seventy-five-thousand records a day, over half of RCA Victor's entire output), neither he nor rock 'n' roll were taken seriously by adults (or by some teenagers), whose hope it was that the raucous noise spreading across the country was merely a fad—an aberration of America's teenage psyche gone temporarily lunatic—that would soon fade away.

Indeed, in order for rock 'n' roll to shed its low-class, outlaw image and become respectable it would need a spokesman acceptable and believable to adults—preferably a white Anglo-Saxon Protestant who projected mainstream, middle-class values and offered some degree of order and decorum. Someone like Dick Clark.

It was at this crucial juncture in the annals of pop music that Clark assumed control of *Bandstand*, the television show that would soon become as instrumental as Elvis himself in altering the face of American popular music. But, fresh off spinning easy-listening standards over WFIL radio, Clark confessed that the increasing popularity of rock 'n' roll music on *Bandstand* had him baffled. "The music I listened to was the last vestige of the big band era," he later said.[34]

He was not alone in not understanding rock 'n' roll. "It was a total turnaround from Jo Stafford and the Four Aces to Fats Domino and Bobby Darin," explained Jerry Ross, who was hired as a WFIL radio disc jockey not long after Clark became host of *Bandstand*. "We were all learning, and being influenced by the new music. It was a very exciting time."

Ross described Clark as a rock 'n' roll novice who "didn't know Chuck Berry from a huckleberry" when he inherited *Bandstand*, and claimed that Tony Mammarella (who, beginning in 1955, shared the task of selecting *Bandstand*'s music with Bob Horn) "screened everything" before it made the show's playlist.

But Clark proved to be an adept learner, attuning himself to the rock 'n' roll scene by relying on promotion men and key disc jockeys in Philadelphia and around the country. Locally, that meant monitoring Philadelphia's two black-oriented but white-owned stations, where Clark relied on the ears of WHAT's Hy ("Hyski Oroony McVouty O'Zoo") Lit, as well as Georgie Woods ("the guy with the goods") and Douglas "Jocko" ("your ace from outer space") Henderson, both of WDAS. Ross contended that when one of those local powerhouse jocks got on a record, Clark "would pick up on that information, verify it, and when he knew that there was good response he would start programming [the record] lightly, and then would increase his rotation."

Lit, who was still learning the game himself in 1956, had specialized in the pop sounds of Frank Sinatra and Perry Como before his friend and future *Bandstand* announcer Charlie O'Donnell hired the deejay to play rock 'n' roll for WHAT radio. It would not be long before Lit broke rock 'n' roll records with the best of them in Philadelphia.

The only white disc jockey at WHAT at that time, Lit said he "went in totally blind" and winged it. "A listener would call and say, 'Play that boss record by Little Richard,' and I'd impersonate the listener and say, 'Here's a boss record by Little Richard.' They'd ask for a record by Fats Domino, and I'd say, 'I don't call *him* Fats, he don't call *me* Fats. Here's *Antoine* Domino.'"

Lit recalled receiving a telephone call from Dick Clark not long after Clark had inherited *Bandstand*. Clark told Lit he listened to his radio program, liked his taste in music, and played many of Lit's selections on *Bandstand*. "He thought it would be nice if we had lunch," recalled Lit, who found Clark to be "one of the nicest guys you'd ever want to meet. We became very good friends, and we always discussed radio and music."

Irv Nahan, who managed Georgie Woods when the WDAS deejay emceed r&b shows held frequently at the local Uptown Theatre, confirmed that Clark also used to call Woods "to find out what black records he was playing that he felt he could play [on *Bandstand*]."

The more Clark listened to the rock 'n' roll programmed by the likes of Hy Lit, Georgie Woods, Jocko Henderson, and Tony Mammarella, the more he enjoyed it, and the more it helped him gain an insight into *Bandstand*'s teenage guests. "I knew that if I could tune into them and keep myself on the show I could make a great deal of money," he said.[35] It did not take long for Clark to put his plan into action. By using *Bandstand* to introduce young white singers less offensive than "Elvis the Pelvis," the show's host did more than any other non-performer to change the face of rock 'n' roll—and amassed a personal fortune in the process.

Rock and roll entrepreneur/eccentric Phil Spector described Philadelphia in its heyday as "the most insane, most dynamic, the most beautiful city in the history of rock 'n' roll," a city in which cash-poor, ambition-filled wheeler-dealers—aspirants to the riches wrought by the creation of a hit record—plotted and schemed around the clock. "Money was a lot of it, of course," conceded Spector, "but there was something else as well: a purist's love of hustle for its own sake."[36] That hustle, observed pop music historian Arnold Shaw, yielded a "tightly knit complex of record labels, distributors, promoters, managers, and singers, all revolving around Dick Clark, which has been called the Philadelphia 'Mafia.'"

They were not the mafia per se, but rather a tight, powerful clique of would-be entrepreneurs who, in their quest for the elusive big score, had been historically overshadowed by neighboring New York City's front-line players.

In the mid-1950s, America's few major record companies, aided by their mighty national distribution networks, ruled the pop music industry. But their dominance was about to be challenged. Since the end of World War II a myriad of small independent labels had appropriated the market in black rhythm and blues, as well as a good part of the jazz and country music fields from the majors. With the rise of rock 'n' roll, which was essentially a product of the "indies," competition between them and the major labels intensified.

Philadelphia's *Bandstand* provided that city's would-be pop music tycoons a venue of their own. Barely recognized outside of Philadelphia, they carved out their niche in a pop music industry still shaped by local spheres of influence, and every so often struck paydirt. (One of the first rock 'n' roll records to make the national charts was Bill Haley and the Comets' "Crazy Man Crazy," issued in 1953 by Philadelphia's tiny Essex label.) None of these entrepreneurs dared imagine that a television show originating from their very own city would soon be fawned over by America's teenagers (and by almost every record company in the country), and that Philadelphia would, for a few wild and wooly years, become the center of the rock 'n' roll universe.

The competition for the exposure of new records in Philadelphia would soon grow cutthroat, giving rise to wheeling, dealing, and scheming on a grand scale. For if there was one underlying axiom for a business as serendipitous as the pop music industry, it was that the most promising song in the world did not stand a chance unless it could be heard by the masses.

A hint of things to come was offered in January 1957, when Bernie Lowe, owner of the recently founded Cameo Records, approached his old friend Dick Clark and offered him twenty-five percent of the publishing rights to the hottest record in Philadelphia in return for a major hyping of that record to the guys who could do best by it—the most influential radio disc jockeys across America. It was an offer Dick Clark did not refuse.

Born as Bernard Lowenthal in Philadelphia in 1917 (d. 1993), Lowe, who was to become the biggest player in that city's pop music industry in the late 1950s and early 1960s, learned to play the piano at an early age, honing his skills playing barrelhouse numbers in former speakeasies after the Prohibition era came to an end. Lowe spent much of the 1930s on the road as a pianist with such name bands as Meyer Davis, Jan Savitt, and Lester Lanin, while also finding the time to perform on a WPEN radio program emceed by Jack Steck.

Just prior to World War II, Lowe and fellow musician Artie Singer landed steady gigs in the Walt Whitman Hotel's house combo in Camden, New Jersey. Lowe spent the war years in the navy, after which he rejoined Singer as a member of WIP radio's studio orchestra, a job which soon proved to be unsteady; because of their high maintenance cost, radio's live orchestras began to fall by the wayside as the 1940s drew to a close. Seeking job security, Lowe and Singer opened the "20th Century Institute of Music" school in Philadelphia, and when Paul Whiteman came looking for a musical combo to appear regularly on his *TV-Teen Club* he chose Lowe to put one together. Artie Singer became the contractor for the new combo.

Another Lowe business associate and right-hand man was songwriter Kal Mann (born Kalman Cohen in Philadelphia in 1917). In the early 1950s, Mann supported himself by writing comedy jingles and song parodies before deciding to take piano lessons at the "20th Century School of Music," which happened to be located just across the street from where he lived. After the first lesson, Bernie Lowe told Mann to go home and practice, at which point the pupil informed the professor that he did not have a piano on which to do so. "Then what are you taking piano lessons for?" queried the talented and crafty Lowe. Intrigued by Mann's song parody skills and aware that the student was already writing lyrics to somebody else's music, Lowe suggested that Mann "might as well write them to ours."

"*Ours?*" thought Mann.[37]

They would pose no threat to Lerner and Loewe or to Rodgers and Hart, but as a songwriting team Bernie Lowe—who intended to supply the music for Kal Mann's lyrics—thought Lowe and Mann would do just fine.

Kal Mann accepted Bernie Lowe's offer, and for a short time they and Artie Singer wrote together. Having no success, however, Singer amicably set out on his own. But it would not be long before Singer reappeared on the scene with what would prove to be one of the most successful songs in rock 'n' roll history—one whose publishing rights Dick Clark would acquire before the *American Bandstand* host gave it a significant promotional boost on his popular television show.

Working on a shoestring, Lowe and Mann cut a deal with local recording mogul Ivin Ballen, who, in exchange for three Lowe-Mann songs, agreed to let the pair work out of his Gotham Records studio in South Philadelphia. But after several months passed and Ballen still had not received his three songs, he began to lean on Lowe. Realizing the time had come to pay the piper, Lowe, not wont to giving away anything of potential value, grabbed Kal Mann's book of unpublished songs and said to his partner, "Let's see the three worst songs ya got!"[38] Lowe gave those three songs to Ballen.

In 1956, after having several of their compositions published and recorded, Lowe and Mann signed a one-year songwriting deal with the powerful, New York-based Hill and Range music publishing company. The songwriting duo from Philadelphia even had the good fortune to have one of their songs, "Teddy Bear," placed on Elvis Presley's recording agenda that year, but in order to do so they had to relinquish control of the song to Hill and Range. Not only did Mann and Lowe lose control of their song, but also, because of the lengthy royalty payment process, it would be at least a year after the record was released before they could reap any monetary gain from their work.

If there was one thing Bernie Lowe coveted more than writing a hit song it was owning his own record company, but he not only lacked the cash necessary to underwrite such an undertaking, he also lacked the nerve required to plunge unwaveringly into a risky business historically dominated by a few major record labels. Agnes Mammarella, who became friendly with Lowe when the two worked on Paul Whiteman's TV show together, remembered Lowe forever talking about producing a hit record, "but he always needed encouragement to get into the business."

Lowe had tiptoed around the edges of the record business for years. He threw in with Artie Singer, and nightclub owner/talent agent/attorney Nat Segal to form SLS (Singer-Lowe-Segal) Records during the early 1950s, but little came of the enterprise. And although he, Horn and Segal were more successful with their Teen and Sound record labels, Lowe was essentially a frustrated bit player in those enterprises. He even formed his own Bernlo label, but lacked the resources and industry contacts to make a go of it.

Lowe finally took the plunge late in 1956. He borrowed $2,000 from his family and formed Bernard Lowe Enterprises, which consisted of Mayland Music publishing and Cameo records.[39] But the first five Cameo releases stiffed and Lowe was broke once again. Meanwhile, he and Kal Mann had written a song called "Butterfly," which they considered to be a potential hit. But they were still under contract to Hill and Range and realized that if they claimed to be the song's writers its publishing rights would revert to Hill and Range, as had been the case with "Teddy Bear." Lowe saw "Butterfly" as his last shot at keeping Cameo records from going under, so he and Mann decided to release it themselves without listing any songwriter.

To record the song, Lowe engaged Charlie Gracie (née Graci), the South Philly son of Italian immigrant parents, who had recorded locally, if unspectacularly, since his days on *TV-Teen Club*, where he had won, among other things, a refrigerator, the first one his family ever owned. All of five feet four inches tall, Gracie recalled that although Lowe "was looking for the tall, sexy, handsome Elvis-type who could sing and play the guitar, it ended up he couldn't find one in Philadelphia, and he wound up with me!" Furthermore, since Lowe, who ran Cameo records out of his Philadelphia row house basement, was broke, he cut a deal with the owner of a local recording studio, giving him a piece of "Butterfly" in return for studio time with which to record the song.

The December session went well, as Gracie sang and accompanied himself on guitar while Lowe played the piano on "Butterfly" and on the flip side of the record, "Ninety-Nine Ways." Lowe "knew what he wanted," recalled Gracie, "and we didn't stop until we got it."

Released locally in the waning days of 1956, "Butterfly," a jilted lover's mid-tempo lament about his two-timing girlfriend, took off like a shot. "We knew within a few days it was going to be a big, big hit," recalled Lowe. But his dream come true was about to turn into a nightmare.

It was an established recording industry practice in the 1950s for record labels to "cover" or copy potential hit songs released by other labels, particularly small labels with poor distribution, such as Cameo. At least a dozen cover versions of "Butterfly" were being rushed out, the most ominous of which was sung by Andy Williams, who had the promotional advantage of appearing regularly on a network TV show. Lowe, who realized he lacked the means to distribute Gracie's original version of the song around the country, would not only suffer a loss of record sales revenue because of the cover versions; because no writer's name was listed on the tune he would lose the songwriting royalties as well.

Lowe's dream—not to mention the last of his borrowed cash—was about to go down the drain. But as he told a 1960 House subcommittee investigating music industry payola, "I was pretty determined not to go just back to songwriting."

Less than two weeks after "Butterfly" was released he approached Dick Clark, who, after a half-year as *Bandstand* host, was already a major force in local pop music circles and was fast becoming ensconced in a coast-to-coast web of influential disc jockeys. "I think I have finally hit one," Lowe told Clark. "Orders are coming in and it is being played around town, and everybody tells me it is going to be a big one." He then asked if Clark would tout Charlie Gracie's recording of "Butterfly" to disc jockeys around the country as the original version and tell them "there is no shame to play it, because it is a hit."[40] For doing as much, said the label owner, he would give Clark 25 percent of the publishing rights to the song.

Clark, who stands on the thirty-year-old payola investigation record and prefers not to discuss its particulars, revealed to congressional investigators in 1960 that he told Lowe he "would be very happy" if the Cameo owner was able to score his first hit for the label, and he agreed to tell disc jockeys across the country that "Butterfly" was already big in Philadelphia. Clark maintained that he told Lowe "it wouldn't make any difference one way or the other" if he received a portion of the song's royalties, but "Lowe insisted that I take a financial interest in the song. I again said it was unnecessary and the discussion ended."[41]

The discussion may have ended, but "Butterfly's" rainbow ride to worldwide success had just begun. Clark, who played Gracie's version of "Butterfly" on *Bandstand* from the onset, subsequently invited the artist to appear on the show to plug his hit. He also took a copy of Gracie's recording to a New York meeting of disc jockeys from across the country, "to vouch for the fact that the record had done well in Philadelphia." [42] ("Butterfly" was number one in that city within several weeks of its release.)

Charlie Gracie's and Andy Williams's versions of "Butterfly" both sold well nationally, "but we had it in the groove," recalled the South Philly singer. "Of course, we also had Dick Clark with us."

In fact, the song sold so well that things soon reached a point "where we had to have somebody's name on there as a writer" in order to earn songwriting royalties, Lowe recalled in 1960. [43] He decided to credit "Butterfly" to "Anthony September"—the *nom de plume* of Anthony Septembre Mammarella—who had previously been listed as the writer of the flip side.

"Butterfly" went on to become a worldwide hit and proved to be one of 1957's biggest sellers. Some months later, after Lowe reaped the financial rewards for the song's publishing royalties and for record sales of Gracie's Cameo version, he approached Clark and told him he was "very grateful" for Clark's promotion of "Butterfly" and that "things are working out pretty good." In fact, things were working out so good that Lowe told Clark he had $7,000 from "Butterfly's" publishing royalties, and "I want to give it to you."

What happened next remains in dispute. Clark said he told Lowe "again that the payment wasn't necessary," while Lowe maintained that Clark's response to the record man's offer was, "Well, O.K., if you want to give it [the $7,000] to me." What is certain is that in December 1957, Clark accepted a $7,000 check "on the account of 'Butterfly'" from Lowe's Mayland Music, drawn, at Clark's request, to his mother-in law, Margaret Mallery ("for the education of her children and the operation she needs," Clark later explained). But after realizing he or his mother-in-law might be liable for federal income tax on the money, Clark returned the check and had Lowe make out a new one payable to Click Corporation, a company owned by Clark. Click Corp. subsequently received a second $7,000 check from Mayland "on the account of 'Butterfly.'" [44]

Clark revealed in his 1976 autobiography that he did not realize in 1957 that he would "live to regret [his] decision to take the money" from Lowe. [45] But having done so made for an uncomfortable situation when, during the 1960 congressional investigation of broadcasting payola, the government attempted to bolster its contention that the money Clark received from Lowe was paid in exchange for Clark's promotion of "Butterfly." Clark denied making any agreement with Lowe concerning "Butterfly," but congressional probers proceded to produce a letter from Clark to Mayland Music in which Clark made reference to his and Lowe's "oral agreement in which you [Lowe] gave me twenty-five percent of the publisher's share of the song 'Butterfly.'"

When Clark was asked what exactly he had agreed to do for a share of the song's publishing rights, the *Bandstand* host straight-facedly replied that he had "agreed to do absolutely nothing." [46]

Due to the success of "Butterfly," Dick Clark reaped his first song publishing booty. If he had been unaware of the fast bucks that could be earned from a hot rock 'n' roll song, Bernie Lowe set him straight. As it turned out, "Butterfly" was only the first such song that the new *Bandstand* host would benefit from financially. As for "songwriter" "Anthony September" Mammarella, who, according to his wife Agnes, allowed Lowe to use his name as a favor to the owner, he ended up with somewhat less than Clark did. Mayland Music made payments totalling less than $7,000 to the *Bandstand* producer—a sum equal to what Lowe identified as "the one-third that I said I would give him to put his name on" "Butterfly" and "Ninety-Nine Ways." [47] Meanwhile, the real songwriter, Kal Mann, would not receive credit for the song until 1960 and only received half of the royalties due to him years later.

· · ·

In January 1957, just as "Butterfly" was breaking big around the country, Bob Horn returned to Philadelphia to stand trial on the vice charges lodged against him. Just six days before his scheduled court appearance he steered his big green Caddy in the wrong direction on a one-way street, striking a car going the correct way, and injuring a family of five in the other vehicle. The hapless Horn was discovered raving incoherently at the accident scene and was arrested and charged with drunk and reckless driving. Once again his name was splashed in bold headlines throughout Philadelphia as the *Evening Bulletin* reminded its readers that Horn already faced two trials before this latest arrest.

Horn was the last of the Philadelphia vice defendants to stand trial, and in one of life's subtle ironies Lee Stewart, who Horn had helped sabotage as his *Bandstand* cohost and who subsequently found work as a reporter for the *Camden* [N.J.] *Courier Post,* was assigned to cover the courtroom proceedings. The trial commenced on January 28th, with the much-excoriated defendant facing four counts of statutory rape. The prosecution's sole witness was Dolores Farmer, who testified that she and Horn had sexual relations on at least four occasions, the first occurring when she was just fourteen. [48]

Farmer claimed the relationship ended when she and the former *Bandstand* host both realized "it was wrong." [49] But Horn said he told Farmer to stay away from him after he realized she was a psychopathic liar. "I don't believe Dolores Farmer dislikes me or intended to hurt me," Horn testified on his third day in the courtroom. "I can only say that for her this trial is the spotlight."[50] The only point on which the two parties agreed was that they stopped seeing each other near the end of 1955.

In an effort to discredit Farmer, sixteen-year-old Jerry Blavat testified to her "bad reputation"[51] and Horn's attorney deemed her accusations "baseless and dastardly,"[52] and Farmer "not worthy of belief."[53] The prosecution fought to counter these accusations by praising Farmer's forthrightness and courage, but after seven hours of deliberation, the jury announced that it was dead-locked with "no possibility of agreement."[54]

So it came to pass that on the heels of a lurid four-month sex scandal and a highly publicized trial, *Bandstand*'s tenuous rehabilitation remained incomplete until the state of Pennsylvania retried Bob Horn. A hostage of circumstance, Dick Clark remained under public scrutiny, which, in his words, caused him to appear "as pure as the driven snow," lest he be accused of "jumping on one of those thirteen-year-olds" on his afternoon dance show.[55]

Bandstand was now seen in the Philadelphia area on WFIL from 2:30 to 5:00 P.M., followed by ABC's network feed of Walt Disney's *Mickey Mouse Club*. Those locals who needed an additional dose of dancing teens obtained their fix by tuning to WPFH in nearby Wilmington, Delaware, where the *Grady and Hurst Show* went on the air at 5:00 P.M. After months of flat ratings, few believed *Bandstand* capable of reaching greater heights, but then again, few people knew Dick Clark. *Billboard*'s Bob Rolontz noted in 1958 that the show's initial high rating from the Bob Horn era did not begin to increase until Clark's "under-emotional, relaxed 'all-American boy' personality began to attract the kids—and the adults—possibly because it contrasted so sharply with the brashness of Horn."[56] Indeed, it was during the winter of 1957, with Horn temporarily out of the news, that Clark's *Bandstand* ratings surpassed those of his predecessor for the first time.

While *Bandstand*, in the words of Jack Steck, was "a sensation from the start," it took some time for the show's format to catch on elsewhere around the country. *Billboard* reported in November 1954 that although most well-known radio deejays had given TV a try during the last five years, "their survival-average has been low."[57] Aided and abetted by the relentless rise of rock 'n' roll, however, by 1956, successful *Bandstand* clones existed in major cities across the U.S. The most popular of them included ex-bandleader Ted Steele's *Teen Bandstand* in New York, Jim Lounsberry's *Bandstand Matinee* in Chicago, Don McCleod's *Detroit Bandstand*, and Jim Gallant's *Connecticut Bandstand*.

That same year, the NBC network dispatched a representative to Philadelphia to determine whether or not *Bandstand* was suitable for network status. Although NBC ultimately informed Tony Mammarella that it was not interested in televising WFIL-TV's hit show nationally, the network's fleeting interest in *Bandstand* caused Clark and Mammarella to believe it was simply a matter of time before another network embraced the show's concept. Furthermore, NBC's flirtation with *Bandstand* heightened the duo's fear that their show might be shut out of a prestigious network shot by one of its successful counterparts. "By then there were two or three copies of it and they were all successful," said Clark. "I firmly believed that it would be a national phenomenon."

It would be. Not on NBC or CBS, but on the American Broadcasting Company (ABC), which, by 1957, was the country's third major network. Although ABC had sixty affiliated television stations (accounting for about 12 percent of America's TV stations), any suggestion of parity with its two powerful rivals was fanciful delusion. Offering a patchwork system of national coverage, and broadcasting in black-and-white while its competitors splashed tantalizing color images across America's home screens, ABC was light years behind NBC and CBS. In the words of network chronologist Huntington Williams, ABC remained "just one step ahead of the bill collectors."[58]

ABC had its beginnings in 1943, when, in compliance with a U.S. Supreme Court ruling that no entity could own more than one broadcasting network, NBC, which owned the Red and the Blue networks, sold its less-prestigious Blue to Life Savers candy magnate Edward J. Noble. Renamed the American Broadcasting Company by Noble, the network immediately became a stepchild among broadcasting giants. With his new creation on the brink of bankruptcy in 1951, Noble hammered out a merger deal with Leonard Goldenson, who headed the financially solvent United Paramount Theatre chain. Desperate to enter the world of TV broadcasting, Goldenson begrudgingly made uncharacteristic concessions to Noble, not the least of which was Goldenson's pledge to keep his hands off of ABC's management for a three-year period. As a result of the protracted and acrimonious UPT-ABC merger wrangling, bad blood flowed freely between Noble and Goldenson. The latter chafed as the need for change at ABC became apparent to him, but as Goldenson (who declined to be interviewed for this book) said in *Beating the Odds: The Untold Story Behind the Rise of ABC*, each time he proposed a solution to a problem, "there were twenty ABC executives coming up with 210 reasons why it wouldn't work."[59]

When Ed Noble's grace period expired in 1956, ABC's corporate headquarters reeled, as Goldenson sacked network president Bob Kintner and brought in Ollie "the Dragon" Treyz, a highly touted Madison Avenue marketing whiz who had previously been with the network from 1948–1955.

Given ABC's lowly status among the three leading television networks (Goldenson said ABC was "still desperate for programming and experimenting with all sorts of strange ideas, trying to come up with something totally different"), it was the most likely to give the *Bandstand* concept a try.[60] Since the TV programs shown on NBC and CBS appealed mostly to an older audience set in its watching ways and in its buying habits, Treyz (who did not even respond to several requests to be interviewed for this book) decided that ABC would concentrate on developing programs with which younger viewers would more likely identify.

Treyz's decision to play to America's youth was not borne of whimsy. Since the end of World War II the country had experienced an unprecedented population explosion that had only begun to show signs of slight abatement. By 1957, high schools all across America prepared to accommodate a national body of teenagers whose numbers were on the rise. Author and history professor Robert Sobel observed in *The Manipulators: America in the Media Age*, that the baby boomers of 1946–55 "would upset the nation for the rest of their lives . . . whenever they entered the next stage in their development." As it was, in just a few years from 1956, the next stage in the development of the first wave of baby boomers would be the newly confirmed and coveted status of teenager, and it was already a given that the ranks of this recently recognized demographical group would swell for years to come. America, wrote Sobel, "would respond by a hurried effort to accommodate them."[61] Ollie Treyz and his youth-oriented television network prepared to do likewise.

In addition to developing youth-oriented programming for ABC, Treyz also planned to move ABC into daytime hours in 1957, so that the network could "play with blue chips at the main table."[62] But since ABC was still preoccupied with developing its prime-time schedule, Leonard Goldenson asked Treyz to see if his network could acquire from an affiliate a local daytime show that could be broadcast nationally.

Because WFIL-TV was an ABC-affiliate, Jack Steck was privy to the network's programming strategy. He received word in May that ABC was about to abandon its afternoon movie and was in the process of querying its affiliates as to a possible cost-efficient replacement "to fill a couple of hours [on the network] in the afternoon."[63] Thinking that *Bandstand* could fill ABC's bill, Steck buttonholed Tony Mammarella and suggested he urge Dick Clark to tout the show to ABC's assistant director of programming, Ted Fetter.

Steck's suggestion would ultimately result in Fetter being regarded at ABC as the man who discovered Dick Clark, but Fetter, who at the time Clark came calling considered himself fortunate just to have a job at ABC, said the claim was "not true. Dick Clark discovered *me*."

By the time Theodore (Ted) Fetter joined CBS-TV in 1949 he had a college degree, acting and producing experience in the theatre, and a songwriting cousin named Cole Porter. The following year Fetter left CBS to become coproducer of NBC-TV's *Your Hit Parade* show, but he returned in 1953 to produce Jack Paar's morning TV show. He remained at CBS until 1956, when Bob Kintner—a close friend since their college days—offered Fetter a job at ABC just weeks before Leonard Goldenson took over and proceded to clean house.

The day Kintner was ousted from ABC, Fetter received a message from Goldenson's office that the new boss wanted to see him. "This is it," thought the new employee, so certain he was about to be fired that he immediately cleaned out his desk. But after resolutely making his way to Goldenson's office to meet his fate, Fetter was taken aback when Goldenson, who had a great interest in television but no experience with the medium, picked Fetter's brain rather than fire him, and proceeded to find out "everything he could about the program department."[64]

Although *Bandstand* was doing well—it was drawing up to 65 percent of the Philadelphia-area daytime audience—there was a remote possibility that Roger Clipp and George Koehler would drop the show in favor of the new network feed. Dick Clark, who believed he had taken *Bandstand* as far as he could as a local show, saw the opportunity to advance the show (and himself). He asked Tony Mammarella for a kinescope of *Bandstand*, which he intended to take with him to ABC's Manhattan headquarters in an attempt to persuade the network to air the show nationally. But Clark was told that Koehler had sent a kinescope of the show to ABC a month earlier, and had not heard back from the network. As further discouragement, a record plugger friend of Clark's who had gained access to one of ABC's executive meetings by masquerading as a sponsor reported back that ABC execs thought Clark had "droopy eyes and a lousy set."[65]

Undaunted, Clark contacted ABC. Although by his account he initially spoke directly with Ted Fetter, Fetter thought someone from the office of Jim Aubrey, ABC-TV's director of programming, told him about "this fellow in Philadelphia who has a local show doing very well in the ratings and he wants to come up and talk with us about it." Fetter's first inclination was to check *Bandstand*'s ratings, "and they were very, very high," he said.

But Fetter, who had been involved in television production since 1950, remained skeptical about the popular Philadelphia-area show called *Bandstand*. He explained in 1993 that back in 1957 ABC "had stuff coming in over the transom from every local station, saying 'We've got this show that would really be a big hit on the network.'" ABC had gone so far as to briefly try one or two of the unsolicited programs, "but I was very skeptical of the local shows," said Fetter. He sought to dispense with the "fellow in Philadelphia" by firing off a "don't call us, we'll call you" letter to Clark, which he closed with the platitudinous invitation for Clark to "drop in and say hello" if he was ever in New York.[66]

Taking Fetter at his word, Clark, who happened to be on vacation, hopped aboard a plane and was in New York at the drop of a hat. Surprised to see him, Fetter, who by that time had viewed the kinescope of *Bandstand*, did his best to discourage the show's host. "Dick, networks can get into a lot of trouble putting on shows that have done wonderfully well locally, but are just local shows [that] . . . don't catch on network," he told the *Bandstand* host. "I hesitate to put this show on because its just kids *dancing*!"

Clark, who later maintained that he knew if he could get *Bandstand* seen elsewhere, "it would probably enjoy the same success," told Fetter, "You're missing the point. This is their own world. It could come from . . . anywhere; it doesn't matter. It happens to be here in Philadelphia." There was something about *Bandstand* that "people watch," he emphasized, "and I think they'll watch it nationally."[67]

Despite Clark's exhortations, everything Fetter knew from his years in the business told him that *Bandstand* was wrong for the network. "On the surface of it," he recalled, the show "did not have anything that would really grab people and [cause them to say] 'I gotta watch that tomorrow!'"

That might have been the end of their conversation had Clark not played his trump card, informing Fetter that WFIL was prepared to deliver the program to ABC "for nothing."[68] The only expense to ABC would arise from transmitting *Bandstand* from WFIL-TV's studios to the network feed.

Fetter reconsidered *Bandstand*'s local ratings. "There it was," he said to himself. "It was doing well, people were watching it." He also realized his judgment was not infallible. After all, he had originally balked when asked to produce the televised version of radio's long-running *Your Hit Parade* because he believed the musical show lacked both action and suspense and was destined to flop. Eventually persuaded to coproduce *Your Hit Parade*, the show became a TV staple for the better part of a decade. Now Fetter wondered if that would be the case with *Bandstand*.

It would be a stab in the dark for ABC to add Clark's show to its schedule, but in obtaining *Bandstand* free of charge, the network had nothing to lose. All that remained was for Fetter to convince his boss, Jim Aubrey, of *Bandstand*'s network viability. But when he told Aubrey about the "fellow in Philadelphia" who hosted a local show featuring "kids dancing" that was doing well in the ratings, Aubrey remained unmoved. "What else?" he wanted to know.

"That's it!" said Fetter.

"Do they have any guest stars?" asked Aubrey.

"He plays records!" replied Fetter. Sensing that Aubrey was not buying his proposition, Fetter proceded to hit his boss with what he termed *Bandstand*'s "big advantage." "They won't charge us anything for it."

"Really?" replied Aubrey in disbelief.

"Look," said Fetter, "it can't cost us anything to get it on the network. The worst that could happen is we can lose the few stations we have, and who knows?"

"Alright," Aubrey finally told Fetter, "if you really want to give it a try, go ahead. I'll give it two weeks."[69]

That June, Fetter sent Clark another letter, but this one indicated ABC now viewed *Bandstand* with "interest and pleasure" and planned to come to Philadelphia for a first-hand look at the show.[70] So it was that Aubrey, Fetter, and Army Grant, ABC's head of daytime TV, paid *Bandstand* a visit in July. Jack Steck recalled that, "Like all network people, they began saying, 'We'll tell you what we could do to improve this.' They were suggesting all sorts of crazy things that would have loused the show up but good, [until] Tony finally got very impatient."

"Look," Mammarella told Aubrey, "Dick Clark has nursed this show along to where it's *sensationally* successful. Dick has three things in mind in doing the show. The most important thing is the kids. The second most important thing is the music. The third most important thing is for the host to be as unobtrusive as possible." Mammarella pointed out that the show had already proven itself in Maryland, Delaware, New Jersey, and Pennsylvania, and it would do the same nationally. "You've got to take it the way it is, or don't bother with it," he insisted.[71]

Mammarella's level of exasperation was such that his wife recalled him arriving home one evening muttering to himself, "It's a successful show and they want me to change it. You don't change it if it's successful!" But if he had convinced Jim Aubrey of *Bandstand*'s suitability as a network program, Aubrey nevertheless remained noncommital. "We'll let you know," said the ABC executive as he headed back to New York.[72] To the surprise of almost everyone at WFIL, Aubrey called Jack Steck a few days later and told him the network had decided to give the local station's hit show a trial run. ABC planned to call its new show *American Bandstand*.

• • •

While Clark labored to sell *Bandstand* to ABC, Bob Horn's statutory rape retrial—a stripped-down version of his first courtroom battle—took place that June. This time Horn's fate was to be decided not by a jury, but (at the defendant's request, according to state law) by a judge, who subsequently ruled that all testimony would be restricted to what had occurred on the four specific dates on which Horn was accused of improprieties with Dolores Farmer. The ruling worked to Horn's advantage because it prohibited Farmer from mentioning the alleged sexual encounters she had with him prior to those specific dates in question.

Then, on the third day of the trial, the judge unexpectedly ruled that the prosecution had failed to set forth in the bills of indictment that Horn was sixteen years old or older when the alleged sexual encounters with Farmer occurred. Since such proof "was necessary to make out a charge against him of statutory rape," he found Horn not guilty of all the charges.[73]

The ruling freed Horn, the apparent benefactor of an inexplicable blunder by the prosecution, without ever addressing the matter of innocence or guilt. Had the case not turned on a technicality, the adjudicator's decision would have been difficult to predict. Although Farmer was not the only underage female with whom Horn was rumored to have been involved (almost everyone interviewed for this book who knew the former *Bandstand* host said his salacious behavior had reached the point where it became commonly accepted), the predilection for a family involved in such cases to shield a daughter from harmful publicity by refusing to press charges, rendered Farmer's case the strongest—if not the only one—that the prosecution could muster.

But the character and credibility of Farmer was suspect from the start. Compounding matters was a string of bizarre revelations by Farmer's father, who testified in court that he had known Horn for four years, that on one particular occasion he overheard Horn invite his daughter to Horn's apartment to pick up a record player, that Horn had visited his daughter at their home at least eight times, and that he, Farmer, had been home the day Horn allegedly arrived to take his daughter on a trip to the Jersey shore. Taking everything into consideration, the judge might have seen things Horn's way.

No matter. Awaiting disposition of his two drunk driving cases and an impending lawsuit stemming from his second automobile accident, Horn did not quibble over his acquittal by virtue of a legal technicality. He quickly returned to Houston, but Philadelphia was destined to hear more about Horn's activities. His forthcoming federal income tax evasion indictment, in which it was revealed that Horn had regularly received payments from local record distributors—allegedly as inducements for him to play their records on *Bandstand*—served as a harbinger of the coming payola scandal of 1959 and 1960. During that gloomy episode, many disc jockeys were fired for allegedly taking money to play certain records on the air, and highly publicized congressional hearings focusing on bribery and other nefarious broadcasting practices rocked the music and the broadcasting industries to their foundations, threatening the very existence of *American Bandstand* and the career of Dick Clark.

• • •

Despite the fact that Clark had to convince ABC to broadcast *Bandstand* nationally, the teenage dance show meshed nicely with the network's new emphasis on music-related programs. Soon after he took over the helm at ABC-TV, Ollie Treyz blustered that the network's lowly status was actually advantageous in that it afforded his network the opportunity to "take chances and experiment" with its programming.[74] One such experiment undertaken with the hope of luring a younger audience to ABC was its flirtation with the controversial rock 'n' roll music.

Since musical programs were one of the most cost-efficient (read: cheap) forms of programming, ABC-TV traditionally relied on such fare to fill out its network schedule. The struggling network discovered the power inherent in national TV to create a hit record early in 1955 when "The Ballad Of Davy Crockett," which was taken from an episode of *Disneyland*, ABC's first blockbuster TV show, became the number one song in America for five consecutive weeks, selling upwards of four million copies in sixteen languages. Furthermore, ABC's highly popular *The Adventures of Ozzie and Harriet* situation comedy launched the rock 'n' roll career of child star Ricky Nelson when Ozzie's younger son made his singing debut on that program in April 1957. One month later ABC afforded New York based disc jockey Alan Freed (at that time the nation's most prominent rock 'n' roll spinner) two prime-time rock 'n' roll specials with the assurance that, should Freed's TV ratings prove respectable, a prime-time rock 'n' roll series would be in the offing. In the wake of Freed's specials ABC announced that, beginning in July, *Alan Freed's Big Beat*, a thirty minute show consisting of artists lip-synching their latest hit records, would begin a thirteen-week run on the network.

But ABC's national experiment with Freed's brand of rock 'n' roll proved apocalyptic when, on the third episode, black singing star Frankie Lymon, who had appeared on the show as a guest that evening, was caught by the cameras dancing with a white girl. "I remember saying to the director, 'This could get us into trouble,'" recalled Ted Fetter. "At the time there were a lot of Southern stations that would have questioned that." Question it they did.

ABC's southern affiliates and national sponsors went berserk, and Freed's *Big Beat* TV show was dropped by ABC one week before *American Bandstand* was set to make its network debut.

It has been said by some that the emergence of rock 'n' roll music in the 1950s served to break down more racial barriers than did *Brown v. Board of Education*, the historic Supreme Court ruling in 1954 that declared segregated public schools to be unconstitutional; but as evinced by the Frankie Lymon incident, rock 'n' roll also caused many of its more fanatical opponents to decry the mixing of the races as one more evil it had brought about.

Although it seemed as though ABC, which was about to introduce a new program that featured integrated rock 'n' roll, was on the proverbial hot seat, Ted Fetter maintained that Freed's cancellation did not cause the ABC programming executive any trepidation over his decision to give Philadelphia's *Bandstand* a network shot. While the TV shows of Freed and Clark both centered around rock 'n' roll, Fetter believed their formats to be significantly different. He thought Freed's show had "sort of a wild party feeling" similar to the deejay's tumultuous live theatre shows, which resulted in spontaneous and chaotic dance floor action as well as frequent cut-ins and partner changes—all of which proved conducive to race-mixing in the studio and trouble for the network. On the other hand, *Bandstand* was a more controlled and scripted show, on which the studio guests "got up and they danced with each other for a dance. You could see before it started who was going to dance with whom."

Still, ABC was aware that airing *Bandstand* nationally posed a potential racial problem for the network. The bottom line, recalled Fetter, was "just be careful we don't have blacks and whites dancing together."

That was a highly unlikely scenario, considering the *de facto* segregation of *Bandstand*'s studio audience, which was drawn primarily from four area high schools. Although the public school system's John Bartram High and West Philadelphia High were racially mixed, the same could not be said for the two parochial schools—West Catholic for Girls and West Catholic for Boys—situated nearest the WFIL studios, from which the majority of *Bandstand*'s audience was drawn. Because few blacks were of the Catholic faith, not many of them attended parochial school. So it was that while almost a quarter of the 400,000 students attending Philadelphia's public schools in the mid-1950s were black, only a small handful of blacks attended the city's parochial schools.

As a result, *Bandstand* originated as a predominantly segregated show and commenced to blend unnoticeably into the lily-white format of early 1950s television. But by the mid-1950s, as the show became imbued by black-derived music and dance, racial segregation in the TV studio persisted. Dick Clark told writer Henry Schipper in 1990 that when he took over the show in 1956, "a few blacks were allowed in the audience, just a smattering."[75] (Out of approximately seventy-five photographs published in *The History of American Bandstand* that showed teenagers on the set during the 1950s, only one reveals any blacks—a couple and two girls, surrounded by a sea of white faces.) Weldon McDougall, a black who lived just blocks from the WFIL studios and attended West Philadelphia High, conceded there were always some blacks on the show, "but it was maybe one or two people. It was a clique [of white teenagers] from all over the city, and the biggest crowd was from South Philly."

That is not to say that in the beginning many blacks even sought admittance to *Bandstand*. During the show's early years as a strictly white pop venue it was of little interest to them. McDougall, a member of the (Philadelphia) Larks vocal group, described the white pop played on *Bandstand* as "bullshit music . . . that didn't have a beat," and claimed that most blacks simply did not care about attending the show or dancing to its music.

Bandstand eventually did offer its dancers rhythm and blues, but by that time membership cards were needed to gain admittance to the show. Because the *Bandstand* crowds had grown so large, however, new cards were seldom issued, "And that's how [blacks were excluded]," claimed McDougall.

Fellow West Philadelphian Lee Andrews, who, along with his vocal group, the Hearts, attended Bartram High, agreed that *Bandstand* was "systematically set up" to be segregated, that there was "always some reason black kids couldn't get into" the WFIL studio. It may have been because they did not have a membership card, or perhaps they did not meet the dress code, but for whatever reason, "everybody began to understand, 'Hey, this is a show for white people!'" charged Andrews.

Whatever the case, by the time *American Bandstand* appeared in August 1957, featuring the largely black-derived idiom of rock 'n' roll, the show's studio audience remained segregated to the extent that viewers around the country did not have an inkling that Philadelphia contained one of the largest black populations in America.

Ironically, *American Bandstand*'s misrepresentation of Philadelphia's ethnicity began during a year that was historic in the area of civil rights. As the South (and many areas in the North, including Philadelphia) dragged its heels in complying with the Supreme Court's integration decree, the civil rights movement continued to gather steam. The tension of intersectional confrontation hung in the air throughout the summer of 1957, as the United

States Congress was locked in a fierce, protracted battle over the first enact-
ment of a major civil rights bill since the post-Civil War reconstruction era;
segregationists warned that President Eisenhower might use powers granted
to him in the bill to send troops to southern states to enforce the integration
orders of federal courts. (Eisenhower countered that he could not imagine any
circumstances that would cause him to do such a thing, but a month later, on
September 24th, he did just that when Arkansas governor Orval Faubus
defied a federal court order to integrate Little Rock's all-white high school.)

Not all of the fingerpointing could be directed at the South either, as racial
tensions also flared close to *American Bandstand*'s home town. The same week
the show made its bow, a debut of another kind took place in Levittown,
Pennsylvania, a lily-white postwar suburban community of 16,000 homes
located on the northeast outskirts of Philadelphia. The first black family to
move in was greeted by nightly gatherings of rock-throwing, name-calling
mobs of up to four hundred. The intimidation went on for ten days until
police finally dispersed the crowd with riot clubs and made several arrests.[76]
Meanwhile, two suburban communities just to the south of Philadelphia were
about to announce an end to racial segregation in their school districts.[77]

As it was, the volatile topic of race relations was foremost in the minds of
many Americans in all areas of the country at the time when Dick Clark
offered his rock 'n' roll dance show. To those viewers of *American Bandstand*
who were intimidated or appalled by the historic civil rights moves being
made by the federal government—reminders of which were brought into
their living rooms nightly by televised news reports—*Bandstand*'s whiteness
may have offered an affirmation of their futile yearning to retain the status
quo. On the other hand, to those national viewers who empathized with those
involved in the integration process then taking place, *Bandstand*'s whiteness
was a reminder that the complexion of its studio audience would eventually
be unacceptable.

WFIL, which opted to preserve the racial status quo, was not alone in
doing so. "There was little positive response to the rock 'n' rollers' experiment
with desegregation," observed history professor and author David Nasaw in
Going Out: The Rise and Fall of Public Amusements. "Instead, the public commentary that greeted [Alan] Freed and the disc jockeys who promoted live
shows with integrated audiences focused entirely on the degraded state of the
music and the rowdy behavior of the teenagers."[78] (ABC incurred no racial
problems in airing *American Bandstand*, but in order to be on the safe side,
each artist or group—black or white—who performed on the program was
subsequently whisked directly to the autograph table, thereby precluding any
repeat of the Frankie Lymon incident.)

• • •

Although the soaring cost of TV advertising caused each of the networks to experience increasing difficulty in selling airtime to national sponsors in 1957 (prompting *Variety* to report that "the panic button is beginning to ring at the networks"[79]), and Leonard Goldenson revealed that ABC was still experiencing difficulty "finding both daytime programs and sponsors,"[80] there was cause for guarded optimism as the network readied *American Bandstand* for national exposure. ABC's advertising rates remained lower than those of NBC and CBS and, although still the third-place network, ABC continued to gain additional TV affiliates in major marketing areas.

If *American Bandstand* proved even marginally acceptable in its trial run it would be added to ABC's fall line-up, when, for the first time, the network would have a TV affiliate in each of the country's major metropolitan markets. Cognizant that a successful fall line-up would finally put ABC on a competitive basis with NBC and CBS, Ollie the Dragon roared about ABC's "almost overnight advent" as a network.[81]

Following ABC's announcement that it intended to air *Bandstand* nationally, one Philadelphia critic wrote of Dick Clark's "great break," noting that ABC had cast "a fatherly eye" on Clark and viewed him as a "potential favorite of teenagers."[82] But Roger Clipp, who, from the start had been as lukewarm to the prospective success of *American Bandstand* as ABC executives had been, maintained higher hopes for Clark than he did for Clark's new teen-oriented network outing. The *Philadelphia Daily News* reported that WFIL "feels it is only a question of time before Clark is whisked to New York for bigger and better things."

It seemed nobody besides Clark was enamored by *American Bandstand*'s prospects for success. "Ironic, isn't it, that Philadelphia's first network contribution in years should be no more significant than a teen-age dance party," concluded one local critic. "Surely we can do better than that."[83]

In a year's time Clark had progressed from a controversial replacement host of *Bandstand* to the show's greatest booster. What is more, by single-handedly convincing ABC to air his teenage dance show nationwide, he had pulled the proverbial rabbit from the hat. But it is uncertain exactly why Clark believed so strongly that *Bandstand* would catch on nationally when nobody else gave it a chance. Part of his desire for ABC to pick up *Bandstand* undoubtedly stemmed from the possibility that WFIL was about to cancel the show (or at least scale back its air time) in favor of ABC's forthcoming afternoon network feed to its affiliates. But the chance of that happening was negligible, and by itself could not have motivated Clark to act as vigorously as he did in selling the show to ABC.

Clark is on record for stating that ever since his days at Syracuse University he was intrigued by the business aspects of broadcasting more than the announcing aspects. Although sustaining his career was foremost in his mind at the time he inherited *Bandstand*, Clark firmly believed that if he could carve out a niche on that show he stood to make "a great deal of money." The advancment of rock 'n' roll, a music Clark professed to know nothing about when he inherited *Bandstand*, was of secondary importance to him.

But an individual with Clark's intelligence and drive did not need his college degree in business to recognize that the pop music industry had recently entered a boom era. From the introduction of the 45 RPM single record in 1949, unit sales had increased by an annual average of 3 percent through 1954. Then, with the advent of rock 'n' roll, unit sales advanced 30 percent (an increase of 64 million units) the following year, and jumped another 36 percent (an incredible 100-million-unit sales increase) in 1956. Total unit sales for 1956—the year Clark succeeded Bob Horn—were 377 million, almost double the figure of two years earlier.[84]

Clark's self-taught crash course in rock 'n' roll, not to mention his windfall profit from the success of "Butterfly," led him to recognize that there was big money to be made in the pop music business, and little investment necessary to do so. At some point it occurred to him that he might be able to meet both of his goals—to perpetuate his career and make a lot of money—through the exploitation of rock 'n' roll. The business opportunities afforded a nationally known TV figure, along with any designs he harbored to join the flourishing rock 'n' roll game from the inside (as he ultimately did), make it easier to understand why Dick Clark pushed so hard for ABC to broadcast *Bandstand* nationally.

CHAPTER 4

Philadelphia, U.S.A.

D ick Clark's graduation from Syracuse University ensured him not only of a business degree, but also of what he described as a "sound" business education.[1] After having the exploitable position of *American Bandstand* host bestowed upon him, Clark discovered, as had Bob Horn, that the opportunity to make money—lots of it—came with the territory. Bernie Lowe had helped Clark to see the future, and now the future was at hand.

During the time when "Butterfly" was still soaring high on the charts, Clark had invested $1,000 to form Click Corporation in order to handle his song publishing and record hop revenues. Then, in May 1957, he paid $125 for a quarter interest in a failed record company called Jamie Records that, having issued a string of flops in 1956, was $400 in the red. What would become of Jamie, a subsidiary of Philadelphia's Universal Record Distributors, was anybody's guess, but whatever it amounted to, Clark would be entitled to 25 percent.[2]

Clark also discovered that money would come to him even when he was not actively seeking it. Record distributors, label owners, music publishers, and promo men now queued up outside Clark's cubby hole office at WFIL as they attempted to get him to play their records on *Bandstand*, and some even offered him the publishing rights to a particular song if he would do so, a practice that was common in the music business long before Clark came upon the scene.

Further opportunities to make money came about in July, when Clark, accountant Bernie Binnick, and record label owner Bob Marcucci formed the Binlark Company to bankroll the rock 'n' roll exploitation movie *Jamboree* in an attempt to cash in on the fad started in 1956 by Alan Freed's low-budget surprise moneymaker *Rock Around the Clock*.

Clark was not the only one in the record business interested in capitalizing on the growing industry of rock 'n' roll music. Bob Marcucci would soon make a name for himself as a scout and promoter of teenage idols. Born and raised in South Philadelphia, Marcucci graduated from South Philly High and went on to manage a band in which his friend Peter DeAngelis played. The duo began to write songs in 1951, and after peddling their demos to various record labels they decided to start their own record company. Since Marcucci's brother ran the dining room at the Chancellor Hotel in Philadelphia, they decided to call their label Chancellor. Marcucci used the Chancellor Hotel for his office while he waited tables to "keep everything going," much the same as Bernie Lowe ran Cameo Records from the basement in his home.

Marcucci and DeAngelis struck paydirt with local songstress Jodie Sands, when her pop ballad "With All My Heart" became a national best-seller in the spring of 1957, about the same time that "Butterfly" topped the charts. Am-Par Records, a subsidiary of the American Broadcasting Company, took notice and offered to buy the master from Marcucci and DeAngelis, but the duo declined to sell. Instead, they worked out a deal giving Am-Par the national distribution rights to that song and to future Chancellor releases.

Assured of national distribution, Marcucci now envisioned greater opportunities for Chancellor. All around him, young stars were popping up, achieving national success—not just Elvis Presley, the undisputed king of rock 'n' roll, who had just turned the Bernie Lowe/Kal Mann composition "Teddy Bear" into the number one song in America, but also younger, safer, less threatening (and thus more marketable) singers like Ricky Nelson and Charlie Gracie. Thanks to the promotional value of a weekly singing spot on his parents' ABC-TV situation comedy, Nelson now sold a lot of records. And Charlie Gracie, from Marcucci's own neighborhood, no less, had attained worldwide fame with his hit "Butterfly" in a matter of months. These and other Presley spin-offs (except for the intimidating Gene Vincent, perhaps), exhibited no threatening behavior and were welcomed into most of America's living rooms. "It looked like teenage idols were making it," recalled Marcucci, who determinedly set out to discover one for himself, even if he had to teach them to sing!

He decided to contact a young trumpet player named Francis Avallone, who lived in the neighborhood and performed with a local band called Rocco and the Saints, to see if he knew any young singers who might want to make a record. Avallone, who now called himself Frankie Avalon, suggested he check out the Saints' lead singer.

Marcucci attended the band's next gig and conceded that the Saints' blond-haired, blue-eyed singer was good enough to record, but "there was something about him that didn't hit me as the idol type." Then, as Marcucci was about to leave, Avalon got up to sing his obligatory nightly number, which stopped Marcucci in his tracks. "He just had something that was unbelievably charismatic," recalled the Chancellor co-owner. "He had everything!" But when Marcucci told Avalon that *he* was the singer the record executive wanted to record, Avalon "looked at me like I was crazy," and protested: "I'm not a singer, I'm a trumpet player!"

"You're the one I want," Marcucci reassured him, and into the recording studio they went.

Avalon's first record for Chancellor stiffed, but Marcucci, who had already produced his share of failed records, realized that he had something special in this young, raw talent. "We took Frankie on the road to the record hops and saw that the reaction to him was just unbelievable!"

It was while Marcucci readied Avalon's next release that he was approached by Bernie Binnick about investing in the movie *Jamboree*. Recognizing the promotional value inherent in such a venture, Marcucci threw in with Binnick and Clark and formed the Binlark Company to produce the film. As part of the deal, filmed performances of Jodie Sands, Frankie Avalon, and other Chancellor artists singing their upcoming releases were included in *Jamboree*. Charlie Gracie and a passel of other current artists also appeared in the film, as did a group of notable disc jockeys from around the world. The most prominent role among them went to Dick Clark.

Bandstand's success had already established Clark as a local promotional force among Philadelphia's record manufacturers and distributors. With the nationally-televised version of *Bandstand* due in August and the release of *Jamboree* set for that fall, Clark's promotional stock soared to a national scope. Thanks to the success of Charlie Gracie's "Butterfly," Bernie Lowe was able to move Cameo records out of his basement. Furthermore, Gracie's next record, "Fabulous," became a hit in the spring of 1957. This not only led to Gracie's appearance in *Jamboree*, it also caused Lowe to believe he had finally signed a consistent hitmaker. As ABC geared up to broadcast *American Bandstand* to an unsuspecting nation, visions of unfettered national exposure for his budding young singing star danced in Lowe's head.

Charlie Gracie and Frankie Avalon were not the only Italian-American teen idols to come out of Philadelphia. Gracie, whose Sicilian grandparents had their surname of Graci Americanized when they arrived in their new home in the early 1900s, lived near Bobby Rydell (née Ridarelli), who lived on 11th Street, several doors up the street from Fabiano "Fabian" Forte and just two blocks east of Frankie Avalon (who lived on 13th).

The neighborhood's common denominator was the noted South Philadelphia High School for Boys, located at Broad and Jackson Streets in the extreme southwest corner of the heart of the Italian community. Given the deep musical traditions inherent in so many Italian families (in the1940s and early 1950s several of their talented sons and daughters—including Frank Sinatra, Perry Como, and Dean Martin—became pop singing stars), South Philly High's prodigious number of singing alumni is not surprising. Many, in fact, honed their talents in the subway station at Broad Street and Snyder, adjacent to the school. "A lot of famous people graduated from there," said alumnus Charlie Gracie, before reciting a litany of names that included Mario Lanza (née Alfredo Cocozza), Al Alberts of the Four Aces, Al Martino, Armando "Buddy" Greco, Eddie Fisher, Frankie Avalon, James Darren (Ercolani), Fabian, and Chubby Checker (Ernest Evans). "Chubby was the only non-Italian," he quipped.

While a handful of these would-be teen idols were already local stars, the process of hyping Philadelphia's singing sons on a national basis was about to begin. Shortly before Dick Clark's national TV show made its debut, Bernie Lowe released Gracie's third record, "I Love You So Much It Hurts." Just days before *American Bandstand* hit the airwaves, Clark, commenting on the importance of young rock 'n' roll singers to the music business, pointed out that although "six months ago, no one ever heard of [Gracie], to us he's a big, big name."[3] Gracie, who was on tour in England when Clark bestowed this glowing praise upon him, could have been forgiven for having the same heady thoughts as Bernie Lowe. He was an international singing star who recorded for a man who was tight with Dick Clark. "We had a nice thing going," recalled Gracie. "Everything was perfect."

• • •

Clark, who was then putting in eighteen-hour days including personal appearances at dances six nights a week, told the press on the eve of *American Bandstand*'s debut, "This is more than I dared hope for right now." Going network was "about the greatest thing that can happen to a young fellow in this business."[4]

Clark was at the WFIL studios early on the hot and muggy Monday morning of August 5, 1957, hosting his radio program *Music Break* (which aired weekdays from eleven A.M. to one P.M.), and proceded to radiate enough nervous energy to drive everyone crazy by lunch time. Although ABC head of programming Jim Aubrey had granted Clark a couple of weeks to convince ABC that the country's burgeoning teenage market would show an interest in their peers dancing in Philadelphia, the skepticism initially exhibited by Ted Fetter about whether a show of such provincial origin could possibly garner enough national interest to sustain itself was held by many others at ABC. Nevertheless, a telegram arrived from Army Grant in New York, wishing Clark good luck.

Irv Ross, then supervisor of WFIL's engineering department, recalled that the station's TV crew was proud *Bandstand* had become a network show. He said the national program did not change a great deal from what it had been in its local days. "We added some production values [but it] was still our show and we simply fed it to" ABC.

Nevertheless, ABC did insist upon certain changes. For one, the network redesigned the *Bandstand* set, scrapping the canvas backdrop simulating a record store in favor of a wall of framed gold records. The network also introduced a new, smaller podium, perhaps to enhance Clark's image and impact on the TV screen. There also were attempts to homogenize *Bandstand* for national consumption. Teenagers interviewed by Clark would no longer be permitted to state their high school on the air (a practice now deemed too provincial), and Clark would henceforth refer to record sales across the entire country as well as those in Philadelphia.

At precisely three P.M., millions of viewers on ABC's forty-eight affiliated stations from coast to coast caught their first glimpse of the Philadelphia regulars dancing as they had danced for the previous five years. But now—at least on the network portion of the show seen from 3:00 to 4:30 P.M. (WFIL continued to televise the show locally from 2:30 to 5:00 P.M.)—the camera lens peered through a cutout map of the United States as it focused on the studio dance floor.

Then came the show's host. "Hi, I'm Dick Clark," he told millions of curious Americans that first afternoon. "Welcome to *American Bandstand*. You and I have got an hour and a half to share together with some of my friends here, lots of good music, and our special guest stars."[5]

But almost before the show began, disaster threatened. Technicians belonging to the National Association of Broadcast Employees and Technicians (NABET) in Chicago, Los Angeles, San Francisco, and New York walked off their jobs, protesting that ABC's employment of WFIL-TV's local technicians—represented by the International Alliance of Theatrical and Stage Employees—had deprived NABET members of work. The wildcat walkout caused program transmission problems to many ABC affiliates, and during what was thus far the most crucial moment of Dick Clark's career, many stations across the country had no choice but to display "Please Stand

By" messages to their home viewers. Fortunately for Clark, the interruption lasted only a few minutes before the technicians were appeased and returned to their duties.

In an attempt to attract the widespread audience sought by ABC and its advertisers, Philadelphia pop songstress Kitty Kallen, the Chordettes, and Billy Williams—each of whom enjoyed a current hit record and, more importantly, projected the innocuous image demanded by the networks—made guest appearances on *American Bandstand* that first day. Telegrams of congratulations from numerous celebrities were read over the air, among them Pat Boone and Frank Sinatra, both of whom happened to have their own shows slated for ABC-TV that fall. To get an immediate pulse on *American Bandstand*'s nationwide popularity, Clark and Tony Mammarella engineered a contest called "Why I'd Like a Date With Sal Mineo," in which viewers were asked to mail in their reason for requesting a date with the hot young film and recording star who had been a frequent *Bandstand* guest during the show's local days.

Long familiar with *Bandstand*'s fare, the Philadelphia press observed that "except for a more grandiloquent title . . . and a few fancy scenic trimmings," ABC's new show was "pretty much the same dance-disc-and-din mixture as before."[6] The national press was not so tolerant. The *New York Times* opined that viewers beyond voting age might find ABC's new network offering "something of an ordeal" to sit through. But the *Times'* conceded that *Bandstand*'s dancing teens were "an attractive group of youngsters . . . [with] no motorcycle jackets and hardly a sideburn in the crowd," and that Clark was a "well-groomed young man richly endowed with self-assurance," indicating that rock 'n' roll (and Clark himself) could be fashioned in a consumer-friendly manner.[7]

American Bandstand was initially broadcast on a sustaining basis (supported by ABC because the show did not yet have sponsors), with the hope that advertisers, national as well as local, would eventually sign on. Since the one thing potential sponsors and their advertising agencies dreaded was controversy, Clark was under pressure from ABC to present the most benign show possible. With Alan Freed's recent *Big Beat* TV debacle fresh in their minds, ABC executives realized they were taking a gamble in airing *American Bandstand*, but they trusted that the show's calm, controlled atmosphere and the easy image of Clark would soon attract sponsorship to its new afternoon show. There was some basis for such trust.

The Hidden Persuaders, Vance Packard's controversial expose on advertisers' subconscious manipulation of consumers, was in the midst of a six-month run on the national best-seller list and was a favorite topic of the media at the very time ABC mulled over the prospects of putting *American Bandstand* on the air. Coincidentally, perhaps, much of what was asserted in Packard's book supported ABC's decision to give *American Bandstand* and Clark a go.

According to *The Hidden Persuaders*, motivational analysts had discovered that sales of products on television were found to increase substantially when programs of a more easygoing nature and that did not depict crime were substituted for shows that induced "emotional frenzy" in their viewers. *American Bandstand* more than filled the bill on that account. But a more telling facet of Packard's motivational research expose was the recognition of the basic "good guys" versus "bad men" pattern in children's television, whereby the villains were found to be older men, perhaps symbolic father figures, while the "good guys" were young men in their twenties who were seen "as a sort of older brother (and not a father symbol)."[8] It is not surprising then that ABC stipulated that if Triangle Publications (the parent company of WFIL) could not deliver the immaculately groomed, coat-and-tied Dick Clark—television's quintessential "good guy"—as host of *American Bandstand*, the deal was off.

Hip to ABC's low-key designs, "good guy" Clark made it a point to tell an inquisitive America that although *Bandstand*'s teenage guests might yell and scream and even cry over guests like Pat Boone, Tab Hunter or Sal Mineo, "they don't go in for tearing buttons and clothes off people."[9]

• • •

American Bandstand had been on the air for a week when Ted Fetter wondered how it was doing. A check of the A.C. Nielsen Company ratings indicated that some twenty million viewers had watched ABC's new show during that period, but even more startling to Fetter was his discovery that during that span "three or four new stations had joined the [ABC] line-up." When *American Bandstand*'s two-week trial run ended, Fetter received a call from Jim Aubrey. "Ted, strange things are happening," he said. "Another fifteen or twenty stations have joined this thing. Try it for another week."[10]

Meanwhile, in Philadelphia George Koehler was telling Clark, "I don't think there's any question about it. They [ABC] want this show."[11]

ABC now signed an average of three new stations a week to broadcast *American Bandstand*, and the number of affiliates carrying Clark's show quickly rose from forty-eight to sixty. Ironically, although Fetter was the only executive who had pushed to get *American Bandstand* on the network, he remained unimpressed with it. "And yet, there it was," he said. "It was doing well; people were watching it." What did impress Fetter "was the fact that stations were joining up" to broadcast the show. That also impressed Jim

Aubrey. After four weeks *American Bandstand* was added to ABC's schedule on a permanent basis.

In *Rock, Roll, & Remember* Clark promulgated the chummy image of himself and Tony Mammarella working on *American Bandstand* "as partners."[12] Very unequal partners, it seems, for soon after Clark's show joined ABC-TV's line-up, he approached Roger Clipp and said: "In order to do this, we've got to have a corporate set-up. Assign us the rights to [*American Bandstand*], for which we'll pay you a royalty."[13] But Clark's references to 'we" and "us" did not refer to himself and Mammarella, they referred to Click Corp., which Clark planned to use as a production company. As for Mammarella, his widow pointed out that "Anthony just worked there."

Unlike his "partner" Tony Mammarella, Clark would no longer work directly for Walter Annenberg's Triangle Publications. Nor, contrary to popular belief, would he work for the ABC network (not yet, anyway). Under Clark's corporate design, for $2,000 a week, Click Corp. was to supply Triangle/WFIL with *American Bandstand*. Triangle would then charge ABC $3,175 a week to air the show nationally. Although *American Bandstand* was produced by Clark's own company, and to the home viewers, the show appeared to be in his fiefdom, in reality the show remained within the province of Triangle, which retained the right of approval of all radio, TV, and film appearances by him. Triangle also had the last word on Clark's endorsement of products or services, and, as originator of *Bandstand* and *American Bandstand*, Triangle retained exclusive control of both titles.

No tears needed to be shed for Clark, however. After one year on Philadelphia's *Bandstand* he had combined his meager WFIL salary with revenues earned from hosting nightly record hops (sometimes even two a night) to earn at least $50,000, in his estimate. "I was making a killing, racing around trying to get all the money I could," said Clark of his record hop activities. "My tentacles went in every direction."[14]

With *American Bandstand* assured a network life, Triangle Publications launched a nationwide publicity campaign to boost its new program. *TV Guide* ran two feature articles on Clark's show in September and October, 1957, emphasizing *Bandstsand*'s well-groomed and well-behaved teenage guests. "We don't try to preach to anybody," Clark was quoted as saying in his first national press opportunity, "but we help set a good example for the people watching at home."[15] In addition, Walter Annenberg's TV bible dubiously touted the "handsome, youthful, glib, unruffled" Clark as "TV's first national disc jockey."[16]

By the end of October *American Bandstand* was the number one program in its time period. It drew a 62 percent higher share of the audience than

CBS, a 35 percent higher share than NBC, and more than doubled ABC's previous share of the late-afternoon time slot. "Clark was the beginning of daytime television on ABC," recalled Ted Fetter. "You can't count those English movies as daytime shows."

Besides snaring the anticipated teenage crowd, *American Bandstand* afforded ABC the unexpected bonanza of corralling the American homemaker. While TV marketing studies in the mid-1950s indicated that more than half of the American women at home during the day did not listen to radio or watch television at all during that time—presumably because they were not interested in game shows or soap operas—*American Bandstand* had an undeniable appeal to the nation's housewives. No doubt many of them, not all that far removed from their own teenage years (American women were marrying at increasingly younger ages in the 1950s), vicariously relived that lost period in their lives by watching Clark's show. ABC wasted no time sending a press release with the headline, "Age No Barrier To *Bandstand* Beat," to each of its affiliated stations, informing them and their local sponsors of *American Bandstand*'s extended appeal to the nation's housewives, some of who danced in front of their TV sets using pillows, named after their husbands, as partners. On the air Clark unabashedly implored the "housewives" who were watching to "roll up the ironing board and join us when you can."[17]

In effect, *American Bandstand* challenged entertainment's "fourth wall" by blurring the boundaries between the "players" and those who watched from the sidelines. It was theatre-within-a-theatre, in which the show's millions of young viewers and housewives tuned in to watch the studio audience who, in turn, danced and watched guest stars lip-synch their records. To Clark, what enticed those millions of viewers was "the kids—and what they wear. Older people looking at younger people. Younger people looking at their contemporaries. It's a little soap opera. . . ."[18]

"The kids" was it in a nutshell. From the beginning, *Bandstand*'s predominantly Italian-American studio audience—who, apart from their families, was influenced most by streetwise peer groups that reflected the blue-collar sentiment of their forbears—emerged as the show's surprise hook and went on to greatly affect it. Like most of the area's high school students who cared enough to investigate *Bandstand* in the show's early days, sisters Joanne and Carmen Montecarlo drifted into WFIL's studio B simply because it was on their way home, and there was not much else going on at that hour anyway. But after paying a visit to *Bandstand*, most of them were smitten by the party-like atmosphere and beguiled by the local notoriety provided by the television cameras. To many of the area's teenagers, like Carol McColly (Kirkbride), who was there in studio B that first fateful day, her *Bandstand* experience "was such a thrill" that she subsequently ran "all the way every day to get there."[19] Although the show's first visitors attended mostly out of curiosity, it was not long before area teens began to be drawn to *Bandstand* for reasons of their own.

Mothers, it seems, were a strong motivating factor. Kenny Rossi had no interest in *Bandstand* until his mother urged him to attend, "because she wanted to see how I looked on TV."[20] When Justine Carelli returned home in tears after being turned away from the show because she was too young (Justine, who was only twelve, had gone there on a dare by some older friends), Mrs. Carelli gave the distraught Justine her older sister's birth certificate to show at the door. The ruse worked, and Justine soon became a regular on *Bandstand*.

Some, like Frank Brancaccio, who lived in one of the toughest sections of South Philly and had no friends he could relate to in the neighborhood, found friends on the television screen "right there in my living room."[21] The next logical step for such lonely souls was to join their "friends" on the *Bandstand* set.

Before long, the show's regulars begat others of the same sort. Arlene Sullivan was invited to attend *Bandstand* by Justine after the two met by chance at a neighborhood party. Rosemary "Little Ro" Fergione (not to be confused with Rosalie "Big Ro" Beltrante) invited Nino Bambino on her birthday, and after Bambino sang "Happy Birthday" to her on the show, he began to receive fan mail, "and suddenly I was a regular."[22]

Like Kenny Rossi, Bob Clayton of nearby Wilmington, Delaware, had no interest in appearing on *Bandstand*. The smooth-stepping blonde Adonis was already a regular dancer on Grady and Hurst's local dance show, which was broadcast from his home town. But one afternoon Clayton happened to turn on *Bandstand* and spotted the blonde beauty known as Justine. From that moment on his goal in life became to "go there and dance with her."

Fortunately for Clayton, the last period of his school day was a study hall, which enabled him to leave school early, jump in his car, and "haul ass" to Philadelphia. The day after setting eyes on Justine, he gained admittance to *Bandstand*, cockily approached the pretty young girl and told her: "Before this summer's over, you're gonna be my girl."

She was, and by the time *Bandstand* went national a year later the blonde, fair-skinned Bob and Justine went from being Philadelphia's star couple to America's couple. "It all just exploded," recalled Clayton. "We became national TV stars, for no other reason than that we happened to be in the right place at the right time."[23]

The only *Bandstand* couple to come close to receiving the amount of attention that came Bob and Justine's way were Kenny Rossi and Arlene Sullivan. If the fair-haired, light-skinned Bob and Justine were All-American in appearance, the dark-complexioned, wavy haired Rossi and Sullivan were All-South Philadelphian. In fact, Rossi and Sullivan looked so much like brother and sister that the day they first met inside the studio (she was a regular; he was a newcomer) Sullivan introduced her future dance partner to her *Bandstand* comrades as her brother. But the couple was soon forced to divulge their "sibling" hoax. "We found out we got along together and we danced well together, so it just went from there," recalled Arlene.[24]

Dancing with Sullivan or Pat Molitierri, Rossi became one of the show's premier dancers. He said at first he "just went to dance, really," and that "everything else happened later."[25]

"Everything else" began with the first *American Bandstand* telecast in 1957. It was then that America began to stand vigil over Clark's teenage brood, dominated by Philadelphia's third-generation Italian-Americans, whose ethnicity struck a participatory chord with the rest of the nation. As adult female viewers became surrogate parents to the well-groomed adolescents with familiar faces who appeared each afternoon on TV screens across America, and as millions of teenage peers coast-to-coast enviously eyed their Philadelphia counterparts, it was difficult to imagine that the grandparents of these new darlings of America had been ostracized and berated by the same country that now fawned over their descendants.

The regulars were inundated by unsolicited gifts of jewelry and clothing. Sometimes admiring viewers sent complete wardrobes that they wanted to see their favorite dancer wear on the show. After Justine innocently mentioned on camera that she liked to wear tiaras she received a diamond tiara in the mail the very next week. Carol Scaldeferri, who was partial to headbands, received more than her share of them from admiring fans.

The *American Bandstand* regulars also set grooming and fashion trends. Carmen and Yvette Jiminez dyed blonde streaks in their bangs, which prompted a nation of female adolescents to do likewise (In later years the sisters fittingly opened a beauty salon), while most of Justine's mail concerned her famous blonde locks, "what I used to wash it with, how I rolled it."[26] As for fashion statements, there were the double-layered, rolled bobby sox on which the Catholic girls of *Bandstand* hung tiny bells and pom-poms in order to divert attention from the unhip saddle shoes they were required to wear as part of their school uniform. Much of young America soon did likewise. Carol Scaldeferri, for one, disliked the saddle shoe/bobby sox look so much that she began to wear a ballerina-type shoe that laced up the ankle and calf with ribbon, and *voila*—another fad quickly swept the nation.

The Catholic school uniforms were also responsible for what became known nationally as the "Philadelphia collar." Parochial school officials did not take kindly to the luring of their young ladies to *Bandstand* (teenage boys and rock 'n' roll were viewed as the Devil's combination if ever there was one), but they could not prohibit the girls from attending. However, they could (and did) ban the wearing of school uniforms while the students were on camera.

Since most of the girls went directly from their nearby schools to *Bandstand*, this was cause for great concern. Necessity truly being the mother of invention, many of the Catholic females on the show took to bringing sweaters, and even complete changes of clothing, to school with them. The WFIL ladies' room doubled as a teenage dressing room, but often there was no time for a complete change of clothing. Whenever that happened, a sweater would be thrown on or buttoned up, covering the school uniform, except for "this white, sort of abbreviated Peter Pan collar" protruding out of the sweater, recalled Joanne Montecarlo.

Although parochial school officials never caught on to the disguise, the disguise caught on with much of an unsuspecting young America. What began as a desperate masquerade quickly developed into a national fashion rage. In a matter of weeks Montecarlo and her girlfriends on the show began receiving letters saying, "Hey, where can I get myself one of those Philadelphia collars?" [27]

Despite the interest in clothing and fashions, the most passionate interest *American Bandstand*'s home viewers had concerning the regulars involved their social lives. "If so-and-so didn't happen to be dancing with his regular partner that day, a few days later there'd be thousands of letters asking what was wrong, were they ill, had they broken up," recalled the late Billy Cook. [28] The most popular regulars received thousands of pieces of mail each week, and many of them had national fan clubs. "Bags of mail were in the downstairs hall," noted Jack Steck. "You couldn't move!" Kenny Rossi, for one, received so much mail that it took his entire family to answer it all. "It was just unbelievable, how intense the viewers were with the regulars," recalled Bob Clayton. [29]

As expected, this outpouring of adulation over an otherwise very ordinary group of teenagers had a dramatic effect on them. Although never impressed with herself, Carol Scaldefierri was impressed by the fact that "people seemed to get to know me just by watching me on TV, and that fascinated me." Arlene Sullivan said *American Bandstand*'s home viewers "all felt like they knew us, because we were in their living rooms for over an hour a day, five days a week." "The craziest part of it was so many of us became these instant celebrities, yet none of us really had any talent," thought Ed Kelley. [30]

While some of *American Bandstand*'s regulars did become instant celebrities, pitfalls awaited any regular who dared try to capitalize on his or her celebrity status while a member of Clark's cast of characters. They were expressly forbidden to turn professional, and for good reason. Had any of them joined the actor's guild (AFTRA), Clark would have been liable to pay them scale for their on-camera appearances. The show operated on a thin budget and could not cover appearance fees for all of the recording artists, much less the student dancers. Still, each weekday afternoon a crowd of would-be managers and publicists was drawn to the WFIL studios, proffering deals that would make Clark's regulars genuine stars. "That became a dilemma for some kids," recalled Frank Brancaccio, "having to decide if it was unreasonable not to take the money or if it was more important to them to stay on the show."

The ban on professionalism nonwithstanding, life as a regular on *American Bandstand* was not a total cakewalk. Many of the swooning females watching at home had real-life boyfriends—extremely jealous boyfriends, in many cases—who did not take lightly to their steadies' idolization of Bob or Kenny or Frank or whoever. Clark's regulars may have been loved from coast to coast, but in Philadelphia they "literally could not go out to a lot of public places because there would always be mobs of people outside threatening to beat us up," explained Brancaccio. "It was very schizoid in a way." In some cases a police escort was required to get the regulars in and out of the studio or to and from dances and record hops safely. "We were hated in Philadelphia," said Brancaccio. "You walked down the street and you were a '*Bandstand* faggot.'"[31]

The girls had their own set of problems with their celebrity status. "If you went to a local dance you could feel the animosity," said Joanne Montecarlo, who received her share of telephone threats.[32] Justine Carelli said she never got used to being "so loved and so hated by total strangers."[33]

For the most part, however, life as a *Bandstand* regular was a fantasy world come true. As Ed Kelly put it: "We were just kids who lucked out . . . and found ourselves in the midst of this amazing soap opera with the rest of the country."[34]

None of this escaped Clark, who, recalled Jack Steck, "had that certain amount of charm, and was smart enough to not dominate, at least apparently not dominate, everything that went on. Actually he did dominate. He had a very shrewd tight hand, but it was always fronted by a kid."

ABC executives soon realized that *American Bandstand* was no flash-in-the-pan. In what show business bible *Variety* termed a "startling . . . ratings coup," the upstart network demolished its rivals throughout the fall season, outdrawing its competition by as much as a seven-to-one margin in *Bandstand*'s afternoon time slot.[35] "It made a hero out of me," chuckled Ted Fetter.

The network's afternoon blockbuster, which featured Clark as ABC's version of the *The Hidden Persuaders'* "good guy," had no difficulty acquiring lucrative national sponsors, including General Mills (which was eager to pitch its Betty Crocker products to America's homemakers), 7-Up, and, perhaps Clark's best-remembered sponsor from those halcyon years, Clearasil pimple cream. By November, ABC's station affiliate count had risen to sixty-three.

There are those who have wondered if *American Bandstand* could have achieved such national status under Bob Horn's stewardship. WFIL's Jack Steck believed the local show "was so good itself that it could have made the network, but I don't think it could *ever* have been the mammoth corporation that Dick Clark Enterprises became. I don't think Bob thought on that large a scale." As great an affinity as Jerry Blavat had for Horn, in the eyes of the Geator the fallen WFIL personality "could never have taken that show nationally. Even though [Bob] had the rapport with the kids, he just did not identify with the kids the way that Dick Clark did. Bob did not fit the image of young America at the time."

Considering Horn's grating personality and questionable image, and recognizing the pivotal role Dick Clark played in convincing ABC to air *Bandstand* ("The whole thing was really Dick," recalled Ted Fetter), it is highly unlikely that the show ever would have made it to ABC under Horn's tutelage.

Thanks to Clark, things would never be the same at WFIL. Jack Steck pointed out that once *Bandstand* began to be aired nationally it "became . . . so big that it was a separate operation for itself, and it was strictly an operation that Tony and Dick ran with the aid of one secretary." Clark and Mammarella "were very smart . . . to organize committees," he added. "They delegated a lot of the detail work like sorting out the mail and running the errands."

On the heels of *American Bandstand*'s startling success all of television began to follow ABC's lead in addressing the power of America's growing teenage population. CBS announced it was adding a "Teen Age Special" feature to singer Patti Page's weekly *The Big Record* music show, and Ed Sullivan, whose long-running and top-rated variety show was also seen on that network, let it be known that he would increase the appearances of singers who appealed to teenagers. Over at NBC, the easy-going crooner Perry Como, whose popular Saturday night variety show had been a forerunner in spotlighting rhythm and blues and rock 'n' roll talent on national TV, increased the frequency of appearances of such acts.

As 1957 drew to a close then, rock 'n' roll performers had more access to national television than ever before. While the more traditional TV shows such as Sullivan's and Como's offered one rock 'n' roll slot per week, *American Bandstand* had several spots to fill each *day*, five days a week. This not only created a heretofore unheard of amount of performing opportunities, it also meant that an artist stood a good chance of appearing on *Bandstand* at the most crucial of times—just as the artist's record was beginning to move in local markets throughout the country.

As Clark stated in 1994, "One of the remarkable contributions of [*American Bandstand*] in the long run was it gave a lot of people who never, ever would have gotten the opportunity to be on television the chance to be there. We had the audience, we had a lot of guest spots available . . . so that a whole world was opened up to the people who made music." Because it was able to offer the immediacy required in the "here today—gone tomorrow" world of pop music, *American Bandstand* became the premier venue for televised rock 'n' roll, and an appearance on Clark's show became the goal of almost every artist with a new record to promote. "Everybody in the world" tried to appear on *American Bandstand*," recalled Jack Steck, and "all the big stars came so willingly."

Rock and roll artists particularly enjoyed appearing on *American Bandstand* because they knew they would receive preferred treatment by the show's producers and an enthusiastic welcome by the studio teens, whereas the audiences on adult-oriented TV variety shows hosted by the likes of Ed Sullivan, Perry Como, and Steve Allen often greeted rock 'n' roll performers coolly or worse. Singer Sam Cooke's disastrous national TV debut exemplified the desultory manner in which rock 'n' roll artists were treated on adult-oriented TV shows in the 1950s. On November 3, 1957, Cooke was the final performer of the evening on the *Ed Sullivan Show*. The live variety show was running late, and as the young singer appeared on stage and mouthed the first two words to his rising hit, "You Send Me," the performance was abruptly terminated. Cooke continued to mouth the words to his song for a few seconds and then walked off the stage, having been humiliated in front of a national audience.[36] In contrast, when Cooke made his first *American Bandstand* appearance two months later he was afforded the respected he warranted.

In an era when most TV producers were unfamiliar with rock 'n' roll, televised live performances—as seen on Como's show, and sometimes on Sullivan's—tended to be inferior in arrangement and aural fidelity, and as a result, hit songs sounded nothing like the recorded version that teenagers were used to hearing. Rock and roll artists who appeared on *American Bandstand* lip-synched their original hit records, a format that was preferred by most young audiences.

The impact that the dozen or so weekly national promotional slots proffered by *American Bandstand* had on the pop music business cannot be overestimated. Before *Bandstand*, it was not uncommon for a rock 'n' roll artist or group to experience a hit record—sometimes several hit records—without once being seen by the public. Fans seeing a particular artist or group for the first time were not only amused to discover what that artist looked like, they were often surprised to discover that an artist they thought to be white was black—or vice versa.[37]

A prime example of this pre-*American Bandstand* visual ambiguity involved a rhythm and blues group from Brooklyn, New York called the Rays, consisting of Hal Miller, Walter Ford, David Jones, and Harry James. Signed to a contract by New York independent producers Frank Slay and Bob Crewe, the Rays released one record on the Chess label in 1956 that went unnoticed.

The following year Slay and Crewe wrote a ballad called "Silhouettes," in which a young man became heartbroken after discovering what he believed to be the silhouette of his girl and another guy smooching behind a window shade, only to discover that he was on the wrong block looking at the wrong window, and that all was well between him and his baby. After the Rays recorded "Silhouettes," Slay and Crewe issued the song on their own XYZ label near the end of the summer. A copy of it somehow made its way to Hy Lit, who introduced it in Philadelphia, and when "Silhouettes" began to move up the local charts, a guest spot for the Rays on ABC's new *American Bandstand* show was in order. But Dick Clark was resistant to have on the show any artist whose record was not distributed nationally, as was the case with XYZ.

Fortunately for the Rays, Bernie Lowe took an interest in the song and was able to pull a few strings. "Silhouettes" had been covered by a white group from Canada called the Diamonds, and their copy version was beginning to give the Rays' original recording a run for its money. Lowe, who knew all too well about having a potential hit covered by another label (see "Butterfly"), told Slay that if the Rays' "Silhouettes" should happen to appear on Lowe's Cameo label, then his friend Dick Clark would play it on *Bandstand*. But, added Lowe, if the song did not appear on Cameo, Clark would then play the Diamonds' version of "Silhouettes" on his show.

Whether this was simply a case of Lowe blowing smoke in an attempt to score a hit for Cameo is uncertain. Although Lowe had exerted what Slay characterized as "a little bit of pressure" on him for Cameo to acquire "Silhouettes," Slay was uncertain "who put the pressure on whom, and I don't know who did what to whom." But singer/producer Teddy Randazzo, who has known Clark since the *Bandstand* host's days as an unheralded WFIL radio disc jockey, pointed out that in many dealings Clark "kept himself buffered. He had all of these other people dealing for him and they would play the games and he would be mister clean."

Clark laughed in 1994, when told of Lowe's alleged remark. He professed to have no inkling of the label owner's machinations, but he thought Lowe's purported threat to Slay was "probably" something that the Cameo owner would have said, ultimately conceding that "it's very, very possible" Lowe did make such an assertation to Slay. Clark added that he has been "credited with so many things that are figments of peoples' imaginations. . . . More people have had lunch with me than any other human being," he quipped. Although such negotiations and "threats" cannot be proven, it is probably not a coincidence that the Rays' version of "Silhouettes" was ultimately transferred to Cameo and that Clark began to play that version on *American Bandstand*, just as Lowe had promised.

In September the Rays made their national TV debut on Clark's show to promote the song. But when the group anxiously arrived at WFIL's studios the day of their scheduled appearance on *American Bandstand*, they were stopped at the door and asked who they were and what they wanted.

"We're the *Rays*," said Hal Miller, the lead singer on "Silhouettes." "We're here to *perform*."

"Get outa here, don't give me that," they were politely told. "The Rays are an *ofay* [white] group!"

"We laughed," said Miller, who laughed all over again in 1994 as he recalled the incident, taking the time to explain that the Rays were thought by many to be a white group because, in order to ensure radio airplay on major stations, "Silhouettes" was recorded in a style that "fit into the [white] type sound." As the group stood at the WFIL-TV studio door in disbelief, Tony Mammarella appeared in the nick of time and said "These *are* the Rays, let them in!"[38]

Two weeks after their *American Bandstand* appearance, the Rays entered *Billboard*'s Top 100, where they remained for twenty weeks while "Silhouettes" rose to the number three position in the country. Despite the song's top ten status, the group did not receive great monetary return for their monster hit. Miller said the Rays got "shafted, just like every other group at that point. We saw money [from Cameo], but we didn't see nearly half as much as what we should have seen." This development did not come as a complete surprise to the group, however. When "Silhouettes" was originally transferred from XYZ to Cameo, Cameo executives introduced the Rays to the group's new "manager," a company figurehead who, they were informed, was to receive a percentage of the Rays' royalties. "I said, 'What damned manager?'" exclaimed Miller, recalling the incident with more amusement than bitterness in 1994. "And there went 16 percent of our checks . . . before we even knew what was happening!" Miller, who left the music business long ago and is now retired, said he "paid [his] dues" and did not mind the financial shortcomings so much. "I loved being on the stage, I loved performing, and to meet Dick Clark was a thrill."

Despite feeling somewhat "pressured" into the deal with Cameo, Frank Slay became good friends with Bernie Lowe, who the producer characterized as "a lot of fun to be with, . . . an enjoyable personality . . . who could sit around and tell great stories." Slay and Crewe continued to make records for Cameo, just as they did for Dick Clark once the *American Bandstand* host decided to get into the record business himself.

• • •

It was during the 1950s that America's merchandisers first began to cultivate teenagers as a social phenomenon—all the better to tap into an unmined consumer source—and pre-teens aspired to the status and life of apparent frivolity experienced by that group. For the first time, not only did teenagers enjoy a separate sense of identity, unlike their predecessors they had money to spend—and the Madison Avenue advertisers jumped to cash in on this movement, particularly in the areas of clothing and music.[39]

When it came to selling popular music, nothing in the 1950s was more successful at doing so than was *American Bandstand*. When Bobby Charles appeared as a guest on Clark's show during the fall of 1957, the singer unexpectedly announced to the nation (as well as to the show's embarrassed host) that he had been told by disc jockeys across America that "Dick Clark has got us dead," meaning that the power and influence of the local jocks now paled in comparison to that of Clark and his juggernaut national audience.[40] The flustered Clark meekly replied to Charles's obviously unrehearsed outburst that he hoped that was not the case.

But it was. Years later, Clark admitted: "Every kid in the country was watching the show, and as a result, program directors had their secretaries watching the show to copy down the records we played. In other words, whatever we played, everybody else had to play because a kid, say, in Keokuk, would call a station and say, 'I heard it yesterday on *Bandstand*. How come you're not playing it?'"[41]

Across the country phonograph record dealers installed TVs in their record departments and invited teenagers to watch *American Bandstand*, the show that was already being hailed by some dealers as "the greatest stimulant to the record business . . . ever known."[42]

"If it wasn't on *American Bandstand* it wasn't a hit," recalled disc jockey Hy Lit, who moved from WHAT to rock 'n' roll radio powerhouse WIBG in 1957. Because Dick Clark was constantly on the lookout for records that were breaking in local markets—records he might add to *American Bandstand*'s playlist—Philadelphia stations received intense promotion from a myriad of record companies who hoped to get their latest entries in the hit sweepstakes aired on Clark's show. "Some West Coast record companies would come to Philadelphia and try to get their records started," said Lit. "They'd come and they'd see the Hy Lits and the Jockos and get their records played on [local radio] and kind of force *American Bandstand* to get on it."

That was the dream—get it played on *American Bandstand* and it might well become a national hit. Artie Singer, who would soon produce and record the classic hit "At the Hop" for Danny and the Juniors, said that as far as promotion went, *Bandstand* was "the top of the line. That was it! 'At the Hop' proved it. It was [just] a local hit, [but] once it got on [*Bandstand*] it became the giant that it turned out to be."

Other performers who made their national TV debut in 1957 by way of *American Bandstand*, and who benefitted from Clark's unprecedented promotion, included Jerry Lee Lewis, Gene Vincent, Paul Anka, Buddy Holly and the Crickets, the Everly Brothers, the Diamonds, Jimmie Rodgers, Jackie Wilson, Johnny Mathis, Chuck Berry, and a teenage duo that went by the name of Tom and Jerry (and later found fame using their own names of Paul Simon and Art Garfunkel).

As rock 'n' roll's popularity continued to increase, so did that portion of teenage America's $9 billion in spending money that went for phonograph records. Between 1955 and 1957, retail sales of records more than doubled, to $400 million annually. Not surprisingly, Dick Clark took notice.

Although he and Tony Mammarella shared a tiny office at WFIL's studios where song publishers and promo men obsequiously queued in hopes of facilitating fortune and fame, the *Bandstand* majordomos (who received up to 175 new records each week) and a passel of promo men from Philadelphia's abnormally large contingent of record distributors met elsewhere to make the crucial determinations as to which records would—and which would not—be aired on *Bandstand*.

The rendezvous point was the Brown Jug, an earthy Market Street Irish saloon located one-half block from the WFIL building. In the rear of the popular lunchtime hangout was a dreary back room that contained a lone table and a handful of mismatched chairs, a room in which "some of the biggest record deals of the fifties were made,"[43] according to Clark.

The local promotion men who frequented the Brown Jug "were all nice guys and Dick trusted them because they knew better than to give him a bad line," said Jack Steck. "They had to be honest. They'd tip him on a record that had not yet come up, but was showing on other markets. . . . They wouldn't lie to him about it because they knew if they did they were through."

As 1957 drew to a close, Bernie Lowe, himself no stranger to the Brown Jug, realized that his newly acquired status as the honcho of Philadelphia's rapidly coalescing rock 'n' roll scene was already imperiled. Lowe had recently reaped the rewards of the Rays' "Silhouettes," but he had also suffered the ignominy of having his bookkeeping challenged by his rebellious teenage recording star Charlie Gracie. It seems that while Lowe dispensed thousands of dollars of "Butterfly's" profits to Dick Clark, he was more disposed to shower Gracie with praise rather than with the royalties the singer believed to be his due. According to Gracie, "Butterfly" sold over three-and-one-half million records, "and the guy wants to pay me for 700,000."

Gracie's manager implored him to keep his mouth shut, telling the singer that if he came up with enough hits, "you won't need [Cameo]." But Gracie went ahead and sued Lowe for what he believed were royalties owed him, and although the upstart singer received an out-of-court settlement from Cameo, he lost out big time in the long run. Despite Gracie's nearly twenty appearances on the local Philadelphia *Bandstand* and hefty words of praise from Dick Clark, the lawsuit caused him to fall out of grace with Bernie Lowe, according to the singer, and Gracie was subsequently never given the opportunity to appear on the national *American Bandstand*.

Lowe was contractually required to release three more of Gracie's records, but after the two had their falling out Lowe declined to promote them, leaving his ungrateful artist to twist in the wind. Gracie remained shackled to Cameo for almost a year—an eternity in the meteoric life of a pop music star—out of sight and out of mind of his audience, and by the time Lowe did cut him loose, the singer had lost his shot at becoming a teen idol. "Charlie was a damn good singer," said Kal Mann, looking back on the sorry episode. "He should have been a bigger star." When asked his opinion of what had happened with Gracie, Dick Clark said in 1994 that "in all honesty I lost track and I don't know anything about him whatsoever."

Gracie never appeared on *American Bandstand*, thereby foregoing any chance he had to become a teen idol, but over the years Clark has been deprecated for his robust promotion of other teen idols from Philadelphia, most notably Frankie Avalon, Fabian, and Bobby Rydell. "You know," said Clark in his own defense, "the shameful part of that is, [people] always speak disparagingly of teen idols, forgetting that Elvis Presley was a teen idol, the Beatles were teen idols, Bing Crosby and Frank Sinatra were teen idols." [44]

True enough, but those pop icons possessed more than a modicum of talent and were largely responsible for their own success, whereas the teen idols that followed in the wake of Elvis were, for the most part, totally contrived.

America's tradition of younger generation idol-worshipping is almost as old as the record industry itself. In the first quarter of the twentieth century numerous vaudeville and recording stars became quite popular among their peers. The first pop idol to be revered by America's youth is generally thought to be Rudy Vallee, who blossomed during the Great Depression, before being succeeded by Crosby, who is widely credited with inventing the pop singing style. The first pop hero to tap into mass teenage hysteria was Sinatra, who, two years after gaining popularity as Tommy Dorsey's vocalist, struck out on his own. Sinatra's now-legendary appearances at the New York Paramount beginning in 1942 are widely credited with the birth of "modern pop hysteria," which reached new heights during the teenage revolution that blossomed in the 1950s to cast Elvis as the nation's premier teen idol. [45]

Elvis's overtly sexual image kept a large part of the American public at bay, however, leaving enough room for others to try their luck. (Indeed, Presley's manager Colonel Tom Parker could not get his "boy" into the army fast enough to recast Elvis as a red-blooded All-American.) Bernie Lowe thought he found the answer to Elvis in Charlie Gracie, but Gracie, as things turned out, was removed from the picture after refusing to play by Lowe's rules.

Meanwhile, Bob Marcucci and his would-be idol Frankie Avalon did not fare much better than Lowe. While the rock 'n' roll film *Jamboree* did well enough to return Marcucci's investment, the publicity it afforded Avalon's second record ("Teacher's Pet") did nothing to spur sales of the song. But it did enable Marcucci to secure for Avalon an appearance on *American Bandstand* (under the guise of promotion for *Jamboree*), despite the fact that the singer was unknown outside of Philadelphia.

Without yet having come face to face with Clark, the aggressively ambitious Marcucci booked Avalon onto *American Bandstand* in September 1957, to commemorate the singer's eighteenth birthday. For good measure Marcucci also arranged for a cake to be delivered to Avalon while he was on the set—the first in a string of "crazy" promotional stunts engineered by Marcucci to elevate his young singer. Marcucci's chutzpah did not set well with Clark, who fumed: "Who the hell is this maniac to come on *Bandstand* and do things like this? He has no right!" [46]

In the end Clark suffered Marcucci's overblown hoopla, Avalon's fans came out to *American Bandstand* en masse, "and it was very, very big on television," recalled the Chancellor Records executive. But it was not big enough to interest the nation's teenagers in buying Avalon's recording of "Teacher's Pet," proving early on that the mere performance of a song on *American Bandstand* did not automatically make it a hit.

Undaunted, Marcucci took Avalon back on the local record hop circuit where throngs of frantic, adoring teenage girls continued to swoon over the handsome singer. Returning from the pandemonium one evening more convinced than ever that he had a potential teen idol under his wing, Marcucci told his partner, "Pete, we've got to write him a hit song!"

The pieces were now almost all in place for the *Bandstand* era to begin in earnest. Bob Marcucci and Peter DeAngelis would write that hit song for Frankie Avalon (and Marcucci would discover the duo's next star literally sitting on a South Philly stoop); Bernie Lowe would find his own teen idol to replace Charlie Gracie; Dick Clark himself would enter the record business; and *American Bandstand* would begin to alter the face of pop music, not only in Philadelphia, but across America and around the globe.

CHAPTER 5

At the Hop

Rhythm and blues acts were traditionally shunned by network television, so when the Five Satins plugged their pop-styled ballad "To the Aisle" before a national audience of millions during an *American Bandstand* appearance in 1957, the group did not dare contemplate how, if at all, their anomalous national TV spot boded their future. Fred Paris, the founding member of the group whose "In the Still of the Night" has become one of the best-remembered ballads of the 1950s, called rhythm and blues-oriented groups such as the Five Satins the true "pioneers" of rock 'n' roll. "And pioneers always get kicked in the ass."

As the rock 'n' roll era began to flourish and white acts came to the forefront, classic rhythm and blues groups such as the Five Satins, the Moonglows, the Spaniels, and the Flamingos continued to take care of business on the black entertainment circuit, staking their careers on local theatre gigs throughout the East and Midwest, and on radio airplay from black disc jockeys across the country. Paris emphasized that it was local radio, and not television, that "kept our music going" in the 1950s. "How often [could the Five Satins] get on a national TV show?" he rhetorically stated.

But other black acts, one in particular being Philadelphia's own Lee Andrews and the Hearts, did manage to find an open door to *American Bandstand*. In the process they became the envy of less fortunate counterparts. "We were unique," said Andrews. "We had such a pop sound. If you were too R&B or too black sounding you didn't get on.[1] There was a certain standard being held there, and everyone understood the standard and what was happening."

Despite the fact that Andrews and the Hearts were accepted by the white record-buying public, the group's live appearances remained largely confined to the black performing circuit. Andrews recalled singing in New York at

Harlem's famed Apollo Theatre and being aproached by other black groups who marveled at the fact that the Hearts had appeared on *American Bandstand*. "We were sort of envied in that way," he said. "It was like, 'Who do you guys know?'"

It seems they knew the right people. Formed in 1954 while its members attended West Philadelphia's John Bartram High, Lee Andrews and the Hearts (the original group consisted of Arthur Lee Andrew Thompson, whose father sang with the legendary Dixie Hummingbirds gospel group, Royalston "Roy" Calhoun, Thomas "Butch" Curry, Jimmy McAlister, and John Young) were originally known as the Dreamers, a group with an abundance of talent and enough savvy to hitch their fortunes to Kae ("The Jet Pilot") Williams, one of Philadelphia's leading R&B deejays. Williams became the Dreamers' manager, but after a name change to Lee Andrews and the Hearts, two failed records, and a grueling string of live performances (all of which netted the group "not one dime," according to Andrews), the Hearts and Kae Williams acrimoniously parted company. They signed with Ivin Ballen's Gotham label, but when several of their records failed to sell outside the Philadelphia area, Ballen cut them loose.

In 1957 the group decided to try the disc jockey route again, this time signing on with Douglas "Jocko" Henderson. In addition to hosting popular radio programs in Philadelphia and New York, Jocko was a business associate of Barry Golder, who co-owned Philadelphia's Main Line Record Distrubutors. Jocko and Golder planned to start their own record label and were looking to sign local recording talent, and Lee Andrews and the Hearts fit the bill nicely.

Early that year the group cut the plaintive ballad "Long Lonely Nights," written by Andrews and fellow group member Roy Calhoun. The song was subsequently released locally on Main Line and nationally on Chess. Thanks largely to Hy Lit, who lived near Andrews and was close friends with the singer, "Long Lonely Nights" broke big in Philadelphia during the summer. Backed by Chess' effective national distribution, the song also became a hit in key markets around the country, exposing the group not only to a much larger market, "but also the *white* market," said Andrews.

"Long Lonely Nights" began to break nationally at precisely the time that *American Bandstand* made its debut on ABC-TV. Golder and Henderson arranged for their group to appear on Clark's show during its first week on the air, and, in what was perhaps the most-watched debut of any rock 'n' roll group, black or white, Andrews and the Hearts were introduced to America on August 9, 1957. Three days later, "Long Lonely Nights" entered *Billboard*'s Top 100, on its way to becoming a national hit.

But instead of an exhilarating experience, appearing on the most influential rock 'n' roll show of that era proved to be a bittersweet one for Andrews and his group once they learned that a condition of their *Bandstand* debut was to sign their TV performance earnings back to Click Corp.

"It undoubtedly was true," said Clark, speaking of the kickback process in 1994. "check exchanges [his euphemism for the practice—author's note] were very common." He maintained that the practice was necessitated by *American Bandstand*'s limited talent budget and the show's demand for up to ten live acts each week. "ABC had a budget of $1,500 a week for all five shows. When we ran out of the budget the check exchanges happened." Clark was more candid with Joe Smith in explaining how record companies worked what the *Bandstand* host described as a "kickback system. . . . Artists would come on the show, and the record company would allegedly pay them for their performance. We'd pay for maybe half the people who came on, and when our money ran out, we'd say, 'We'll book them and you'll pay them.' It wasn't illegal, nor was it immoral."[2]

Although the most direct method of kickback was for an artist to return his or her check to Click Corp., a more circuitous return route was sometimes employed. The Silhouettes' Rick Lewis, who experienced the practice, viewed it with a jaundiced eye. "Since the record distributor [that booked a particular act on *Bandstand*] was pushing the record, it would be their obligation to pay" for the record's promotion, he explained. Clark paid the performers the required AFTRA union scale, which was then reimbursed by the distributor. Clark's checks to the performers were then endorsed by the recipients and sent to the distributors. "It was a ruse in order to facilitate the rules of the union," said Lewis. "It was just like a little circle of money that never really went to anybody."

Few artists failed to comply with the practice, for not doing so meant forgoing the unprecedented national exposure afforded them by their *American Bandstand* appearance. In 1960, Clark stated that *Bandstand*'s reimbursement policy was discontinued in October 1958, "because of a change in policy in the number of performers appearing on the show, some relaxation as to the amount of available budget, and my own preference."[3]

But according to Sy Kaplan, comanager of Little Joey and the Flips, who plugged their hit, "Bongo Stomp," on *American Bandstand* in 1962, "before the guys even appeared we had to endorse their performance check right back over to the show's producers."[4] And other artists who performed on *American Bandstand* after 1958, who asked to remain anonymous, stated that the kickback policy remained in effect after that date. When asked in 1994 if the kickback practice did indeed end in 1958, Clark replied, "Oh, I haven't any idea."

Whether the check exchanges were legal or not, perhaps the performance fees were not so crucial to the recording artists. The success of "Long Lonely Nights," coupled with the fact that Lee Andrews and the Hearts played by the system's rules and performed the song gratis on *American Bandstand*, enabled the group to become what Andrews described as "pretty well connected" with the show to the extent that their managers "could call Dick Clark and say, 'Can I get Lee Andrews and the Hearts on?' and it would be done."

Jocko Henderson and Barry Golder had the wherewithal to land Andrews and the Hearts on Clark's show, but the group discovered to their dismay that, in their case, at least, there was a price other than a kickback fee to pay for being so "connected." When "Long Lonely Nights" was released, the songwriters credited on the label (who, as such, received a share of the song's sales royalties) were "Andrews, Henderson, Uniman, and Abbott." Andrews and Henderson are self-explanatory. Mimi Uniman was Hy Lit's wife, and "Abbott" was thought to be influential Philadelphia disc jockey Larry Brown. The flip side of the record ("The Clock") was credited to "Curry, Golder, Davis, and Binnick." Along with Hearts' member Butch Curry, who was the actual writer of the song, the other "writers" were Bernice Davis, the fiancee of influential Philadelphia deejay Georgie Woods, and Bernie Binnick, who was one of Dick Clark's partners in the film *Jamboree* and was soon to be a partner with Clark in a record company. The publishing rights to both songs went to G and H Music, standing for Golder and Henderson. "It was a form of payola," Andrews ruefully remarked. But it was the price that a singer or a group often had to pay in order for a record to be promoted or—in extreme cases—released during that era.

Andrews and the Hearts' "Teardrops" was a ballad similar to its predecessor, and although the song eclipsed "Long Lonely Nights" and became a national top twenty hit during the winter of 1957–58, the group's acceptance among America's white baby boomers remained tenuous. Despite the widespread popularity of Andrews and the Hearts, the apparent light at the end of the confining rhythm and blues tunnel was in reality the headlight of the onrushing future of rock 'n' roll—young, good-looking white artists, many of whom possessed minimal musical talent and experience.

"The beauty of American capitalism," observed Nelson George in *The Death of Rhythm and Blues*, "is that it can assimilate anything into its production machine, package it, and sell it as if it were a new item."[5] Once rhythm and blues began to spread to white society, many of the owners of small record labels, who, in the early 1950s, had eked out a modest living selling black records to the black community, recognized the opportunity at hand. By 1957 it was obvious to many of them that rock 'n' roll was here, if not to stay, then at least long enough to enable the more fortunate of them to strike it rich. These indie label disseminators of early rock 'n' roll began to dilute (whiten) the black sound in order to generate broader acceptance and bigger profits.

This supplantation of black rock 'n' roll artists by white counterparts was the latest instance in white America's tradition of usurping facets of black culture. The purveyors of rock 'n' roll records were primarily concerned with selling *records*, not peddling rock 'n' roll. Had teenagers bought opera or polka records at the rate they bought rock 'n' roll discs, those businessmen would have accommodated them willingly. And had it been possible for those entrepreneurs to expand the rock 'n' roll market to its fullest potential by using black artists, they also would have done that, too. Instead they found themselves in competition with the major record labels who controlled the pop music industry and were not about to surrender their domain to the upstart indies without a fight.

Many executives of the major labels were long-time veterans of the music business who personally disliked rock 'n' roll (as did a majority of adults), but they also feared the loss of control of their industry due to the rise of rock 'n' roll. When it became apparent that white teenagers had a growing affinity for black music, the majors retaliated by issuing "cover" records of certain rhythm and blues hits.

Perfectly legal so long as songwriting and publishing royalties were paid to the proper parties (only the singer being covered stood to lose, as particular arrangements of songs could not be copyrighted), the practice of covering records was not new. In the late 1940s and early 1950s, song publishers sought to get their compositions recorded by as many vocal artists as possible, and it was not uncommon for a particular song to be recorded by up to a dozen artists. Some record companies even had their pop artists cover hit records from the smaller country and western and rhythm and blues fields. Crooner Tony Bennett, for one, had great success covering Hank Williams's songs and, to a lesser extent, rhythm and blues hits, in the early 1950s. But with the rise of rock 'n' roll, the covering practice amounted to open warfare on black artists (although there were a few instances whereby black artists covered other blacks, as well as whites).

Ironically, the most notorious pop whitewasher of all did so not for a major company, but for a tiny independent label in the South. Recording for the Tennessee-based Dot Records, Pat Boone sold more records during the 1950s —many of them pale imitations of black hits by Fats Domino, Little Richard, and others—than any artist except Elvis Presley. Boone, who today describes those covers as "antiseptic, sterile-sounding, [lacking the] raw, natural quality" of the black originals, nevertheless defends them and justifies his role as a "catalyst, unwittingly and unintentially," for rock 'n' roll's acceptance. If his whitewashed hits had not sounded as they did, they would never have been played on white radio, and "the likelihood of the music being accepted by mainstream America might have been nonexistent."[6] (As it was, ABC did its part to spread Boone's sanitized sound and demeanor throughout America when the network afforded the singer his own weekly prime-time TV show during the late 1950s.)

The major labels placed their pop 45 singles on racks in suburban super-markets and other retail stores, and developed mail-order record clubs to get their wares (45s and LPs) directly into America's households. "They'd copy our records," recalled Ahmet Ertegun, one of Atlantic Records' cofounders, "except that they'd use a white artist. And the white stations would play them while we couldn't get our records on."[7] Danny Kessler of Okeh Records (the black subsidiary label of Columbia Records), said that if a black record looked like it would become a hit, "the chances were that a white artist would cover —and the big stations would play the white record. . . . There was a color line, and it wasn't easy to cross."[8]

Then, just as white covers of black records reached new heights in 1956, Elvis Presley burst upon the national scene. Presley, who, unlike Pat Boone, flaunted his black mannerisms and diction, helped legitimize the black artists he admired. By the end of the year pop cover songs no longer overshadowed the black originals they imitated, a sure sign that young white record buyers no longer tolerated such copies. But still and all, the teenage market had not yet fully exploited, for even though rhythm and blues and rock 'n' roll provided many whites with their first taste of black culture, white identifica-tion with black artists had its limitations.

Rhythm and blues and black rock 'n' roll was the most exciting form of music most white teenagers of the mid-1950s had ever heard, but while they became instantly enamored of the genre and its practitioners, a substan-tial portion of the white record-buying public had minimal, if any, contact with blacks. Sam Phillips—the man who discovered and first recorded Elvis —pointed out that although black records appealed to white teenagers, "there was something in many of those youngsters that resisted buying this music. . . . They liked the music, but they weren't sure whether they ought to like it or not. So I got to thinking how many records you could sell if you could find white performers who could play and sing in the same exciting alive way."[9]

So it was that in 1957 black artists encountered a tragically ironic situation. Although they were more popular than ever on the white charts, their success, for the most part, was about to be eclipsed by the rise of white rock 'n' roll performers. Nowhere was this more evident than in Philadelphia, which had its own vibrant, if insular, rhythm and blues community.

Lee Andrews and the Hearts may have been the most famous rhythm and blues group out of Philadelphia that year, but they had plenty of company back home. Black streetcorner vocal groups of the early to mid-1950s included the Blue Notes, the Buccaneers, the Capris, and the Castelles—the latter being pioneers of the distinct "Philly sound," which embodied high tenor lead vocals and harmonies. To most of white Philadelphia, this music was nonexistent. But it existed for many working class Italian youths, whose close proximity to the city's blacks resulted in an appreciation of this peculiar ethnic sound.

Lee Andrews observed the phenomenon each day at Bartram High in West Philadelphia, which, unlike the tight knit Italian community of South Philadelphia, exhibited a more ethnic mix, with Italians, Irish, blacks, and others living in close proximity to each other. Not far from the WFIL studios, and within a few blocks from each other, lived Charlie O'Donnell, who became the announcer on *American Bandstand*, and disc jockey Hy Lit, both white, and members of the vocal groups Lee Andrews and the Hearts and the (Philadelphia) Larks, who were black. (Not that the traditional black ghetto did not exist in that neighborhood; it did, several blocks north of the WFIL studios, separated from the rest of the neighborhood by a great open field the locals called "the dusties.")

"The rhythm and blues market was really beginning to open up," recalled Andrews. "I would go to school and see white kids as well as black kids who recognized who I was." What he did not realize was that many of those whites who took rhythm and blues to heart were about to duplicate the black form in their own white manner. Then, aided by Dick Clark's national forum —which was located right in their own neighborhood—those white singers would, on the fast track to stardom, leapfrog those black artists.

As Lee Andrews and the Hearts rejoiced in their newfound popularity, rock 'n' roll's future arrived in the form of Danny and the Juniors, a group of white teenagers from West Philadelphia who attended Bartram High. Thanks to a big boost from Dick Clark and *American Bandstand*, they were about to unleash one of the biggest rock 'n' roll records of all time on the public.

In 1955, Dave White (Tricker), Frank Maffei, Joe Terry (Terranova), and lead singer Danny Rapp (who had been a frequent dancer on Bob Horn's local *Bandstand*) formed a singing group called the Juvenairs. As youngsters they had been influenced by two musical sources—the pop harmony of groups such as the Four Aces and the Four Freshman heard on the radio, and the earthier black streetcorner sound heard firsthand at such gathering spots as West Philly's Haddington Recreational Center. Sometime in the spring of 1957, the Juvenairs were overheard by would-be producer/songwriter John Medora, who thought they exhibited promise. Medora, who happened to be taking voice lessons at the time, introduced the Juvenairs to his instructor, Artie Singer.

Once partners with the crafty Bernie Lowe, Singer had been stirred by Lowe's success with "Butterfly." "If Bernie can do it, why can't I?" he thought, before setting out with local WPEN disc jockey Larry Brown to produce a hit record of their own. One of the songs sung by the Juvenairs at their audition for Singer was "Let's All Do the Bop," which was written by Dave White after being inspired by a West Coast dance craze of the same name. Singer had the Juvenairs cut a demo of the song, which he brought to old friend Dick Clark for an appraisal. What happened after that is uncertain.

In *Rock, Roll & Remember*, Clark wrote that he liked the uptempo beat of "Let's All Do the Bop," but was dissatisfied with the lyrics. (Ostensibly, it made no sense to Clark to record a song based on a dance fad that most likely would have been forgotten by the time the record was released.) Clark, who was in the midst of conducting a string of some eighty record hops in sixty days that summer, claimed he suggested to Singer and Brown that they rewrite the song to describe those dance experiences, and that they "could call it 'At The Hop.'" [10]

Singer claimed that after Clark listened to "Let's All Do The Bop" he told him to "redo the whole thing," and that it was he, Singer, who thought of the record hop angle and suggested to Clark: "Why don't I revise it and do something with 'Let's Go to the Hop?'" Singer also contended it was he who rewrote the song and "made it what it is" in some twenty minutes.

Complicating matters further, Joe Terry insisted it was the Juvenairs who made most of the revisions to "At the Hop," after which Singer and Brown altered "a word here and a word there" to come up with the finished product.

In the end, songwriting credit went to Singer, Medora, and White. Singer subsequently changed the Juvenairs' name to Danny and the Juniors, and that September produced and recorded the song at Reco-Art Studio, the facility where Charlie Gracie's monster hit "Butterfly" was spawned. Perhaps lightning would strike again.

Singer and Brown had five thousand copies of "At the Hop" pressed on their Singular label and Dick Clark began testing the song at record hops. Clark discovered that the teens invariably went wild over it and told Singer: "Artie, this is gonna be a smash!"

Since it was Clark's practice not to play songs on *American Bandstand* that did not have national distribution (and thus were unavailable to his national audience), Clark did not play "At the Hop" on *American Bandstand*, although on several occasions prior to the song's national release the group lip-synched "At the Hop" on the locally broadcast portion of *Bandstand*.

Broken in Philadelphia by Hy Lit (who "was bangin' that record!" in Artie Singer's words), and given another boost by Larry Brown's heavy airplay on WPEN, "At The Hop" took off like a shot locally. "Everybody knew it was going to be a giant hit and everybody wanted the record," recalled Singer. Because he lacked the capital and the distribution to handle a national hit, Singer began to entertain offers from larger record companies to purchase or lease "At the Hop" for national distribution. One major firm exhibiting a keen interest in the song was the American Broadcasting Company's Am-Par Records.

Recalling Am-Par's designs on "At the Hop," Singer claimed that he was told by Clark: "They *want* it, and it would make *me* happy" if they got it. But Singer was careful to add that any "pressure" he felt for Am-Par to acquire "At the Hop" emanated not from Clark himself, but "from the fact that Dick was connected with ABC."

Singer also revealed that because of *Bandstand*'s initial promotion of "At the Hop" at the local level, he "felt a little obligated" to lease the song to Am-Par (not to mention the fact that Singer was tight with one of the owners of the Philadelphia distributorship that handled Am-Par records in that city). In the end that is just what he did.

Once Am-Par acquired "At the Hop," Clark began to play the song on *American Bandstand* and Danny and the Juniors graduated from the local spotlight to the national limelight. They lip-synched the song to a national audience on December 2, 1957, which, according to Joe Terry, "really kicked the record off." "At the Hop" roared onto *Billboard*'s Top 100 and in a matter of weeks it was the number one song in America. (Ironically, two weeks after the group's *American Bandstand* performance, rocker Gene Vincent appeared on Clark's show to plug his latest release—a song titled "Dance to the Bop.")

"At the Hop" eventually became one of the biggest rock 'n' roll hits of all time, yet Joe Terry believes that without the exposure Danny and the Juniors received via Clark's show, "people would have a tough time knowing who we are today. The enormity of *American Bandstand* really had an awful lot to do with it . . . so we gotta thank Dick Clark an awful lot."

Truth be known, Clark was abundantly thanked. When Am-Par acquired "At the Hop" from Singular, half of the song's publishing rights were assigned to Clark's Sea-Lark (or C-Lark, a play on the spelling of his last name) publishing company, an acquisition he considered to be "a return on my creative energies" for having revised "Let's All Do the Bop."[11] Clark maintained that Singer and Brown told him: "We'd like you to have half of the copyright for your publishing company," because "At the Hop" would not have been a hit had he not suggested the rewrite.

Asked to explain how Clark's "creative energies" merited half of the publishing for "At the Hop," Artie Singer grew reticent and declined to comment. Joe Terry, who claimed that he and the other Juniors then "knew nothing" of the behind the scenes jockeying regarding the song, thought Clark deserved his publishing windfall because "without that title change 'Do the Bop' would probably have been some also-ran song."

How and why Dick Clark became the recipient of the publishing rights to "At the Hop" aside, Danny and the Juniors were suddenly one of the hottest acts in the business. (Over the next two years they were to have six additional releases for Am-Par, and performed each one on *American Bandstand*.) Bolstered by the startling success of the show and of songs like "At the Hop," ABC began to tighten its focus on America's ever-expanding teenage population, 75 percent of whom were white. "And why not?" asked Clark. "After all, teen-agers have $9 billion a year to spend."[12]

Since *American Bandstand*—then the greatest promotional vehicle in pop music history—was televised by the American Broadcasting Company, which also manufactured and sold phonograph records, it is almost inconceivable that the network did not in some way attempt to capitalize on the combination of the two.

ABC's Am-Par record division (whose records were released on the ABC-Paramount label) was formed in 1955, in an attempt to broaden the company's base in the entertainment industry. (Rival NBC had ties to the RCA Victor label, as did CBS with Columbia) Shunning the costly development of its own stable of recording stars, Am-Par instead focused on purchasing completed masters from small labels such as Singular, and releasing them nationally. But prior to the inception of *American Bandstand*, ABC's record division managed to crack the national top ten just once (in 1956, with George Hamilton IV's "A Rose and a Baby Ruth"), and was awash in a sea of red ink. Then Am-Par stumbled upon a talented fifteen-year-old Canadian singer/ songwriter named Paul Anka.

It is uncertain whether Am-Par executives encouraged ABC to add *American Bandstand* to the national network, but they wasted no time in capitalizing on Clark's new national music forum. As ABC readied the show for national consumption, Anka's first ABC-Paramount release, "Diana," began to take on the trappings of a smash hit. The young singer plugged his fast-rising song on *American Bandstand* the third day the show was on the air, and three weeks later Am-Par assigned the copyright of the flip side of the song to Dick Clark's Sea-Lark publishing company, ensuring that Clark would receive a royalty on every copy of "Diana" that was sold.

And "Diana" sold a lot, most likely over a million copies.[13] The song became Am-Par's biggest success by far, reaching number two on *Billboard*'s Top 100 and remaining on the charts for twenty-nine weeks. Like a shark that has just tasted blood, Am-Par Records grew frantic to repeat its success.

But Am-Par soon discovered that, with or without its corporate pipeline to *American Bandstand*, marketing hit records would not be an easy task. Joe Bennett and the Sparkletones' "Black Slacks" was given a hefty boost when, in a rare live performance, the group sang the tune on Clark's show (this time the publishing rights to the flip side went to New York deejay Alan Freed), but Paul Anka's follow-up to "Diana" proved to be a dismal failure. Artie Singer said Am-Par was "in big trouble, and then 'At the Hop' came along."

Independent record producer Lee Silver made reference to a "very strong connection" between Am-Par and *American Bandstand*, and he, if anyone, should know. During the summer of 1957 Silver and his buddy Leo Rogers recorded a song called "Short Shorts" by a New Jersey group called the Royal Teens. The song, whose entire lyric consisted of eight monosyllabic words ("Who wears short shorts? We wear short shorts!"), was cowritten by group member Bob Gaudio (later one of the Four Seasons), who thought so little of the number that he implored Silver not to release it. Perhaps Gaudio was right, for when Silver tried to peddle the master recording he found that nobody was interested.

Finding no takers, Silver and Rogers pressed up one thousand copies of "Short Shorts" and released it on their tiny Power label in November. In an effort to generate airplay for the record, Silver and Rogers headed straight for Philadelphia. But Tony Mammarella, perhaps recalling all too well the Bob Horn/Dolores Farmer incident, rejected "Short Shorts" because any song about boys ogling girls in short shorts "might be a little too sexy" for *American Bandstand*.

Desperate for airplay, Leo Rogers gave old buddy Alan Freed half the publishing rights to the song, and New Yorkers soon began to hear "Short Shorts" nightly (sometimes several times each night) on Freed's famed "Rock and Roll Party."

"As soon as we got some airplay I got calls from seven different record companies [wanting to purchase 'Short Shorts']," recalled Silver, no longer in such a rush to sell the master. Each time he refused an offer for the song, the offers escalated. Then Silver received a telephone call from Am-Par president

Sam Clark (no relation to Dick Clark), who said he would make "one offer" of $15,000—at the time, the largest advance ever offered for a master recording —for "Short Shorts." Silver and Rogers accepted. The deal was finalized at ABC's New York headquarters, after which Sam Clark picked up the telephone, called *American Bandstand*, and said triumphantly, "I got it!"[14]

Within a week or so, "Short Shorts" was being played regularly on *American Bandstand*. During the first week in February, 1958, the Royal Teens made their network debut, lip-synching the song on Clark's show, after which it entered *Billboard*'s Top 100 and quickly rose to the number three position.

Once Am-Par purchased "Short Shorts" from Power and the song began to receive airplay on *American Bandstand*, Alan Freed's business associate Jack Hooke thought perhaps Freed and Clark could "help each other" by playing each other's records. Hooke, who, with Freed, owned Figure Music publishing, went to Philadelphia and met with Tony Mammarella in hopes of establishing such a relationship, but the *Bandstand* producer apparently had bigger fish to fry. After all, with free access to airplay on *American Bandstand*, Mammarella (and Clark, for that matter) had no need to cut deals with anyone. "We had a talk that to Tony wound up meaning shit," revealed Hooke. "We didn't get down to any nitty gritty. It was just, 'Hi, I'm so-and-so.' It was a very awkward situation, so I left without making any deal. . . . I was a little disappointed."

Since Am-Par went to great lengths to acquire potential hits such as "At The Hop" and "Short Shorts," it would seem to follow that the company would have made certain such acquisitions received a shot on *American Bandstand*. Dick Clark said that was never the case. He characterized Am-Par's Sam Clark as being "a very aggressive guy," but denied there was ever any pressure from Am-Par, or, for that matter, from anyone else at ABC, to play the company's records on his show. "No," the former *Bandstand* host flatly insisted in 1994, "they didn't exert any pressure."[15]

But Alan Freed swore that Am-Par did attempt to get him, Freed, to play the company's records. Freed testified during the 1960 payola hearings that when ABC hired him in May, 1958, to broadcast his rock 'n' roll show over WABC, the network's flagship radio station in New York, the company attorney who drew up Freed's contract said to him: "I trust that you will be sure to lay very heavily on ABC-Paramount records now that you are in the family." In addition, Freed swore that Sam Clark complained "lots of times" to Freed that the deejay was not playing enough Am-Par records.[16]

If Am-Par sought to have Freed play its records locally in New York, it is difficult to imagine that ABC's record division was not even more intent on having its records aired to a national audience via *American Bandstand*. For one, ABC was not adverse to altering song lyrics deemed inappropriate for airplay on *American Bandstand*. In 1958 Lloyd Price re-recorded a sanitized version of his hit, "Stagger Lee," expurgating the violent lyrics contained in his initial waxing of the classic blues number. Price claimed it was Clark who insisted on the sanitized version ("He felt that all that shooting and blood weren't right for his TV audience, even though I had already appeared on *American Bandstand* several times and even on his Saturday night show," recalled Price).[17] But Clark maintained the song was remade after ABC objected to the original lyrics. (Whichever way it occurred, the expurgerated version of "Stagger Lee" is now referred to as the "*Bandstand* Version.")[18]

If, as Clark claims, he was not pressured to play Am-Par's records, there is at least one documented instance that gives cause for speculation that he did indeed unduly hype ABC's product, perhaps out of loyalty to the company. During the time "At the Hop" was developing into a national hit, an instrumental record called "Tequila," played by a group called the Champs, was also beginning to happen. Although most radio stations across America played the Champs' version of the song, there were those—including Dick Clark—who played a cover version by Eddie Platt, which was issued by Am-Par. In fact, Clark remained faithful to Platt's copy long after it was clear the Champs' original version was the bigger hit. His long and hard lean on Platt's cover of "Tequila" (Clark eventually abandoned Platt's copy in favor of the original version) has been written off as an example of the *Bandstand* host simply "guessing wrong" on a song's potential (something he readily admits he has done), but the fact that Platt's record was released by Am-Par has never been factored into the equation.[19]

Whether or not Clark exhibited favoritism towards Am-Par records, a comparison of *American Bandstand*'s guest list and Am-Par's artist roster indicates that if any of Am-Par's artists did record a potential hit song, they became shoe-ins for a *Bandstand* slot. In the first six months Clark's show was on the air, Paul Anka, Johnny Nash, Joe Bennett and the Sparkletones, Danny and the Juniors, George Hamilton IV, and the Royal Teens—all with potential hit records released by Am-Par—appeared on *American Bandstand*.

On the other hand there is Teddy Randazzo, who left the Three Chuckles in 1957 to sign with Am-Par. Randazzo, whose first hit as a solo artist was "Little Serenade" in 1958, claimed he "never felt . . . at all" that it was easier for him to get on Clark's show during the years he recorded for Am-Par. "I got on *Bandstand* just as many times when I was on RCA Victor," he pointed out. "There was no difference." It was not the record label, so much as the fact that Paul Anka, Danny and the Juniors, and the Royal Teens were simply hot, opined Randazzo. "It was time!" He thought Am-Par simply "gravitated towards what they thought the kids wanted, and so they pulled in those kind of people."

With or without Am-Par's influence for the company's singers to appear on *American Bandstand*, ABC's recording artists apparently enjoyed an open door to Clark's show, and the airplay their records received there undeniably helped expose them to a national audience, thereby accelerating the hitmaking process. Furthermore, Am-Par's access to *American Bandstand* also gave that company tremendous leverage over its competitors in acquiring master recordings for national release. Whereas "A Rose and a Baby Ruth" had been the only top ten record Am-Par turned out in the two years prior the advent of *American Bandstand*, ABC's record label produced four national top ten hits—Paul Anka's "Diana" and "You Are My Destiny," Danny and the Juniors' "At the Hop," and the Royal Teens' "Short Shorts"—in a little over half a year after the show's inception.

• • •

Realizing that his position as the popular host of *American Bandstand* "could be a precarious one to sustain," Clark, after receiving his "At the Hop" publishing windfall from Artie Singer, set out to expand his base of operations and look for investment opportunities. It was "most natural for me to look to the music industry, the field I knew best, for such investments," he later explained.[20]

By the end of 1957, Clark's Sea-Lark publishing held the copyrights to several major rock 'n' roll hits, and the queue of persons prepared to offer him the publishing rights to one potential hit or another seemed endless. One of Clark's earliest publishing benefactors was New York record mogul George Goldner, who in his latest effort to create hit records (he had been responsible for Frankie Lymon and the Teenagers' hits on his Gee label), formed Gone and End records in 1957. Goldner (who died in 1970) unabashedly told the 1960 congressional subcommittee investigating payola that he assigned tunes to Clark's publishing firms "looking for favor or hoping to gain favor with Dick Clark . . . hoping that he would play my records."[21]

Thanks to Goldner and other similarly motivated record company executives, song copyrights continued to come Clark's way, and the *Bandstand* host established several additional music publishing firms to accommodate those musical properties. "All of a sudden I found myself going into the music publishing business, artist management, record pressing, every conceivable angle of music I could get into," he told Joe Smith in *Off the Record*. In December 1957, with Jamie Records still lying dormant, Clark formed Swan Records with Tony Mammarella and Bernie Binnick, with shares of 50 percent, 25 percent and 25 percent respectively. Binnick, who was one of Clark's fellow investors in the movie *Jamboree*, oversaw the everyday operations of Swan, but Clark revealed in 1960 that all of the label's releases were approved by either him or Mammarella, and that "no decision of any importance" was made without the duo's "approval and advice."[22]

The record business had boomed since 1955, but although it seemed a most propitious time to enter the fray, there was also a risk in doing so. Of the three hundred or so popular recordings released each week, perhaps a dozen received serious consideration for airplay. In addition, the almost six hundred independent record labels that existed were dependent on local distrubutors to serve as the middlemen with retailers. A distributor could sometimes make or break a small record company by delaying payment on the label's share of the profits from a hit record. If the record company did not have a follow-up hit to use as leverage against the distributor, it often went bankrupt. It followed that, without their own distribution, small independent record companies such as Swan were virtually hostage to local distributors, who, wrote Russell and David Sanjek in their history of the popular music business, "realized the largest profit from a hit record."[23]

Hoping to gain a niche in the Philadelphia record distributorship hierarchy (where that city's unusually high number of companies rendered the competition particularly cutthroat), as well as to eliminate the worry of dealing with the all-important middleman, Clark, Harry Chipetz, and Bernie Lowe created Chips Distributing Corp., each with a one-third interest, at the same time that Swan Records was formed. "In those days it was an absolutely normal thing to have a hand in everything," Clark recalled in 1986. "After all, I wasn't making any big money then on television, so I had to make it somewhere."[24]

With Dick Clark and Bernie Lowe now partners in a record distributorship, while still competing as the heads of Swan and Cameo Records, respectively, a peculiar working relationship arose between the two men whose friendship extended back to Paul Whiteman's *TV-Teen Club* days. For instance, shortly after the advent of *American Bandstand* Lowe issued Mike Pedicin's "Shake a Hand" and, as a favor to Clark or as an inducement for Clark to play the record, the Cameo owner coupled the song with a number called "The Dickie-Doo," the nickname of Clark's son, Richard. Clark's wife Barbara received half the writing credit for "The Dickie-Doo," and as such would have received sales royalties for the song had "Shake a Hand" become a hit. As it was, Clark gave "Shake a Hand" heavy airplay on *American Bandstand*, but he could not make a national hit out of it.

Record producer Frank Slay said relations between Cameo and Swan were "friendly, but really competitive. Those slots on *Bandstand* were extremely valuable. If Dick was playing a Swan record it meant fewer chances for a Cameo record, and vice-versa."

Swan's debut was an auspicious one. The label's first two releases became substantial hits despite the fact that one was originally considered to be a B-side throwaway and the other one was previously rejected by Cameo. "Did You Cry" and "Click Clack," the songs comprising Swan's first release, were recorded by aspiring singer/producer Gerry Granahan, who sang all of the voices on both numbers. "The band was just pick-up guys." said Granahan, who took the finished master recording to Clark.

"I think you've got something, that's a hit," Clark told the singer/producer after listening to "Did You Cry." But his plans to release the song on Swan hit a snag when Granahan informed Clark he was legally signed to another label and could not put his name on the record.

Perhaps recalling the song "The Dickie-Doo," Tony Mammarella said, "Call 'em Dickey Doo and the Don'ts," which is how the artist was ultimately listed on the record label. "We all laughed at it," said Granahan. "I figured, 'Who cares?'"

After a week of steady *American Bandstand* airplay that commenced even before the song was officially released, it became obvious that Clark had guessed wrong about the hit potential of "Did You Cry."[25] He should have played the flip side. It is not certain who turned the record over (it was not Clark), but "Click Clack" began to receive requests in certain radio markets around the country. By January, 1958, Clark had the song in heavy rotation on *American Bandstand*, and an appearance by "Dicky Doo and the Don'ts" was hastily arranged. Since no such group existed, auditions were quickly conducted to find a band to appear with Granahan, and three weeks after the pseudogroup lip-synched "Click Clack" on *Bandstand* the song entered *Billboard*'s Top 100, on its way to number twenty-eight.[26] Although the throwaway "Click Clack" may have become a hit without the airplay it was afforded on *American Bandstand*, it is certain that the difficult process of persuading the music industry to play the flip side of a failed song was facilitated by Clark's lead on national television.

Independent producers Frank Slay and Bob Crewe, who worked out of New York at the time of "Click Clack's" success, were also "hitting pretty good in Philadelphia," according to Slay. When the pair's next batch of recordings were completed, Slay, as he had done in the past, "took the masters down to Bernie [Lowe] to see if he was interested."

Lowe was very interested. Of the four completed sides, two were by a black lounge act duo called Billy and Lillie (Billy Ford and the Thunderbirds and

Lillie Bryant), and two were solo efforts by Bryant. As it turned out, Lowe wanted all four sides—two for his own release on Cameo and two to resell to Bernie Binnick at Swan.

Bernie Lowe was "very active in trying to get masters for Swan . . . just for Dick's good will," said Slay, adding that the frugal owner of Cameo Records had an ulterior motive for doing so. "Bernie thought he could buy the records from me at half the cost. [That way] he'd get the two that he wanted and put the two that he didn't want off on Swan."

But first Lowe would have to take a stab as to what he thought would succeed in the hit record sweepstakes. He opted to retain Lillie Bryant's solo sides and offer the Billy and Lillie recordings to Binnick. Lowe ostensibly touted "La De Dah" (which happened to be suitable for a popular *Bandstand* dance called the Chalypso, a cha-cha done to calypso music) as a natural for Clark's TV show, and Binnick grabbed it in a heartbeat.

As he did with "Did You Cry," Clark previewed "La De Dah" on *American Bandstand* before Swan Records was even operating.[27] Ultimately, he gave the song more airplay than he gave to "Click Clack," and in a matter of weeks "La De Dah" bounced into the national top ten. Meanwhile, the Lillie Bryant record Bernie Lowe selected to release on his Cameo label turned out to be a flop.

Needless to say, Clark's viewers had no inkling of what was taking place behind the cameras. Furthermore, not only did the host of *American Bandstand* fail to disclose to his viewers his interest in the songs he touted on his television show, his comments to the press appear somewhat disingenuous as well. As "At the Hop," "Click Clack," and "La De Dah" simultaneously rode high on the nation's hit record charts, Clark told the *New York Daily News'* Kay Gardella: "I admit there are a lot of free-swinging deals made in the disk business. But on my part I must say ABC pays me enough" to preclude the need to become involved with them.[28]

Apparently Clark was also reluctant to let music industry insiders in on the extent of his behind-the-scenes business dealings. Frank Slay, who worked closely with Swan over the years, claimed he was unaware that Clark even held an interest in that label. "As far as I was concerned, Tony [Mammarella] and Bernie [Binnick] owned Swan. I kept my nose out of their business."

• • •

Thanks to *American Bandstand*, the rock 'n' roll scene in Philadelphia really began to catch fire in 1958. New releases shipped across the country with the hope that one might catch on locally and be overheard by Clark, who would then add the privileged song to *Bandstand*'s coveted playlist, made their way to Philadelphia radio stations in record numbers. That city became "the greatest test market" for a record, said Lee Silver. "You knew what you had within a week or two. If it sold there, then you could bring it anywhere!"

Considering the success of his first two Swan releases, Clark had entered the recording fray with a big splash. Now it was Bob Marcucci's time. Despite two failed records by Frankie Avalon, Marcucci continued to bring the teenage heartthrob to record hops, where the label owner saw that the reaction to his young singer remained "just unbelievable!" Since neither Marcucci nor Peter DeAngelis (who despised rock 'n' roll) were adept rock 'n' roll songwriters, the new song they wrote for Avalon consisted of little more than a number of song titles of current hit records strung together. They called it "De De Dinah."

The day Avalon recorded the song, he suffered from a heavy cold and "was singing with this crazy nasal sound," recalled Marcucci.

"Frankie, that's great!" said the label owner, who discerned a catchiness to the peculiar sound Avalon was producing.

"Pete'll kill me," replied the singer.

"Pete doesn't even know you're singing right now," said Marcucci, "so go ahead and do it."

Avalon did it, and sure enough, recalled Marcucci, when DeAngelis heard the finished take of "De De Dinah" he "went insane. Poor Frankie was scared to death!"

Eager to get "De De Dinah" pressed and on the market, Marcucci feigned agreement over the poor quality of Avalon's record, but he told DeAngelis they would have to release it as it was because they did not "have any money to come back and bring the musicians in again."

"De De Dinah" was released on the first day of December, and five days later, "it was a smash hit," said Marcucci The following week Avalon lip-synched the song on *American Bandstand* and never looked back. "We went out and sold a million records," recalled the Chancellor co-owner. ("De De Dinah" reached number seven on *Billboard*'s Top 100.)

It was the success of "De De Dinah" that finally brought Marcucci and Dick Clark together. Although Clark may have continued to believe Marcucci was "insane and crazy," the *American Bandstand* host gained a healthy respect for the scheming ways of the ostentatious producer/manager. Marcucci said he and Clark became "very friendly. Dick kind of believed in me and believed in what I was doing," trying to create a teenage singing idol.

Plucked from the sidewalks of South Philadelphia's Italian enclave, Frankie Avalon became the prototype for that city's teen idols. Marcucci, who also managed the young singer, became a respected player in the hit record sweepstakes. The relationship between himself, Dick Clark, Bernie Lowe, and Bernie Binnick was one of "friendly enemies . . . all very close to each other," said Marcucci. "We knew we were in competition, but we all helped each other." Indeed they did. Cameo, Swan, and Chancellor were destined to become three of the most influential independent record labels of the *Bandstand* era. Although Clark had no financial stake in Chancellor, Am-Par did, distributing Marcucci's label nationally. It must have warmed the corporate hearts of Am-Par executives to see Frankie Avalon become a giant star and a *Bandstand* favorite.

• • •

Thanks to Cameo, Swan, and Chancellor Records and *American Bandstand*, Philadelphia took the pop music industry lead in developing and marketing teen idol singers. And early in 1958, when Danny and the Juniors sang "rock 'n' roll is here to stay" in their prophetic follow-up to "At the Hop," they demonstrated to America that Philadelphia's new crop of young white artists were not necessarily of the "one-hit wonder" variety. Group member Joe Terry, who claimed Danny and the Juniors "probably did *Bandstand* more than any other group alive," credits Clark's show with having had an "instant effect on audiences," changing the music world in much the same manner televised news did in comparison to newspapers. Indeed, the focus of America's teens on ABC's afternoon dance forum reshaped the music industry's traditional method of song promotion. Before the advent of *American Bandstand*, it was necessary for artists to make numerous promotional appearances throughout the country in order to help their records build momentum. But a single appearance on Clark's show made an artist seem "bigger than life, instantly," said Terry. "If you went on the show and the kids liked the record and they liked you, they immediately ran to the stores to get the record, the record took off and you hit the charts quickly."

Boom times in the pop record business continued into 1958, as more and more white artists appeared on the scene. Meanwhile, Clark's role in that business grew more complex. The American Broadcasting Company owned both a record company and the only nationally televised rock 'n' roll show. Clark, thanks to his ownership of the publishing rights to the flip side of Paul Anka's "Diana" (given to him by Am-Par), profited from the sales of songs he played regularly on *American Bandstand*. This conflict of interest only deepened after Clark formed Swan Records and Chips distributing, for he then profited from playing records owned and distributed by those companies. Clark's unwillingness to let industry insiders such as Frank Slay in on what he was doing was yet another instance whereby Clark sought to portray himself as something less than he actually was. The fewer people who realized the extent of his behind-the-scenes involvement in the music business, the better.

Everything seemed in perfect order. Not only was *American Bandstand*'s power as the premier promotional vehicle within the pop music industry undisputed, ABC-TV now looked for a way to unleash Dick Clark on its prime-time viewing audience.

CHAPTER 6

Saturday Night

Not only were ABC executives stunned by the success of *American Bandstand*, they were also impressed with Dick Clark's facile manner. When ABC originally contracted for its teenage dance show the network viewed Clark as being indispensible to the show's success; now ABC realized that *Bandstand*'s personable young host was everything they had expected—and then some. "We saw that he was a property in himself," recalled Ted Fetter. "Here we had a guy who was obviously a star. He had something; he had a knack, and so we said, 'How can we develop this thing?' It was just in the cards that we were going to try our best to capitalize on this guy."

ABC wanted Clark in prime time. Just two weeks after *American Bandstand* was added to ABC's permanent schedule the press noted that he was "reportedly set" for his own nighttime program on the network, which was supposedly going to air on Saturday evenings from New York City and follow a similar format to *American Bandstand*.[1] But plans to develop a new show for Clark fell victim to ABC's longstanding practice of employing the bottom line to determine network programming. Instead of developing an entirely new show for Clark, the network decided to institute a live Monday night version of *American Bandstand*. Since *American Bandstand* was making money in the afternoon, why not also air the popular program at night?

Fetter, who thought that prime time was "not the time" to air *American Bandstand*, objected, telling his fellow ABC executives it was not a good idea. But rather than pay attention to what was appropriate for the time slot, ABC considered only the cost-effectiveness of showing *American Bandstand* during evening hours and decided to broadcast a special edition of the show one night a week simply because it was the cheapest programming available to fill that particular time slot. (Clark said in 1994 that he had "no idea" who at ABC made the decision to air the night version of the show.)

It was ABC's hope that the Monday night version of *American Bandstand* (which made its debut on October 7, 1957, from 7:30 to 8:30 P.M.), would prove to be a strong lead-in to another new music-oriented show scheduled to make its debut on ABC that same evening, hosted by popular singer Guy Mitchell. But in order for the prime-time version of Clark's show to live up to the network's expectations it would have to overcome obstacles not inherent in its popular afternoon time slot. For one, the afternoon show's core audience —teenagers and housewives—was otherwise preoccupied in the evening hours. Also, most family breadwinners—fathers, who had little or no interest in *Bandstand*—were home by 7:30 P.M., and many commandeered the family TV set for themselves. In addition, Monday night *Bandstand* faced stiffer competition from rival networks and local stations than it did in its afternoon time slot.

It was no surprise then, that nighttime *Bandstand* proved to be a ratings disaster. Clark, who agreed to do the show "without thinking," soon regretted having done so at all.[2] All he could recall about the ill-fated program in 1994 was that it "didn't last but a minute in time and it didn't make much of an impression on me." Likewise, Ted Fetter was unable to recall anything about Clark's Monday night show, "because it was brief and it was a failure, both of which make you forget."

Fetter said ABC realized within a matter of weeks that its prime-time spinoff of Clark's afternoon hit show would not work at night, and, seeking a new format and time slot for the show's personable host, "that's when we devised the Dick Clark Saturday night show." Word leaked out in November 1957 that ABC was preparing a Saturday evening show for Clark, "styled along the same teen-age record hop groove" as *American Bandstand* but under a different name.[3] In compliance with ABC's latest design, Monday night *Bandstand* was to be discontinued when the new show began. (It was actually taken off the air in December, over a month before the debut of Clark's new show.)

ABC's latest decision to air Clark's show on Saturday nights presented a new challenge for the *Bandstand* host. Since most 1950s' households possessed only one TV set, if they contained any at all, and home videotaping was still a distant dream, Clark would need the unwavering support of his budding teenage constituency—the same following that failed to support him on Monday nights—if he was to survive against the adult-oriented Saturday night competition. What is more, Clark's new show was slated for the 7:30–8:30 P.M. time slot, portending a head-to-head scuffle with CBS's hot new "Perry Mason" law series and NBC's firmly entrenched variety show hosted by popular crooner Perry Como. But Clark had already gained a measure of respect in broadcasting circles. Factoring him into the Saturday evening ratings battle, one columnist opined that "the Perrys might get hurt!"[4]

Although Clark's Saturday night foray came hard on the heels of his Monday night debacle, the show's host maintained that he was "not at all" reluctant to give prime time another try. "At that point I wouldn't have been knowledgeable enough to have even recognized the failure," he recalled. "I was just happy to have the work."

Clark pointed out on the eve of his new show that it was about time a major network took aim at the teen age market, the "most entertainment-starved group in the country."[5] To be sure, America had always had its share of teenagers, but never before had so many of them existed at one time. And unlike its predecessors, this adolescent group had cash in its pockets and leisure time to burn—a dream-come-true for any Madison Avenue ad man. But the teenagers of the 1950s had yet to be corraled by Saturday night television.

Meanwhile, the exact format of Clark's new show remained undecided. ABC executives, whom Tony Mammarella derided as never having had "any connection with the modern popular song and singer of the day," were not united in how their network should go about affording rock 'n' roll prime time status. Ted Fetter, who at one time coproduced the televised version of radio's long-running *Your Hit Parade* on which the week's most popular songs were performed by a regular cast of singers, "injected some of the techniques" from that show into Clark's new program. He also recommended one significant change. In the pre-rock 'n' roll era that spawned *Your Hit Parade* it was the songs, not the specific artists who sang them, that were the show's drawing card. But as the former ABC executive pointed out in 1994, in order to attract viewers during the rock 'n' roll era, "you had to have the specific recording artist" who was responsible for the hit version of a particular song.

This made sense to everyone but the ABC brass. Tony Mammarella said a "wide difference of opinion [existed] between people in New York . . . about the type of music and the type of performer" that would be featured on Clark's new show. It was Clark himself who broke the logjam by insisting that he and Mammarella (whom Clark had already named as the associate producer of the yet-to-be formatted program) be given "total control of the artists who appear" on it. When ABC finally assented, Mammarella and Clark "got together and came up with a format" for the show.[6]

The Dick Clark Show originated from the heart of Manhattan in ABC's

Little Theatre, a converted West 44th Street radio facility that seated less than three hundred. The production emerged as a live rock 'n' roll stage show featuring artists with current hit records, on which Clark also revealed the *American Bandstand* top ten songs for the week. The show was put together each Saturday, with an afternoon dress rehearsal in front of an audience conducted before the televised show was aired that evening.

Clark's new show debuted on February 15, 1958, a cold and blustery day during which a driving blizzard developed. As some overly exuberant teens began to arrive at the theatre early that morning and the snowflakes began to fly, Clark eyed the frigid throng with trepidation. He pulled twenty-five dollars from his pocket and dispatched a crew-member to buy hot drinks for the kids, only to later reveal in his autobiography that this action did not occur out of sympathy for the youngsters; but came from "the heart of a cunning capitalist" who did not want to lose his audience to the inclement weather.[7]

Just before showtime the fifteen hundred true believers who lined Manhattan's sidewalks watched in dismay as two ice-encrusted busloads of fans from Philadelphia pulled up and were given choice seats for the evening's festivities. One reporter assumed that Clark reserved the seats because he figured he "owed priority to his hometown fans," but observed that the preferential treatment prompted "catcalls and despair" from those who had been waiting patiently, if numbly, in line for several hours.[8]

Word must have leaked out about this special treatment, for when the buses arrived at the theatre a policeman climbed aboard and warned the *Bandstand* regulars not to leave the vehicle under any circumstances until he returned. "We all looked at each other and wondered what was up," recalled Joanne Montecarlo, before being startled by "this incredible screaming and all of a sudden this crash and thump and the bus began rocking from side to side." Arlene Sullivan opened one of the icy windows a wee bit to peer out and saw that the bus had been surrounded by a group of New York fans. The angry crowd was quickly forced away from the buses by police, who then formed a wedge and escorted the Philadelphians into the theatre, two-by-two. "Kenny Rossi had the clothes ripped off his back [and] . . . our hair was getting pulled on the way in," recalled Montecarlo. "Dick didn't bus us up to the show again after that, and I couldn't blame him."[9]

At precisely 7:30 P.M. millions of Americans who were tuned to ABC-TV heard the show's announcer say: "From New York, in the Little Theatre on 44th Street, just west of Broadway, it's time for music, fun and excitement with your favorite recording artists—and your Saturday night host, Dick Clark!"[10]

In a scene reminiscent of bygone gala on-the-street movie premiers, Clark was first seen outside the theatre, after which the cameras shifted into the lobby to catch the Royal Teens, clad in black short sleeve shirts and tan bermuda shorts, mouthing the words to "Short Shorts" as they followed a pretty girl from a telephone booth to center stage. It was uncertain who was more excited at that moment, the millions of ABC viewers or Am-Par's Sam Clark, whose record label released "Short Shorts."[11]

The electricity on Clark's new show was supplied by the tempestuous Jerry Lee Lewis. When informed that he was expected to lip-synch his songs that night (apropos the show's policy), Lewis told Clark he did not "give a damn what everybody else does. . . . I ain't no puppet, and I didn't come all the way up [from Memphis] to play charades." *Variety* duly noted that the Killer's live performance "stood the teenage pewsters on their ears."[12]

Also on Clark's opening-night bill was songstress Connie Francis, who had recently made her national TV debut on *American Bandstand*. Unlike the contentious Lewis, Miss Francis offered no objection to lip-synching her first hit, "Who's Sorry Now," which was one of the fastest-rising pop songs in America.

Over the years, Clark has tended to downplay the promotional value of an artist's appearance on his show, maintaining that he could not create a hit simply by playing a particular song. But his treatment of "Who's Sorry Now" offered a glimpse of the other side of the promotional coin: although Clark could not make a hit indiscriminately, airplay on his show could prove invaluable to a song with hit potential.

Few who tuned in to Clark's show that night were aware that Francis, with ten failed recordings under her belt at the tender age of nineteen, was on the verge of quitting the business when, at her father's urging, she recorded a song that had originally been a hit in 1923. When Francis' version of "Who's Sorry Now" was released in November 1957, it seemed as if the only person besides the singer's father who liked it was the Philadelphia record distributor who handled her record label. He urged Francis to come to Philadelphia to promote the song, but when she declined, he undauntingly took it to Dick Clark.

Considering her dismal track record, Francis was not surprised that a month after the release of "Who's Sorry Now," no one had played it. Consequently, when she tuned in *American Bandstand* on New Year's Day, 1958, and heard Clark talking about "a new girl singer who's headed straight for the number one spot," she was shocked to hear him play her own latest recording. "And he continued playing it until it sold a million," recalled Francis. "Without Dick Clark I wouldn't have stayed in show business. I was ready to go back to school to study medicine."[13]

Press accounts of Clark's new show were mixed. One Philadelphia reviewer described the production as "a sort of sit-down version" of *American Bandstand* whose songs were mostly "hideous efforts by no-talent performers." *Variety* was kinder, describing Clark as "a young, wholesome type who makes with hip chatter" and handles his emcee chores "pleasantly and informatively." Ironically, it was one of rock 'n' roll's most acerbic critics, the *New York Journal-American's* Jack O'Brian, who put Clark's Saturday evening show into the most accurate light, warning that "anyone past the blue-jeans age shouldn't be expected to appreciate or even understand" the program, which, wrote O'Brian, "doubtless will delight the audience just past the Mouseketeer age." [14]

Clark later retorted that he was fortunate that when it came to television, "popularity does not depend on what the critics say. I can't say that I've been pleased by some of the things that were written about me. . . . But I wasn't surprised." [15]

There was no reason for Clark to be surprised about O'Brian's comment. As was the case with *American Bandstand*, nobody loved Clark's new show but the audience—and lucky for ABC and Clark, this audience was one of significant numbers. Over half of Clark's viewers were said to be adults, and his initial Saturday night broadcast was credited with "cutting deeply into the competition on the other networks," more than doubling ABC-TV's previous rating in that time period. [16]

As popular as Clark's new show was, it did not yet have a sponsor when it went on the air. Perhaps recalling ABC's Monday night *Bandstand* debacle, network sponsors had displayed no interest in the program, and ABC was forced to air it on a sustaining basis, in hopes that it would develop a following and thereby draw advertisers. "We had a time period to fill, and we just filled it," said Ted Fetter.

But before any large national accounts could react to the prime-time success of Clark's new show, sponsorship was secured by Beechnut Foods, a company anxious to promote its new spearmint chewing gum, which was said to contain the secret ingredient "IFIC." (as in, "it's flavor-ific.") [17] Ticketholders to Clark's third Saturday night production were caught off guard when they received from the Little Theatre ushers complimentary Kelly green packets of Beechnut's new product and large green "IFIC" buttons to pin on themselves.

Ironically, while gum-chewing remained forbidden on *American Bandstand* the practice was abetted on Saturday nights and quickly became de rigueur for Clark's New York audience. Everyone on the set, from the producer on down to the cameramen, chewed the sponsor's product, and ad-lib camera shots panning across the masticating young audience—"IFIC" buttons proudly displayed—became a recurring feature of *The Dick Clark Show*.

Clark, of course, did not chew his sponsor's product. He sold it, invariably foregoing the prepared script to ad lib his pitch. One Madison Avenue ad man noted that whenever Clark threw away his copy and winged it, "the commercials [came] out even better than we wrote them." Citing the massive teenage audience attracted to Clark's Saturday night show, the ad executive emphasized that the program "was the kind of show we wanted to hang our hats on."[18] So successful was Clark in associating his sponsor's product with his new show that the two became inexorably linked to the extent that the program came to be referred to as *The Dick Clark Saturday Night Beechnut Show.*

As they chomped on their spearmint gum few, if any, of Clark's home viewers realized that the owner of Beechnut Foods was none other than Ed Noble, the original owner of the ABC network. Upon seeing a kinescope of Clark's show Noble reportedly remarked that it was "terrible . . . the worst thing I've ever seen. But it'll sell a lot of my gum."[19] Although he no longer ran ABC, Noble remained its largest stockholder, which was reason enough for some to wonder if he had cut some sort of "sweetheart" sponsorship deal with the network.

Ev Erlick, who handled the Beechnut advertising account before he become an attorney for ABC, described Noble as "Machiavellian . . . brilliant . . . very subtle . . . [and] very farsighted." But also "such a cheap S.O.B. that he wouldn't buy programs for Beechnut anywhere but ABC" and would not accept any deal "until he pushed ABC flat against the wall."[20] Ted Fetter was not certain how much influence Noble exerted to acquire sponsorship of Clark's show, but the former ABC programming executive thought that Beechnut, although "not in the bag, . . . [was] a very likely sponsor" at the time Clark's show made its TV debut.

Despite his cozy deal with ABC and the added promotion through Clark's chewing studio audience, Noble expressed concern that he had squandered his advertising money and, the "IFIC" campaign nonwithstanding, would not sell any gum by sponsoring Clark's show and thus was considering backing out. This may simply have been a renegotiation ploy engineered by the Machiavellian business tycoon to squeeze a more favorable advertising rate out of ABC, but when Clark got wind of Noble's ploy he sprung into action. The loss of Beechnut's sponsorship would affect Clark financially because ABC was obligated to pay him $750 per sponsored show as opposed to only $500 for each unsponsored show—and that was only if the network chose to return the show to a sustaining (unsponsored) basis. It was also possible that if Clark lost his sponsor the show might be cancelled altogether. Why Clark then telephoned Jerry Lee Lewis's manager, Judd Phillips, of all people, and told him Beechnut was not very happy with the show, is unclear. "I need to come up with something fast," said Clark. "I was hoping you could help." [21]

Judd Phillips, the affable and gregarious older brother of Sam Phillips, the quiet and reserved owner of Sun Records (for which Lewis recorded), thought he could help. Acknowledging that Lewis' current record "Breathless," "isn't movin' very fast and you ain't movin' enough gum," Phillips proposed that Clark's TV viewers send in five Beechnut gum wrappers along with fifty cents to obtain a copy of Lewis's record through the mail.

Clark liked the idea, but wanted Phillips to be the one to sell it to the ad men who handled the Beechnut account. The deal was cut, and on April 5 Lewis reappeared on Clark's Saturday night show to sing "Breathless," after which Clark, in the words of one reporter, "begged America to take him up on his once-in-a-lifetime offer." [22] (Interestingly, two of Sam Phillips' unknown artists, Carl McVoy and Ray Smith, as well as Bill Justis—who had not been on the pop charts for months—were subsequently booked onto Clark's Saturday night show, although there is no evidence that this was part of the deal.)

Three days later, Clark's office was inundated with tens of thousands of green gum wrappers and hundreds of pounds of loose change. By week's end Beechnut had reportedly sold more spearmint chewing gum than it had since the product's introduction, "Breathless" began to move up the record sales charts again (it eventually reached number seven on *Billboard*'s Top 100 and purportedly sold one million copies), and Ed Noble signed a $2-million, fifty-two-week pact to sponsor Clark's show.

As part of the Clark/Sun Records deal, Jerry Lee Lewis waived his royalties for the almost forty thousand copies of "Breathless" sold in conjunction with it. In addition, the song's publishing royalties were waived by Sam Phillips, who also agreed to supply the records free of charge. It was later reported that the deal was carefully arranged so that no costs would be borne by Clark, and that the profits—described by Sam Phillips as "slim"—were split evenly with Clark. [23]

In the wake of the "Breathless" promotion Clark told Judd Phillips he would "never forget what you and Jerry have done for me." But just months later, when Lewis became embroiled in controversy over the disclosure of his marriage to his thirteen-year-old cousin, Myra Brown, Clark nevertheless shunned the controversial twenty-two-year-old performer, as did most of the nation.

The series of events leading to the near-destruction of Lewis's career began in the spring of 1958, as the "Killer" prepared for a performance on Clark's Saturday night show designed to kick off an extended tour of England. The volatile singer stunned Judd Phillips by revealing his intention to disclose his clandestine six-month marriage on Clark's show, "so the whole country'll know I'm married to Myra."[24] Never one to suffer from insufficient ego, Lewis believed he was big enough to withstand any controversy generated by his matrimonial announcement, but Phillips realized that such a move on Lewis's part would be suicidal to the singer's career.

Determined to save his calamitous artist from himself, Phillips called Beechnut's advertising agency and told them of Lewis's intentions, reminding them it would not be advantageous to Beechnut if Lewis, after having recently done the "Breathless" co-promotion for that company, was publicly crucified. The advertising agency called Clark and informed him that it was in both his and their best interests to cancel the upcoming Saturday night appearance of Lewis. Meanwhile, Judd Phillips disguised his voice and called Clark anonymously, warning him to be careful because "all hell's fixin' to break loose."

Caught between the proverbial rock and a hard place, Clark weighed his options. Despite the favors Lewis had done for him, Clark, in what he later described as "a very cowardly act," opted to yank the plug on Jerry Lee. Clark not only scratched the controversial singer from his upcoming Saturday show, he also held off on further bookings of the contentious artist.

As Lewis railed about Clark's ingratitude, the complicit Judd Phillips let the television host take the heat. That April, Jerry Lee headed for England referring to Clark as "Judas." Once in England, Lewis disclosed his marriage to Brown and was virtually driven out of the country. Even worse, when the tempestuous singer returned to America he discovered that radio stations there would no longer play his records. Judd Phillips pleaded for a guest spot on one of Clark's shows for the beseiged Lewis, and Clark replied that if it was up to him he would have the controversial singer on "every week. But you know my sponsors are the harshest critics and I don't think they'll back me up on this. Jerry's too hot for me to touch right now."[25] As it was, Clark did not have Lewis on *American Bandstand* again for four years.

. . .

Almost overnight, *The Dick Clark Show*, which boasted a waiting list of seven months to attend, became ABC's hottest ticket. In effect, the show was an adjunct of *American Bandstand* on which the half dozen available weekly guest appearance slots were highly coveted.[26] Johnny Maestro, lead singer of the Crests, a popular vocal group that appeared on Clark's new show, thought the reason for its success was that in the 1950s, "anything on TV that had to do with rock 'n' roll was a major event. It was very . . . [seldom that] you'd see a rock 'n' roll show or a rock 'n' roll act on TV." Ted Fetter agreed that Clark's new program "really opened up a whole thing in television."

Acts fortunate enough to be booked on Clark's new Saturday night national rock 'n' roll showcase had to be on their toes however, for its host ran an extremely tight ship. No one understood that better than the Silhouettes (Rick Lewis, Bill Horton, Raymond Edwards, and Earl Beal), a Philadelphia vocal group who recorded "Get a Job," the lively, albeit almost unintelligible, lament of an out-of-work guy being nagged by his wife.

The song was not even intended to be the hit side of the Silhouettes' record. The ballad "I Am Lonely" was released in December 1957, by the tiny Junior label, which was owned by Philadelphia disc jockey Kae Williams. (Ironically, although Bernie Lowe was looking for a potential hit for his Cameo label, he passed up the opportunity to release "Get a Job.") "I Am Lonely" sold well in Philadelphia, but disc jockeys elsewhere began flipping the record over, causing "Get a Job" to move in other breakout markets. Clark would not play the record even though he "smelled a smash hit" and wanted to do so "in the worst way," however, because the Silhouettes' label had no national distribution. As it was, a copy of "Get a Job" lay on his desk for two weeks.

But after the nationally distributed Herald-Ember label acquired the rights to "Get a Job" (and subsequently awarded half of the song's publishing rights to Tony Mammarella's Wildcat Music), Clark began to play it on *American Bandstand.* "When I walked into the office the morning after he played it, there were telegrams with back orders for about 500,000 records underneath the door," recalled Herald-Ember owner Al Silver. "It was unbelievable." [27]

"Get a Job" hit *Billboard*'s Top 100 in January and reportedly sold a million copies in just three weeks. By February it was the No. 1 song in the country. The infectious song had already peaked on the national charts by the time Clark's Saturday night show came into existence, so when the Silhouettes were booked into the Little Theatre that March they were slated to reprise their hit and introduce their follow-up record, "Headin' For The Poorhouse."

Interrupting a Florida tour, the Silhouettes flew into New York the Saturday morning of Clark's show and headed for Ember's Brill Building offices. They spent the better part of the day there before going out to shop for new tuxedos to wear during that night's TV performance. Unfortunately, when the Silhouettes arrived at the Little Theatre that evening an irked Clark said, "You guys were supposed to be here for rehearsal this morning, why weren't you here?" Rick Lewis, who wrote "Get a Job" and sang lead on the song, claimed the Silhouettes were never informed by Herald-Ember of any afternoon rehearsal for Clark's show.

"What are you going to say to the man, 'We've been up at the record company . . . all day and they didn't tell us to come down here?'" Lewis lamented. According to the singer, Clark then informed the group that since they had missed the show's rehearsal they would not be permitted to introduce their new record that night. "Headin' For The Poorhouse" was not heard by Clark's national audience and the song subsequently failed to make *Billboard*'s Top 100. "And that's how we got screwed," recalled Lewis.

Lewis's claim notwithstanding, there was no guarantee that the follow-up to "Get a Job" would have cracked *Billboard*'s top 100 even if the Silhouettes had performed the song on Clark's show. Vito Picone and the Elegants could attest to that.

The Elegants (Picone, Carmen Romano, James Moschella, Frank Tardogno, and Artie Venosa), who hailed from Staten Island in New York, were well-known in that borough by early 1958, after winning local contests by singing "Little Star," a tune that had been adapted from the old "Twinkle, twinkle, little star" nursery rhyme. The number was so popular with live audiences that Picone was certain "we were winning more with the song" than because of the group's talent. "Little Star" became so well-known on Staten Island that another neighborhood group planned to record it. When the Elegants found that out, Picone said they jumped on the ferry to Manhattan, headed for the Brill Building, and "just started knocking on doors" of record companies. The first door they knocked on belonged to Hull Records. "We hit 'em with ['Little Star'] . . . and the next thing I know, we were in the studio." Released just days after it was recorded, "Little Star" proceded to take off that June.

Picone said the Elegants "knew right away that we had a monster by the tail, we just never figured how big and how long it was going to last. All we wanted to do was get some kind of air play and get back to the neighborhood and pop some buttons on our chest." But Hull's owners had more grandiose plans for "Little Star." Realizing that the song was too hot for their tiny label to handle, they worked out a national distribution arrangement with Am-Par Records while the Elegants remained totally unaware of their goings-on.

As "Little Star" entered *Billboard*'s Top 100 in July, Am-Par not only booked the Elegants onto *American Bandstand*, but onto Clark's Saturday night show as well. Picone recalled that the group was in a jovial mood as they drove from New York to Philadelphia, "which we thought was a million miles away." Then, during the obligatory post-performance interview conducted after the Elegants lip-synched their hit on *Bandstand*, Clark asked how they had arrived at their name. Unaware of the liquor industry's voluntary (and network supported) television advertising ban, Picone unabashedly replied that it was inspired by a whiskey advertisement, "*Schenley, The Whiskey of Elegance.*" The irreproachable Clark died a thousand deaths on camera as he realized that millions of viewers were watching him and a group of underage teenagers violate that ban by promoting alcohol on the air. "He almost had a heart attack," recalled Picone.

"Little Star" became the number one record in America that summer, causing the Elegants to be invited back to Clark's show despite their whiskey-promoting gaffe (ABC took no action against Clark). But the group's follow-up record, "Please Believe Me," was not released until October, and despite the Elegants' performance of the song on Clark's Saturday night show it failed to make *Billboard*'s Hot 100 (the chart name Top 100 was changed to Hot 100 in August 1958). In an unprecedented move, Clark brought the group back for a national reprise of the song two weeks later, but despite this concerted effort at national promotion, "Please Believe Me" died unceremoniously.

Ironically, the magnitude of "Little Star's" success may have contributed to the Elegants' downfall. As it was, Picone blamed the group's inexperienced management for not knowing what to do with them after their giant hit. "What they did was keep us out on the road too long," he explained. "We worked and worked and worked, and did not go back into the studio to concentrate on releasing a follow-up. By the time we came back and recorded . . . the style was already copied by about six or seven different acts, the song was already played out, and the Elegants now had to start playing catch-up. And that's where we got hurt."

According to talent manager Ernie Martinelli, the longevity of most hits during the 1950s was "a month and a half to two months. If you were out [touring], making three dollars a night during that time period, by the time you came back your record was dead [and] . . . if the company didn't have another record to come behind it, your career was over!" It was certainly over for the Elegants, whose management had overlooked the crucial window of opportunity that had been opened up by "Little Star." Unable to produce a follow-up hit for Am-Par, the Elegants were dropped from the label in 1959.

In contrast Dion and the Belmonts, a similarly styled group, released their first hit, "I Wonder Why," two months before "Little Star," but their record company released a follow-up, "No One Knows," eight weeks later, and had the group perform it on *American Bandstand* and on Clark's Saturday show rather than wait until interest in the first hit died down. By the time the Elegants released their *second* record, Dion and the Belmonts' third hit, "Don't Pity Me," was already in record stores, enabling them to gain a foothold as America's premier white rock 'n' roll group while the Elegants faded from public view. "It's like we were the world's greatest disappearing act," lamented Picone.

Clark's often unpredictable Saturday evening line-up was a product of the serendipitous world of popular music, the demands of having to book a half-dozen guest artists each week, and the fact that the show's host had to cater to a broad-based prime-time audience.

One of the most anomalous hitmakers ever to appear with Clark was local Philadelphia TV actor/personality John Zacherle (b. September 26, 1918), better known around Philadelphia in the 1950s as "Roland," the ghoulish undertaker/host of a local TV station's late-night horror movie. A former actor with a bachelor's degree in English literature, Zacherle not only introduced *Shock Theatre* movies, he intermittently "appeared" in them by having another camera focus on his macabre image while he reacted with his own zany studio antics to the characters in the movie. (As a rule of thumb, the worse the movie, the greater was his role in it.) "And it worked!" he later exclaimed. "It seemed like the funniest thing we'd ever done in our lives." Bernie Lowe's daughter thought it was so hilarious that she urged her father to cut a record on Zach. As it was, Lowe did not need much encouragement to do so.

Down and disconsolate, Lowe had not only lost his budding teen idol Charlie Gracie and outsmarted himself by virtually handing the hitbound "La De Dah" to Swan Records' Bernie Binnick, he had also failed to put a record into the top forty during the past six months. The thirty-nine-year-old actor-turned-TV ghoul Zacherle, who may have been the farthest thing there was from a teen idol, was the one who would restore Lowe's fragile confidence.

Lowe tuned in *Shock Theatre* and saw Zach carrying a basket, containing a head from which dripped chocolate syrup, as the eerie figure recited a canni-balistic limerick about being the main course for a dinner at Dracula's house. The next morning Lowe got on the telephone with Zacherle and asked him to make a record reciting his ghoulish limericks, with "some funky music behind it." Zacherle remembered Dick Clark thinking the finished product "was a little too bloody for TV," which sent Bernie Lowe into a panic. Realizing "Dinner With Drac" would be next to worthless if Clark refused to play it on *American Bandstand*, Lowe had Zach record a "cleaner" version of the song.

Released about the same time that Clark's Saturday night show made its debut, "Dinner With Drac" sold well enough locally for Clark to book Zacherle on his new program. Zach describes his performance there as "an early attempt at a music video," in which he sat at a table as dancers dressed as monsters appeared onstage and began jumping around, "while I was reciting stuff about how dinner was served for three at Dracula's house. It was strange!"

"Dinner With Drac" entered *Billboard*'s Top 100 the week of Zacherle's appearance on Clark's show and eventually reached number six on that chart. It became Bernie Lowe's biggest hit since "Silhouettes" and was one of the most popular novelty hits of 1958.

Clark noted that "every single human being in the record business" wanted to appear on his shows, and a look at those who, besides Zacherle, did appear there bears him out.[28] Some nights, such as the evening Jerry Lee Lewis, Paul Anka, Jimmy McCracklin, the Shirelles, and the Everly Brothers were featured on the same show, Clark's program was a rock 'n' roller's dream come true. But on other occasions the show's excitement was tempered by schlock pop artists—the likes of Somethin' Smith and the Redheads, Hugo and Luigi, Janice Harper, Pat Suzuki, and Don Cornell—many of whom did not even have a hit record to promote. Worse yet was the appearance of totally unknown artists such as Ann Reynolds, Pat Shannon, and Wally Lewis.

Clark's uneven line-ups were the product of a longstanding industry practice whereby a booking agency, when committing a hot artist to a particular appearance, also included one of its new or lesser-known acts as part of the package. "That was the politics of the business," recalled Jack Hooke, who booked and produced Alan Freed's legendary 1950s stage shows. "They used to say, 'Don't cherry pick, buy my shit, too, because we have to build new acts.'" Clark wanted to present the hottest stars of the day, but in doing so he was also forced to expose some of the culls of the business. Of course, those fortunate enough to secure a highly coveted ticket to his Saturday show did not particularly care who was booked on any given night. The teen set, which strove desperately to be a part of Clark's rock 'n' roll zeitgeist, came to the Little Theatre in droves, no matter who was on the bill.

Bandstand producer Tony Mammarella echoed Clark's belief that no amount of air play could "make a hit out of a dog," but Mammarella was quick to add that "if a record is potentially a hit and Dick plays it, it would be known almost overnight."[29] Indeed, having a particular record "known almost overnight" propelled many a recording artist to the upper echelons of the pop charts, a fact demonstrated most clearly during the career of Rock 'n' Roll Hall of Fame guitarist Duane Eddy, who made more appearances on *American Bandstand* and on Clark's Saturday night show than any other artist.

Had *The Dick Clark Show* been created with just one artist in mind, that artist would have been Eddy, a handsome young guitar picker who, in a three-year period coinciding with *Bandstand*'s salad days, produced a string of twelve top forty rock 'n' roll hits. It was a run elipsed only by Elvis Presley's and Ricky Nelson's, who happened to be the only two well-known recording artists of that era who never appeared on Clark's shows. Clark understood that Presley and Nelson were beyond his realm, not only because his shows could not afford them, but because Elvis and Ricky were already so big that they stood to gain absolutely nothing from appearing with him.

But Duane Eddy was something else. Cynics maintain his string of TV appearances on Clark's shows occurred solely because Clark had an interest in Eddy's record company (Jamie) and in his management (SRO Artists). On the other hand, fans of Eddy point to the quality of the guitarist's records as the sole factor behind those appearances. The truth lies somewhere in between.

Born in upstate New York, Eddy developed an affinity for the guitar at an early age. When he was thirteen he moved to Tucson, Arizona, where he befriended disc jockey Lee Hazlewood, himself an aspiring writer/producer. When Hazlewood turned to full-time production in Phoenix, Eddy, who did a lot of session work on Hazlewood's recordings, also conducted some sonic experimentation with him. With Eddy playing melody on the bottom strings of his guitar as if it was a bass, and running the sound through a powerful amplifier, he and Hazlewood composed and recorded a tune called "Movin' n' Groovin'" (described by Eddy as nothing more than "two riffs thrown together"). Hazlewood then took the recording to Hollywood where, to fill out the sound, he overdubbed the rasping saxophone of Plas Johnson onto it. Now all Hazlewood needed was a label on which to release the song.

Eddy's road to Dick Clark and *American Bandstand* led through Hollywood and music business veteran Lester Sill (d. 1994), a mover and shaker in the Los Angeles rhythm and blues scene since the 1940s. If there was a music business deal that Lester Sill could not do, it was one that nobody could accomplish. Sill, who happened to be friends with Hazlewood, had music business connections in every part of the country, including Philadelphia, where he was tight with promo man Harry Finfer and with attorney Harold Lipsius, the majority owner of Universal Record Distributors. Because of this connection, Sill and Hazlewood leased their production of the Sharps' "Sweet Sweetheart" to Jamie Records in which Universal shared ownership, in early 1957.

As a result of Sill's exhortations to Finfer and Lipsius, Jamie issued "Movin' 'n' Groovin'" in February, 1958, and the song sold about 100,000 copies and became the label's first chart success. Sill and Hazlewood promptly formed a business partnership whose main resource was Duane Eddy.

Hazlewood again overdubbed a sax and this time added rebel yells to

Eddy's second Jamie release, "Rebel-'Rouser," which entered *Billboard*'s Top 100 that June. In July Eddy and his combo, the Rebels, packed their equipment into a U-Haul trailor, hitched it to the guitarist's '56 Chevy, and headed out on Route 66 for Philadelphia. They made their television debut on *American Bandstand* that month, miming "Rebel-'Rouser" and "Movin' N' Groovin'" to a national audience. Later that summer "Rebel-'Rouser" reached the number six position in the country.

Eddy's national television appearance was his introduction not only to Dick Clark, but to Clark's *American Bandstand* fiefdom, where the young guitarist quickly learned that the rules and regulations of that province were strictly enforced. One such rule, which stemmed from the Bob Horn debacle, involved the projection of a wholesome image by everyone involved with the show.

Eddy's lesson occurred when Steve Douglas, his traveling sax player, arrived for the group's *Bandstand* appearance sporting a mustache. "He was twenty years old at the time and he thought, 'This'll be cool, I'm goin' on *American Bandstand*, I'll have me a little mustache and really look grown-up and everything,'" recalled Eddy. But the display of any facial hair was verboten on Clark's show, and Douglas was forced to shave before he went on. Which, said the guitarist, "really pissed him off."

Unlike Douglas, Eddy understood and agreed with Clark's demand that all *Bandstand* guests set good examples. "It was bad enough that they were puttin' us down for our so-called long hair at that time," he explained. Besides, chuckled the guitarist, Douglas's moustache made the sax player "look kinda sleazy anyway."

Because Clark was busy at the time, Eddy went in and mimed his song, but did not say much to him during their first meeting. He evidently made a favorable impression on the show's host, however, for Clark later invited the guitarist to perform on his Saturday night show on location in Miami.[30] Eddy jumped at the offer.

When he and the Rebels arrived in Miami, Clark wanted to know if he had a manager. Eddy told him that Hazlewood and Sill were acting in that capacity temporarily, to which Clark replied: "Well, I know a lot of good ones and a lot of bad ones. One of the good ones happens to be here today, do you want me to introduce you?"

Eddy did, and Clark introduced him to Al Wilde, who ran SRO Artists.[31] "And the next thing I knew," recalled the guitarist, "Al Wilde was my manager."

During rehearsal for Clark's Miami show, on which Eddy was slated to mime "Rebel-'Rouser," Clark told the guitarist he would also like him to open the telecast by playing "Movin N' Groovin'" in place of the regular pre-recorded theme, and also asked if Eddy had anything with which to close the show. Eddy and the Rebels, who did not have much experience playing together because the touring Rebels were different from the studio musicians who backed the guitarist on his records, were at a loss for another song until Eddy suggested a number that he and Al Casey had recorded in Phoenix in 1956, called "Ramrod." The combo ran through it a number of times before playing it for Clark, who said, "I love it, that's great!"

When Clark's show ended and the credits rolled, Eddy and the Rebels played "Ramrod" to young America. The tune was a bit ragged around the edges, if not a tad repetitive, but the following Monday morning Jamie Records received orders for 150,000 copies of the song, which was yet to be recorded. Hazlewood called Eddy—who was still in Florida—in a panic. No problem, said the guitarist. He would go into the studio to record "Ramrod" as soon as he returned to Phoenix.

"They want it now!" exclaimed Hazlewood, who then took matters into his own hands. On Tuesday he located the original "Ramrod" master from 1956, onto which he overdubbed a saxophone, handclaps, and vocal yells. He then speeded the whole thing up a wee bit before making a master copy. "Ramrod" was pressed on Wednesday, shipped that night, and was in the stores by Friday, less than a week after it had been heard live on Clark's show. In a matter of weeks it was in *Billboard*'s top forty, proof that there were times when Dick Clark could create a hit.

Eddy's first three chart smashes were uptempo rockers, but he and Hazlewood were set to release a slower, softer number called "The Lonely One" next. An appearance to promote the song on Clark's Saturday night show was scheduled before Clark even heard the song, and when he finally did hear it he was certain the slow number would not appeal to Eddy's fans. "Uh-uh," he told the guitarist, "this is not gonna get it."

Only then did Duane Eddy have his first inkling that Clark had more than a passing interest in the guitarist's fortunes. "I thought Dick was just lookin' after my career," he explained. "I didn't realize he owned a part of it."

At twenty years of age, with a major hit record already under his belt, contractual details did not matter to Eddy, who was preoccupied with looking after his combo "and the logistics of gettin' from here to there, and makin' enough money" to keep touring. He periodically heard rumors attesting to Clark's involvement in Jamie Records, but he paid no attention to them and "had no idea" that Clark had an interest in the label. "How could he do that and run a nationwide television show?" the guitarist naively wondered at the time.

Clark said in 1994 that Eddy "might not have known that Jamie was owned partially by me and Harry Finfer and another guy . . . [but] I think he must have known I was his manager because Al Wilde and I were partners" in SRO. But Eddy claimed he did not know Clark was Wilde's partner at the time.

Now aware that Clark was a part of the "team," the day before his scheduled appearance to plug "The Lonely One" on Clark's show Eddy flew from New York to Phoenix to cut a song more to the *Bandstand* host's liking. Despite the recent business revelations, he respected Clark's professional instincts and bore him no animosity. If Clark wanted a song other than "The Lonely One," that is what he would get. After working in the studio all day Friday to complete the number, Eddy "got back on the ol' DC-6 again, flew all night to New York, got off and went to the hotel and cleaned up and went down to the Little Theater." He was greeted there by Clark and Al Wilde, who took the acetate from him, went backstage and played it, "and came out all smiles."

The new uptempo number, called "Cannonball," cracked *Billboard*'s Hot 100 on November 3, 1958. Eddy not only performed the song on *American Bandstand* two weeks later, he also plugged it on Clark's Saturday night show in December. "Cannonball" reached number fifteen nationally and became Eddy's second-biggest record to date. At that point Dick Clark discovered that Eddy's fans were receptive to just about anything released by the guitarist. "The Lonely One" was released as the next single and it, too, became a hit.

Eddy did not progress from what he termed a "handshake deal" with Jamie Records to a signed, four-year contract calling for a 3 percent royalty on all the records he sold until the success of his second record, "Rebel-'Rouser." Although the guitarist had heard that 3 percent was the going rate for a beginning artist, and had no reason to question the deal when he received a "huge check" from Jamie towards the end of 1958, he was later to discover that "it was only half of what I should have gotten."

A look at the murky history of Jamie Records, which had released twelve flops before it began issuing Eddy's recordings, reveals that the company had numerous partners—among them Dick Clark, Harold Lipsius, Harry Finfer, Lester Sill, and Sam Hodge—each of whom purportedly owned a 25 percent share.[32] "I never really gave it a hell of a lot of thought at the time . . . [but] there were about six people that had a *quarter* of Jamie," Eddy recalled with a laugh.

Without knowing who did or did not own Jamie Records, Eddy and Hazlewood turned out hit records for the label at an unprecedented pace, a feat no doubt aided by the regular appearances of the agreeable and talented guitarist on Clark's national TV shows. As successful as Eddy was in 1958, he proved to be even more so in 1959, when Jamie released five records by its star property and all five became top forty hits.[33]

The Duane Eddy/Jamie Records hit machine was enough to give even a super promoter/manager like Bob Marcucci cause to marvel. Whenever Eddy had a new release ready to go, the guitarist would usually make promotional appearances on both of Clark's TV shows, and Clark would afford the record a strong national sendoff by giving it steady airplay on *American Bandstand*. After the record ran its course and sales dipped, Jamie released the guitarist's next record. "We'd just wait 'til it slipped and put out another one," recalled Eddy. And when they did, Clark invariably jumped off of the old and onto the new, with never a gap of more than several weeks in airplay on *American Bandstand*.

Duane Eddy, Lee Hazlewood, Dick Clark, and Jamie Records together comprised one of the greatest hit-producing machines in rock 'n' roll history. Eddy performed fifteen of his first sixteen Jamie releases on Clark's national TV shows, and the guitarist's first eighteen releases for the label appeared on *Billboard*'s Hot 100. Beginning with "Rebel-'Rouser" in 1958, Eddy remained on *Billboard*'s Hot 100 chart for an almost uninterrupted three-year period.

Inducted into the Rock and Roll Hall of Fame in 1994, Eddy—with fifteen top forty chart hits—remains the most successful instrumentalist in rock 'n' roll history. He agreed that Clark's airplay did render his hitmaking "a speedier process," but the guitarist, who, during the course of his career sold more than one hundred million records worldwide and influenced countless teenagers all over the globe to take up the guitar as a rock 'n' roll instrument, pointed out that in order for his records to consistently become hits, they had to be good to begin with. "Look at the rest of the world—Australia, England, the Netherlands, the Scandinavian countries, Germany—I had hits in all those countries" without the aid of Dick Clark's promotion, he pointed out.

Working hand in hand over the years, Clark and Eddy developed a genuine friendship. Clark "just loved the group," recalled the guitarist. "He'd come and he'd watch us every time we worked. . . . We became friends and actually hung out together." Their friendship grew so strong that Clark named his second son Duane.

• • •

Clark's Saturday night show, for which ABC was inundated by 750,000 unfilled ticket orders, remained as popular as ever in 1959. Because it was a live production, some of the program's memorable moments went unnoticed by its viewers, at home and in the studio. Despite daytime rehearsals, during which each act had its production number blocked out by the show's director, once the televised nighttime performance got under way nobody knew quite what to expect.

"On TV you're lighted, you have a mark, and you're supposed to stay there, because . . . that's where the cameras are, where they're shooting," explained Bobby Rydell. But when the audience began to scream during the first of his seven Saturday night appearances with Clark, Rydell wanted to encourage "the reaction from the kids." But in doing so he inadvertently overstepped the pre-staged boundaries outlined for his number and ventured past the director's mark, out of range of the stage lights. "All of a sudden, I'm in black," recalled Rydell. "The director came out of the booth in the back, and he's telling me to get back to my mark. I didn't know what the hell he was talkin' about!"

Frankie Ford was another young singer who got more than he bargained for on Clark's show. It happened on the Saturday night he lip-synched his hit "Sea Cruise" from atop a raft being rocked by stage hands who were concealed from the audience. "The wardrobe guy got these sailor jeans and cut 'em off and faded 'em and everything," said Ford, "but when it came time for dress rehearsal they were too tight and Dick said, 'Get those off, get him some other pants, immediately!'"

But that was only half of Ford's surprise. His number also called for a mermaid ("a great big buxom woman in a strapless costume") to come aboard the raft during the song's instrumental break. "I was to bend down and two stagehands would try to put her up on the raft," explained the singer, but "every time we tried to get her on the raft, somethin' would fall out! We finally had to scrub that. It was quite amusing to me, though, I enjoyed it."

Other acts also received crash courses in anticipating the staid and stern demeanor of the show's emcee. As the Silhouettes had already discovered, Clark may have appeared easy-going on camera, but he was dead-serious when it came to putting his show together. Johnny Maestro and the Crests, who made their national TV debut the Saturday night they performed "Sixteen Candles," had already run through their afternoon dress rehearsal, at which time they lip-synched the song from a boat onstage. (The director of Clark's show was evidently determined to get all the mileage he could from that prop — as well as from the spiral staircase set used by many acts.) The group was then informed of an additional rehearsal, to be filmed for a kinescope, scheduled to take place prior to the actual TV production that night. But the Crests were erroneously told to be at the kinescope performance an hour later than they should have been, and "when it came our turn, the curtains opened and we weren't there," recalled Maestro with a hearty laugh. Clark did not laugh the night it happened, however. "They had to start the whole show over again," said Maestro, "and Dick never lets us forget about that!"[34]

Besides the gaffes inherent in appearing on live shows, other surprises awaited uninitiated guests. What Joe "Speedoo" Frazier, lead singer of the Impalas, a vocal quintet from Brooklyn, who had a hit with "Sorry (I Ran All the Way Home)," remembered most about their national debut before an audience of millions was what the group was forced to wear that evening. Clark's producer "wasn't familiar with the record, so when he saw the title [which contained the reference to running 'all the way home'] they constructed a facsimile of a baseball diamond on the stage and gave us baseball uniforms to wear," explained Frazier. A cute concept, perhaps, but since the Impalas' song had absolutely no connection to the sport, the group felt humiliated performing it in baseball regalia. (At least they were not asked to do their number in the boat.)

Just as there was a level of activity to which Clark's performers, but not his audience, were privy, there existed a business level that even the performers knew nothing about. Before the advent of Clark's Saturday night show he was not directly employed by ABC. Clark (as Click Corp.) was an independent producer who supplied *American Bandstand* to WFIL, which then passed the show along to the network. Clark therefore was not subject to ABC's edicts, so long as he displayed acceptable comportment in his role as host of the show. But unlike *Bandstand*, Clark's Saturday night show was owned and produced by ABC, which meant that, for the first time, its host became an employee of the network.

As such, ABC locked Clark into a seven-year deal, during which time he was to accept no other network radio or TV offers without ABC's prior approval. His new network identity led to some twisted situations, such as the time in 1958 when Clark, who had previously appeared as a guest panelist on CBS's *I've Got a Secret*, was approved by ABC for a return spot, only to have it cancelled at the last minute by the show's sponsor. As it was, the advertiser also sponsored Art Linkletter's *People Are Funny*, a show broadcast by NBC opposite Clark's Saturday night outing. Since Clark had already cut into Linkletter's ratings, Linkletter's sponsor was not about to give a rival personality exposure on one of its own programs.

As evinced by the *I've Got a Secret* cancellation, Clark was in a confining position for someone with an outlook as expansive as his, but he accepted his lot as the cost of being affiliated with ABC, and looked upon his new relationship with the network as one that could be altered more to his advantage once he further established himself. Besides, there were immediate advantages to Clark's projected long-term network affiliation.

Having discovered that he was indeed "a property unto himself," ABC positioned itself to get as much mileage as possible out of its new star. Being nobody's fool, Clark sought to maximize his own potential as part of the deal. ABC now exerted some degree of control over Clark's outside appearances, but this constraint was more than offset by a merchandising agreement in his new contract which gave ABC the exclusive right to use "and to license others to use [his] name, voice, biographical material, representation and likeness in any and all media" in conjunction with the show, with the net proceeds to be divided equally between himself and the network. In addition, Clark was to receive 30 percent of the net profits from the network's sale of national time on his show, as well as 50 percent of the net proceeds from its syndication.[35]

Still playing catch-up to its rivals, ABC entered the deal harboring considerable aspirations for its bright young TV personality, and Clark was not about to disappoint. His music business holdings had expanded commensurately with his television air time, to the point where Clark not only owned song publishing firms, pieces of record companies, and a record distributorship, he also shared in the management of Duane Eddy, one of rock 'n' roll's most promising artists. The public, however, knew little of Clark's business involvements, as demonstrated by Eddy's ignorance, and Clark—possibly not unintentionally—continued to preserve his low profile in the industry.

Of equal, if not greater, significance to Clark's destiny (and to ABC's), was the fact that his Saturday night show was owned by the network, thereby rendering him an employee. While Clark's new status proved to be a boon for ABC's immediate fortunes, in the not-too-distant future it was to become a tremendous liability.

CHAPTER 7

A Television Personality

Before Dick Clark's Saturday night show catapulted him to another level of stardom, his TV niche was thought by many to consist of little more than bantering with teenagers and playing rock 'n' roll music on daytime television. But just as *American Bandstand* demonstrated that Clark possessed more than provincial allure, *The Dick Clark Show* proved that his constituency consisted of more than housewives and acne-fearing teenagers. It also rendered ABC's budding TV personality an entertainment force to be reckoned with.

Just months after the inception of his Saturday night show Clark was the center of an extensive media blitz that included a favorable profile in the conservative *New York Times* (which was a first for a proponent of the scandalous rock 'n' roll music), feature articles in at least three national adult magazines, a five-part series in the *Philadelphia Daily News* ("Philadelphia's Pied Piper"), and a nationally televised interview at his home by Edward R. Murrow. In addition, Clark made nearly a dozen appearances on other national TV shows, and Walter Annenberg's *TV Guide* splashed the *Bandstand* host's face across its cover (the first of many of that publication's cover stories about him), touting Clark as the "Nation's No. 1 rock 'n' roll salesman."[1]

By the summer of 1958 Clark had received a dozen movie offers, he was being compared to TV greats Arthur Godfrey, Perry Como, and Garry Moore, and he was considering making a record of his own. ABC's new star received thousands of pieces of fan mail each week, and the network mailed out hundreds of thousands of Clark's photograph to his admirers. Clark expressed mixed emotions about his sudden transformation into what Murrow described as a "television personality," telling *Time* magazine that "It's all a little frightening," and *TV Guide* that "It's a wonderful thing for a guy to be 28 and make so much money and have so much influence."[2]

Appearing on ninety of ABC's affiliates from coast to coast, *American Bandstand* continued to draw one of daytime TV's biggest audiences (about eight million viewers daily) and the crush of teenagers seeking admittance to WFIL's studio forced the station to institute a policy whereby between thirty and fifty seats were set aside each day to guarantee access to out-of-towners. As new sponsors signed on with the show, the network's advertising revenue continued to increase. Clark's suave sincerity, which dated from his pitchman days on Paul Whiteman's *TV-Teen Club*, was a sponsor's biggest asset. "Sponsors wait in line to buy what the boys on Madison Avenue refer to as a personality with 'a great sell,'" observed columnist Hy Gardner. One ad agency executive who fretted about the outcome of a commercial that Clark practiced reading just once saw him do the spot on camera and observed that it was "as perfect as if we had taken three days to film it."[3]

ABC regarded Clark as one of its "most valuable properties," and *Variety* noted that the network was "out to get as much mileage as possible" from him. ABC announced in the fall of 1958 that it was about to give Clark his third network TV outing, a Sunday evening panel show called *Take a Good Look*, which was designed to appeal to all ages and would be sponsored by Ed Noble's Beechnut peppermint gum. Presumably the adult studio audience would not be expected to chew the sponsor's product during the show. Rumors flew that Clark was ready to jettison his popular afternoon dance show, but they were quickly scotched by the man himself, who told one reporter, "It'll be a cold day in Hades when I drop *Bandstand*."[4]

Take a Good Look was scrapped at the last minute in favor of the western, *Colt 45*, but *American Bandstand* continued to establish itself as the bellwether of ABC's limited daytime TV schedule. In fact, the show was doing so well that the network planned to use *American Bandstand* to lead its foray into the daytime television business. In a bold move that would fittingly coincide with the first anniversary of Clark's afternoon dance show, ABC intended to enter the 11 a.m. to 3 p.m. broadcasting time block that fall.

Not only had Clark's status in broadcasting risen sharply after less than a year on national television, he was also regarded as the most powerful figure in the multi-million-dollar pop recording industry, where it was said that a song's "surest start to gold record status" (one million sales) was to be played on *Bandstand*.[5] But as Clark's business relationship with ABC grew more complex he continued to downplay his expanding role in the music industry. In a *Billboard* article published shortly before Clark's Saturday show made its debut, he lamented about the cutthroat competition in the record business, in which new labels appeared almost overnight. "I almost hate to think about more new labels," Clark told the music trade publication. "As it is now, I listen to between 50 and 75 new records a week, and there are many others I never even get to hear."

When the reporter from *Billboard* pointedly asked Clark, whose music business ventures had become the subject of whispered speculation, what he thought about disk jockeys with interests in other facets of the music publishing business, Clark responded that "the matter depends on the individual. . . . If a man knows what's good for him—what side his bread is buttered on— and he's intelligent and honest with himself, then there's nothing wrong with it at all."[6]

Although Clark's music-related interests were expanding, he made it clear that his principal interest remained his TV shows, which provided "plenty to keep [him] busy."[7] Indeed they did. He was on the air for at least thirteen hours per week—eight of them on network—and each Saturday morning he traveled to New York to rehearse and broadcast his weekly TV show. And even though Clark was forced to cut back on his record hop appearances (he made at least 180 of them in 1957), he still found time to conduct several of them each week.

He also complained to the *Billboard* reporter that rumors of his involvement in the record industry with at least eleven different labels were "way out of proportion. The truth is that I have an interest in one label and in one publishing firm only." But in fact, when Clark made that statement he already had interests in Jamie and Swan Records, as well as an interest in Chips Distributing.

In addition, at the same time Clark openly preached about "almost hating" to see new record labels arise he was busy forming another record label of his own. Clark's business dealings with ABC grew further entangled when he organized the Globe Record Corporation and a wholly owned subsidiary called Kincord Music Publishing in March 1958. Globe's records were to be issued on Clark's new Hunt label, which was to be distributed nationally by Am-Par.

Clark told Joe Smith in *Off the Record* that the rags-to-riches record business of the 1950s was an "exciting period. . . . You found a record breaking in Cleveland or Columbus, and you'd charge in there and find some guy who didn't have the wherewithal, and you'd lay a few dollars on him, take the master, give him a piece of the record, put it on the air, and the next day it would explode all over the country."[8] There also were occasions when Clark did not have to spend any of his own money to obtain a song to release on one of his record labels—such as the time Am-Par gave him a master recording to use as Hunt's first release.

As Clark's power within the pop music business increased (commensurately with his music-related holdings), so too did the whispers that the *Bandstand* host was apt to give an extra ride to those songs in which he had an interest. In response, Clark continued to minimize the importance of airplay on his show, maintaining that he could not "make the kids buy a record they don't like. I can play a tune every day for a month and it won't go anywhere if the kids don't like the sound."

Clark was right, as far as he went. The underlying issue was not that he could create a hit anytime he wanted, however, but rather that he was able to give unparalleled exposure to any records he chose—including his own. As it was, the fate of Hunt's initial release, the Five Stars' "Pickin' On the Wrong Chicken," inadvertently proved Clark's point. He played the record steadily for a six-week period on *American Bandstand* during the spring of 1958, but it nevertheless failed to crack *Billboard*'s national Top 100.[9] In fact, Hunt would have no chart success until its fourth release, but when a hit record did come the label's way—courtesy of a black vocal group called the Quin-Tones from nearby York, Pennsylvania—it proved to be worth the wait.

The Quin-Tones were discovered in 1957 by Harrisburg, Pennsylvania disc jockey and dance promoter Paul Landersman, who was so impressed with the group (who sang in much the same vein as George Goldner's Chantels) that he reportedly boasted to them, "if you stay with me, I'll have you on *American Bandstand* within a year."[10]

The debut record of the Quin-Tones, who signed with Landersman while still in high school, went unnoticed. Meanwhile, the group began to include in their live performances a new song they had written called "Down the Aisle of Love." Noticing that audiences invariably went wild over the number, Landersman realized it was then or never to make good on his *Bandstand* promise. He sought out music business veteran Irv Nahan, whose contacts in the Philadelphia record industry ran deep, and Nahan agreed to record "Down the Aisle of Love" on Red Top, a small label he ran as a sideline to his other activities.

A slow number known as a "drag," which had a beat almost anyone could dance to, the Quin-Tones' song was tailor-made for *American Bandstand* and proved to be an instantaneous smash in the Philadelphia area when released there in June 1958. Sensing he was onto something big, Nahan took the record to Dick Clark and "Down the Aisle of Love" was transferred from Red Top to Hunt (with a reported 95% of the song's publishing rights going to Clark in the process). When asked in 1993 how the transaction came about, Nahan made reference to a "Philadelphia connection" and said that his partner Red Schwartz (for whom Red Top was named) "was very friendly" with

Clark. Whatever the circumstances were, Quin-Tones member Phyllis Carr, who was not privy to the behind-the-scenes machinations between Red Top and Hunt, recalled that after the record was switched to Hunt, "Dick Clark began playing it a lot."[11]

Indeed he did. Once Hunt released "Down the Aisle of Love" nationally Clark instituted daily airplay of the song. He played "Down the Aisle" on his afternoon show every day but four in August—the first month it appeared on *Billboard*'s Hot 100. That September the Quin-Tones performed their hit on *Bandstand*, after which, without ever acknowledging that he owned the record label it appeared on, Clark played "Down the Aisle of Love" almost daily for another eight weeks until the song began to descend from its peak chart position of number twenty.

The song reportedly sold close to a million copies, for which Clark received sales royalties, but Phyllis Carr told writer Wayne Jancik in 1990 that the Quin-Tones had "yet to receive royalties" for their big hit. "Never, not ever, did we get anything," she lamented. "We were just kids, too young, didn't know nothin'!"[12]

Having finally broken his newest record label nationwide, Clark was eager to keep Hunt working for him. While "Down the Aisle" was still at the height of its popularity, the Quin-Tones recorded a follow-up record, "There'll Be No Sorrow," which Clark previewed on *Bandstand* six days later. But he inexplicably held off playing the song again until "Down the Aisle of Love" disappeared from the charts some two months later. Clark played "There'll Be No Sorrow" thirteen times on *Bandstand* during November and December, and also gave thirteen spins to Hunt's next release, Doc Bagby's "Muscle Tough," but neither record became a national hit.

Hunt did not issue another record until 1959, when, after almost two months of steady airplay on *American Bandstand*, the lively instrumental called "Guitar Boogie Shuffle" by a local group called the Virtues edged its way onto *Billboard*'s Hot 100 that spring. "Guitar Boogie Shuffle" subsequently reached number five on *Billboard*'s Hot 100 and became one of the biggest instrumental hits of the year. Clark gave the Virtues' next two releases nine plays each on *American Bandstand*, but in the long run he could no more develop a follow-up hit for them than he could for the Quin-Tones. Despite open access to airplay on *American Bandstand*, Hunt had no further hits.

Meanwhile, Clark's business involvement with Am-Par grew more complex. A joint project was hatched whereby ABC's record division, supervised by the *Bandstand* host, was to produce two *Dance With Dick Clark* long-playing record albums (ABC-Paramount LP 258 and LP 288; released in the fall of 1958 and 1959, respectively) and a non-LP single that was played on

American Bandstand. Nine of the twenty-four instrumentals performed by a studio group known as the Keymen were published by Clark's companies. In addition to his share of the publishing royalties for those songs, Clark received mechanical (recording) royalties for the estimated 60,000 to 80,000 LPs that were eventually sold.[13]

But it seems that not everyone received the royalties that were due them. Duane Eddy claimed in 1994 that he never saw the *Dance With Dick Clark* albums until a few years prior, and was surprised to see his song, "Duane's Stroll," written by himself and Lee Hazlewood, featured on the second of these albums. At that time, he thought, "'Hmmm, somebody's covered my song, let's see how they played it.' So I played it and it was my record. It was me!" Eddy then recalled recording "Duane's Stroll" after being told by manager Al Wilde that the number was "for a special deal, a charity thing or something . . . Dick wanted to do," but had forgotten about it immediately after. Informed that "Duane's Stroll" was published by one of Clark's companies, Eddy remarked, "I don't think I've ever gotten a royalty check from Sea-Lark. Very interesting, isn't it?"

In May 1958, not long after Clark formed Hunt Records, and just prior to the release of the first *Dance With Dick Clark* album, he teamed up with Bernie Lowe, his partner in Chips Distributing, in yet another enterprise. Clark and Lowe each put up $7,500 to purchase from Ivin Ballen's Gotham Records a pressing facility, Stenton Music, which they renamed Mallard Pressing Corp. Long before the formation of Mallard it was known in the pop music industry that certain pressing plants were controlled by individuals who for one reason or another could influence radio airplay. The owners of small labels often felt behooved to have their records pressed at such a facility in order to increase the chances of getting those records played on the air. Some industry insiders believed that Mallard existed only on paper and was set up to take advantage of that practice, while Stenton continued to do business as usual, buoyed by the additional work orders of record manufacturers who sought to have their records played by Clark.

In 1960, Clark stated that Mallard "had a contract with Stenton Music Co. to produce records at a certain price," which may or may not have been the case, but those close to Clark apparently took Mallard's interests to heart.[14] Shortly after Clark acquired the pressing facility, the Crests' "Sixteen Candles" began to sell in large numbers, causing Universal Distributors' Harry Finfer to suggest to the owners of the small label on which the song had been released that if they were overloaded on orders, "there was a pressing plant at Philadelphia called the Mallard Pressing Plant" that could be of service.[15]

"There were no real rules about all this stuff," said John Zacherle, who, over the years, developed a friendship with Clark. "It was just a question of what did it look like to invest in a company that was pressing records when you were a big star playing records on TV." (Shortly after Clark came under fire when the payola scandal erupted in 1959, he sold Mallard to Ivin Ballen's son, Morris.)

With an interest in two music publishing companies (January Corp. had recently been added to Sea-Lark), three record labels, a record distributorship, a record pressing plant, and a share of a talent management agency, Clark was now "vertically integrated" within the music business. Not only could he inject a hand into every facet of an artist's career (see Duane Eddy) and give the major record labels a run for their money, he also held the rock 'n' roll music business trump card. In his own words, Clark was "now the No. 1 plug in the country."[16]

As Clark's reputation as the premier kingmaker within the popular music industry increased, ABC could not have been more delighted with the success of its budding young star. Buoyed by the continued strength of *American Bandstand*, the network remained optimistic about "Operation Daybreak," its recently launched, ambitious move into full daytime TV that was designed to make it the equal of NBC and CBS as a "full-service" network. "Operation Daybreak" made six new daytime shows available to ABC's affiliates, but *American Bandstand*, which led the network's foray into daytime TV and whose advertising time was sold at a higher rate than the time on ABC's new daytime shows, was not part of the daytime package. Ted Fetter explained how, by that time, ABC regarded *American Bandstand* as "a very successful daytime show [and] the powers that be were now making money" on it. Because of a 1958 rate increase to its sponsors, Clark's afternoon show was to yield an even higher dollar volume in network advertising during its second year than it had during its first.

Meanwhile, Clark's Saturday night show, which now boasted an eight month wait for tickets, remained so hot that the ABC affiliate in one Oklahoma town reportedly received a number of letters about the show that exceeded the town's entire population. Record company officials called an appearance on that venue "the hottest plug in the industry," and *Variety* tabbed Clark as "perhaps the hottest ABC-TV property next to *Maverick* (the network's revolutionary western series).[17]

While Dick Clark gained a firm foothold in the pop music business during *American Bandstand*'s first epic year, the show introduced a formidable array of pioneering rock 'n' roll artists to America. In that group were future Rock 'n' Roll Hall of Fame members Chuck Berry, Johnny Cash, the Coasters, Eddie Cochran, Sam Cooke, Bobby Darin, Dion DiMucci (who first appeared on *Bandstand* as a member of Dion and the Belmonts), Duane Eddy, the Everly Brothers (whom Clark initially dismissed as "hillbillies who would never sell"), Buddy Holly (with the Crickets), Jerry Lee Lewis, Simon and Garfunkel (as Tom and Jerry), and Jackie Wilson.[18]

Meanwhile, the changing of the guard continued. Less than three years earlier, rock 'n' roll had been almost exclusively the domain of black artists—including the likes of Fats Domino and Little Richard—who enjoyed widespread acclaim when rock 'n' roll emerged as a specific musical genre. By the time *American Bandstand* appeared on the scene, however, rock 'n' roll's ever-increasing popularity among white teenagers caused an unorganized, yet industry-wide, effort to "whiten" the music in order to increase record sales.[19] White artists began to wrest control of the rock 'n' roll domain from blacks, who thus faced a new struggle to keep from being reclassified by the white mainstream as rhythm and blues singers.

For black recording artists, the distinction was crucial. Being regarded by the white broadcasting establishment as a black "pop" group (such as the Platters and Frankie Lymon and the Teenagers) as opposed to being labeled "rhythm and blues " (such as the Five Satins, the Dells, and the Spaniels) afforded an artist or a group a tremendous promotional advantage when it came to national television appearances and radio airplay on stations catering to large white audiences. Consequently, it greatly enhanced record sales as well. A major rock 'n' roll hit could sell millions of copies and expose the song's artist to an even greater audience, whereas a significant rhythm and blues hit rarely topped sales of a half million, and usually sold much less than that amount. Perhaps no one knows the price black recording artists paid for failing to cross over onto the pop charts than does Rock 'n' Roll Hall of Fame member Bo Diddley, who was the recipient of the Rhythm and Blues Foundation's 1996 lifetime achievement award. "We went up and down the highways at night, riding in raggedy buses," recalled Bo, "and the promoters went away with the money."[20]

Ironically, while *American Bandstand* afforded national exposure to more rock 'n' roll groups than ever before, their black identity was concealed by the recording industry in hopes of increased sales. Session guitarist Renee Hall, a member of Ernie Freeman's studio instrumental combo of black musicians (who in addition to having records released under Freeman's name had hits as B. Bumble and the Stingers, the Marketts, the Routers, and Billy Joe and the Checkmates), played anonymously on over two hundred hit records. Hall told writer Jim Dawson that if one of the combo's records became a hit, "we'd have to put together a young white group to send out on the road and promote it."[21]

Although Frankie Ford denies it, his 1958 hit "Sea Cruise" may have resulted from the pop music industry's tendency to promote white artists over black ones. "Sea Cruise" was originally recorded by Huey Smith and the Clowns, who were black, and was intended to be the Clowns' next release, but it has been written that label owner Johnny Vincent subsequently erased Clown vocalist Bobby Marchan's vocals and overdubbed Ford's, so as to have the song sung by a white teen idol–type. Ford, who was backed on "Sea Cruise" by the Clowns, insisted the erasure story was "wrong, very wrong," and that Vincent told Smith just before the song was released: "You don't need the record now, let's put this out on Frankie."

"That's how haphazard and spontaneous that business was," maintained Ford.

Of course, the leading black stars could not hide from their fans. For them, the white mainstream was where fame and fortune awaited, and the surest way to incur such mass acceptance was to appear on *American Bandstand*. The most successful black group to do so in the 1950s were Little Anthony and the Imperials

The driving force behind the Imperials was Brooklyn-born Anthony Gourdine, who was determined at an early age to become a singer. While still in high school in 1956, Gourdine organized a quartet called the Duponts, who made two records before they broke up the following summer. Anthony next joined forces with the neighborhood foursome of Ernest Wright, Jr., Clarence Collins, Tracy Lord, and Glouster "Nate" Rogers to become the Chesters (Sammy Strain and George Kerr eventually replaced Lord and Rogers in the group), who made one record before being guided to New York record mogul George Goldner. It was under Goldner's tutelage that the group —rechristened the Imperials—recorded the now-legendary ballad, "Tears on My Pillow." ("Little Anthony" was added to the group's name only after Alan Freed referred to them that way on his radio program one evening.)

After "Tears on My Pillow" was released during the summer of 1958 and immediately took off in the New York area, Goldner wasted no time wielding the power he commanded within the pop music industry to secure national exposure for his new group. Just weeks after "Tears on My Pillow" debuted on *Billboard*'s Hot 100, Little Anthony and the Imperials made their national TV debut on Dick Clark's Saturday night show, where they lip-synched their hit. Two weeks later they did likewise on *American Bandstand*.

Anthony "really didn't notice" how the Imperials' numerous promotional spots on Clark's shows were arranged. "I was a kid," he explained. "They told me I was going to be on Dick Clark's show, and that was the only thing I thought about. I was ready to go!" Looking back on his almost forty years in the business, however, Anthony recognized that "politics" wrought by the wiley Goldner played a hand in those appearances with Clark. The singer of seven top forty hits now admits what Goldner knew back then: Although "Tears on My Pillow" began to gain popularity before the Imperials appeared on *Bandstand*, it was Clark's promotion of the song (and many songs like it) that proved vital in projecting it beyond the limited rhythm and blues market to broad national acceptance.

In addition to providing immediate national exposure for a particular song, Clark's show also possessed the unique capacity to visually promote an artist, a phenomenon exploited to the utmost by the Imperials. (Anthony called *American Bandstand* "the MTV of that time.") Because of Anthony's distinctly gentle voice, many radio disc jockeys and much of the record-buying public "thought I was a girl at first, and many stations thought I was Caucasian, [that] the whole group was Caucasian," recalled Gourdine. They "could not believe that a black singer had that enunciation." Whereas, a year earlier Anthony and the Imperials would have had a more difficult time in establishing their true identity, just two national TV appearances with Clark in 1958 solidified their visual image. As Clark's audience continued to grow at a rapid pace, more people became familiar with the faces of the Imperials— faces that were clearly different from the average group seen on *Bandstand*.

Thus, a performance on one of Clark's shows was particularly alluring to black artists. Anthony believed that each time his group made such an appearance it set them apart from other black groups who had routinely been consigned to the rhythm and blues field, and reinforced their image as mainstream entertainers. The Imperials Ernest Wright said they "were always considered a pop group more so than a soul act because of that exposure by Dick Clark."

Even though most black singing groups continued to be hampered by conservative mainstream tastes in their struggle to gain current status, a smaller category of racially integrated groups faced an even more daunting situation. Until 1958, the most notable integrated rock 'n' roll group was the Del Vikings, who enjoyed two national top ten hits in 1957 and appeared on *American Bandstand* that year. But the Del Vikings were soon split asunder by military service obligations and contractual disputes, and the distinction of being the premier racially mixed rock 'n' roll group passed to the Crests.

The Crests were formed on New York's Lower East Side in 1956 when black bass singer Jay Carter and his friends (Tommy Gough, Harold Torres, and Patricia Van Dross) joined forces with the strong-voiced Italian John Mastrangelo (who would soon call himself Johnny Maestro). Recording for a tiny Brooklyn-based label, the Crests had a modest New York area hit during the summer of 1957 with "My Juanita," for which Maestro claims he received a total of seventeen dollars in royalties.

In 1958 the Crests were introduced to ex-bandleader and long-time music publisher George Paxton, who sought to cash in on the burgeoning rock 'n' roll market by starting his own record company. The Crests auditioned for Paxton, who liked what he heard and signed the group to a recording and a management deal with his new Coed label. In retrospect, allowing Coed to manage the Crests "wasn't a very smart thing for us," thought Johnny Maestro as he recalled the incident. "Who [could] we go to when we want[ed] to say, 'We want this from the record company?'"

To make matters worse, the Crests got off to an inauspicious start when their initial Coed release failed to crack *Billboard*'s Top 100 that spring. Not much happened when their next record, "Sixteen Candles," was released that September, either. Fearful of going zero-for-two with his newly signed vocal group, Paxton asked Universal Distributors' Harry Finfer (Coed's distributor in Philadelphia) if Finfer could get Dick Clark to play "Sixteen Candles" on *American Bandstand*. Sure enough, Clark played the song twice in September and once in the middle of October, but it showed no movement in any of the country's break-out markets, and Clark did not play it again.

Despite his dubious claim that "Sixteen Candles" was doing "fairly well" in several markets, Paxton proceeded to assign the song's copyright to Clark, because "every little bit helps. . . . I thought it was possible that he could make something singlehanded."[22]

Paxton's partner Marvin Cane, who initiated the "Sixteen Candles" arrangement with Clark's publishing company, contended that the move was "just a brainstorm" on his part to gain airplay on Clark's show. "Dick Clark was probably the most popular disc jockey in the country and . . . it looked like a good business proposition." Cane insisted there was never any agreement or understanding that the assignment of the song copyright to Clark would guarantee any airplay. Rather, he "just assumed" that if Clark accepted the copyright, "it would naturally be to my advantage to have the No. 1 man participating in the same record."[23]

It only facilitated matters that Vera Hodes, who administered Clark's song publishing companies, had spent many years in the business working for Mills Music, Morris Levy, Phil Kahl, and George Goldner, was already friendly with Cane, and was familiar with the common practice of assigning song copyrights to influential parties.

Of course, the Crests, who Johnny Maestro said "really had no inkling at all" about the potential of "Sixteen Candles" and hoped that the flip side of the record would become a hit, were not privy to the behind-the-scenes copyright transfer from George Paxton and Marvin Cane to Dick Clark. The Crests only concern was to make records "and go on the road and perform," recalled Maestro. "We were very naive as far as business went. We didn't care about that at all." But Maestro admitted in 1994 that even if he had known about the copyright transfer of "Sixteen Candles" to Clark, he would have been in favor of it.

And why not? On November 28, 1958, just after Clark acquired the copyright to "16 Candles," it cracked *Billboard*'s Hot 100. The Crests lip-synched the rising number on Clark's final Saturday night show of 1958, and "Sixteen Candles" soared all the way to number two on *Billboard*'s Hot 100 early in 1959. The song remained on that chart for an incredible twenty-one weeks, prompting the music trade publication *Cashbox* to name the Crests "Most Promising Vocal Group of 1958." (Despite recording five top forty hits on Coed, Maestro claimed that because of expenses that were continually levied against their royalties, the Crests "never got a penny" from the record company. Maestro also suspects that Coed underreported record sales in order to keep royalty payments down—a common practice in those days. "I couldn't believe that we could be number two in the country [with "Sixteen Candles"] and [not] sell a million copies.")

For his part, Clark contends that he did not begin to promote "Sixteen Candles" because he obtained the song's copyright, that he did so only when the song began to become popular. Like the chicken and the egg conundrum, whether the airplay or the hit came first could be argued endlessly, but in Clark's promotion of "Sixteen Candles"—just as with "Down the Aisle of Love" and numerous other hits (see Appendix II)—he unabashedly pushed his own record without divulging that he stood to gain financially from doing so. Although this practice was not illegal at the time (and was adhered to by other disc jockeys who had financial stakes in various records), it was most definitely deceptive, and it would soon return to haunt Clark and jeopardize his role on *American Bandstand*.

• • •

As *American Bandstand* celebrated its first anniversary in August 1958, the teen idol phenomenon that Clark was excoriated for aiding and abetting was not yet in full bloom. In Philadelphia, which would soon be viewed as the crucible of the genre, only Bob Marcucci began to hit his stride.

Despite a kickoff performance of "You Excite Me" on *American Bandstand*, Frankie Avalon's follow-up to "DeDe Dinah" did not do as well as its predecessor and stalled at number forty-nine on *Billboard*'s Top 100. Avalon rebounded strongly that summer, however, when "Ginger Bread" became his second top ten hit. "Frankie Avalon had made it," recalled Marcucci, who nevertheless refused to rest on his laurels. Inspired by a photo of Ricky Nelson that appeared on the cover of a local weekly newspaper magazine, he set out to find another teen idol, but "nothing hit me that knocked me out."

Then, as Marcucci drove through his South Philadelphia neighborhood one spring day in 1958, he spotted an ambulance parked in front of the house of his best friend, John Palmieri. When Marcucci stopped to see if anything was wrong he was told that his friend's next-door neighbor, Dominic Forte, had suffered a heart attack. It was at that fateful moment that Marcucci spotted the stricken Forte's sixteen-year-old son, Fabiano. "He had the look, he had the face—*exactly* what I was looking for," recalled Marcucci, who turned to his friend's wife and asked, "Can this kid sing?"

"I don't know and I'm not gonna ask him," she replied. "His father's being pushed into an ambulance and going to the hospital!"

Legend has it that Marcucci directly engaged Fabian that fatal day, a story with which Fabian concurs, claiming that the brazen record executive "was rude enough" to ask the good-looking teenager if he was interested in "being in the singing business," despite the fact that Marcucci knew Fabian's father had just suffered a heart attack. Fabian "couldn't believe the balls" on Marcucci and told him "to go to hell."[24]

Marcucci went home, but he did not forget about the kid with the face. As he drove past the Forte residence each day, the idolmaker observed Fabian as he swept the floor at the corner drug store where he worked after school. "Finally one day I just got enough nerve to go knock at the door," he said.

When Marcucci knocked, Fabian answered, turned to his mother and said "Mom, that crazy man, the friend of our neighbor, is here. What should I do?"

"Be nice," she cautioned her son, "He's your neighbor's friend."[25]

Young Fabiano Forte wanted no part of Bob Marcucci's crazy promises of teenage stardom, but Marcucci simply would not take no for an answer. Concerned primarily for his stricken father, with his family now in a financial bind, Fabian eventually acceded to Marcucci's wishes in order to earn some money for them. "That's how it started," he said. "It was part love of rock 'n' roll, but mainly it was to help my family."[26]

Marcucci's friend John Palmieri recalled Fabian's audition with Marcucci, held at Palmieri's house: "Fabian sung the best way he knew how, and Bob was not impressed with his voice. He said, 'John, he doesn't have that good a voice . . . but I'm gonna make this kid a star!'" Marcucci's latest protege could not sing a note, but the label owner/manager sensed he had a tiger by the tail. His first step was to create a local following for the good-looking teenager.

Marcucci unveiled Fabian to the public at a local record hop, where the singer was introduced to the young crowd as "an up-and-coming star who's gonna make it real big." Jim Testa, of the South Philadelphia vocal group the Four J's (consisting of Testa, Junior Pirollo, Bob Finizio, and Joe Milaro), was at the same hop, plugging their first record, "Rock 'n' Roll Age," and recalled that Fabian "came out and the girls went crazy," even though he did not have a record out yet.

Ironically, the Four J's, who lived within a few blocks of Fabian and Bob Marcucci and would soon be recruited by Marcucci to sing back-up for Fabian as the "Fabulous Four," got off to a more auspicious start than did the soon-to-be-star. "Rock 'n' Roll Age" became a modest hit in Philadelphia, Baltimore, and Washington, D.C., and the group appeared at numerous record hops and on *American Bandstand*.

Now ready for the next step, Marcucci gave Fabian a song to take home and learn. Only then did he muster enough chutzpah to introduce Fabian to his rock 'n' roll-hating partner Peter DeAngelis, telling him, "This kid has everything we're looking for!"

"But he's not a *singer*," protested DeAngelis.

"Does it really matter anymore in this day and age?" replied Marcucci.[27]

The Chancellor owners then took Fabian into the studio where, with plenty of assistance, he recorded "Shivers," a song that the pair had written especially for him. In an interview for *Redbook* in 1960, Fabian shared how his records were made. After singing a song "maybe 20 times . . . the engineers take over," he revealed. "They listen to the tape for hours before deciding . . . if I hit a wrong note" or whether to enhance the vocal with an echo chamber, speed up the tape, or snip out a segment of the song and replace it by one taken from another part of the tape. "And if they think the record needs more jazzing, they emphasize the accompaniment. By the time they get done with their acrobatics, I can hardly recognize my own voice."[28] It was a process that was destined to exceed even Marcucci's wildest expectations—but not just yet.

Because Marcucci's success with Frankie Avalon had made a believer out of Dick Clark, Marcucci was able to book Fabian onto *American Bandstand* even though the would-be singer had no previous recording experience. Although "the reaction to him was unbelievable" according to Marcucci, Fabian's first record stiffed.

"They all thought I was totally insane for even trying to make him a star," said the Chancellor co-owner. "ABC-Paramount [which distributed Chancellor] only went along with it because I had Frankie Avalon, and he was making money for the label."[29]

But Marcucci and Clark recognized there was something about Fabian that drove the little girls wild. They both knew it had taken Avalon three tries (and a couple of *American Bandstand* apearances) to score a hit, so, with that in mind, Fabian was brought back into the studio to record "Lilly Lou," another number Marcucci and DeAngelis wrote especially for him. The balky idol plugged "Lilly Lou" on Clark's Saturday night show in June 1958, but Fabian's second release did not fare any better than "Shivers." Marcucci doggedly kept Fabian on the record hop circuit, noting that "wherever we took this kid—with or without a hit record—he was becoming unbelievably big." Observing the phenomenon, Dick Clark told his pal, "You gotta find this kid a hit record!" [30]

* * *

Clark's shows not only broke new ground with their hit records, in certain cities such as Atlanta, Georgia they broke ground in race relations. Traditionally, audiences of public entertainment in the South, if not limited to either the white or the black race, were segregated in one manner or another. Blacks (or whites) were often confined to a theatre's balcony, or the two races were kept apart by dividing the theatre in two, sometimes by nothing more than a rope extended down the building's center. But the most bizarre seating configuration occurred when the stage itself was used to divide the two races, with seats located both in front of and behind the raised platform, rendering it impossible for an act to face one race without turning its back to the other.

Lee Andrews, who toured extensively in the South during the 1950s, was often subjected to that awkward situation. "Could you in your wildest dreams imagine what a theatre like that looked like?" he asked. "We were on the stage, performing to both sides, and you could not favor one against the other." To solve the dilemma diplomatically the group "sang to a wall."

Not only were audiences in the South segregated, the talent was often segregated, too. When the Crests performed in that region they occasionally encountered the situation described by Lee Andrews, but usually their audience was divided in front of them, "black on one side and white on the other side," said Johnny Maestro. "And I would have to perform on the side with the white, and the other guys would be on the black side."

Lou Christie, who was responsible for five top forty hits in the Sixties, beginning with "The Gypsy Cried" in 1963, recalled being the only white act on an otherwise all-black show touring the South. In Atlanta, Christie was told that when it was his turn to sing, "the band had to leave the stage and play on the floor. As a white person, you can't be on the same stage" with blacks. (Certain Southern cities had local ordinances that prohibited white and black performers from appearing on the same stage.)

Southern social mores and laws presaged trouble in Atlanta for Dick Clark, who, via his Saturday night show—scheduled to be held in that city on October 11, 1958—was about to deliver a double whammy to the local populace. Because ABC received some 50,000 ticket requests for the 12,000 available seats, tickets for Clark's show—on which black singer Sam Cooke was set to appear on the otherwise white bill—were distributed on a first come, first serve basis, guaranteeing that the show's cast *and* its audience would be integrated.

There had been much pre-show publicity over this fact, and, not surprisingly, the production crew received letters and anonymous telephone calls threatening violence if the show went on. Security remained tight and the atmosphere grew thick with tension as Clark and his troupe prepared for an afternoon rehearsal in front of an audience before the national telecast took place under the stars that night. Clark outlined the grim situation for Cooke, telling the singer that there would be National Guard members and Ku Klux Klanners in the audience and that he could not guarantee Cooke's safety. "I'm going on," replied the singer. "I gotta go on. That's all there is to it."[31]

The rehearsal went off without a hitch, as did the TV show later that evening (despite a bomb threat just before showtime), the latter climaxed by a huge display of fireworks that spelled out B-E-E-C-H-N-U-T- G-U-M in the Atlanta sky. Somewhere, Ed Noble must have had a smile on his face.

Clark wrote in his autobiography that the integrated Atlanta show "was one of the few ballsy things I ever did. We went up against the authorities and told them they either took us as we were or the hell with them."[32] When it came to integrating *American Bandstand*, however, Clark was a lot less ballsy.

In the year after he inherited *Bandstand* there were no racial incidents on the show, but the composition of the studio audience remained almost totally white. Like America itself, many areas of which continued to drag their heels in complying with federal efforts to promote integration, *American Bandstand* did not remain unaffected by the pervasive influence of black-derived rock 'n' roll music and the growing civil rights movement. While the racial policies of Clark's afternoon dance show were quietly accepted by the white majority, a vocal minority began to cry foul.

In his 1976 autobiography, Clark alluded to the increasing dilemma he faced in realizing that rock 'n' roll and *Bandstand* "owed their existences to black music and the black artists who sang it," while the program continued to tacitly refuse to recognize the existence of black citizens. In 1994 Clark stated that when *American Bandstand* originated he and producer Tony Mammarella "alone decided that we had to get more [blacks] on the air because we knew as we went on with the show and it got to be seen nationally, [segregation] couldn't be. It wasn't anything that we did as do-gooders or [that] we were politically inclined, or anything other than the fact, 'this made sense.'"

In 1990 Clark told Henry Schipper he was "terrified" the first day he ever spoke to a black youth on the air because he "didn't know what the reaction was going to be" in the South. Ultimately there was no reaction. "From that day forward, nobody ever called, and it just happened," he pointed out.[33] But it did not happen quickly.

The racial climate of *American Bandstand* was initially addressed in an in-depth series that appeared in the *New York Post* in September 1958, in which an anonymous veteran of the show claimed it was a "practice" of WFIL-TV to admit "only eight or nine" blacks per day, "and not to focus the camera on them."[34] When the reporter asked ABC's Ted Fetter about the dearth of blacks on Clark's program, Fetter cited the brouhaha that had occurred a year earlier when Frankie Lymon was seen dancing with a white girl on Alan Freed's ABC-TV rock 'n' roll show. "Observers believe the presence of Negroes as *Bandstand* guests [the rules don't seem to aply to entertainers] is controlled to the point where few even bother to go," wrote the reporter.[35]

When Clark was asked about the dearth of blacks on his show and the alleged ban on showing them dancing, he deftly sidestepped the issue, telling the *Post* in 1958 that the show's doors were "open to anyone who wants to attend," adding that he had "nothing to say about camera shots" of the studio audience.[36] (In 1959 the black newspaper *New York Age* saw fit to editorialize about a "matter which has never seemed to bother many people. This is the question of Negro participation on the various bandstand programs." The newspaper championed Alan Freed's efforts at racial integration and asked: "Have you ever seen Negro kids on Dick Clark's program? Perhaps, a few times, but the unspoken rule operates—Negro kids simply have been quietly barred from the *American Bandstand*."[37])

Clark insisted in 1994 that "there was never a rule not to show" blacks on *American Bandstand*, and "as the years went by—'58, '59—more black kids attended. They didn't turn up in great numbers because they hadn't been welcome for so many years."

In fairness to Clark, it should be noted that racial problems were inherent throughout the genre of TV dance shows of that era. Segregation was openly practiced on some TV bandstands, including "The Buddy Deane Show," which originated in Baltimore in 1957 with a "whites only" teenage committee and became the top-rated local TV program in the country. The Baltimore TV station on which Deane's show was broadcast solved the race dilemma by setting aside one day per month on which only blacks were admitted to the studio. "It sounds ridiculous now, but that's the way it was done," recalled the show's host. "There might be a white performer on with the black group of youngsters and there might be black performers on with the white group of youngsters, so the artists was not where the fear was. The problem was the social integration on the program that would bring about complaints."

Over the years, however, the facts surrounding the integration of *American Bandstand* have been muddled, portraying Clark as more of an activist than he was at the time. In a 1995 profile of him in *The Saturday Evening Post*, it was written that Clark "doesn't duck controversy. A year after taking over *Bandstand* in 1956, he insisted that the dance floor be open to African-American kids. He issued no fiery statement about equality, but quietly made sure that young black students were well represented in the studio audience."[38] Although *Bandstand* eventually underwent peaceful integration, free of boycotts or comments from the show's viewers and sponsors, that process did not happen because of Clark's forcefulness, and it did not occur until well into the 1960s.

• • •

As 1958 drew to a close, ABC was faced with more pressing problems than the integration of *American Bandstand*. For one, the network's record division was unable to match the continued good fortune of Clark's two hit TV shows. Not since the summer hits of the Elegants ("Little Star") and the Poni-Tails ("Born Too Late") had Am-Par been able to cash in on the exposure of its artists on the parent company's TV shows hosted by Clark. The label's early gusher of hits aided by *American Bandstand* had run dry.

Even more troubling to ABC, three months into "Operation Daybreak," disappointing ratings dampened the network's initial optimism over its foray into daytime TV. The previous summer ABC had guaranteed to deliver to its charter daytime advertisers a 25% share of the TV audience, but despite the fact that *American Bandstand* remained consistently over that mark, the network's new daytime shows drew a disappointing 12–15% collective share— less than half of what rivals NBC and CBS each boasted. *Variety* noted that if ABC's ambitious move into daytime TV failed, the chances of the network ever getting another opportunity were pretty slim.

Not about to go down without a fight, ABC again looked to Dick Clark and *American Bandstand* to rescue it from a perilous situation. As 1959 began, the network attempted to appease its daytime advertisers by offering each of them one minute of coveted commerical air time during Clark's afternoon show for every four quarter-hours per week they purchased under ABC's original daytime plan.

As Clark and ABC tiptoed their way through the integration of *American Bandstand*, he and the network faced more pressing concerns. As Clark's popularity among teenagers increased, the barbs aimed at him grew more vitriolic. Detractors charged that his program "might be a documentary on incipient idiocy," and that *Bandstand*'s performers were, "for the most part, egocentric incompetents, entirely lacking in talent but wallowing in wealth and adulation because of their hypnotic effect on their young worshippers." As for Clark, he was said to possess "no musical gifts beyond the highly commercial one of guessing which samples of caterwauling dissonance are likely to be hit records."[39]

Although such negative reaction to someone championing a commodity as controversial as rock 'n' roll was to be expected in the 1950s, Clark discovered that a potentially greater problem—one indigenous to the pop music business itself—also came with the territory he now commanded. As Philadelphia became entrenched as the rock 'n' roll capital of the country, rumors of disc jockey payola, the nefarious practice of paying to secure airplay for certain records, increased. Ironically, it took the unsightly wreckage of Bob Horn's career to confirm the rumors as fact and augur the forthcoming downfall of many Philadelphia broadcasting personalities who not long ago chortled at Horn's own misfortune.

Philadelphia was reintroduced to the hapless Horn in April 1958, when the federal government indicted the deposed deejay on charges of income tax evasion stemming from alleged payola he received during his tenure as *Bandstand*'s host. To many local citizens, it seemed as if the disgraced Horn would never leave their presence. In 1957 and 1958 he underwent two highly publicized trials to settle the statutory rape charges leveled against him, and Philadelphians were also subjected to two more trials later in 1958, each for a separate drunken driving arrest. Convicted both times, Horn was fined $300 and given one year's probation for the first offense and a six-month prison sentence for the second.

With the announcement of Horn's imminent trial for tax evasion (the case was ultimately resolved by a plea bargain), the talk of payola increased.[40] The *Philadelphia Bulletin* editorialized that while the practice "certainly does not reach to all disc jockeys and record companies . . . where it does, it is evidently a profitable source of extra income."[41] This only served to focus the spotlight on Dick Clark, who not only held sway over the most coveted airplay in America, but also happened to be making a great deal of money from his

music business investments. Informed that Bob Horn had extracted significant sums of money from certain parties eager to have their records heard on
WFIL-TV's local *Bandstand*, many citizens about town wondered how much
cash surreptitiously came Dick Clark's way.

Payola "only goes on with the people who need the money," said Clark in
his defense. "God help me if I ever need money that badly." [42]

Clark would never need money that badly, yet he was unable to shake the
growing payola stigma. By then a one-man music conglomorate who not only
owned all or part of song publishing firms, record labels, a pressing plant, a
distributorship, and a talent management company, Clark also commanded
the number one rock 'n' roll pulpit in America. But in the consolidation of
such power a concomitant problem developed. Success, especially a highly
visible success, oftentimes breeds suspicion, and although Clark did his best
to downplay his growing involvement in the music business he was nevertheless thrust into the public spotlight. The public, for the most part, remained
unaware of his privileged status within the music industry, or simply did not
care. But to Clark's competitors, who did not have open and unlimited access
to *American Bandstand*, he became an unrestrained force in the business. As
rumors of rampant payola coursed through Philadelphia's pop music business,
the recently anointed majordomo of rock 'n' roll heard his name mentioned
more frequently.

Clark was particularly vulnerable to payola's double-edged sword, for at the
same time his lofty *Bandstand* position caused people to suspect him of
receiving payoffs, some of those companies Clark held an interest in did business as usual distributing payola. "It was not illegal in those days," Clark said
in 1992. "We kept an accounting, and we reported it as a business expense." [43]

Payola was not a federal offense, nor was it a crime in any state. Or so most
people thought, if they thought about it at all. But when push came to shove,
certain states—Pennsylvania included—were to discover laws on their books
that could be used to render both the acceptance and the payment of payola to
be illegal. Dick Clark would be at the center of the controversy.

CHAPTER 8

Rubicon

Bob Marcucci and Peter DeAngelis had a proven hit-maker in Frankie Avalon, but they had yet to break Fabian. DeAngelis had his doubts that they ever would. "For some strange reason Pete and I weren't able to write songs for him," said Marcucci. "We weren't capable of giving him the kind of songs that he needed." So he and DeAngelis enlisted the services of the crack songwriting team of Doc Pomus and Mort Shuman, who penned a tune called "I'm a Man" (not the Bo Diddley song of the same title) for Fabian's third release.

Marcucci arranged for Fabian to introduce the song on *American Bandstand* in December 1958, and "I'm A Man" hit *Billboard*'s Hot 100 several weeks later. With a hit record to his credit, the crowds of swooning teenage girls surrounding Fabian grew even wilder.

When it finally happened, success came hard and fast at Fabian, who "took off like a bat out of hell" according to Jim Testa, a member of the Four J's, who backed the would-be singer in the studio and on the stage. As it was, the young heartthrob was completely unprepared for the perils of stardom and encountered great difficulty dodging the frenzied hordes of teenage girls who dogged him wherever he went. The crazed fans "would shake cars and shake trucks," said Testa, who noticed that Fabian "was really scared when we went on tours." The situation grew so perilous that Marcucci's young protege had to be secretly transported to and from shows in an armored car.

"It was terrible," Fabian told Wayne Jancik in 1990. "I was out in front of people, lip-synching my record, feeling very strange, and very awkward. . . . You'd think it would be flattering, but it was unwielding (sic) . . . so out of control."[1]

The song Marcucci said "really launched" Fabian was "Turn Me Loose," the Pomus-Shuman follow-up to "I'm A Man" that was introduced on *American Bandstand* in March 1959. Two weeks later the song rocketed onto *Billboard*'s Hot 100 on its way to the top ten.

Thus the die was cast. Avalon, who Marcucci and DeAngelis were pleased to discover "really had a nice little voice," would sing the dreamy ballads written by Chancellor's owners, while Fabian would give his all to what Marcucci termed "the rock 'n' roll stuff" of Pomus and Schuman.

The plan worked to perfection, and during the golden year of 1959 Chancellor's co-owners could do no wrong. The Philadelphia-based label issued records by Avalon and Fabian almost simultaneously, and each one became a hit. Two of Avalon's releases went all the way to number one on the national charts and three of Fabian's five records made it into the top ten that year. So frequent were their appearances on *American Bandstand* and Clark's Saturday night show that many viewers came to believe the two stars owned the shows (or vice versa).[2]

Clark "knew what was right and what was wrong for his show, and he wouldn't put just anybody on there unless there was something that made sense to him," said Marcucci. "Fabe and Frank made sense to him." That "sense" caused a ripple effect throughout the pop music industry as record companies that once searched for the next Elvis now made their elusive quarry good-looking, virile teen-idol types who could be exploited on *American Bandstand*.

Over the years, Fabian has borne the brunt of the abuse for everything wrong with rock 'n' roll between 1958 and 1964, when the Beatles arrived in America. But if anyone should be taken to task for the direction taken by rock 'n' roll during that allegedly fallow musical era it should be those who commanded the power in the business, not an impressionable teenager whose family was in dire financial straits at the time Bob Marcucci persuaded him to make a record. Even if money had not been a factor in Fabian's decision, what red-blooded teenager would have turned down the record label owner's offer of wealth and stardom?

As Chancellor, Cameo, and Swan Records capitalized on their proximity to *American Bandstand*, record companies from coast to coast strove to do likewise. One non-Philadelphia label that was particularly adept at tapping into *Bandstand*'s teen idol TV promotion was Ace Records, a tiny regional company located in Jackson, Mississippi. By 1959 Ace was one of many independent rhythm and blues labels that had foregone a steady if unspectacular source of income from making recordings aimed strictly at the black community, to pursue the potential windfall of riches made possible from recording white teen-idol types. As *American Bandstand*'s popularity (and its influence on record sales) continued to grow, Ace owner Johnny Vincent (born Vincent Imbragulio) eyed the show with envy.

Vincent had already cultivated a rudimentary working relationship with Dick Clark. After Huey Smith and the Clowns, one of Ace's more commercial black acts, recorded the rollicking "Don't You Just Know It," a song with nonsensical lyrics, a great dance beat, and loads of teen appeal, Vincent "loaned" Clark the publishing rights to the song, assigned a portion of its copyright to Clark's Kincord Music, and subsequently sent Clark a royalty check for $2,000.[3] The Clowns performed the song on *Bandstand* in April 1958, and it went on to become a national top ten hit as well as Ace's most popular recording to that point (also the label's most profitable; Vincent ultimately derived so much money from the success of "Don't You Just Know It" that he was forced to incorporate for financial reasons). The following January, Vincent entered into a licensing agreement with Sea-Lark publishing in which the Ace owner gave the publishing rights for "Don't You Just Know It" to Clark's company in exchange for a one-half-cent royalty per record sold.[4]

Having blazed a trail to *American Bandstand*, Vincent set out to capitalize on America's expanding white teenage market. He already had under contract seventeen-year-old Jimmy Clanton, who was a student at Louisiana State University. Vincent reasoned that if Huey Smith and the Clowns could have a national hit, so could the good-looking and personable Clanton. Vincent had the would-be singer record a teen-oriented ballad called "Just a Dream" and then arranged for his young artist to plug the song on *Bandstand* in his national TV debut. The day after Clanton lip-synched the song on Clark's show, Ace received over 100,000 orders from distributors around the country.[5] "Just a Dream" appeared on *Billboard*'s Top 100 several weeks later, and that summer it became the number four song in America.

"Just a Dream" was a dream come true for Johnny Vincent, who, after years of recording and promoting black artists, finally hit the bigtime with his own teen idol. And just as Bob Marcucci did after he established Frankie Avalon as a star, Vincent began to cast about for a second teen idol. He wasted no time in signing Frankie Ford (Guzzo), an eighteen-year-old Louisianian of Italian-American descent who had been in show business ever since he could remember.

Backed by some of the best rhythm and blues musicians in New Orleans, Ford recorded "Cheatin' Woman," a song that became a regional hit in the South. But although Vincent arranged for Ford to lip-synch the song on *American Bandstand*, "Cheatin' Woman" failed to catch on nationally.

Ford's next record was the high-spirited and rocking "Sea Cruise," which took an unusually long time to break out of the South. Ford recalled being on a promotional tour somewhere in that region, riding in a car with his manager at the wheel, and being half-asleep when he was jolted awake by the sound of "Sea Cruise" on the car's radio. Ford's manager was beside himself with jubilation as he excitedly told the singer, "We sell records [in the South], Dick Clark will pick it up."

"And, of course, after Dick picked it up, the ball game was over," said Ford. Vincent booked his budding star to lip-synch "Sea Cruise'" on *Bandstand*, which "was a great shot for the career," recalled Ford. "Once Dick Clark played it, it was a hit. There was nothing bigger than that!"[6]

Johnny Vincent and Ace Records caught teen idol lightning in Jimmy Clanton and Frankie Ford, but Dick Clark's own Swan label had fallen upon hard times. During its first year of existence Swan issued a total of twenty-five records—all but six of them played at least once on *American Bandstand*—but despite a degree of national airplay that any other label owner would have sold his soul for, Swan's sales were disappointing after its initial flush of success. In fact, the majority of Swan's releases failed to dent *Billboard*'s Top 100. Aside from the records of Dicky Doo and the Don'ts and Billy and Lillie, the only other Swan release to crack that coveted list in 1958 was the Upbeats' "Just Like in the Movies," which required twenty-eight plays on *Bandstand* just to get the song onto the chart, where it then stalled at number seventy-five.

In addition, Swan's early hitmakers were unable to duplicate the popularity of their initial recordings. Frank Slay claimed that the notion that people would go out and buy a record simply because they heard it on *American Bandstand* was erroneous (see Appendix III), and, as proof, cited Billy and Lillie's "Happiness," which sold only 35,000 copies despite the fact that Clark "must have played it for six weeks." "Finally," said Slay, who had an independent production arrangement with Clark's label, "we got on the ball."

The ball was carried by Freddy Picariello, an Italian-American who hailed not from South Philadelphia, but from Lynn, Massachusetts. As Freddy Karman and the Hurricanes, the seventeen-year-old Picariello recorded "rock 'n' roll Baby," a tape of which somehow found its way to Slay. The producer did not think much of the song, but his attention was drawn to one brief portion of the number that featured a pronounced thumping beat. "I heard that and I thought, 'boy that's different,'" recalled Slay, who signed Picariello to a contract and took the would-be recording artist into a Boston studio to put "Rock 'n' Roll Baby" on wax. But to Slay's dismay, the finished product—which included alterations of the lyric and a title change to "Tallahassee Lassie"—sounded no better than it had on tape. "It was just awful!" said the producer.

Slay nevertheless made the rounds in an attempt to sell the recording, but "everybody in the world turned the record down!" Everybody but Swan's Bernie Binnick, that is. Binnick showed an interest in "Tallahassee Lassie," but "was such a coward about it, he said that he'd have to get Dick Clark's approval before he would buy it," said Slay. "He went to Dick with the record and Dick said, 'Yeah, I think this has really got something.'" But Clark also thought that the pronounced thumping part on the record, which was very brief, should be repeated.

Slay held his head in despair when Binnick told him of Clark's suggestion. "How the hell am I gonna do that?" he wondered. "I'll have to go and re-record the damn thing. I'll never get it to sound like this again."

Instead of attempting to re-record "Tallahassee Lassie," Slay simply copied the brief drum-thumping part and spliced it into the song. "When you hear '*She dances to the bop, she dances to the stroll*,' you're hearing exactly the same thing repeated the length of the record," he revealed.

Freddy Karmon became Freddy Cannon, a suggestion the singer said "probably came from Bernie Binnick and Dick Clark," and "Tallahassee Lassie" was released in April 1959. Cannon lip-synched the song on *American Bandstand* on the first day of May, and in less than two weeks it appeared on *Billboard*'s Hot 100, eventually reaching number six. The song became one of the biggest hits of 1959, and thrust Cannon and Swan Records into the teen idol sweepstakes.

"I don't know what really would have happened if it wasn't for Dick Clark taking that much interest in me, especially since he really hadn't even met me initially—when he first heard 'Tallahassee Lassie,'" said Cannon. "I guess he liked what he heard and thought it had a hit sound to it. . . ."[7]

It pained Bernie Lowe, who was still looking for a teen hitmaker of his own, to watch Frankie Avalon and Fabian make Bob Marcucci a rich man. Lowe sought to emulate Marcucci's success by "making records strictly for *Bandstand*," recalled Slay. "He would go into Dick's office and would play his latest production, and if Dick didn't like it, Bernie just dropped it in the trash can. It was never released."

Still, Cameo was unable to crack the teen idol sweepstakes. Lowe, who now emptied his trash all too frequently, grew so desperate that he signed South Philadelphia resident Bobby Rydell to a recording contract late in 1958, even though the sixteen-year-old veteran of Paul Whiteman's *TV-Teen Club* had been turned down by every other record label in town.[8]

Rydell's first Cameo record, "Please Don't Be Mad," was issued in January 1959, just about the time that Fabian was gaining stardom, and although the song went unnoticed, Dick Clark nevertheless booked Rydell on *Bandstand* to lip-synch his second Cameo release, "All I Want Is You." But when that song also failed to catch on, Rydell said he "was ready to give up" the singing business.

Cognizant of the fact that it had taken Frankie Avalon and Fabian several releases and numerous promotional spots on *American Bandstand* before they hit the bigtime, Bernie Lowe kept the faith. Besides, who else did Lowe have to offer? "And then," said Rydell, "all of a sudden they came up with 'Kissin' Time.'"

Taking a page from the success of "Tallahassee Lassie," Kal Mann and Dave Appell (who taught at Bernie Lowe's music school in the early 1950s, and whose combo, the Applejacks, served as Cameo's house band) constructed the uptempo "Kissin' Time" around its own catchy, thumping hook. Still and all, considering his dismal track record, Rydell was not optimistic about the song's hit potential. But not long after the song was recorded he and a group of friends were at the Jersey shore resort town of Wildwood when Rydell's grandmother, who ran a boarding house there, came running out to the beach, calling out, "Bobby, Dick Clark's playing 'Kissin' Time'!"

The song hit *Billboard*'s Hot 100 toward the end of June, and Rydell was booked to lip-synch the number on Clark's Saturday night show. "Kissin' Time" went on to become a huge summer hit, and by the time Rydell reprised his Saturday night performance on *American Bandstand*, he was a star. For Bernie Lowe the circle was now complete. In signing Rydell, who, ironically enough, had literally been under Lowe's nose all the while, the Cameo Records owner secured the consistent hitmaker that he previously lacked.

When it came to hyping a record Rydell likened Clark to an all-star baseball player. He said Clark wanted to know if there were sales reports that "the record was moving in different markets" around the country before getting on it. "In other words, you'd get three men on base before Dick would start playing your record. . . . Then he would step up to the plate and knock it over the wall on *American Bandstand* . . . [with] immediate exposure across the United States." With Clark's help (and Rydell's records), Cameo was headed nowhere but up.

As the teen idol phenomenon gathered momentum, young white artists from other parts of the country sought to become part of the movement and a trip to the City of Brotherly Love for an appearance on *American Bandstand* remained the Holy Grail for veteran singers and newcomers alike. One of the most popular new faces on *Bandstand* that year belonged to sixteen-year-old ex–Disney Mousketeer Annette Funicello (sans mouse ears), whose ample bosom and three *Bandstand* appearances in 1959 caused adolescent boys from coast to coast to develop a heightened interest in Clark's afternoon TV show.

Other teen idols to emerge that year who appeared regularly on *Bandstand* in the near future included Johnny Tillotson, Bobby Vee, and Ray Peterson.

Born in Denton, Texas, Peterson began singing while being treated for polio at a Texas hospital. He cut his first record in 1957, but did not have a hit until "The Wonder of You" in 1959. Peterson made his first appearance with Dick Clark that December when he lip-synched his next hit, "Goodnight My Love (Pleasant Dreams)," on Clark's Saturday night TV show. Clark was "usually on top of the marketplace, so that was the best show to do," recalled the singer, who has made so many appearances with Clark that he has lost count of them. "If you were on [with] Dick Clark, you made it."

During the teen idol phenomenon, white vocal groups continued to displace their black forebears, and a number of them, including the Fleetwoods, Skip and Flip, the Teddy Bears, and the Skyliners appeared on *American Bandstand* in 1959.

Appearing on Clark's afternoon show, the Skyliners (Jimmy Beaumont, Janet Vogel, Wally Lester, Jack Taylor, and Joe Verscharen) lip-synched their first hit, "Since I Don't Have You," whose sophisticated orchestration and arrangement caused Clark to mistakenly announce the song as an old standard even though it had been written that very year. Lead singer Beaumont recalled that after "Since I Don't Have You" broke in New York and in their home town of Pittsburgh, a *Bandstand* appearance "really kicked it off nationally. . . . Within a couple of weeks' time it was top twenty (peaking at number twelve), just from that shot." (Beaumont maintained that although the Skyliners did get paid for their *Bandstand* performance, the group would have done almost anything, including forgoing their performance fee, in order to appear on Clark's show.)

Another young white singing group just starting out then was the Delicates — Peggy Santiglia-Davison, Arlene Lanzotti, and Denise Ferri. "We sang outside school, we sang walking home, we sang in front of the dining room mirror," recalled Santiglia-Davison, an ardent *American Bandstand* fan who "used to come home from school every day and watch Dick Clark and practice my dancing with the refrigerator door handle." The Delicate's first record, "Black and White Thunderbird," was released in June 1959, and because of the airplay the song received in the New York area, the young trio from New Jersey was afforded a spot on *Bandstand*. Santiglia-Davison, who was to go on to become the lead voice of the Angels (teaming up with sisters Barbara and Phyllis "Jiggs" Allbut) and have a number one hit with "My Boyfriend's Back" in 1963, recalled being fourteen and "petrified," not by the magnitude of a national appearance on Clark's show, but by the fear of not being accepted by *Bandstand*'s studio dancers, who, in her eyes, were the true stars of Clark's show. "There was a rumor that if they didn't like you . . . they gave some kind of secret signal and the other people wouldn't applaud," she recalled. But if some secret *Bandstand* signal existed, the Delicates did not receive it. "They cheered," said Santiglia-Davison. "I just couldn't believe it. It was great!"

Not everyone thought that the producer-dominated teen idol phenomenon was great, however, including some of those who had been pawns in the very movement they criticized. Teddy Randazzo, who, after splitting from the Chuckles vocal trio, was marketed as a teen darling, offered a disparaging opinion of the concept. "We were the stars at the time," he recalled. "We were the images that most people were running after, so they used us to death. We never got paid [much] for it, we got [union] scale. Big deal!"

The teen idol sweepstakes was "not a matter of good singers, because nobody was a good singer in those days," Randazzo candidly opined. He thought the talent level "didn't make any difference, it was all bullshit! Paul Anka was bullshit. There was nothing phenomenal about him or any of those other people that were there. They were all terrible, but it was just time!" (Ironically, Randazzo was one of the first singers to be marketed as a teen idol and sang his biggest hit, "The Way of a Clown," on Clark's Saturday night show.)

Reaction to the teen idol phenomenon extended across the Atlantic, where British bandleader Vic Lewis bemoaned "the obvious deterioration in the field of popular music. Any thinking person knows the teenage idols are largely the creation of self-seeking wirepullers with little principal and less artistic discernment." But as Lewis wondered if the stars of the future were "to be drawn exclusively from the three-chord guitar bashers and bawlers of gibberish" fellow-countrymen "guitar bashers" John Lennon, Paul McCartney, and George Harrison—soon to be the Beatles, a group that was to have a profound effect on *American Bandstand*—were busy honing their rudimentary skills in a skiffle group called the Quarrymen.[9]

Despite receiving its share of harsh criticism, the teen idol phenomenon continued to gather momentum. Jimmy Clanton and Frankie Ford appeared regularly on both of Clark's TV shows, and Johnny Vincent ran Ace Records as if his label was located in Philadelphia, and not in Mississippi. Closer to *Bandstand*, Bob Marcucci and Peter DeAngelis had their hands full at Chancellor with Frankie Avalon and Fabian. Bernie Lowe had replaced Charlie Gracie with Bobby Rydell, and Dick Clark—through Jamie and Swan Records—had a vested interest in Duane Eddy and Freddy Cannon.

According to the *Philadelphia Bulletin*, "pandemonium broke loose" in front of Philadelphia's Fox Theatre on the night of November 11, 1959, as

Fabian returned from Hollywood to plug his first motion picture, *Hound Dog Man*.[10] A crowd of 8,000 frenzied teenagers surged against the barricades set up along Market Street as the teen idol's motorcade, led by Dick Clark, arrived at the theatre. But as Clark introduced Fabian to the cheering audience inside the grandiose movie palace he was preoccupied with a more pressing issue than that of appeasing a crowd of screaming teenagers, for in a matter of hours he would be forced by ABC to make the most compelling decision of his life. Clark would have to either divest himself of his myriad music-related companies or relinquish his *American Bandstand* and Saturday night TV shows.

· · ·

It had been a hellish whirlwind of a week for America's broadcasting companies. On Monday, November 2, 1959, the nation was held spellbound by the network TV appearance of the personable and engaging Charles Van Doren, the Columbia University professor who two years earlier had won $129,000 on NBC-TV's quiz show *Twenty-One*. Van Doren, who earned $4,000 a year teaching at Columbia, became an American folk hero of sorts, and even had his picture splashed across the cover of *Time* magazine.

But when Van Doren appeared before the House Subcommittee on Legislative Oversight that November day he tearfully told America it had all been a sham; that most of the big-money TV quiz shows had been rigged, and that he was "involved, deeply involved," in the deception.[11] The broadcasting networks at once realized they had a major problem on their hands.

The House Subcommittee on Legislative Oversight, created in 1952, during the height of the anticommunist furor of the McCarthy era—ostensibly to investigate and monitor the morality of the nation's radio and television programs—had since bedeviled the TV industry and the Federal Communications Commission with antitrust allegations and inconclusive hearings concerning televised sex and violence. After being pressured in 1955 to look into the operating practices of the television networks, the subcommittee issued a report in 1957 calling for sweeping changes in the broadcasting industry, including placing the networks under FCC control. After vehemently protesting that their loss of autonomy would destroy the structure of American broadcasting, the networks were able to retain their independence, but they remained wary of FCC control. With the TV quiz show rigging now confirmed by Charles Van Doren, it was anybody's guess as to what action the FCC might take.

The great TV quiz show battle had been precipitated in 1955 by the surprise success of CBS's *The $64,000 Question*, after which NBC and CBS traded high-stakes quiz show blows until the rigging scam began to unravel. Spurred by disgruntled contestants' allegations of chicanery, during the summer of 1958 the New York District Attorney's office began an investigation into the alleged duplicity, only to discover the rigging of TV quiz shows was not a crime. That October, the House subcommittee announced it would begin public hearings on the subject, affording the scandal heightened exposure and abruptly ending the 1950s' claim to be an age of innocence, while plunging the nation into a collective state of shock.

Never a major player in the TV quiz show battle, ABC was spared by the rigging brush that tarred NBC and CBS. Ted Fetter said his network's lack of involvement with the tainted shows "was a relief," and that the prevailing feeling at ABC was, "Aren't we lucky!" Not that ABC's lack of involvement with the big-time TV quiz shows was any part of a grand moral design. "We just couldn't get one," Fetter confessed, laughing as he recalled the episode.

Leonard Goldenson breathed a deep sigh of relief and proceded to gloat on the sidelines as ABC's rivals backtracked furiously in an attempt to distance themselves from the revelations of deceptive practices that had been employed on their highly popular quiz shows. But Goldenson basked in a false sense of security, unable to foresee that public attention would be galvanized to the subcommittee's activities when the panel turned to the matter of broadcasting payola.

The House subcommittee believed that the quiz rigging revelations had finally given it a significant issue to use against the television broadcasters, whose power within the industry had increased alarmingly over the past few years, but subcommittee attorneys were subsequently unable to discover any federal law that had been broken by the show riggers. Thus, the hearings became a vehicle by which Congress strove to demonstrate to the American public that such legislation was necessary. It was hoped that the quiz rigging revelations would cause a national outrage and spur the demand for federal legislation rendering such deception illegal, while at the same time curtailing the broadcasters' autonomy. To the legislators' dismay, however, a majority of the American public considered the rigged quiz shows to be good entertainment, and many viewers expressed a desire for such programs to return to the air—which goes a long way in explaining why the legislators then opted to mount a vengeful attack on broadcasting payola.

The scrutiny of the payola situation by the subcommittee was instigated by the American Society of Composers, Authors, and Publishers (ASCAP), a song-licensing guild formed by composers and lyricists in 1914 to protect the copyrights on their music through the regulation of performance rights.

ASCAP's elite songwriting membership—the Gershwins, Kerns, Porters, and Berlins—had historically controlled the publishing rights to what was considered "good music," while it haughtily shunned the genres of rhythm and blues, country and western, and rock 'n' roll to the extent that that music came to be licensed for performance by the rival Broadcast Music Incorporated (BMI), an organization formed in 1941 by the broadcasters themselves, in a response to a hefty increase in ASCAP's song licensing fees. With the growing popularity of post-World War II country and western and rhythm and blues, BMI began to license an increasing amount of the music broadcast on the radio, and when BMI-licensed rock 'n' roll gained predominance in the 1950s, ASCAP cried monopoly, pointing out that the same individuals who selected the music to be broadcast also owned the song licensing organization that stood to profit from its airplay.

"The people who held the pocketbook strings in those days, the music publishers, the old-line writers, the artists, the record companies, they were concerted in their effort to squash [rock 'n' roll] because they were going to lose money," said Dick Clark, who thought the congressional payola investigation was "absolutely founded" upon rock 'n' roll's challenge to ASCAP-dominated music.[12]

ASCAP had long contended that payola was the prime factor in determining what songs were selected for radio airplay and what records the public was "surreptitiously induced to buy," but the truth of the matter was, by the late 1950s, when rock 'n' roll reigned supreme on America's airwaves, ASCAP's members had grown so out of touch with the pulse of popular music (and out of touch with the substantial licensing royalties being reaped by BMI) that many of them discounted any appeal held by rock 'n' roll and truly believed that disc jockeys played such music simply because of payola.[13]

ASCAP sought to make its latest assault on BMI and the upstart rock 'n' roll by way of Representative Oren Harris's subcommittee—a panel of nine middle-aged, conservative white congressmen who all faced reelection in the coming year.[14] Seeking to generate favorable press for the voters back home, the subcommittee members did their best to accommodate the song-licensing guild. Prompted by ASCAP's charges of rampant payola in the music business, the panel announced it would turn its attention from the completed quiz show phase of the hearings to payola and other deceptive broadcasting practices.

This announcement greatly alarmed ABC, which not only employed Dick Clark—the sole national rock 'n' roll disc jockey—but was also in consort with him in various business deals, deals that some members of the subcommittee were sure to find deceptive, at best. Having survived the quiz show investigation unscathed, ABC, thanks to *American Bandstand*, was about to be dragged into the muck and mire of the payola probe.

Clark had been stunned the morning ABC-TV president Ollie Treyz summoned him to ABC's New York headquarters. At Treyz's side was Leonard Goldenson, who only recently had been briefed on the allegations of rampant payola in the music business and informed that the House subcommittee was about to launch an investigation into payola and other deceptive practices in the broadcasting industry. Goldenson was not in a jovial mood.

Although ABC (and other broadcasting companies in the United States) was not controlled by the FCC, the network was beholden to that governmental regulatory agency for granting its broadcasting license. If the FCC found sufficient cause it could revoke the network's license or refuse to grant a renewal when that license came up for review. When Leonard Goldenson learned of ABC's possible payola complicity he had cause for grave concern. Fearful that Clark's position as the nation's most powerful disc jockey might somehow link ABC to the escalating scandal, the ABC head suddenly faced the shocking prospect that Clark and *American Bandstand* "might go down the drain."[15]

The "only show that I remember there being any question about" at ABC was Dick Clark's, recalled Ted Fetter in 1994. "We were concerned about it." As the ABC executive who was responsible for putting *American Bandstand* on the air to begin with—and thus the individual with more at stake than any of his network peers—Fetter counseled Goldenson: "Let's get [Clark] up here and lay it on the table and tell him . . . what we want and what we don't want."

What ABC did not want was to discover any link between Dick Clark and payola. What Goldenson did want the morning he confronted Clark in Ollie Treyz's office was to know everything about Clark's operations, from top to bottom. He pointedly asked if the *Bandstand* host had ever taken payola in any form. Clark said he had not.

According to Goldenson's 1960 testimony before the House Subcommittee on Legislative Oversight, he also asked his star TV personality if he had any interests in music publishing, record manufacturing, "or any other information that would relate to our analysis of this problem."

Clark replied that he did have such interests, and Goldenson admonished him that "they should have been brought to my attention by you." The ABC chief said he would "assume" that Clark had not taken payola, but he coolly added that he did not think, "in order to achieve objectivity, that you should ever have your judgment challenged, and the only way to insure that is to divest yourself of any interest that would put you in an inconsistent position. Unless you are prepared to do that, we will have to give consideration to taking you off the air."[16]

According to Ted Fetter, Clark took issue with ABC's top executive, telling him, "Look, here I am, a guy goofing along trying to make some money. I make a little bit of money, where am I going to invest it? I don't know anything about the hot dog business; I don't know anything about the steel business. The thing I know about is the music business. Why shouldn't I invest in the music business?"[17]

Looking back, Fetter thought Clark's question was "pretty hard . . . to answer on that basis." But at the time, Goldenson would have none of it. Clark then challenged ABC to "see whether there's any evidence that I favored songs from my own companies" and assured Goldenson that his involvement in various music-related businesses "is perfectly all right; it doesn't affect my judgement in what I do."

Goldenson took issue with Clark, claiming Clark's music investments "could affect your judgment, and we will not find ourselves in that position." The network president also informed Clark that if he was going to remain on the air, "as far as we are concerned you are going to have to divest yourself immediately."

"Can I think about it overnight?" asked Clark.[18]

Goldenson said he could.

In retrospect, Ted Fetter thought Clark "did a very good job" in that he had a "real tough position to defend." Clark thought his position was anything but indefensible. "Nothing I did was illegal," he told Henry Schipper in 1990. "It may not have been without a conflict of interest. And that was when ABC came to me and said, 'What do you want to be, in the broadcasting business or the record business?'"[19]

The rapidly unfolding chain of events took an unexpected turn for the worse for Clark soon after he rushed back to Philadelphia for that afternoon's *Bandstand*. He encountered Tony Mammarella at the tiny office the two shared at WFIL and hurriedly told his producer that he wanted to meet with him later that evening to discuss what had taken place in New York that morning. Clark said that Mammarella "seemed strangely reluctant" to do so, but finally agreed to meet with him after dinner, "and that he would bring his lawyer."

That evening, Clark told Mammarella he intended to make a statement to ABC that he had never taken payola and asked Mammarella to make the statement with him. The request prompted Mammarella and his attorney to withdraw to another room for a private discussion, after which the *Bandstand* producer allegedly told Clark: "There are some things that I have done that will be difficult to explain."

Clark wrote in his 1976 autobiography that he was "staggered" by the response of his close friend and business associate, was unable to look him in the eye, and "didn't really know what to say. Tony's words hung in the air." (In 1994, Clark claimed he did not recall Mammarella's exact words from that evening, only that Clark "couldn't believe what I heard.")

If Clark did indeed struggle for an appropriate reply to the man he had previously referred to as his "right arm," it would seem that someone in his position would, at that moment, have wanted to know more about the things "difficult to explain" that Mammarella had just mentioned. But instead, Clark inexplicably instructed his friend: "Fine, don't tell me about them. I don't want to know at this point."[20] Mammarella then purportedly informed Clark of his decision to resign from WFIL.

As a follow-up to their initial meeting in Ollie Treyz's office, Dick Clark met with Leonard Goldenson the next day to reveal whether he would remain in the television business or opt for the music business. In what Clark termed "a pistol-to-your-head decision," he decided he would "stick with TV" and divest himself of his music-related investments.[21]

Observing how the music industry had expanded over the years, Clark told a reporter in 1989 that selling his music interests "may have been the worst mistake" he ever made.[22] He reiterated in 1994 that, "As years have gone by [he was] obviously very sorry" over the decision to divest, because those properties would have been worth "millions and millions of dollars. I noticed a lot of other people were able to [invest in the music industry] and I wasn't. But then again, I was a test case."

But Clark also revealed that when the payola scandal erupted he "wanted to be in the broadcasting business" so badly that he never seriously considered giving up American Bandstand. "Music was just an avenue to augment the income. I wasn't making a great deal from television, but I knew that was my dream, so it wasn't a hard decision to make."

That decision having been made, Goldenson sought to protect ABC's position in the face of the gathering payola storm. Clark's business activities had never been a concern of the ABC president, but now he told his imperiled TV star, "I don't know anything more important than to get to the very depths of everything you are doing in this field." Goldenson wanted a complete account of all of Clark's holdings and activities in the music business. "I want to know any gifts of any nature that you have received. I want to know everything about this field, and I want you to put this under oath."[23]

Goldenson instructed ABC attorneys that he wanted an affidavit from everyone employed by the network who had anything to do with music selection stating that they had not engaged in any payola practices and that they did not hold an interest in any music-related companies. Although Goldenson would later maintain that this payola document was based on the questions he had asked Clark ("the language may have been different, but the principles were exactly the same"[24]), Clark later admitted when he testified before a Washington, D.C. subcommittee investigating payola, that he would not have been able to agree to the statement contained in ABC's document because, at the time, he did hold interests in music-related companies.[25]

The next day, Friday, November 13, ABC sent its payola affidavit to company-employed disc jockeys and other individuals who participated in the selection of music broadcast by the network. Unaware of Tony Mammarella's disclosure to Clark two days earlier that he intended to quit, WFIL's Roger Clipp and George Koehler informed the *Bandstand* producer of ABC's demand for a signed affidavit, whereupon Mammarella tendered his resignation.

Agnes Mammarella claimed that "because there were a lot of people that really liked [Anthony] and thought he was a gentleman," her husband was tipped in advance that ABC was going to require the affidavits "because [the network] didn't want to sell Dick down the tubes." Ironically, the Mammarellas had already been talking about the possibility of the producer leaving WFIL because of the amount of time he spent away from home. "He used to do *Bandstand*, they would do the Saturday night show, and then Dick got a Sunday show" (*Dick Clark's World of Talent*, a live nighttime talent show from New York that made its debut in September 1959), said Agnes. "Put it all together, it made twenty-four hours a day, seven days a week. Dick was making a lot of money with all of this. We weren't."

Considering that Tony Mammarella and Bernie Binnick had Swan Records, "and he liked that type thing anyway," the producer's wife urged her husband to leave *Bandstand* in order for them to have more time together. "Believe it or not, it wasn't devastating to him to leave," she stated. "Of course, the overall [payola] thing was very difficult."

Clark, who was scheduled to meet again with Goldenson on Sunday, realized he had better ascertain exactly what it was that Mammarella had done that had caused him to resign. On the Saturday prior to the meeting, he, his attorney Charles Seton, and Mammarella met in the New York office of Clark's manager, Marvin Josephson, to do so.

Although Josephson and Seton did not yet know why Mammarella had resigned, they planned to use his resignation to defuse any payola issue surrounding Clark. According to House investigator James P. Kelly, Josephson told Mammarella: "Look, you are out now, and we don't want to get caught with our pants down." Mammarella recalled in his testimony that Josephson and Seton informed him he "should tell anything that they could use in Dick's behalf, even though it might be against me." Josephson and Seton also warned Mammarella that the divulging of "any confidential information that would be detrimental" to him would be used by Clark's attorneys, "if we have to."

Realizing "there were some things" in his background that Mammarella should tell Clark, so as "not to throw Dick a curve," Mammarella thought it "only fair that Dick know" about his receipt of payments from various record companies and distributors, especially since they were "all friends."[26]

Beginning in 1956, Mammarella had received monetary payments from at least seven companies: Chess Distributing; Universal Distributors; Edward S. Barsky, Inc.; Cosnat Distributors; Gotham Records; Marnell Distributors; and David Rosen Distributors. He claimed the funds were remuneration made to him for "advice" he had given to distributors "on overcoming deficiencies in their distribution," and to recording companies for assisting them "in the selection of the recordings which they should place their label on." To the best of his knowledge, Mammarella did not think Clark had been aware of the payments. Clark agreed that it was only "from that point on" that he knew about them.[27]

The list of personages present at the Sunday meeting held at Leonard Goldenson's residence attested to the gravity of the situation as ABC saw it. Representing the network's interests were Goldenson, ABC vice president Sy Siegel, WFIL head Roger Clipp, and two ABC attorneys. Present on Clark's behalf were Marvin Josephson, Charles Seton, and Clark's tax attorney. "For greater privacy, we used the projection room of my home theatre," recalled Goldenson, who revealed that he and the ABC attorneys "went at it all day long and well into the evening. We grilled Dick in great depth, went over everything related to his record business and his ABC show."[28]

Up to that point, the situation boded well for Clark, but the volatile act of Mammarella's receipt of monies from record companies and distributors remained unknown to Goldenson. When Clark informed him that Mammarella would not sign the payola affidavit, Goldenson demanded to know why not.

Clark explained that Mammarella refused to divest himself of his music holdings. "He said he has been doing some things wrong, and I would rather not disclose the nature of what those are. I don't think it will serve any purpose, since he has already quit."[29]

Earlier that day Clark had produced his own payola affidavit, in which he used the narrowest of payola definitions to proclaim his innocence, asserting that only a specific agreement between a disc jockey and another party to play a particular record constituted payola. Now Goldenson—who ultimately was informed by attorney Charles Seton of the details of the payments to Mammarella—sought to neutralize the Mammarella wild card by having Clark insert a paragraph into that affidavit acknowledging the recently resigned producer's revelations, as well as Clark's unawareness of them to that point.

Clark objected on the grounds that Mammarella was close to him, that he "felt warmly about him and did not want to, did not feel it was appropriate at this time to use harsh language," and Goldenson finally accepted a more nebulous paragraph that stated: "Early yesterday morning one of my programming associates revealed to me certain information which he had concealed from me. I had no previous knowledge or suspicion of these facts. His resignation has been accepted." The Sunday meeting concluded with Goldenson satisfied "that Dick was clean."[30]

With Mammarella now ABC's "designated culprit" in the escalating payola scandal, Goldenson, himself an inveterate high-stakes casino gambler, decided to back Clark on Clark's word alone and let the chips fall where they might in the coming investigation. But the ABC president also hedged his bet. Since he "most wanted to know if [Clark] had ever promoted his own records" on *American Bandstand*, Goldenson declared that if it were to be proven that Clark had indeed favored songs in which he held an interest on the afternoon dance show, such a determination would be grounds for Clark's dismissal.[31]

Clark's decision to divest himself of his music-related interests made a big splash in the next day's newspapers. Tony Mammarella was quoted as saying that if he thought his programming of Swan Records, in which he had a financial interest, was wrong, "I wouldn't have done it. I never demanded nor solicited payment for thousands of favors I did for worthy and needy artists or their sponsors." The best answer to any question of profiteering illegally from his *Bandstand* position was his "financial status," said the former *Bandstand* producer, who asserted that he had $15,000 in savings and lived in a home worth $19,000, "with an $11,000 balance on the mortgage, after working in this business for over nine years."[32] (Mammarella's widow said in 1992 that even though Clark and her husband "were always trying to think of what they could do to make money, Dick always made the money and we always ended up on the other end.")

Marvin Josephson attempted to downplay the newspaper accounts, emphasizing that there "never was any secret" concerning Clark's outside interests. But when the show business newspaper *Variety* noted that his music empire "has become the first casualty of the current Congressional war against payola in the broadcast industry," it was clearly time for Clark to initiate damage control. Having overnight become the subject of unflattering newspaper headlines from coast to coast, the embattled *Bandstand* host now sought some reassurance from ABC that the network had "confidence in [his] integrity."[33]

And he got it. On Wednesday, November 18, ABC issued a press release exonerating Clark of any wrongdoing and conveying the network's confidence in its TV star. That afternoon the *American Bandstand* host greeted the show's millions of viewers thusly: "Hello. You and I have talked many times in the past. Maybe some of you are looking today for the first time. If we've never met, my name is Dick Clark. You know it's always been the ambition of every television performer, every entertainer, every singer, every night club performer to get his name in the papers. My name has been in the papers, on television and radio quite a bit the last 24 hours. You've probably wondered what on earth it's all about. All this morning and a good part of this afternoon, people have called me, said wonderful things and sent me telegrams, and patted me on the back and said, 'Don't worry, everything will be all right.' It's a very wonderful thing to know you have friends, amongst which I hope I count you. Now if by any chance you haven't heard as yet of the ABC statement in my behalf regarding the investigation of the music business, I would like to read it to you, because if you haven't read it I'd like to have the opportunity of my telling you about it."

Clark then read ABC's statement, which indicated that in light of the recent payola allegations, the network was "thoroughly investigating its own programs with particular emphasis on those which feature disc jockeys." The statement went on to say that ABC had "examined all evidence available" to them concerning Clark's programs and then concluded that he "has neither solicited nor accepted any personal considerations, money or otherwise, to have any performer appear, or to play records, on any of his programs."

ABC's statement also indicated that the network, in order "to avoid any potential conflict of interests and to insure impartiality and objectivity in the free selection of music on its programs," had adopted a new policy whereby anyone who was involved with music programming would be required to divest themselves of all music-related holdings, noting that Clark "has volunteered to divest himself of such interests. We are satisfied that the American Broadcasting Co. has been apprised of all pertinent details relating to the various Dick Clark programs and his related activities. We have concluded our investigation with renewed faith and confidence in Dick Clark's integrity."[34] There was no mention of Tony Mammarella.

After reading the statement, Clark told his audience: "I want you to know as a friend that I appreciate, as I said before, your kind words and encouragement and the fact that the people I work for stand behind me." Press accounts noted that as the show's familiar "Bandstand Boogie" theme began to play, the teenagers in the audience applauded.[35]

ABC's words of support for Clark sounded convincing, but in fact the network had made no investigation of their star property beyond the questions he was asked at Leonard Goldenson's home three days earlier. The only evidence of Clark's innocence possessed by ABC was his self-composed payola affidavit. As one subcommittee investigator later noted, ABC relied "solely on their appraisal of the individual whom they suspect of wrongdoing."[36]

The aura of uncertainty that surrounded the future of Clark and *American Bandstand* was eerily reminiscent of the situation whereby Clark had rescued the popular program from Bob Horn's disastrous wake three years earlier. Now, however, instead of having to tilt with the ghosts of Horn's transgressions, Clark was confronted with his own questionable business practices—not to mention those of Tony Mammarella, who underwent a three-hour grilling from House subcommittee staff investigators the very afternoon Clark proclaimed his innocence to America.

Agnes Mammarella said two government investigators questioned her husband for about two weeks before he was subpoenaed to testify in Washington. She recalled that "originally these men were really quite nasty," playing "good cop/bad cop" as they examined the couple's financial records with a fine-tooth comb. "They classified everything as payola. . . . Everything you can possibly dream of!"

She said the investigators especially had a "problem" with the payments her husband had received from Bernie Lowe for Mammarella's purported writing of "Butterfly," payments Mammarella allegedly agreed to return to the label owner. "It looked like we had gotten all this money, which we did not get," said his widow. "We got the checks and gave them [back] to Bernie." Asked how Mammarella's name came to appear on "Butterfly" and "Ninety-Nine Ways" to begin with, Mammarella's widow replied, "That was Anthony just being a nice guy and being stupid." Nevertheless, "that was one of the big things that they had on [Anthony]. . . . They wanted to know where all that money was." Lowe eventually "did say he had it, and they straightened that part out, and then at the very end [of the investigation], the last day or two, they were really nice to Anthony [and] said they were sorry."

It was the belief of subcommittee investigator James Kelly that ABC felt it could weather the payola storm, provided the bribery allegations were confined to Mammarella. Kelly said Josephson told him ABC insisted that Clark insert into his payola affidavit the paragraph implicating Mammarella, because the network "wanted to keep its skirts clean."[37] But the former *Bandstand* producer remained tight-lipped during his inquisition and refused to discuss the payments he had received during his tenure on the show. The only thing Mammarella talked freely about was his complicity in Bernie Lowe's "Butterfly" songwriting scheme.

After questioning Mammarella, House subcommittee investigators met with Clark that evening. Stymied by Mammarella's reticence, they wanted to know exactly what the *Bandstand* host knew about the payments to his ex-producer and about Mammarella's sudden resignation from WFIL. Clark refused to divulge any information, telling investigators that "Mammarella had not told him . . . [and he, Clark] did not want to know" what Mammarella had done, "because it would impose an obligation on me when I was questioned about it later."[38] (At that point Clark apparently knew exactly what Mammarella had done. He later told the subcommittee it had not been his intent to conceal anything from them; that he simply preferred any information pertaining to Mammarella come from the man himself.)

"In many ways Tony was like a brother to me," Clark recalled years later. "We had sat across from each other in that tiny office, sharing the joys and sorrows that came along as *Bandstand* grew. But in the end I found I really didn't know him. I certainly didn't know he had received money from several record companies in exchange for consultation."[39]

Many in the music business wondered how it could be that Clark had been unaware of the payments made to Mammarella. After all, as Clark himself pointed out, for the past three years he and his former producer shared a telephone and sat face-to-face in an office "so small we could reach out and touch all four walls," a room in which "the promotion men came in and out at will." [40] Furthermore, Clark, Mammarella, and Edward Barsky, the owner of one of the record distributorships that made some of the payments in question, were partners in a company that manufactured jewelry for teenagers and *American Bandstand* record-carrying cases bearing Clark's likeness. On top of that, Agnes Mammarella and her husband had been "good friends" with Clark and his wife Barbara, had "always traveled together . . . to the New York shows," and had socialized on numerous other occasions prior to the payola episode.

Did Clark at least have an inkling of the payments from record manufacturers and distributors to his producer? Did he decide, prior to his meeting with Mammarella, that the payments were something he simply did not want to know about on the record?

"Anthony was very hurt with what Dick said," claimed Mammarella's widow in 1992. "He was truly hurt by it." Although her husband and Clark remained friends and continued to see each other after the payola scandal, she claimed the friendship "never went back to where it was."

In 1994, Clark maintained that he and Mammarella remained "intimate friends . . . until the day he died." But he admitted that their relationship was "strained" for some time, that all they did was "send messages [such as], 'I'm thinking of you, I hope all is well.' That's all we could say to one another." Looking back on what he called a "brutal situation," Clark reasserted that Mammarella had been one of his "dearest and most intimate friends, but he, we just never shared the secret he held." In the face of the implausibility of such a claim, Clark steadfastly maintained that "it just happens to be the truth. It was true then; it's true now."

Given the dubious assumption that Clark did not know of Mammarella's transgressions until he was appraised of them by the *Bandstand* producer, it was still possible that ABC attempted to assuage public opinion (and that of the FCC) by exploiting Mammarella's vulnerability. Network president Leonard Goldenson maintained at the House payola hearings that ABC had not concerned itself with the details of Mammarella's activities because by the time it learned of them the producer had already resigned from WFIL, making it impossible for ABC to compel him to cooperate. But the Silhouettes' Rick Lewis, for one, remains convinced that Mammarella "took the fall, took the weight [for ABC] because he didn't have a future in the industry. He could see that the big money for him was in the record industry, not in television, because he wasn't a personality."

In retrospect, WFIL's Jack Steck believed Mammarella received a raw deal from ABC, but he would not elaborate, saying only that the scandal "hurt a lot of people that didn't deserve to be hurt," before adding cryptically: "I happen to know an awful lot about that, and I'm not going to tell it. All I can do is hurt people."

The day after Clark and Mammarella met separately with subcommittee investigators, the *Philadelphia Bulletin* splashed the headline: "Dick Clark's Ex-Producer 'Wrote' And Split Royalties for 'Butterfly' Hit," augmented by a huge photo of Charlie Gracie as the singer appeared on the cover of the sheet music to "Butterfly." [41]

"I was flabbergasted when I woke up that morning," recalled Gracie. "You had to commit murder to get your picture in the paper that big!" Gracie suspected it was someone privy to Lowe's "Anthony September" songwriting ruse who called *Bulletin* reporter Frank Brookhouser and "spilled the beans. Evidently somebody dropped a dime [revealed inside information] on these guys and they probably thought it was me . . . [but] I had nothing to do with it." Gracie, who, at the time of the "Butterfly" disclosure was striving to overcome his reputation as a rebel within the recording industry, ruefully recalled in 1992 that the payola episode "put the nail in my coffin."

(Gracie had signed with Decca Records after his Cameo contract expired, but he suffered the misfortune of having his first record for the label issued simultaneously with Buddy Holly's first posthumous record since the singer's fatal plane crash early in 1959, the ironically titled "It Doesn't Matter Anymore." When Holly's record became a huge hit, Decca put all of its promotion behind that song, and Gracie's record was lost in the shuffle. Gracie's final Decca release was issued just before his picture appeared in the *Philadelphia Bulletin* in conjunction with the payola scandal, after which no radio station would touch the record.)

Thus began what Dick Clark termed "a reign of terror that didn't end until the following June." The unfolding scandal brought the pop music business in Philadelphia to a screeching halt. One press account noted that the House subcommittee had "amassed a wealth of information about the practice of 'payola' on Philadelphia radio and television" and its investigation had "given some local radio and television personnel a bad case of the jitters." Three days after ABC issued its statement backing Clark, it was reported that payoffs "running into thousands of dollars" to disc jockeys were alleged by record company officials in Philadelphia and Cincinnati.[42]

Despite ABC's support, Clark continued to take hits in the press. After noting that Clark had helped popularize "Get A Job," a song in which Tony Mammarella had a publishing interest, one Philadelphia record distributor claimed that he (the distributor) regularly paid "cash, checks, and gifts" to local disc jockeys in order to get records played in the City of Brotherly Love, a ward that suddenly brandished the reputation of being the worst place in the country for payola.[43]

Given Philadelphia's preeminence as a hitmaking city, such a reputation was not surprising. Music business veteran Jack Hooke pointed out that the competition to get records played on the air there (and in other key markets) was so intense (there were hundreds of new releases each week, only a handful of which could be added to a disc jockey's playlist) that "there was no other way to get your record played other than to pay somebody. . . . Practically every disc jockey—ninety-nine out of one hundred—was available to take something. That was a way of life."

Payola may connote the image of shady disc jockeys extorting money from vulnerable record company owners, but in many cases those owners, feeling a debt of gratitude to influential disc jockeys such as Dick Clark and Alan Freed, actively sought them out for reward. Hooke recalled that at the time of the payola scandal Leonard Chess (co-owner of Chess records) told him that when he first started in the business he was "sleeping in a fuckin' car. I could-n't afford a hotel room. If it wasn't for Alan Freed I wouldn't have all this. How can anybody tell me I can't give him anything?"

Gone/End Records owner George Goldner, a frequent visitor to the Mammarella household, "wanted to put in a swimming pool for us and he wanted to buy us a Cadillac," said Agnes Mammarella. "He said to Anthony, 'Look at all this money I have made. I want to do something [for you]!'"

Payoffs were "part of our industry," explained talent manager/booker Ernie Martinelli, who preferred to call the practice "promotion." "You had to go and work the record, and Philadelphia was one of those towns" where such pro-motion was utilized. I mean, you work in the drug business, they give you free cigarettes, or free drugs to the doctors [and] . . . that's not considered payola."

Nervous broadcasters, fearful of losing their licenses, did not want to know about such rationalization for payola. In New York, noted disc jockey Alan Freed refused to sign ABC's company-authored payola affidavit and was summarily fired from his WABC radio program. Stung by what he viewed as the network's preferential treatment of Dick Clark, Freed told columnist Earl Wilson, "I feel this guy should be investigated. If I'm going to be a scapegoat, he's going to be one, too. He's on about 300 stations. I'm on one." [44] (Jack Hooke maintained that Wilson plied Freed, who had a drinking problem, with alcohol to get the embittered deejay to talk.)

Just weeks after the scandal broke, Clark celebrated his thirtieth birthday mired in adverse publicity. Adding to his woes, ABC announced in the face of the gathering payola winds that Clark's new *World of Talent* show was to be discontinued (it left the air on December 20, 1959). The network maintained that its decision to scrap the show was based on "poor ratings" (indeed, most critics panned the ill-fated program during its dismal thirteen-week run) and had "absolutely nothing" to do with the payola investigation, but *World Of Talent's* untimely demise only served to sharpen the public's perception of Clark's culpability in the growing scandal. [45]

Although Clark fulfilled the vow he had made to become a millionaire before he reached the age of thirty, with the impending loss of his music empire now a foregone conclusion and a flop TV show on his resume, his heretofore unblemished image had changed. [46] Clark's career appeared on the verge of unraveling, and everywhere he turned it seemed he was the focus of yet another investigation.

CHAPTER 9

Clarkola

Dick Clark's fate, as well as the future of *American Bandstand*, hinged on the outcome of the House subcommittee's payola investigation. ABC's initial contract with Triangle Publications for the delivery of *American Bandstand* stipulated that if, "for any reason whatsoever, [Clark] no longer serves as Master of Ceremonies of the said programs, we [ABC] shall have the right to terminate this agreement forthwith."[1] Because of that contractual right, any proof the House subcommittee could provide of Clark's favoritism in programming records in which he held a financial interest would most likely kill the show. To clarify the point, Leonard Goldenson maintained that such verification would be grounds for Clark's removal from *American Bandstand*.

The House subcommittee probe was the most visible inquiry into payola, but it was not the only one. The Federal Trade Commission, for one, declared payola to be a deceptive, unfair business practice and was conducting its own investigation. Seeking to determine Clark's involvement with Jamie Records and Chips Distributing—two of the firms on the FTC's list of alleged payola violators—the FBI entered the case on November 25, 1959, only to discover that Clark's name "does not appear among incorporators" of Chips or Jamie.[2] To be exonerated by the FTC was small vindication, however, for when it came to meting out punishment for payola infractions, that regulatory body was a paper tiger whose standard payola remedy was to secure from the companies in question consent orders under which, without conceding any past violations, they agreed not to give payola. The favorable determination by the FTC notwithstanding, Clark had bigger problems with which to contend.

In New York, the Manhattan District Attorney's office—which was responsible for unravelling the TV quiz rigging conspiracy—began a criminal investigation into broadcasting payola pursuant to a state commercial bribery law pertaining to dishonest or corrupt employees. Because the Manhattan D.A. had the power to subpoena witnesses, Clark, whose Saturday night show originated from that borough, said he "lived like a fugitive for seven months, sneaking into New York" for his Saturday show "hidden in the back seat of a car" to avoid being subpoenaed.[3]

A rather unlikely scenario, perhaps constructed by Clark to gain a degree of sympathy. If indeed Clark was imperiled by a subpoena from the New York D.A. (and he was not, according to Joseph Stone, the assistant D.A. in charge of New York City's payola investigation), surely the NYPD would have found a way to serve it.

The payola investigation that sent chills down the spine of the broadcasters was the one conducted by the Federal Communications Commission, a regulatory body with power to revoke broadcasting licenses or refuse to grant a renewal of said licenses when they expired. The FCC warned that radio and TV stations found to have permitted payola for record plugs were indeed in danger of losing their licenses.

But the payola investigation that hit closest to home in Philadelphia—and the one which would be of major concern to Clark, since two firms that he co-owned would figure in it—was one that might never have taken place had it not been for a tip from a local newspaper reporter. In December 1959, Philadelphia D.A. Victor H. Blanc (who died before research for this book began) was appraised of an obscure and untested section of Pennsylvania's penal code that related to bribery of servants and employees, which stated in part that "whoever offers or gives any agent, employee or servant of another . . . any commission, money, property or other valuable thing, without the knowledge and consent of the principal, employer or master, as an inducement, bribe or reward for doing or omitting to do any act . . . is guilty of a misdemeanor."[4] The law applied in the same way to the employee or to the servant who received or accepted valuable things.

Since payments by record distributors to disc jockeys were commonplace in the business, the discovery of such a bribery law posed a potential threat to most of them. As Philadelphia disc jockey Ed Hurst put it: "I knew in the end we were all gonna get caught up in this thing because somebody [who was given money to play a record] was gonna not deliver and the whole deck of cards would fall in on it."

Which is exactly what happened. Somebody who was paid to play a particular record failed to do so, and "the guy [who paid for] the record got very upset and decided to blow the whistle," explained Hurst.

Learning of his state's obscure commercial bribery law, Victor Blanc

announced that his office would begin an investigation into payola in Philadelphia, directed by first assistant D.A. Paul M. Chalfin. This was an investigation worthy of attention, for unlike the House subcommittee's inquiry, the
Philadelphia D.A.'s probe was not a benign fact-gathering foray. And unlike
the FTC's investigation, it would not result in a mere slap on the wrist to
those found guilty. A conviction under the Pennsylvania statute carried a fine
of up to $500 and a jail term of up to one year.

But in undertaking its payola investigation, the Philly D.A.'s office was
about to enter uncharted waters. Chalfin, now a retired city judge who practices law in Philadelphia, pointed out that the obscure statute the city intended to hang its payola case on had never been used "for this purpose or any
other purpose." And since no appeals had ever been taken under the statute
there were no decisions of appellate courts relating to it.

Unlike an orthodox bribery or embezzlement action, the payola case
proved "much more difficult to prosecute," said Chalfin, who explained that
the use of the state's untested law "was the only tactic that could be used to
bring criminal charges involved." The investigation was not the kind of clear-
cut case that prosecutors favored, but Chalfin had no choice. It was the only
avenue available to him, and he was "not at all certain what the answer would
be."

If such prosecution appeared uncertain to the D.A.'s office, however, some
party involved on the wrong end of the case nonetheless felt its heat. Philadelphia police detective Emil Bucceroni, who, along with his partner Thomas
McDermott did the legwork of the investigation, said that while they were in
Florida on an unrelated extradition case, someone from Philadelphia
appeared and offered the now-retired detective $5,000 to reveal "how much
was involved with this investigation [and] how serious we were with this
case." Bucceroni duly reported the incident to his superiors, but nothing further came of it.

As the various payola investigations gathered momentum, Dick Clark
continued to undergo a public thrashing. A month into the scandal the *New
York Post* reported that Clark still possessed "widespread interests in almost
every phase of the music industry," adding, "it appears that Clark's interests
extend much farther" than his admission of interest in Swan Records and several music publishing firms. The report cited Clark's "potential links" to
Cameo records, a probable connection to Jamie, and a "reported interest" in
Chancellor Records. Although a Chancellor spokesperson reiterated that
Clark had "no stock, no interest, no connection whatsoever" with that label or
its artists, Bob Marcucci did not help to quell the hearsay when, addressing

the rumor that Clark had a 25 percent interest in Frankie Avalon and Fabian, he facetiously replied that "I always heard it was ten percent."[5]

Meanwhile, investigators continued to try to draw Clark into the payola morass. Chips Distributing, in which Clark held an interest, had recently been cited by the FTC for making payola payments to local disc jockeys, as was Bernard Lowe Enterprises, and federal investigators worked feverishly to establish a business link between Clark and his long-time friend Lowe. Clark's "potential links" to Tony Mammarella's Wildcat Music were also mentioned, and one record manufacturer who remained anonymous told the *Post* how Clark's outside music interests affected others:

> I had a good record, one that I thought would be a big hit. When I notified my Philadelphia distributor about it, he said, "Look, why not have some of the platters pressed at Mallard? Dick would like it and I'm sure they'd do a good job with them."
>
> I figured—I want a hit, I need a ride on Clark's show, I'd better have those discs pressed at Mallard. Nobody in Clark's organization put it to me like that. Why would they have to? I've got brains. I can figure it out.

Befuddled by the bad press he continued to receive, Clark stopped speaking with reporters.

The public rumination of Clark's professional activities caused ABC, which had initially vouched for Clark, to have second thoughts. "I'm damned if I know," replied an ABC spokesperson asked about the status of Clark's music-related holdings. "I doubt if anyone [at the network] knows."[6]

Deciding that the network had to display a firmer grasp on *American Bandstand*, ABC's Ted Fetter hired Chuck Barris, who was to go on to become one of the most successful TV game show producers in Hollywood, perhaps best-remembered for his bizarre and often raunchy *Gong Show*, "to watch over the whole situation there [in Philadelphia] so that we could say, 'Look, we have a man that does nothing but supervise this thing!'"

Every weekday Barris, who Clark termed "the network spy," would make the daily commute by rail from ABC's New York headquarters to Philadelphia and back. "The *American Bandstand* personnel hated my guts," Barris recalled. (Clark said in 1994 that despite their inimical introduction, he and Barris eventually became "lifelong friends.")

After taking stock of the situation, Barris said the names of the companies with which Clark had been affiliated would not be made public at that moment. But although he insisted that Clark was divesting himself of his music-related companies, Barris conceded that even he was "not quite sure myself how many companies there are."[7]

Meanwhile, Clark was busy divesting himself of his music-related holdings. His Binlark partnership with Bob Marcucci and Bernie Binnick had already been dissolved. Before 1959 ended Clark sold his Sea-Lark, January, and Arch publishing firms to songwriter Aaron Schroeder and Vera Hodes (the latter had administered those firms for Clark). Clark's interest in BAE and Request Music ended when he sold his share of Swan Records to Tony Mammarella and Bernie Binnick. Clark also relinquished his interest in SRO management to Al Wilde, sold his interest in Chips Distributing to Bernie Lowe and Harry Chipetz, sold his half of Mallard Pressing to Morris Ballen, and sold his interest in Jamie Records back to that company. Globe Records and Kincord Music were dissolved early in 1960.

As Clark's divestiture proceeded, the white-hot glare cast upon him by the payola investigations ultimately began to affect both the professional and personal aspects of his life. He realized after the first week of the investigation that most of his friends and business associates were avoiding him. "The investigators had immobilized the town," he recalled. "No one looked anyone in the eye, long-standing friendships fell by the wayside. Some of the local disc jockeys left town in the middle of the night."[8]

Nevertheless, Clark and *American Bandstand* continued to survive while others involved in the Philadelphia music business tumbled. Rock 'n' roll radio powerhouse WIBG rid itself of top disc jockeys Joe Niagara, Tom Donahue (who was to become a pioneer of 1960s FM rock radio) and Hy Lit, but denied that payola was at the root of their dismissal.

Lit, for one, candidly admitted that payola flourished during that era, and that disc jockeys such as he "made more money on the street than at the [radio] station. Record companies would come in and they were throwing money at everybody, trying to get their records exposed. Promotion men would be standing outside the radio station; they would come to my house, come to the dances, find out my habits; where I eat, where I go, what I do. They tried in any way possible to get on the good side of me, because I was breaking records in Philadelphia, one right after another." Lit claimed that distributors would bring him ten or fifteen records and say, "Pick two or three" for airplay. He did so, and was paid by the distributor "for being their consultant."

When the scandal broke and WIBG asked Lit (and the other deejays at the station) if he had taken payola, Lit told them he had, and was subsequently dismissed by the station. "I got fired for being honest!" he exclaimed in 1992.

Therein lay the rub. By 1959, payola was so endemic to the rock 'n' roll business that the practice was considered a way of life. In an industry that produced hundreds of new records each week—with only a handful of them able to be squeezed onto a disc jockey's playlist in that span of time—payola became the surest way, and in some cases the only way, to get records played by certain individuals. "Nobody thought [the practice] was illegal," explained Ed Hurst. "We thought it was a favor."

The veteran disc jockey's opinion is understandable, given that payola had been in existence as long as the music business itself, having begun in the Victorian era when composers paid substantial sums of money to influential performers to sing particular songs. That practice became known as song plugging, and by 1905 Tin Pan Alley—the heart of the pop music business—was paying a half-million dollars annually to stage stars to plug certain songs. The term *payola* first appeared in print in a *Variety* front-page editorial in 1916 that decried the practice as "direct payment evil."[9] The advent of the phonograph record eliminated the song pluggers, but it also ensured that payola would someday be rechanneled to the individuals responsible for getting those recordings played on the radio.

Despite the trouble that enveloped Clark, still the nation's lone network TV deejay, *American Bandstand*'s ratings remained strong and he continued to draw new sponsors to the show. (By the end of 1959 the show had twenty-five sponsors, as opposed to twelve for the same quarter of 1958.) Likewise, ABC fared no worse for the payola wear. Nineteen fifty-nine proved to be the network's best earning year in the last four as ABC racked up a record gross of over $172 million (up some $35 million from the previous year), with profits of $8 million (up 49 percent from 1958).[10] In its earliest buying season ever, ABC-TV had eighty percent of its advertising time sold by April 1960.[11]

Still, Clark continued to dwell in the netherworld of payola allegations and innuendos. As 1960 began, the FTC accused five more firms—including Jamie Records, in which Clark held an interest—of payola infractions.

In January, Beechnut gave Clark what was termed "a vote of confidence" when it renewed his Saturday night TV show for an additional six months. ABC went so far as to grant Clark a raise, but the network did not publicly disclose that fact for two months. "Because," noted ABC vice-president Tom Moore, "the less said about Clark at this time the better."[12]

In actuality, ABC was engaged in a shell game in which the network publicly backed the still-popular Clark while it conspired behind the scenes to prepare for the possible dismissal of its star personality in the event it was ever faced with that dire prospect. Both Clark and Leonard Goldenson were soon to be called to testify before the Washington payola subcommittee and, having taken Clark at his word that he was clean, all ABC could do now was stand by and hope his word was good.

As he prepared for his Washington testimony Clark managed to conduct his business—if not "as usual," then at least on an uninterrupted basis. *American Bandstand* required his presence five days a week, there were numerous record hops to emcee during the evenings, not to mention his weekend jaunts to New York for the Saturday night show. In addition, more of Clark's time was now taken up with his expanded movie production activities, which, following the loss of his music empire, began to take on greater significance.

On the eve of his Washington testimony Clark's TV and film enterprises consisted of three wholly owned corporations: 1) Drexel Television Productions (incorporated in July 1958) and the wholly owned subsidiary Drexel Shows Inc. (formed in January 1959)—the former to produce Clark's Saturday night TV show and the latter to produce his ill-fated *World of Talent*; 2) Drexel Pictures Corp., which produced his first film *Because They're Young*, for Columbia Pictures; and 3) Drexel Films Corp., which had recently secured a motion picture contract with United Artists for two films.

Even as Clark's budding entertainment empire appeared ready to fall like a house of cards, it was, in actuality, growing stronger. *Because They're Young* was released nationally in the spring of 1960, and had its Philadelphia premier just a week before he was to testify in Washington. One local film critic noted in an oblique reference to Clark's payola woes that the would-be actor "might very well find another career on the screen, and a less troublesome one."[13] But *Variety* reported that Columbia's rival United Artists was apparently "unbothered by all that payola-probing" of Clark, and had signed an agreement with Drexel Films to produce two more movies.

But even with such successful business ventures, there was still cause for concern in the Clark camp on the eve of his testimony in Washington. For even if Clark managed to hold onto *American Bandstand*, there was no guarantee he would emerge untainted by the payola scandal.

Although payola was the most volatile issue dealt with by the Washington subcommittee, the hearings dealt with four areas of broadcasting abuse. Two of the areas involved broadcaster misrepresentation to prospective advertisers and the extent to which stations delegated control to others. A fourth area pertained to unfair advantages obtained by manufacturers and distributers through the use of licensed facilities for the broadcasting of hidden commercials. Considering the authority ABC gave to Dick Clark to make his own broadcasting-based business deals, the issues of broadcast misrepresentation to prospective advertisers and the extent to which stations delegated control to others may have presented a sticky situation for ABC. But it was the fourth area of broadcast abuse that ABC feared as much, if not more, than payola.

ABC realized that a commercial arrangement between Clark and American Airlines—which occurred at the close of Clark's Saturday night show when the announcer stated: "Travel for *The Dick Clark Show* is arranged through American Airlines"—had been tacitly approved by the network and was certain to be exposed by the Washington subcommittee and likely to be deemed a deceptive practice.

Truth be known, Clark's guests did not travel on American, and in some instances American did not even make the travel arrangements for them. In effect, American paid Clark to get its name mentioned on his TV show, and Clark turned a tidy profit on the deal. (In a January 4, 1960, letter to his manager, Marvin Josephson, Clark wrote that Drexel Television's "profit on the American Airlines deal of last year, after taking into account airline expenses by us . . . amounted to $3, 049.60." Drexel paid Josephson a ten per cent commission on its American Airlines "income item."[14])

Fearing the loss of its broadcasting license, ABC began to hedge on its confidence in Clark's ability to weather the outcome of the multiple payola investigations. The "moral turpitude" clause of his contract—standard in all broadcasting contracts—stipulated that if Clark was found to have done anything which might bring him or the network "into public disrepute, contempt, scandal, or ridicule or which might tend to reflect unfavorably upon ABC television, the sponsors or any of their advertising agencies . . . ," then ABC had the right to terminate the agreement. With Leonard Goldenson already on record as saying proof that Clark had heavily played records in which he had an interest would be grounds for his dismissal, ABC altered the moral turpitude clause in their star personality's contract in a small but significant manner, making such action easier.[15]

ABC was initially limited to terminating Clark's services up to thirty days from either the day on which he committed such an act, or from whenever that act became known to ABC. But under the revisions made on January 20, 1960, ABC deleted the thirty-day limitation, thereby allowing the network to dismiss Clark whenever any violation of the moral turpitude clause "shall have become generally known to the public." Clearly, if ABC was forced to cut Clark loose in order to emerge unscathed from the still-widening scandal, it would do so. (Clark later told the House subcommittee that the network had no discussion with him concerning the changes in his contract and that he did not have "any idea why it was written that way."[16])

Several days after ABC greased the skids for Clark's departure, he hired high-powered Washington attorney Paul A. Porter to engineer his defense. (Although many thought that ABC was instrumental in hiring Porter, who was a former chairman of the FCC, Clark said the hiring "was probably a decision" made by his New York attorney, Charles Seton.) As the Washington subcommittee, set to open public payola hearings in February, sparred with the FTC to secure the same set of documents from Clark, it was noted that Porter "rushed to Philadelphia in an effort to restore order."[17] Porter insisted that the Government limit its investigations and raids on Clark's papers to one at a time, and—inferring that his client had nothing to hide—made it known that Clark, unlike Tony Mammarella, would testify willingly before the payola subcommittee.

• • •

Clark thought he was about to lose his job. "I was terrified," he said in 1994. "It was awful! Probably the worst professional experience I ever had, and it bounced into my personal life too, because I was unable to call my lawyer on my office phone because we were pretty sure it was tapped. In later years we found out indeed they did tap my phone, broke into the house, and a lot of other things.

"It was the beginning of my maturation process," he added. "Prior to that I was a kid, and reasonably worldly. But not in the sense that I got to be after that. I was just flabbergasted by what happened."

Perhaps he was. But Clark's profession of naivté when compared with the cunning perspicuity he demonstrated in his business dealings during that period of his life, approaches disingenuousness.

A recalcitrant Tony Mammarella, who previously refused to discuss with congressional investigators the payments made to him by record companies and distributors, was subpoenaed, and in January, 1960, finally testified behind closed doors in Washington. It was not one of the more pleasant days ever experienced by Clark's normally jovial former associate.

The House subcommittee was particularly interested in the payments— those "things difficult to explain"—made to Mammarella by various record manufacturers and distributors. The former *Bandstand* producer denied that those payments were made in order to get certain records played on *American Bandstand*. He claimed they were made "for many reasons"; some as fees and others as gifts, "for any services that I might have done."[18] But as he grudgingly divulged a minumum of information to the panel, prefacing most of his answers with equivocations such as being unable to "recall," or "not sure . . . [he] followed the intent of the question," or finding it "difficult . . . to say,"[19] Mammarella was not at all convincing. Rep. John Bennett (R-MI), for one, told him, "either you are very naive, which I doubt, or you think the members

(Above) The "Odd Couple." Original WFIL-TV *Bandstand* hosts Lee Stewart *(left)* and Bob Horn. *(Courtesy of Urban Archives, Temple University, Philadelphia, Pa.)*
(Below) Bob Horn's *Bandstand,* June 1955. Jerry "Geator With the Heater" Blavat *(center)* is wearing a dark shirt and white jacket. *(Courtesy of Urban Archives, Temple University, Philadelphia, Pa.)*

(*Above, left*) *Bandstand* producer Tony Mammarella marshalls the show's daily queue, circa 1955-56. (*Courtesy of Agnes Mammarella*)

(*Above, right*) Jerry Blavat and his partner take center stage on *Bandstand*, 1955. The preponderance of females in the studio audience was a constant problem. (*Courtesy of Urban Archives, Temple University, Philadelphia, Pa.*)

(*Below*) Bob Horn displays little enthusiasm for holding a live lion cub, but Tony Mammarella seems to approve. (*Courtesy of Agnes Mammarella*)

Bandstand's Bob Horn Held
For Driving While Drunk

Bob Horn, disc jockey idol of the teenage jitterbug set, was arrested today on a charge of drunken driving.

For four years Horn has conducted Bandstand, a Monday through Friday afternoon program over Channel 6, WFIL-TV.

It is enlivened by the dancing of the teenagers who flock to the studio daily.

(Left) Bandstand host Bob Horn was arrested for driving while drunk in 1956, at a time when the *Philadelphia Inquirer*, owned by the same company that owned *Bandstand*, conducted a campaign against drunk driving. The rival *Bulletin* gleefully played up Horn's arrest. *(Courtesy of the author)*

(Below) Bandstand host Bob Horn was brought down by a series of highly publicized transgressions. *(Courtesy of the author)*

(Above) Jerry Blavat *(center)* leads the June 1956 protest for the return of Bob Horn as host of *Bandstand. (Courtesy of Urban Archives, Temple University, Philadelphia, Pa.)*

(Right) New host Dick Clark, seen with some of *Bandstand's* regulars in July 1957, as ABC-TV prepared to broadcast *American Bandstand*, a national version of the popular local show. *(Courtesy of Urban Archives, Temple University, Philadelphia, Pa.)*

(Above) American Bandstand in progress. First-time visitors to WFIL-TV's studio were invariably surprised to discover it was much smaller than it appeared on television. *(Courtesy of Urban Archives, Temple University, Philadelphia, Pa.)*

(Below, left) Dick Clark's first wife, Barbara, with their son, Dickie, 1958. *(Courtesy of Urban Archives, Temple University, Philadelphia, Pa.)*

(Below, right) Sheet music for "Butterfly," a song for which "Anthony/September" (Mammarella) received writing credit, and for which Dick Clark received 25 percent of the publishing rights for his promotion of it, from Bernie Lowe. *(Courtesy of Urban Archives, Temple University, Philadelphia, Pa.)*

(Left) In the late 1950s *America[
Bandstand* helped change the
face of rock 'n' roll. The "old"
represented by West Philadelphia's Lee Andrews *(center)* and
the Hearts gave way to the "nev
represented by Danny and the
Juniors *(below)*, who hailed from
the same neighborhood as the
Hearts, not far from *American
Bandstand. (Courtesy of the
author)*

(Right) Frankie Avalon (left) with manager Bob Marcucci. (Courtesy of Robert Marcucci)

(Below, left) Fabian (Forte) the reluctant teen idol discovered on his South Philadelphia row house stoop by Bob Marcucci. "But he's not a singer," protested Marcucci's partner, Peter DeAngelis. "Does it really matter anymore in this day and age?" replied Marcucci. (Courtesy of Whirlin' Disc Records, Farmingdale, NY)

(Below, right) South Philadelphia's Bobby Rydell, who, along with neighborhood pals Frankie Avalon and Fabian, became one of the "boys of Bandstand." (Courtesy of Whirlin' Disc Records, Farmingdale, NY)

(Above) Teenagers line up on Market Street in West Philadelphia for admittance to *American Bandstand*, 1959. Some local teens went so far as to quit school in order to gain a favorable place in line. *(Courtesy of Urban Archives, Temple University, Philadelphia, Pa.)*

(Below) WFIL-TV's 46th and Market Street studios in the 1990s. The station (now WPVI) moved to a modern broadcasting complex on the northwestern outskirts of the city in 1963. Today the old building is used for storage by a local cable TV outlet. *(Courtesy of the author)*

(Above, left) Dick Clark and Tony Mammarella finalize the daily *American Bandstand* song playlist. Note the tiny office that the two shared. *(Courtesy of Agnes Mammarella)* *(Above, right)* Clark had good reason to smile when this photo was taken in February 1959. He became a millionaire later that year. But he soon faced the gravest crisis of his professional career. *(Courtesy of Urban Archives, Temple University, Philadelphia, Pa.)* *(Below)* Despite the looming payola investigation, Dick Clark managed to keep focused on *American Bandstand*. Here he rehearses in November 1959, just six days after ABC told him to divest his music-related businesses or step down as host of the show. *(Courtesy of Urban Archives, Temple University, Philadelphia, Pa.)*

Clark Payola Quiz to Star Philadelphia

Prober Brands Clark 'Top Dog In Payola Field'

Dick Clark Hauled 500G in 2 Years; Is You Is Or Is You Ain't Payola?

Probers Asking: Why Wasn't Clark Fired?

Dick Clark Bows To ABC, to Drop Side Businesses

His Producer Gives Up Job On Bandstand

(Above) Dick Clark was the star witness of the U.S. House of Representative hearings on broadcasting payola in 1960. *(Courtesy of the author)*

(Below) During the payola scandal of 1959, Clark was thankful for any favorable publicity he could muster. Here, less than two weeks after being grilled by federal payola investigators, he receives an award from the Boy Scouts. *(Courtesy of Urban Archives, Temple University, Philadelphia, Pa.)*

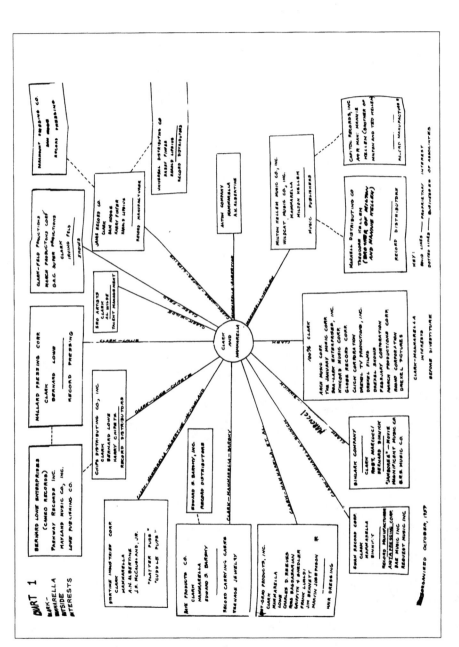

(*Above*) Federal investigators' chart of Dick Clark's music-related business interests. (*Source: U.S. House of Representatives, Responsibilities in Broadcasting Licensees and Station Personnel, 1960*)

(Above, left) Dick Clark starred in three movies. *Because They're Young* was released in 1960. *(Courtesy of the Doug Lumpkin Collection)*

(Above, right) Dick Clark with record producer Frank Slay, 1960. *(Courtesy of Frank Slay)*

(Below) One of rock 'n' roll's greatest hitmaking teams. *Left to right* are Lester Sill, Dick Clark, Duane Eddy, and Lee Hazelwood at the Hollywood Bowl, 1960. *(Courtesy of Duane Eddy Circle/Fan Club)*

(Left) American Bandstand favorite Freddy "Boom Boom" Cannon, whose records were issued by Swan, a company partially owned by Dick Clark. Clark reportedly wanted Cannon to record "The Twist," but the singer declined because a record of his had just been released. "The Twist" was subsequently given to Chubby Checker. *(Courtesy of the author)* *(Below)* Chubby Checker, with a big assist from Dick Clark and *American Bandstand,* changed the way the world danced. *(Courtesy of Whirlin' Disc Records, Farmingdale, NY)*

(Above) The Beatles and Swan Records executives receive an award in 1964 for the group's number one hit, "She Loves You." *Left to right* are Paul McCartney, John Lennon, Tony Mammarella, Ringo Starr, Bernie Binnick, and George Harrison. *(Courtesy of Agnes Mammarella)*

(Below) The Cameo/Parkway Records brain trust, 1964. *Standing left to right* are Dave Appell and Bernie Lowe. *Sitting left to right* are Kal Mann, producer Billy Jackson, and engineer Joe Tarsia. *(Courtesy of Urban Archives, Temple University, Philadelphia, Pa.)*

(Above) After *American Bandstand* moved from Philadelphia to California, the show's dancers began to exhibit a more professional quality, but in the process *Bandstand* lost much of its youthful innocence. *(Courtesy of Photofest, N.Y.)*

(Below) Dick Clark, looking very 1970-ish, welcomes the Fifth Dimension to *American Bandstand* in 1976. *(Courtesy of Photofest, N.Y.)*

(Above and below, left) American Bandstand in 1986. *(Courtesy of Everett Collection, Inc.)*
(Below, right) Dick Clark in 1980. *(Courtesy of Urban Archives, Temple University, Philadelphia, Pa.)*

of this subcommittee are very naive. . . . But I just have the feeling that you have been less than frank in telling us the story."[20]

Mammarella's wife remembered her husband "wasn't happy" about testifying in Washington and that "he didn't say much about it at all" when he returned home.

Meanwhile, the Philadelphia D.A.'s criminal investigation into payola—now in its seventh week—began to encounter setbacks. For the most part, disc jockeys and radio station officials in the city cooperated with the authorities, but when it came to the record distributors—the parties who made the alleged payoffs—that was another matter. According to Paul Chalfin, the distributors refused to open their books or "to come in and make any statements." And, added investigating detective Emil Bucceroni, "They always put [the blame] on somebody else."

In a way, who could fault the distributors for their action (or lack of it). Although, they had traditionally and openly made such payments, carrying them on their books as promotional expenses, the police department now attempted to mount a criminal case against them, contending that what the distributors did all those years was illegal.

Meanwhile, the Washington subcommittee encountered problems of its own. The next round of hearings was scheduled to be held April 26-29, but in the interim, a rift in the subcommittee developed over the date of Clark's appearance (he was slated to be heard on the next-to-last day). Waving a copy of Clark's payola affidavit, Rep. Bennett—who wanted him to testify as quickly as possible because he believed Clark's affidavit "alone makes a stronger case against him than any of the rinky-dink disc jockeys we've had as witnesses so far"—accused the *Bandstand* host of being "obviously quite seriously involved in payola." The Michigan congressman also castigated ABC for its "casual and superficial" investigation of Clark, but the subcommittee refused to be stampeded.[21]

Because Clark's unique situation "requires long, painstaking inquiry," chief counsel Robert Lishman lobbied hard for holding off on calling the *American Bandstand* host to testify. But in doing so he managed to cast further aspersions Clark's way. "His interests outside his broadcasting activities are complex," explained Lishman. "Many persons interviewed are reluctant to talk for fear of reprisals in the form of being denied future opportunity of having their records aired or their talents displayed on his or other broadcast programs. Some individuals associated with him in his various outside business activities likewise are reluctant to furnish information. We have received numerous allegations which turned out to have been inspired by selfish and malicious motives and completely lacking in factual proof." Also skeptical about Clark's alleged divestment of his music-related companies, Lishman publicly questioned whether such divestiture was "genuine."

Hearing Lishman's comments, Clark grew livid. When a reporter caught up with him at the WFIL studios and asked about the latest subcommittee developments, the *Bandstand* host responded "No comment." When the reporter pressed the issue Clark held up his hand and curtly replied, "No comment and goodbye."

Such unfamiliar behavior by Clark was a sure sign that the pressure mounting within him had begun to take its toll. He subsequently asked the subcommittee to be heard a few days in advance of his scheduled testimony in order that he might get it over with, but the request was denied. Citing the "American concepts of due process of law, common decency and fair play," the subcommittee refused to hear Clark earlier than originally scheduled.

Meanwhile, ABC continued to hold its corporate breath. Aside from network vice president Tom Moore, who said he believed his star personality to be "a sincere and honest young man who hasn't given us reason to do anything but support him," it was noted that "all over ABC the executives refused to comment about Clark."[22]

Because the House subcommittee contended that ABC's acceptance of Clark's payola affidavit without any further investigation of him indicated that the network condoned the activities of its star TV personality, ABC regarded the upcoming hearings with as much trepidation as did Clark. And given the extent of Clark's recently divested music-related companies, along with his unique standing as America's most powerful disc jockey and the fact that he was already a millionaire, he was viewed with great suspicion by the subcommittee.

As Clark prepared to testify, the most critical question he faced was: Had he indeed favored those recordings in which he held an interest? As the nation's leading disc jockey, Clark was in a peculiar situation. "It was certainly [a case of] Caesar's wife having to look good as well as really be good," explained ABC's Ted Fetter. In some ways Clark went out of his way to appear as chaste as Caesar's wife. While other record manufacturers, distributors, and broadcasters were frantically "losing" their books and financial records, Clark made his accessible to his accusers, when, in his own words, he "could've burned those motherfuckers in two minutes."[23]

But other of Clark's actions caused him to appear less than chaste. For one, he had accepted gifts (including a fur coat and a ring) for himself and for his wife from the owner of Dore and Era Records. Clark weakly explained that he and his wife Barbara had been reluctant to accept those gifts, but "we kept them because it was difficult under the circumstances to do otherwise" (although he later conceded it "was a dumb thing to do" for someone in his position). He emphasized that he had not received the gifts because of any agreement to give preference to Era and Dore records, and claimed he did not give those records "any special treatment because of those gifts."[24] Nevertheless, Clark realized he would find it "hard to explain to a congressman" that such gifts did not influence someone—even someone making a million dollars a year.[25] Another thing Clark would find "hard to explain" to the Washington subcommittee was his acceptance of money from Bernie Lowe for promoting "Butterfly."

Already concerned with alleged collusion between Clark and Am-Par Records, the subcommittee had its appetite for blood whetted during Alan Freed's secret testimony on April 25, at which time the out-of-work deejay told the panel that at the time he was hired by ABC radio in 1958 he was instructed "to lay very heavily" on Am-Par records and was subsequently pressured to do so.[26] The congressmen also heard from record moguls George Goldner and Bernie Lowe. The former disclosed that he had indeed assigned several song copyrights to Clark's companies with the hope that those songs would be played on *American Bandstand*, and the latter confirmed his own song copyright "gifts" to Clark.

But if there was one witness who aroused the subcommittee's suspicions about Clark's business dealings it was veteran promo man Harry Finfer (who did not respond to requests to be interviewed for this book), who was also the vice-president of Jamie Records. Finfer, who promoted records on *Bandstand* as far back as the Bob Horn days, revealed to the subcommittee that at the same time Jamie paid disc jockeys $15,000 in promotion fees in 1958 and 1959, the record company also paid Clark a "salary" of almost $17,000. Finfer cryptically explained that the money was "compensation" for Clark having provided Jamie "the benefit of his advice and experience with respect to the sale of records." Finfer especially drew the subcommittee's attention when he revealed that Universal Record Distributors, which he managed, had for years made payola payments to local disc jockeys and to Tony Mammarella. But Finfer insisted that Clark did not know of those payments.

Anticipation of Clark's appearance before the subcommittee was heightened when Robert Lishman leaked word to the press that Alan Freed, whom Chairman Oren Harris had characterized as a "cooperative" witness, had "impugned Clark's purity."[27] Lishman, who maintained that the definition of payola offered by Clark "at the suggestion of ABC . . . is phrased in such careful legal draftsmanship as to let him do the substance of the wrong and avoiding the consequence," told the recently fired Freed during his testimony that

Clark said there has to be some sort of an agreement between the two parties in order to constitute payola. Clark was wrong, responded Freed. "If you are going to use the word payola in this investigation, you have got to use it whether you receive money or gifts or something before you play the record, or whether you get them after you played the record because you were a nice guy." Furthermore, said Freed, had the ABC payola document he was asked to sign contained the payola definition offered in Clark's affidavit he, Freed, could have signed that document. In doing so he would have avoided committing perjury and would have appeared "clean as the driven snow," although, "in the common sense" he would have been just as guilty of receiving payola.[28]

Many of those who Clark helped attain stardom had no doubt about their mentor's purity. Frankie Avalon did not think it was improper for Clark to own one business "and an interest in another." The singer saw nothing wrong in bestowing gifts upon the *Bandstand* host, and divulged that he once gave Clark a shirt and a pair of shoes. Fabian, Avalon's Chancellor Records stablemate, thought the accusations leveled at Clark were "a big shame," pointing out that the teenagers who appeared on *Bandstand* "really love Dick. You can always kid around with him." Bobby Darin, with whom Clark was particularly close, said he "couldn't have more respect" for Clark if he was the singer's own brother. Darin thought Clark was "as innocent of doing any harm as any clergymen." Paul Anka made it known he was "a hundred percent Dick Clark man" and suggested that the payola investigators "better get after some other cats."[29]

But those celebrities, over whose careers Clark cast a long shadow, did not sit on the House subcommittee. While Clark realized that the Washington panel had no evidence directly linking him to payola, he also recognized his vulnerability to the charge that he had favored his own recordings on *American Bandstand*. That foremost in his mind, Clark hired a private firm to conduct a survey to determine whether or not he had done so.

The study by a New York firm called Computech was conducted thusly: Each song played on *American Bandstand* through November 30, 1959 was put into one of two categories; Category A, which included all titles in which there could be any direct or indirect financial benefit to Clark, or Category B, which included all titles in which no such direct or indirect financial benefit to Clark existed. A weekly "popularity score" for each song was then determined by subtracting the song's ranking on *Billboard*'s Top 100 from the number 101. In other words, if a song reached number twenty-five on *Billboard*'s weekly chart, the song's popularity score for that week became seventy-six. The popularity scores were then compared to the frequency of plays on *American Bandstand*, and the scores for each group were then averaged.

Utilizing that procedure, it was determined that the average score of all the song titles played on *Bandstand* was .0521; the score of those titles in which Clark held a possible interest was .0585; and the score for those titles in which Clark held no possible interest was .0500. Computech thus concluded there was no significant difference between the categories, and that Clark had not favored those records in which he held a financial interest.[30] Bolstered by Computech's findings, Clark prepared to descend upon Washington.

As expected, the subcommittee did its best to discredit Clark's principal weapon. Three days before his scheduled appearance, two federal statisticians testified that the study "certainly does not support the conclusion" drawn from it, and a Georgetown University statistics professor agreed that "no firm conclusion can be drawn from the data as it is presented." It was the belief of at least one subcommittee member that Computech had been "far more interested in getting the money [for having conducted the survey] than getting the facts."

Computech president and survey author Bernard Goldstein defended his work with the aid of what the press described as "300 pounds of information . . . [and] a series of charts that would have effectively closed any chart gap between *American Bandstand* and the Department of Defense."[31]

But Goldstein's work, particularly its validity, was flawed. To begin with, the study was undertaken by individuals who had no inkling as to how the pop music business functioned. Thus, its misguided premise that a record ranked number one on *Billboard*'s Hot 100 would be played on the radio only twice as many times as one ranked number fifty. Also, the study encompassed too wide a range of songs. It was to Clark's benefit that the study include as many song titles as possible, thus decreasing the percentage of those he played in which he had an interest. One way Goldstein accomplished this was to include in his calculations the show's theme song, "Bandstand Boogie," which was played several times each day, and in which Clark had no financial stake.

In addition, many of the songs in which Clark did hold some interest were legitimate hits that deserved to be played on *Bandstand* no matter who owned them. Their inclusion in the study only served to cloud the picture. However, no study was made of the records in which Clark held an interest and which did *not* become hits, but were nevertheless played on *Bandstand* (see Appendix III). Such a study would have indicated that of the forty-two Swan records released before the payola scandal, twenty-seven of them were played at least once on *American Bandstand*, for a play percentage of over 60 percent (even though over half of the forty-two never appeared on *Billboard*'s top 100). Of the eleven Hunt records released, ten of them were played at least once on *American Bandstand* (a 91 percent play percentage) despite the fact that only two of the songs ever appeared on *Billboard*'s top 100. And of the forty-three Jamie records released before the payola scandal, fourteen were played at least once by Clark (a 33 percent play percentage), albeit that eight of those were legitimate Duane Eddy hits. Overall, Clark's *American Bandstand* airplay included 53 percent of the records issued by the three companies in which he held an interest—an inordinately high percentage of plays for any record company. Clearly, when it came to product promotion, Clark's dual positions of *American Bandstand* host and record manufacturer afforded him an unfair advantage over his record industry competitors.

Flawed as the Clark-commissioned survey was, however, it ultimately served its purpose. Although inconclusive as to whether the *Bandstand* host had favored songs in which he held an interest, the Computech study did serve to obscure the issue. And from Clark's standpoint, that was all he needed. (Clark later boasted that he spent $6,000 on the study, "creating the biggest red herring I could find—something that would shift the Subcommittee's attention away from my scalp."[32])

On Friday morning, April 29, 1960, attired in a conservative dark blue suit, a white, button-down shirt, dark blue tie, and black loafers, Clark made his long-awaited appearance before the subcommittee. Accompanied by attorney Paul Porter, the celebrated witness arrived at the Caucus Room of the old House Office Building—the same room in which Charles Van Doren had endured his quiz show confessional—intent on selling this highly selective adult audience the same moralistic image he had so adeptly sold to America's teens. One national magazine noted that every strand of hair on Clark's head "was neatly lacquered in place," and it was observed that he radiated "the same air of proper respectability he does on TV."

Well aware that the set he now occupied was a far cry from the friendly confines of *American Bandstand*'s comfortable TV studio, Clark jumped to the offensive, reading a thirty-four-page statement in which he cited the press's "prejudgement" of his case. In his opening salvo Clark claimed to have been "convicted, condemned, and denounced" even before he had the chance to tell his side of the story.

Three rows back in the packed gallery, Clark's wife and parents watched and listened intently, but the most interested observers may have been the battery of ABC attorneys dispatched to hear what Clark had to say for himself. "Frankly we're listening and watching," said one ABC executive.[33]

"I want to make it clear, immediately, that I have never taken payola," continued Clark in his familiar low-key manner. After insisting he had never made any agreement to have an artist perform or a song played on one of his shows for a cash payment, "or any other consideration," Clark outlined his extensive business interests, maintaining that it never occurred to him that he was "engaging in any impropriety." He simply "followed normal business practices under the ground rules that then existed," and although some of those practices were guileful, they were nevertheless "legal."

Clark then turned his attention to the thorny subject of Tony Mammarella, conceding he had heard "rumors" about payments to his former producer. But, said Clark, he also heard "many vicious and unfounded rumors" about himself, had dismissed all of them, and assumed Mammarella had done the same about him. When the subcommittee deemed Clark's assertion that he was unaware that Jamie Records had charged promotional fees to Universal Distributors before paying those monies to Mammarella "incredible," Clark attributed his lack of awareness to the fact that he "loved and respected" his fallen associate and had never imagined that Mammarella "would do anything improper, unethical or illegal."

Of the conflict-of-interest charges leveled against Clark, he said such a situation "never clearly presented itself" to him until it was raised by the subcommittee. He then pointed out that the issue was moot since he had divested himself of his music-related interests and could "now program my shows, pick my records and select performers free of any fear that somebody might think that I am playing the angles.'"

Clark attempted to defuse the issue of the potentially embarrasing payments made to him by Bernie Lowe for the promotion of "Butterfly," glibly insisting that Lowe gave him the money because the record company owner "had made a promise [to do so] and that he intended to fulfill his promise and he did."

Of the numerous song copyrights Clark received gratis, he was "very sure" he "never consciously used [his] privileged position as a broadcaster to wrongfully promote or unfairly favor [his] outside interests."

Finally, Clark maintained that when he first saw the results of the Computech study he was "surprised at the high percentage" of plays of songs on *American Bandstand* in which he held an interest (27 percent), and conceded that such a percentage "was high enough to warrant an inference that I was favoring records in which I had some interest." But he was quick to add: "The truth, gentlemen, is that I did not consciously favor such records. Maybe I did so without realizing it."

Clark even pushed the House subcommittee a bit, stating that he "would not be completely frank" if he said he was pleased to be testifying. He did admit that he had "made some mistakes along the way; however, I have always sought to conduct my affairs with honesty and integrity." Then, in a manner described by the press as "even more self-possessed than his experienced counsel," Clark proceded to give the performance of his lifetime.[34]

Clark's alleged favoritism toward his own songs remained unproven. Unable to resolve this crucial issue, the panel took aim where they thought Clark was most vulnerable—his receipt, without charge, of numerous song copyrights, an act which many considered to be a form of payola. Rep. John Moss (D-Calif.), who pointed out that the *Bandstand* host "enjoyed a unique opportunity to exploit" records, no matter who owned them, wanted to know more about Clark's copyright acquisitions.

Clark admitted that he, more than anybody else, could give a song the greatest exposure, and although he conceded that approximately 145 of his 162 song copyrights had been given to him, he pointed out that such receipt of song copyrights gratis was "an established practice" in the business. (It was.) But when he maintained that since no agreement had been made between him and any of the song "donors," his copyright acquisitions could not be considered payola, he moved to less solid ground.

"You say you didn't get payola," remarked Rep. Derounian (R-NY), "but you got an awful lot of royola."

Despite their bluster, the congressmen possessed no proof that Clark had agreed to favor those songs whose copyrights had been given to him. The best chief counsel Lishman could do was to get Clark to concede that some of the song copyrights given to him were received "at least in part because of the fact that I was a network television performer."[35] But there was nothing illegal in Clark's having done so.

Clark also admitted to Rep. Bennett that he never made it known to his audience that any of the records played on *American Bandstand* were owned by him (nor did any disc jockey in a similar situation). "So far as the audience was concerned, they were left with the impression that you had no interest in any record that you were playing," charged Bennett.

"It is a fair assumption," replied an unruffled Clark.

Try as they might, the panel members could not get the better of him. Referring to George Goldner's song copyright "gifts," Rep. Moss asked the *Bandstand* host if he would characterize them as payola.

"No, sir."

"A coincidence?" Moss wanted to know.

"No, sir."

"Gratitude?" asked the congressman.

"A portion of it, maybe," said Clark.

An exasperated Moss told Clark that Goldner and others had been "a little more candid" than he was now being when they testified that exposure by the host of *American Bandstand* "was the precise reason" they gave song copyrights to him.

"I don't deny it," replied Clark.

In the end, the most injurious thing that could be said of Clark's failure to disclose the fact that he had an interest in certain records he played on *American Bandstand* was that the practice was deceptive. But, like the recently divulged deceptive TV quiz show rigging practices, it was not illegal.

Having thus far failed to wound Clark, the subcommittee threw a barrage of charges at him in hopes that one or more might find its mark. Staff investigator James Kelly testified that after he asked Clark if the *Bandstand* host had ever given payola and Clark admitted that he had, "I asked him why, and he said, 'Why not.'"

It may have appeared to some that the panel was at last about to make some headway, but Clark, in his exchange with Kelly, had not meant he had personally given payola, but that Chips Distributing—a company in which the *Bandstand* host had a substantial financial interest—had done so. Kelly swore that Clark "was aware of the fact that this money was paid to disc jockeys, some of them in Philadelphia" (all the more reason then that Clark's "surprise" over the payments to Tony Mammarella remains suspect). The subcommittee staff investigator said Clark's position was that while taking payola "was reprehensible," its payment "was allowable because it was what the industry does."[36]

(It was true, according to a later statement by retired New York City judge and former Manhattan assistant D.A. Joseph Stone, who headed that borough's quiz show rigging and payola investigations. In cases of commercial bribery the taker was "philosophically" viewed as a "dishonest employee" who violated the trust placed in him to be "faithful and dedicated," while the givers of the bribes were "very rarely . . . prosecuted."[37]

Nevertheless, subcommittee attorney Robert Lishman hammered Clark over the fact that Chips regularly made payola payments and billed them as promotional expenses. "Did you know about it going on?"

"That I did," replied Clark, who claimed he had "late knowledge" of the payments, but that it never occurred to him "to look into it in detail . . . this was not a particularly unusual practice in this business."[38]

Clark drew the line with Rep. William Springer's (R-Ill.) allegation that he had "taken part in payola" through the activities of Chips and Jamie, however, labeling Springer's accusation "a terribly dangerous thing from my standpoint." He pointed out that if the case was as Springer stated it to be, anyone who owned stock in a large company such as RCA Victor (recently cited by the FTC for payola infractions), was "as guilty of payola as I am."[39]

Making no inroads there, the subcommittee attempted to prove that, because Clark was so valuable to ABC, he received preferential treatment by the network; specifically, that he had been permitted to submit his personalized payola affidavit to ABC rather than sign the company document that others were forced to sign. Congressman Bennett alleged that Clark's affidavit was "cooked up" between him and ABC "as sort of a public relations operation in order to assure the public this whole matter has been scrutinized and was now taken care of."[40] That prompted Rep. Derounian, who until then had maintained a relatively low profile during the hearings, to spring to life, describing Clark's payola document as a "Christian Dior affidavit, because it was tailored to your need." Echoing the prevailing belief that ABC afforded Clark preferential treatment and elected not to fire him because of the amount of revenue the *Bandstand* host generated for the network, Derounian said "You don't kill the goose that lays the golden egg."[41]

Clark doggedly held his ground, maintaining that his payola affidavit, the only evidence ABC possessed that attested to his innocence, was a "forerunner" of ABC's company affidavit (despite the fact that James Kelly testified that Clark's document had been "dictated to him" by the network).[42] Clark's music business interests may have originally precluded his signing the network's affidavit, he conceded, but he could sign it now, and, "the only important thing is I did divest myself of all of those interests."[43]

The press duly reported that Clark "wiggled off each baited hook flung out" by the subcommittee, which, indeed was the case.[44] When Clark's first day of testimony ended Friday afternoon, his most pressing concern was whether or not he would be able to make it back to Philadelphia in time to appear on *American Bandstand* after the conclusion of his testimony the following Monday morning. Chairman Oren Harris (who, prior to the day's lunch break had helped Clark avoid the mobilized press corps by keeping the subcommittee convened long enough for Capitol guards to escort the day's star witness out a back door) assured the *Bandstand* host that he would be finished in time to do so.

Harris's concern for Clark's well-being may have seemed odd to those seated in the gallery that day, but the subcommittee chairman had good reason to be sympathetic to Clark's plight. During the House subcommittee's 1956–57 investigation of FCC corruption, the panel had discovered (much to its embarrassment) that Harris had acquired (for $500 and a $4,500 promissory note) a 25 percent interest in a TV station in his home town in Arkansas, after which the station reapplied to the FCC for a previously denied power increase. Not only was the license granted this time, Harris never made good on his promissory note. Although those disclosures forced Harris to sell his interest in the station rather than face conflict-of-interest charges, he continued to have jurisdiction over the congressional broadcasting probe—and to treat Clark in an innocuous manner. One of the most pressing mysteries the chairman wanted made clear was, "how you bring about the situation that causes all these fine young people in attendance [at your show] to squeal so loud at a particular time?"[45] (Clark replied off the record that "he would find the answer to that as soon as he found out what makes a woman tick."[46])

(Unlike Harris, most of the panel members and Robert Lishman vigorously attacked the *Bandstand* host—in public at least. In the years since the payola investigation, Clark has expressed dismay over the Jeckyll-Hyde actions of the subcommittee members. He alleges that in session and with the cameras rolling, the congressmen behaved like attack dogs ripping at his flesh, while off the record and out of the camera's eye they cozied up to the TV celebrity. It particularly irked Clark that after being savagely attacked in public by Lishman, the chief counsel "allowed his kid to skip school and took me into the anteroom [during a lunch break] to say would I please take pictures with him and give him [an] autograph. . . . The kid had cut school to get my autograph, and his father didn't seem to mind."[47] On yet another occasion, the wives and children of six of the congressmen on the panel attended Clark's Saturday night show in New York.)

Clark had made a quick exit before the subcommittee's break for lunch, but there was no avoiding the press that evening. When Clark finally met the reporters he did so on his own terms, however. Flanked by two police officers, he slowly worked his way through the fawning crowd outside the Caucus Room, signing autographs as he went. Once outside the building he postured for the television cameras.

Although anyone who appeared on the scene at that moment would have thought Clark had just finished emceeing a record hop, he was not yet completely out of the woods. The next day's press accounts noted that while the *Bandstand* host "still clung" to his ABC jobs, "there were indications his position was somewhat less secure than it was" when Leonard Goldenson had given him a vote of confidence the previous November.[48]

The subcommittee's investigation also encompassed the issue of deceptive practices in broadcasting, and most of Clark's second day of testimony dealt with his tangled web of businesses, and how their ties to ABC may have resulted in a conflict of interest. Rep. Bennett, perhaps Clark's most acerbic critic, took particular issue with a marketing agreement between Clark and ABC involving the sale of *American Bandstand* record cases, an arrangement from which both parties benefitted financially. The cases were manufactured by Raye Products, Inc., the company owned by Clark, Tony Mammarella, and

Edward Barsky, and were promoted by their use as prizes on Clark's daily show. (It was the involvement of Barsky, a local record distributor who made some of the payments to Mammarella—payments about which Clark claimed to have no knowledge—that made this particular deal a red flag in the eyes of the subcommittee. During the payola scandal Clark sold his stock in Raye and resigned his position as one of its three directors.)

In an attempt to further demonstrate the extent of Clark's interlocking business interests it was disclosed that ABC, Walter Annenberg's Triangle Publications, and Clark's Click Corp. and Drexel Productions had entered into a merchandising agreement involving any ABC-TV shows on which Clark appeared, with the profits to be split evenly by all the parties.

Addressing the controversial plug given for American Airlines each week at the close of Clark's Saturday night show, Rep. Moss got Clark to admit that he was "giving a plug just to get American Airlines' name on the program." That, said Moss, was an unannounced commercial. Clark begged to differ, claiming that such a plug was known as something else in the business.

"I do not care what it is known as," Moss angrily erupted. "I can call it Clarkola if I want to."

Through it all, Clark maintained his cool. He told his inquisitors the only "crime, if any" he was guilty of, was that he "made a great deal of money in a short time on little investment."[49]

Continuing in his benign manner, chairman Harris wrapped up Clark's appearance by making known his belief that the *Bandstand* host was "obviously a fine young man" who commanded great influence over his young audience. "I do not think you are the inventor of the [payola] system. I think you are the product that has taken advantage of a unique opportunity in exposing to the public, to the teenagers, the young people, the television productions of this country. . . ."[50] Harris then apologized to Clark for keeping him in Washington all day, after having assured him on Friday that he would finish in time to appear on Monday's *American Bandstand*.

Clark may have missed a *Bandstand* show (ABC showed a tape of a previous show that afternoon), but he also accomplished the seemingly impossible. In a brilliant performance during which he never cowered from the subcommittee's attack, he managed to politely avoid the traps set for him by the panel, often turning its negative questions into positive answers. Even so, some congressmen remained unconvinced of his innocence. Rep. Peter Mack (R-Ill.), for one, believed Clark was "the top dog in the payola field."

All that remained was the testimony of Leonard Goldenson, now a mere formality since the subcommittee had failed to demonstrate that Clark had exhibited favoritism towards his own recordings. Emboldened by Clark's successful bout with the subcommittee, the ABC president took the stand and hung tough in Clark's defense. He claimed to have been "extremely rough" the previous November when he questioned his star employee (and revenue earner) about possible payola activities, pointing out that Clark had narrowly missed being fired at that time. Goldenson also swore that Clark's controversial American Airlines deal conformed strictly with federal regulations, although the broadcasting executive did concede, "I did not alert myself to payola as much as I should have."[51]

Looking back on his Washington ordeal, Clark said the one lesson he learned was to "protect your ass at all times."[52] Asked in 1994 to elaborate on that statement, he said he was referring to his own "maturation process. You find out that large corporate morality is hard to find, and that they have a tendency to cover the trail, burn records, deny, pass the buck; that governmental, elected employees are not necessarily the guys in the white hat. I mean, you sorta get a little jaundiced."

What Clark failed to say is that, up until the payola scandal erupted, he had strived mightily (and mighty successfully) to become a part of that very corporate structure he now castigated. In addition, his insistence that the Washington hearings resulted solely from political motivation has oversimplified the intent of the congressional investigation. Clark would have everyone believe that when the subcommittee members, who "knew little or nothing and cared less" about rock 'n' roll, finished with the quiz show scandal, they recognized they would "hit a responsive chord with the electorate, the older people" by playing the payola card.

True on both accounts, as all of the subcommittee members faced re-election to Congress that fall (and all managed to retain their seats). Politics aside, however, Clark's extensive (and, to his customers, furtive) ownership of the records he plugged on the air was most definitely a deceptive conflict of interest that, coming as it did on the heels of the TV quiz show scandal, ABC could not allow to stand.

Despite Clark's exemplary performance in Washington, one remaining payola hurdle remained. On May 19, 1960, just weeks after the *Bandstand* host testified before the subcommittee, disc jockey Alan Freed and seven others were arrested in New York City and charged with commercial bribery under a law similar to one that Pennsylvania had on its books. Those accused faced fines and/or jail sentences if convicted. If, in the course of Victor Blanc's payola investigation in Philadelphia, anyone at Chips was found guilty of giving payola, Clark, who admitted during his Washington testimony that he had been aware of the payola practices of that company, might also be open to charges that he abetted the crime by not reporting the practice, or ending it himself.

No matter how rosy the picture painted by Clark and ABC in the wake of the House subcommittee's inquiry, neither party would be able to put the payola episode completely behind them until the Philadelphia D.A.'s criminal investigation was concluded.

CHAPTER 10

The Past as Prologue

In an effort to bolster the payola investigation of the Philadelphia Police Department, First Assistant D.A. Paul Chalfin and city detective Emil Bucceroni journeyed to Washington in May 1960, to meet with the Harris subcommittee, the FCC, and the FTC. After it received what Bucceroni described as "a lot of information" from Washington, the D.A.'s office issued thirty-nine summonses for alleged payola violations. Among those summoned were Chips Distributing and Jamie Records, whose officers—and perhaps the corporations themselves—would be subject to prosecution should the alleged violations be proven true. Whether it was appreciable foresight or simply a stroke of good fortune, Dick Clark—who had been a corporate officer in all of the other music-related companies he was involved with—was not an officer of either Chips or Jamie, and thus would not be subject to the D.A.'s investigation. (Chalfin confirmed in 1993 that Clark's name was never on the Philadelphia D.A.'s list of payola suspects, and as far as he knew, Clark "was not involved" in the investigation.)

Others less fortunate could only envy Clark's secure standing. Local disc jockeys and record distributors were asked by Chalfin to explain the incriminating evidence that his office had obtained from Washington. "It was clear that there was enough evidence to support the [commercial bribery] charge," explained Chalfin in 1993. But successful prosecution would require corroboration of the physical evidence he had in his possession, and therein lay a problem. In New York, where the D.A.'s office successfully pursued payola convictions against Alan Freed and several others, the prosecutor had the power to subpoena witnesses and to grant them immunity from prosecution even if they were guilty of commercial bribery. Whatever testimony was elicited from the givers of the bribes was then used to prosecute the bribe recipients.

As was customary in commercial bribery cases, the bribe recipients, and not the givers, were the targets of prosecution. But unlike his New York counterpart, Victor Blanc lacked the power to subpoena witnesses and to grant immunity, and therefore could not compel one party to testify against the other. "There would have been no case to prosecute," confirmed Chalfin, who emphasized that because the givers and the takers of payola in Philadelphia were equally guilty (and did not want to testify), that "turned out to be a fatal blow to the prosecution." As a last resort, Blanc offered the record distributors his verbal assurance that he would not prosecute them if they cooperated, but none offered to testify.

His nine-month investigation at a dead end, the frustrated Blanc announced that his office would make no arrests in the case, but would instead seek a civil remedy of an injunction to halt payola in that city. "What's the sense of making arrests when you know you can't get convictions?" he asked.[1]

In October a city judge handed down an injunction barring twenty-one disc jockeys and eleven record distributors from engaging in payola practices in the City of Brotherly Love. The injunction was similar to the FTC's order of consent, in which, without admitting any prior guilt, the consenting parties agreed not to engage in payola practices in the future. Among those listed were Tony Mammarella and some of the biggest rock 'n' roll deejays in Philadelphia, including Hy Lit, Tom Donahue, Joe Niagara, Kae Williams, Georgie Woods, Larry Brown, and Jocko Henderson. Almost every local record distributor was named, including Chips, Jamie Record Company, and Bernard Lowe Enterprises.

Chalfin, who insisted the D.A.'s office would have needed both subpoena power and the power to grant immunity in order to have mounted a successful prosecution, called Blanc's injunction an "alternative remedy" that was "clearly" the best move the D.A.'s office could make. So it was that after a year of innuendos, allegations, and sensational headlines, Philadelphia's payola probe ended, not with a bang, but with a whimper.

Ironically, while the sources of payola in Philadelphia emerged relatively unscathed, many recording artists—who, for the most part, were removed from the nefarious practice—did suffer from the revelations. "You can say what you want about payola," said disc jockey Ed Hurst, "but a lot of artists owed their popularity to the guys that were being paid" to break their records. This was particularly true in the case of new or unknown artists attempting to break into the business, who were now shunned by disc jockeys and program directors fearful of drawing suspicion to themselves by jumping aboard the bandwagon of an unproven act.

"Jiggs" Allbut Sirico, a member of a group of high school girls from Orange, New Jersey called the Starlets, was as excited as a teenager could be when noted New York deejay Peter Tripp began playing the group's first record late in 1959. Then one day Sirico turned on the radio, only to discover that Tripp was no longer on the air. "He'd just been arrested for taking payola," she said, "so that was the end of our [song]."

Another unknown recording artist who felt the sting of the payola crackdown was Gene Pitney, whose first record, like that of the Starlets, was issued just as the scandal erupted. As a result, said Pitney, when he went out on a promotion tour to plug the record, "people didn't even want to talk to me."

But not every new artist was hurt by the scandal. A group from Virginia called the Rock-A-Teens proved with "Woo Hoo," a frantic instrumental they mimed on *American Bandstand* in September 1959 and on Clark's Saturday night show just two weeks before the payola scandal broke, that if a record had what it took to be a hit, there was no stopping it. Of course, the Rock-A-Teens had one advantage the Starlets and Gene Pitney lacked—national exposure by Dick Clark, who demonstrated that, in some instances, he would do whatever was necessary to promote a new act.

Duane Eddy was another artist not hindered by the payola scandal. "Bonnie Came Back," released just weeks after the scandal broke, turned out to be one of the biggest records of his career, reaching number 26 on *Billboard*'s Hot 100 in January 1960, the same month Eddy performed his hitbound follow-up, "Shazam!" on Clark's Saturday night show. While enjoying his sustained success, the popular guitarist finally discovered that Clark did indeed own part of Jamie Records.

The payola hearings were a revelation to Eddy, who "found out so damn much" about the hijinks that had taken place, "not necessarily with Dick, but with Al Wilde, Lester Sill, and Harold Lipsius." Eddy claimed he and Lee Hazlewood "had no idea" what had been going on behind their backs and had been "pretty well ripped off" by their management and their record company. Truth be known, as the Jamie hits came like clockwork, Eddy had been content with the royalty checks he received. Only later did he learn from what he termed "impeccable sources" that he had received about half of what he should have from the record company.

Aside from the varying effects the payola scandal had on certain recording artists, Ed Hurst thought the ordeal changed "the whole character of the business." Until that time, most disc jockeys had free rein over the records they played, and their programs were their own fiefdoms. Granted, they did not fail to play the most popular hits of the day, for not to have done so would have driven most listeners elsewhere. But each jock also had the leeway to flesh out his or her airtime with "fringe" records not commonly heard elsewhere on the air. It was during such time that a deejay could spin his particular favorites and/or take care of whatever personal "business" was on that day's (or night's) agenda. Perhaps the deejay had been paid to play an unknown record, or maybe the record spinner had a relative or friend (or even a dentist, as was the case with Alan Freed) who had financed a record that the jockey might play as a personal favor. No matter the reason a record was played, what counted most to many listeners was the result: a cornucopia of fresh, exciting sounds — the anti–top forty, so to speak — that often resulted in frantic searches of record shops by avid listeners in quest of a particularly obscure gem of a tune they had heard the previous night. That all ended with the payola revelations, after which disc jockeys were no longer permitted to select their own music, that task having reverted to program directors.

From a practical standpoint, this consolidation of power from a radio station's stable of disc jockeys to one program director did not so much end the practice of payola as it stifled the wide range of rock 'n' roll songs previously heard over the airwaves. It was the loss of this variety in programming that proved to be the most widespread and everlasting result of the payola scandal.

• • •

Although Dick Clark survived the sordid payola episode with his reputation intact, if somewhat sullied, he found his recent ordeal "a difficult thing to talk about." With *American Bandstand* and *The Dick Clark Show* as popular as ever (the former was seen on 135 stations, the latter on ninety-three), he wanted to "put the subject to rest" as quickly as possible. One newspaper columnist likened Clark to an "outpatient with a dubious prognosis: He draws new hope from each positive report."[2]

Even though things were looking up for Clark, from a financial standpoint, the forced sale of his music-related properties (which, in 1960 had an estimated net worth exceeding a quarter-million dollars) left him devastated emotionally.[3] (Clark said in 1976 that just thinking about the divestiture, which, at the time, cost him an estimated $5 to $10 million, made him "want to jump out windows."[4]) Clark realized all too well that he had not reached his millionaire status from the money he earned from hosting *American Bandstand*. With his financial security blanket, woven of a myriad of music-related companies, ripped asunder, his greatest ambition became to reestablish that financial support. Barred from future investment in the music business, Clark needed an alternative means of connecting with the nation's twenty million teenagers, who had access to some $10 billion in spending money.[5] Using his fledgling video and stage productions as a foundation upon which to develop a formidable entertainment conglomorate, he set out to do so with a vengeance.

Because Clark produced his own TV shows (*American Bandstand* through Click Corp. and his Saturday night show through Drexel Television Productions) he already had a toehold on the field of video production, and was afforded an additional revenue-making opportunity with the financial success of his first Columbia picture, *Because They're Young*.

In addition, Clark retained the various non-music companies he had formed prior to the payola scandal. They included: Rosho Corp., which handled Clark's literary rights; March Productions Corp., for his personal appearances and tours; Post-Grad Products, Inc., which, after an aborted try at the cosmetics business, was consigned to the television performance field; and Salutem and Wallingford Realties, corporations Clark used to buy properties in Maryland and Delaware.

No tears needed to be shed for the once again ascending TV personality, who never again would confine his investments to a single field (such as music) that could be wiped out in one fell swoop. With the capital raised through the sale of his music-related properties Clark began to stock his portfolio with a plethora of investments, among them a soft drink company, fast food restaraunts, radio stations, and oil wells.

Clark's refocused investment strategy became apparent to John Zacherle during one of the Cool Ghoul's visits to *American Bandstand*. Just prior to airtime, Zacherle observed the show's host open up the large folding door to WFIL's TV studio, back his car up to it and begin unloading cases of Dr. Pepper soft drink from the car trunk. This occurred shortly after Clark acquired Dr. Pepper as a sponsor for *American Bandstand*, so Zacherle's first thought when he saw Clark unload the merchandise was, here was a national celebrity still not too proud to carry in soft drinks for the kids. Zach told Clark it was "pretty cool [to see] this famous guy" working for somebody else.

Working for somebody else? "I just bought the company!" replied Clark.[6]

But Clark's attempt at financial diversification served as a reminder that knowledge of the top forty did not automatically translate into success in other business ventures. After purchasing the Philadelphia Dr. Pepper franchise, Clark joined forces with a small New Jersey bottler, but the enterprise proved to be so large an investment that they did not have the capital to continue. The franchise soon went bankrupt.

While Clark encountered the pitfalls of diversified investment, ABC began to polish his tarnished image. The network issued a three-page press release biography of Clark, trumpeting the fact that he had made it to "the top of the entertainment industry less than three years after he made his network TV debut." The innocuous puff piece also heralded Clark's six weekly network shows for ABC-TV, the thousands of fan letters he received each day, his more than forty million viewers, and his four starring motion picture roles (including those upcoming in the next eighteen months). It also noted such frivolities as Clark's favorite spectator sport (football), and the fact that he liked to water ski. There was, of course, nary a mention of the recent payola scandal.[7]

Walter Annenberg's Triangle Publications, which still owned the rights to *American Bandstand*, also attempted to boost Clark's stock. In September 1960, *TV Guide* featured the *Bandstand* host on its front cover and ran a feature story titled "Guilty Only of Success," in which Clark claimed to be "all talked out" about his payola experience, stating only that he "was treated decently by [subcommittee chairman] Harris and I was exonerated. I like to leave it at that." But Clark *was* eager to talk about the positive response of *American Bandstand*'s viewers to his recent ordeal. "If I told you the number of letters we got on this thing—and the way they backed me up—you wouldn't believe me," he said.[8] (It was duly noted in the article that Clark received a ten-minute standing ovation from his *Bandstand* regulars upon his return from testifying in Washington.)

• • •

Clark and ABC treated the recently concluded payola scandal as if it had never occurred. And why not. As the summer of 1960 drew to a close, Clark and his *Bandstand* regulars were seen by over eight million people each day, and business for both parties had never been better.

By then, great changes had taken place among Clark's regulars. Since they were required to "retire" once they graduated from high school, there was a constant turnover among the *American Bandstand* regulars, some of whom discovered that leaving their fantasy world of teenage stardom could be a traumatic experience. Being national celebrities and receiving fan mail "really went to their heads," thought Billy Cook, who had to deal with his own withdrawal from Clark's afternoon world. "It made it very difficult to come down to regular life and start to work. They didn't know how to acclimate themselves to being mail room clerks."[9]

When Justine Carrelli graduated from high school her father let her know her stay in what he called "Disneyland" was over and that it was time for her to "rejoin the real world." Justine did not turn to the mail room, but she came close, becoming a steno typist. After being "a national teenage idol to millions of kids," Justine "felt such a void" in her life and "hated every minute" of her six months of typing. "It took me a while to get over *Bandstand*," she recalled. "I loved every single minute of it and wished it would never end."[10] For others, parting was not so difficult. Frank Brancaccio, who "didn't get as much fan mail as a lot of other kids . . . [and] didn't have as many fan clubs" as some of the more popular regulars, found it easier to keep his *Bandstand* retirement "in perspective."[11]

For many regulars, leaving *American Bandstand* brought a new challenge. Since some of the more popular teens who were stars in their own right (or thought of themselves as such) were then free to pursue show business careers, it is not surprising that those who commanded the largest followings were among the first to leave the show and try their hand at real stardom. In most cases Clark's regulars either found that show business life was not for them, or that any interest people had in them no longer existed once they were no longer associated with *American Bandstand*.

America's one-time favorite couple, Bob and Justine, cut a record after leaving *Bandstand*, but sales of "Drive-In Movie" proved disappointing and they broke up shortly thereafter. Justine married bandleader Paul Dino and sang with his combo in Las Vegas for a time, while Bob went to Hollywood and "gave acting a shot."[12] Once there, Bob Clayton discovered that the life of a struggling actor did not appeal to him, and he returned to his native Delaware.

Others kept pursuing their dreams. The *Bandstand* regular who most successfully parlayed his teen celebrity into a Hollywood career was Tom DeNoble, Jr., who appeared in two Hollywood films, was featured on several television series, cut four records of his own, and also sang in nightclubs across America. DeNoble was the exception, however. Most of the *Bandstand* regulars, like Barb Levick, who left the show in order to take an after school job, quietly disappeared from public view under more mundane circumstances.

By 1960, *American Bandstand* viewers had become familiar with a host of new regulars, including Marlon Brown, Joan Buck (Kiene), Ronald Joseph Caponigro, Kathleen "Bunny" Gibson, Charlie "Rubber Legs" Hibib, Yvette and Carmen Jiminez, Ed Kelly, Michele Leibowitz, Gloria Manfreda (Gilpin), Doris Olsen, Jimmy Peatross, Diane Quinto, and Joe Wissert. As more and more of the older regulars who made the transition from the fifties to the sixties fell by the wayside (including Frannie Giordano and Pat Molitierri — the latter had her own unsuccessful record, "Do the USA"), the new faces grew more popular.

In addition, as *American Bandstand*'s cast of characters changed, the show took on a new role within the pop music business, contributing to the homogenization of rock 'n' roll wrought by the payola scandal. Once the nation's disc jockeys lost the power to program their own shows, and station program directors tightened their playlists to include only the "safest" of titles, rock 'n' roll took on a quality of sameness. Exacerbating the situation was *American Bandstand*, which had originally showcased singers from various areas of the country, whose provincial style had been influenced solely by local determinants. Clark's afternoon dance show now began to nurture a generation of artists who, as teenagers, had been inspired by *American Bandstand* itself to enter show business, and whose styles had at least a modicum of similarity where none had previously existed.

When *American Bandstand* made its network debut in 1957, Connecticut high-schooler and future singing star Gene Pitney was among its most ardent fans. After making his national television debut on *American Bandstand* early in 1961, Pitney scored his first hit with "I Wanna Love My Life Away." "Everybody realized how important *Bandstand* was," recalled the singer, who attributed a single guest appearance on Clark's show to "probably twenty, thirty, forty thousand records [sold] the next day."

Lou Christie, an avid *Bandstand* watcher during his teenage years, harbored show business aspirations from the start. Born in 1943 as Lugee Sacco, Christie spent his childhood in the relative isolation of a rural community just outside of Pittsburgh. "There was music in our house all the time," recalled the singer, whose musical tastes ranged from Puccini to polkas to country and western to doo-wop. "It was all music to me. I didn't care about boundaries." *American Bandstand* became Christie's window to what was happening among the youth of America—just as it was to millions of teenagers with similar backgrounds. Christie became "really caught" by the singers who appeared on Clark's show and "started to realize that this was what I wanted, totally." He sat in front of the family television each afternoon and thought, "Oh my god, I've got to be on *American Bandstand*!"

Beginning in 1959, Christie recorded with modest success. Then, in 1962, employing a distinctively piercing falsetto voice, he recorded "The Gypsy Cried," which became a hit in Pittsburgh and was picked up for national distribution early the following year. "The Gypsy Cried" subsequently became a national top forty hit and brought Christie, who only a few years earlier had longingly eyed other singers performing on the show, full cycle. "Lo and behold," he recalled, "there I was, driving to Philadelphia to do *American Bandstand*."

Ironically, as the careers of Pitney, Christie, and others who were inspired to become singers by watching *American Bandstand* began to soar, the influence and prestige of the show from which they derived their inspiration was about to peak. Of course, some of *American Bandstand*'s most influential years were yet to come and the show had not yet begun to lose its status as the nation's most influential pop music program. But the same could not be said about *The Dick Clark Show*.

While there is no indication that ABC's decision to end Clark's popular Saturday outing was influenced by the payola scandal, it did not long survive after that sordid exposé. The decision to axe Clark's Saturday program appears to be another case of corporate bean counters looking to increase the bottom line of the network ledger. Citing the "scheduling shenanigans" the networks routinely indulged in, ABC's Ted Fetter thought Clark's Saturday evening show was cancelled solely because the time slot it occupied had become more valuable to ABC than it originally was in 1958. Fetter pointed out in 1994 that factors such as programming content, "morals, ethical feelings, and politics" were irrelevant to the fate of any TV show, that the only reason why any of them are ever cancelled is financial. "The dollar is all that controls them," he emphasized. Simply put, ABC believed it could generate more revenue from a new show than it could from Ed Noble's bargain-basement Beechnut Gum advertising deal to sponsor Clark.

The Beechnut pact expired in August 1960. Clark's final Saturday broadcast took place the first weekend in September. The next week, ABC showed filmed highlights of Clark's previous Saturday shows, and the following week the network introduced *The Roaring Twenties*, a new action series set in New York in the 1920s. In 1994, as he looked back on the cancellation, Clark professed to have "no idea" why it happened. Then, with more than a hint of satisfaction in his voice, he confessed that he "took great joy in the fact that [ABC] didn't do as well" with *The Roaring Twenties*.

There had been no satisfaction for Clark when the cancellation occurred, however. Besides delivering a blow to his ego and a wound to the total Clark/ *American Bandstand* mystique, the loss of the half dozen or so weekly national promotional spots Clark formerly apportioned diminished his status within the music business. Without missing a beat, he took up the slack by devoting more of his time and resources to his live rock 'n' roll stage productions, which became an integral part of his revamped entertainment empire.

Not that the development of Clark's live stage shows had gone smoothly. On the contrary, it proved to be an uncharacteristically shaky process for him. Mayhem and violence, a stabbing, cancelled show dates, and poor attendance do not come to mind when images of Clark's live rock 'n' roll shows are conjured, but those catastrophes are exactly what the *Bandstand* host encountered as he struggled to get a proper handle on taking rock 'n' roll on the road.

Traveling rock 'n' roll stage shows were an outgrowth of the rhythm and blues tours of the early 1950s, which had grown in frequency and popularity from year to year. Once Alan Freed, in promoting his landmark "Rock 'n' Roll Jubilee Ball" in 1954, had classified black rhythm and blues performers as "rock 'n' roll artists," many r&b productions were called rock 'n' roll shows and for a time they remained primarily a venue for black performers. By the summer of 1958, when Clark gingerly entered the world of live rock 'n' roll by producing an outdoor show at Los Angeles' Hollywood Bowl, things had changed tremendously. White artists now abounded, both on stage and on record.

A year before the payola scandal erupted, Clark had discovered that taking his show on the road could result in pitfalls that did not lurk within the sheltered confines of ABC's Little Theatre in New York. Although his Hollywood Bowl show played to a capacity crowd and grossed what *Variety* termed "a lush $29,000," three days later the same show folded in Minneapolis after only several hundred teenagers showed up on the first day of what was scheduled to be a three-day run.[13] Clark's manager, Chuck Reeves (who preceded Marvin Josephson), put the best spin possible on the closing, stating that Clark "had been taken ill and was suffering from a severe cold and sore throat."[14] That may have assuaged any damage to the public's perception of Clark, but in professional circles his show was deemed an outright flop.[15]

Things went downhill from there. In December a youth was seriously stabbed after a Clark record hop in Pottstown, about twenty miles northwest of Philadelphia. Clark, who had left the premises before the incident occurred and professed to know nothing of it, was "very sorry it happened." He emphasized that after conducting some six hundred hops under similar conditions, "this is the first time there has been any trouble."[16]

In the wake of such adversity, Clark, whose stage shows were originally organized under the aegis of his March Productions—with talent supplied by the General Artists Corporation (GAC) booking agency—strengthened his hand by joining forces with Irvin Feld, then the country's most successful rock 'n' roll promoter. The joint enterprise, known as Clark-Feld Productions, ran contrary to Clark's autonomous business philosophy, but by teaming up with Feld, a pioneer in staging pop concerts in large arenas as well as the first successful rock 'n' roll tour promoter (his highly profitable "Biggest Show of Stars" tours of the 1950s typically played eighty shows in as many days), Clark added stability and expertise to his floundering stage business. Henceforth, Clark's live tours would be billed as "The Dick Clark Caravan Of Stars."

The short-term alliance with Feld, an entrepreneur in his own right who one day would own the Ringling Brothers and Barnum & Bailey Circus, paid immediate dividends. After staging a repeat Hollywood Bowl sellout in the summer of 1959, Clark's road show (on which he did not appear) journeyed to the Michigan State Fair where it proceded to draw a record-shattering total of 58,296 people to the 7,500 seat auditorium during a run of several days.

But just as the gears of Clark's touring "Caravan" were beginning to mesh, disaster reared its ugly head once again. In a scenario reminiscent of Alan Freed's violence-marred performance at the Boston Arena in March 1958, that ultimately cost the deejay his legendary WINS radio program, one of Clark's "Caravan" audiences turned unruly. The incident took place during a performance in Kansas City, Mo. in October 1959, about a month before the U.S. government began to investigate Clark for payola. After repeated pleas for members of the audience to remain in their seats and keep away from the stage, a firecracker was detonated somewhere in the depths of the huge auditorium and people in the startled audience began "swinging at everyone else for no good reason."[17] Duane Eddy, who was on the bill that evening, recalled that the disturbance "was over in a minute, but I guess because of the firecrackers somebody thought it was gonna be a big problem."

A press account of the melee, stating that the fighting continued sporadically until the police ordered the house lights turned up and the show stopped, did not bear out Eddy's recollection. According to the Associated Press account, about seventy-five arrests were made in Kansas City that evening. Unlike Freed's Boston show (after which a stabbing occurred outside the building), no serious injuries were reported.

"I just remember it was blown way out of proportion," recalled Eddy. The guitarist pointed out that similar skirmishes, during which members of the audience suddenly began to "pummel each other around a little bit, the lights would come up, people would rush over and settle it down, and it'd be over," occurred almost nightly wherever the troupe performed. But during a time when rock 'n' roll was mentioned in the press only in reference to riots or other violence-related incidents, Clark's Kansas City commotion fit the bill nicely.

"Rocking, socking teen-agers turned a Saturday night musical show into riot—to the tune of popping firecrackers and swinging fists," the AP wire service reported the following day.[18] Clark, who had not been a part of the tour that played Kansas City, essentially copped the same plea he used after the Pottstown stabbing, when he insisted that his people had left the premises by the time the violence erupted. "What happened was very unfortunate," he remarked, and "reflected the attitude of a very few of the 12,000 people who were there." But the flames had been fanned. Clark's show, scheduled to play Minneapolis the following week, was cancelled by the local police chief, "for the peace and well-being of the city."[19]

Reacting to this latest setback, Clark tightened the reins on his "Caravan" tours. He expressly prohibited ("for insurance, practical purposes") performers from inciting the audience, branding such attempts to encourage people to run to the stage "sheer stupidity. You don't want to see people hurt, killed. You don't want to get sued. If it happens, you've added another nail to the coffin."[20]

To ensure that no further nails would be driven into Clark's "Caravan" coffin, he parted ways with Irvin Feld and took complete control of his live tours. The move did not surprise music business insiders. Anyone familiar with Clark, "knew Dick wasn't going to stay in any one place with other people too long," said Ernie Martinelli, who worked for GAC, the booking agency that administered Clark's live shows in return for a healthy percentage of the profits.

"Now he wanted to own [the shows]," said former Alan Freed associate Jack Hooke. And own them Clark did. In the wake of the payola scandal he established his own company to conduct the tours and then hired Rosalind Ross (who, in Martinelli's opinion, became "like Dick's best friend or right-hand") from the William Morris booking agency to run the new enterprise. Ross, in turn, offered Hooke—who she already knew from his days as talent procurer for Freed—to work in conjunction with Clark's live productions. Because Clark had been affronted by Freed's demand that the payola investigation "Get the guy in Philadelphia," a wary Hooke asked, "How does Dick feel about this?"

"Dick trusts my judgement," replied Ross. "I told him you would be right for the job, and he said to me, 'If you think so, hire him.'"[21] Ross did, and during the time Hooke worked for Clark, Clark never mentioned Freed's name. The two would "talk about a million things," recalled Hooke, "but we never spoke about Alan."

Despite its rag-tag beginnings, Clark's revamped "Caravan" developed into what rock 'n' roll performers came to regard as a smooth-running, professional gig. Lou Christie, a veteran of several Clark tours, said the advance publicity for each show was rolled out like clockwork. "It was full press, full radio coverage, and full television coverage. Every night was a success, every night was a packed audience no matter where we played. Wherever we went, it was the ultimate. It was *Bandstand* coming to your town."

For the performers, however, with the accolades and the packed houses came the drudgery of the road. Routinely subjected to marathon bus rides and spartan living conditions for up to three months at a time, the talent developed a strong fellowship.

Clark, too, "loved the comradery" of the tours. "It was a little microcosm of the world all squeezed together on a bus," he said in 1994. "And the fascinating thing was, the people came from a lot of different areas of the country. It was pretty evenly divided racially, but you got to know people that for some strange reason or other have stayed close over the years without seeing one another."

Gene Pitney, who toured frequently enough with Clark to know, characterized the live shows as "unbelievable marathons." With the well-grounded perspective of a performer whose career has extended into the 1990s, Pitney derided the splendor of modern-day life on the road, pointing out that such comfort (including videotape players, wet bars, and beds) was a far cry from the old days when Clark's acts rode "real buses . . . with park benches in 'em!"

Not only did the performers travel on those cramped buses, they often lived on them. It was not unusual for the troupe to travel as far as six hundred miles to the next town after finishing a show, put on a performance there, and then move on to the next town before checking into a hotel. They sometimes endured three days on the road before savoring the luxury of a hotel bed.

Recalling one of Clark's tours of the United States and Canada that entailed fifty-eight shows in sixty-two days, Pitney said he realized "right in the beginning" he had to do something to make life on the bus more comfortable, "so I found out that I could sleep in the luggage rack." Not only could he do that, the slightly built singer could also turn over in those cramped quarters, "which is the key to being able to sleep. And being as skinny as I was, I got one of those blow-up floats that you put in the ocean, and that was my mattress. I remember Dick saying that he tried it and his belly wouldn't let him do it."

After each show the artists boarded the bus and returned to their usual seats. "You had your own little nest and you'd take the same seat every day, every night," recalled Lou Christie. People in "four or five seats would talk to each other and hang out together. We'd get off the stage and get on [the bus] and drive all night long and land in the morning wherever we were driving to." The artists suffered willingly under such conditions because very few of them saw much money from the recordings they made, and thus were forced to earn an income from other sources. Not that the money they earned from touring was great.

There was "no big money" to be made by recording artists touring in those days, said Ernie Martinelli. When Clark signed Little Anthony and the Imperials (a top attraction in those days) for a thirty-day "Caravan," the entire group received a total of $11,000 (nowadays it is possible for leading rock groups to gross millions of dollars a month by touring). "We were in our glory!" exclaimed Martinelli, who still manages the Imperials.

A much stronger incentive for acts to join Clark's tour was the allure of it all. It was only after hearing other groups come off the road boasting of the great time they had drinking and partying that Anthony and the Imperials practically begged to appear with Clark. The "Caravan" was an ego trip, the thing to do, thought Martinelli. "You weren't anybody until you did it." Not that the Imperials—or any other group, for that matter—ever got to close one of Clark's shows. "The performer who'd get the most screams and probably the highest pay . . . was usually a white teen idol," explained Clark.[22]

Clark's shows ran with precision and lightning speed, as the dozen or so acts on the bill sang only two or three songs, usually their hits. "Those shows moved! " said Lou Christie, who had fulfilled his *Bandstand*-inspired fantasy of becoming a rock 'n' roll star. "The Crystals came out and did their two or three hit records, then it was me, then it was the Supremes, and then it was maybe Barbara Lewis, Gene Pitney, or the Drifters. It just rocked!"

But the fun and comradery of touring ("It was all rock 'n' roll, and we were all a bunch of kids doin' the best we could," recalled Duane Eddy) was tempered by America's dark specter of racial intolerance. Whites and blacks got along fine in the insular world of the tour bus, but "the shocking part was to walk outside the bus and go into a theatre where the blacks sat downstairs or upstairs or on one side or in separate shows," said Clark, who also recalled the tension engendered when his integrated busloads "weren't welcomed in hotels" throughout the South.[23] On more than one occasion Clark's entourage slept on the grass under the stars next to the parked bus after being refused lodging at a hotel. Bookers in many Southern cities were loath to have black acts and white acts perform on the same stage, and when showtime approached, "Dick would look them in the eye and say, 'Listen, we either all go on, or we don't go on,'" recalled Christie.

"It was outwardly segregated and there were no bones made about it," said singer Lee Andrews. "Everybody knew what the deal was. The state troopers actually stopped tour buses and unloaded everybody off the bus—just harassment!" Most restaurants in the South refused to serve blacks, and those that did required them go around to the back door that led to the kitchen. "God knows what you got!" exclaimed Andrews. But the performers did not have much of a choice. "It was either that, or you waited until you got to the town and found the black neighborhood, where you'd eat and stay." Often some of the white artists brought hamburgers and other fast food onto the bus and shared it with those on board.

To illustrate the deep suspicion with which locals in the South regarded integrated rock 'n' roll tours, Gene Pitney recalled the time the "Caravan" finished a show in that region and prepared to move on to the Midwest. Clark and some of the acts boarded one bus, while Pitney and the remaining acts boarded another. But when Pitney's bus arrived in the next town, Clark's was nowhere to be seen. With an afternoon show already scheduled, Pitney took charge and threw together a makeshift band to back the acts already there. Because most of the show's talent was on the missing bus, they had a lot of time to fill.

"It was ridiculous," recalled the singer. "Brian Hyland was goin' out and tellin' all the jokes he knew and singing songs. I was playing guitar, playing piano and singin' some songs. We'd have an intermission and go around and around and around again."

When the wayward bus finally arrived, Pitney and the others learned what had caused the delay. While still in the South, Clark's bus had stopped at a diner located on a hilltop. The driver parked at the bottom of the hill and the racially mixed troupe then "paraded out, up the side of this bank, Dick included." When the proprietor of the diner looked out the window, "all he could think was 'sit-in,' which was happening at the time, so they called the state police."

Although the performers on Clark's "Caravans" did not conduct sit-ins or demonstrations, simply by having whites and blacks sit together at concerts they helped to pioneer integration in the South. Clark "got [blacks and whites] in there together," said the Imperials' Clarence Collins, "and eventually in the South they forgot all about what color you were."

It would be some time before that happened, however. Although the discrimination of the 1950s and early 1960s served to strengthen the bond between the acts on tour ("We were really close," recalled Christie, who likened Clark's troupe to "one big family, sort of 'us all together'"), in order to keep such persecution to a minimum, Clark did not tour in parts of the Deep South. (Rather than suffer the humiliation and indignity of segregation, many black artists chose to forego touring anywhere below the Mason-Dixon line.)

By replacing his cancelled Saturday show with live "Caravans," Clark not only brought *Bandstand* to visit America in person, he developed a profitable addition to his budding entertainment conglomerate. By the late 1960s he had two "Caravan" units of about fifteen acts each on the road simultaneously, and grossed more than six million dollars annually from the operation.

When the sixties had begun Clark's empire teetered on the brink of disarray, and he stood at the crossroads of his career. Although surviving the payola scandal, just months later, in 1960, he had good reason not to want to discuss the issue. Whether or not Clark had favored records in which he had a financial stake, the intricate pop music niche he had so meticulously carved out for himself—one in which he hyped records to a national audience without acknowledging those in which he did command a piece of the action—had represented a conflict of interest. In addition, Clark's admission to the Washington payola inquiry that he had accepted gifts from people who could have benefited from his sales pitch demonstrated that for a person of his stature, he was at least guilty of poor judgement. The payola hearings also showed that the American Broadcasting Company had given preferential treatment to one of its star personalities (and a leading revenue-earner for the network) by allowing Clark to draw up his own payola affidavit instead of insisting that he sign the company payola document (which Clark himself admitted he could not have signed) required of all other ABC employees connected with the broadcasting of music. Then, after Clark was forced to sell his music conglomerate piecemeal, ABC yanked *The Dick Clark Show* out from under him.

On the brighter side, either by design or by good fortune, Clark had managed to insulate himself from the payola accusations leveled at the companies in which he shared ownership. And because the Philadelphia D.A.'s office was unable to criminally prosecute any payola givers or takers, the public's perception of the act itself dimmed in severity as it was generally (albeit erroneously) assumed that since there had been no prosecution, no crime had been committed.

Clark's losses proved to be short term, and may have been fortuitious to him in the long run. He went on to replace his music-related properties with diverse financial investments that gave him a broad-based foundation he did not previously enjoy. In addition, Clark began to seriously develop his TV and movie production capabilities, enabling him to gain an early foothold in that soon-to-be lucrative business. As for the loss of his popular Saturday night show, like all TV productions, it would have eventually run its course and disappeared from the air. But the live rock 'n' roll tours on which Clark placed greater emphasis following its demise proved to be timeless in appeal, and in the long run brought in more revenue than Clark's TV program ever would have produced.

Perhaps of greatest importance, *American Bandstand* remained as popular as ever through the entire payola upheaval, affording Clark the flagship from which he could maintain a high degree of visibility, reinforce his "good guy" persona and design new ways to turn the youth entertainment dollar his way.

From Chubby Checker
to the Beatles

As the 1960s dawned and the payola scandal faded into history, *American Bandstand* did not miss a beat. Nor did Dick Clark, for whom the good times rolled once again. But although the influence of *Bandstand* was about to reach worldwide proportions, its role as a shaper of pop culture through its music and performers, as well as by the dancing that the music inspired, could not continue indefinitely. In fact, not long after Clark's afternoon dance show reached its zenith, events beyond his control began to come into play that caused it to fall from its pinnacle. But not before Clark and *American Bandstand* affected the entire globe.

Although *American Bandstand* did not necessarily invent the dances it featured, the show played a key role in bringing them to the masses. As Chubby Checker has said, "I may have started the whole nation twisting, but I couldn't have done it without Dick Clark and *American Bandstand*."[1]

Popular social dancing in the twentieth century had traditionally served as the great equalizer, enabling Americans separated at home and in the workplace by class, income, and ethnic boundaries to momentarily slip those reins of constraint. As network television's first dance show, *American Bandstand* had a profound impact on that recreational activity, promoting popular dance by projecting it into America's living rooms and creating an awareness among teenagers that they comprised a social group that cut across society's traditional class structure.

Since the turn of the century, each decade has given rise to its own dance crazes. Beginning in 1957, such fads were abetted by *American Bandstand*'s immensely popular dance competitions, which afforded the studio regulars a chance to strut their stuff as they entertained home viewers. The amount of mail generated by these contests also provided ABC executives and television advertisers with an instant barometer of the show's popularity. *American Bandstand*'s initial dance competition drew a response of almost 750,000 letters, and after just several months on national TV it was noted that Dick Clark had "set in motion an unbelievable nationwide dance revival." Within a year's time, *American Bandstand*'s dance contests elicited a million letters each. Since dancing was also a great motivator for teenagers to purchase phonograph records, Clark, through his promotion of new dance crazes, managed to ingratiate himself to record manufacturers and distributors. As the owner of one independent label put it in 1958, Clark's one-man revival of at-home dancing was "one of the greatest things that has happened to this business in years."[2]

But while *American Bandstand*'s dance contests developed into one of the show's more popular aspects, they proved to be a double-edged sword for Clark and for ABC. Historically, moralistic members of America's older generations had imposed taboos on popular dancing. During the 1950s, when the advent of rock 'n' roll enabled blacks and whites to breech theretofore impenetrable color barriers, the injection of the race factor heightened those taboos. (One need only recall the Frankie Lymon incident on Alan Freed's national TV show in 1957 to gauge the emotional hysteria evoked by the fraternization of the black and white races through dancing.)

Spawned in an era stifled by sexual repression and racked by the beginnings of profound and painful social change, *American Bandstand* diminished dancing's sex issue by adopting an unwritten policy that slow and fast records played on the show be alternated, all the better to pry apart couples wanting to "cop a feel" in front of the cameras. Clark's show circumvented the race issue by catering to a minimal number of blacks, and, if the allegations of some are to be believed, affording them minimal, if any, exposure on camera.

Bandstand's dance promotions began during the Bob Horn era, in 1953, when the show played a vital role in generating the bunny hop dance craze. But the bunny hop was anomalous in that the fad was created by white adults, when, historically, America's dance crazes were originated by blacks and later coopted by whites—a pattern that was followed by *American Bandstand*.

Although the show's core of white dancers introduced new steps on TV that they had purportedly devised, by and large those steps originated in Philadelphia's black communities. What *Bandstand*, and later *American Bandstand*, actually did was to act as a filter to make those black dances acceptable to white society. And therein lay the rub. Inevitably, whenever black popular dances did permeate white society they were vilified as being indecent or immoral (a pattern not necessarily racist in origin; Americans in the 1700s decried the European waltz as being vulgar), and because *American Bandstand* played such a vital role in popularizing such dances, the show left itself vulnerable to attack. Unless, of course, the black dances it displayed could be rendered acceptable to society's moral guardians.

The key to such acceptability was the elimination of the fluid hip movement traditionally associated with black popular dance. Such movement was brought to prominence with the Lindy Hop, which originated in Harlem in 1928 and was named for aviator Charles Lindbergh's solo flight across the Atlantic the previous year. When whites danced the Lindy Hop—or "jitterbug"—they generally did so with European decorum: body erect, moving only the shoulders and feet, emphasizing a jerky and staccato up-and-down movement rather than the smooth and effortless horizontal hip movement of the original dance. Veteran rhythm and blues singer Hank Ballard pointed out that when white teens of the 1950s tried to emulate blacks, "they had a way of dancin' where they didn't move their hips, especially on *Bandstand* and those type of shows. And if you dance without movin' your hips it just ain't happenin'!"[3]

It simply was not allowed to happen in white America during the 1950s, a fact evinced by the storm of controversy whipped up by Elvis ("the pelvis") Presley, a brouhaha due as much to the singer's suggestive hip gyrations as it was to the music he sang.

As America's leading proponent of popular dance, Dick Clark's task was to excise the controversial body movements from the black-inspired dances introduced on *Bandstand*. As often happened, a studio regular on the show would discover a new dance, bring it to Clark, "and if Dick liked it and it was approved, he would put you in the spotlight dance," recalled Jimmy Peatross, a dancer on Clark's show during the late 1950s. Chances were, those new dances originated in black neighborhoods before being "discovered" by white teenagers, many of Italian descent, who attended Philadelphia's integrated inner city high schools.

"That's absolutely correct," said Clark. "Black kids always found [the latest dances] and we've always pointed that out."

The evidence suggests otherwise. *American Bandstand* regulars did pass off black-inspired dances as their own creations. In doing so, most of them did not think they were stealing from their black counterparts. "But we were," said Joe Fusco, a regular dancer on Clark's show who admitted that it "wasn't fair, really, when you think about it," that whites received all the credit for originating the dances featured on *American Bandstand*.

In 1959, Jimmy Peatross and dance partner Joan Buck (Kiene) introduced

Clark's national audience to the strand, a dance they claimed as their own, despite having learned it from blacks with whom they attended high school. Years later, Peatross claimed that when he and Kiene demonstrated the strand on *American Bandstand* they had been forced to say they made the dance up but "weren't allowed to say that black people taught us."

In 1994, Clark termed Peatross's charge "fallacious" and exclaimed: "That never happened!"

Joan Buck Kiene agreed with Clark, claiming the *Bandstand* host had simply caught the couple by surprise that afternoon when he asked them where they had learned the strand, and that she and Peatross "didn't really want to say" that blacks taught them the dance.[4]

With or without encouragement, whites did take credit for originating *Bandstand*'s dances, while young America watched and danced with enthusiasm, oblivious to the debt of gratitude owed the black community. "I mean, rock 'n' roll was their music, really, yet they weren't allowed to make good on it themselves for the longest time," recalled Bunny Gibson, another of *Bandstand*'s regular dancers from that era. "I owe a lot to those black kids back then."[5]

Not only were viewers of *American Bandstand* unaware that many of the dances featured on the program had been originated by blacks, they also did not know that the show's host stood to gain financially from a number of those dances. Although Dick Clark did not have a financial stake in every dance record he promoted on *American Bandstand*, his ownership of a particular song did not hurt its chances of success.

Two of the earliest dances promoted by Clark on *American Bandstand* were the bop and the chalypso. Although both originated during the time *Bandstand* was only a local show, Clark managed to parlay them, and his forthcoming national exposure on *American Bandstand*, into entertainment for his viewers and riches for himself. As the show's host pointed out, new dances were almost always "tied closely with hit records," and no one was in a more advantageous spot than he to capitalize on that fact.[6]

The bop, in which partners faced each other, jumped up and down, and ground their heels into the floor when they landed, was allegedly brought to Philadelphia by a Southern California couple who visited Clark's show during the summer of 1957. At Clark's urging, the Californians taught the dance to the *Bandstand* regulars. The bop, of course, begat "At the Hop," which soon became Clark's most lucrative song copyright (see Appendix II).

Clark and Tony Mammarella came up with the name "chalypso" after observing *Bandstand* regulars doing a dance that combined the cha-cha and steps done to calypso tunes. One of the most popular chalypso records was

Billy and Lillie's "La De Dah," a song Clark and Mammarella issued on their own Swan record label. After "La De Dah" became a hit early in 1958, Clark "commissioned" writers Frank Slay and Bob Crewe "to come up with a similar tune," which they called "Lucky Ladybug."[7] Because both songs were hits, and both were used by Clark for his *Bandstand* dance contests, he was able to play them daily, for weeks on end.

The stroll was reminiscent of the Virginia reel, but performed with a calculated urban cool by lines of boys and girls who faced each other and danced in unison from side to side as couples took turns sashaying down the aisle between them. The stroll was inspired by Chuck Willis's 1957 hit, "C. C. Rider," and became extremely popular on *Bandstand*. But no disc jockey could play any record indefinitely, including Dick Clark, who recognized that in order for the stroll to remain popular it would need a new dance floor anthem.

Never short of contacts in the pop music business, Clark approached his good friend Nat Goodman, manager of the singing group the Diamonds, for help. When the Diamonds made one of their numerous promotional appearances on *American Bandstand* Clark told his buddy about the new dance the youngsters were doing to "C.C. Rider," and then remarked: "If we could have another stroll-type record, you'd have yourself an automatic hit." When Goodman and the Diamonds returned to *American Bandstand* to promote their next release, it was no coincidence that the song was called "The Stroll" (purportedly cowritten by a thirteen-year-old who was inspired by watching the dance performed on Clark's show).[8] "We stick it on the air and it's a smash," recalled Clark.[9] "The Stroll" went on to reach number four on *Billboard*'s Top 100.

Whether it was pure coincidence or a stroke of business acumen, the song copyright to the Diamonds' follow-up hit, "The High Sign," was given to Clark by Goodman. Published by Sea-Lark Music, "High Sign" became a top forty hit that spring.

Besides bringing Clark a measure of financial reward, *American Bandstand*'s promotion of popular dance brought home viewer participation in a television show to new heights. Dance fads arrived and departed more rapidly than ever before, as teenagers and young housewives no longer had to leave the friendly confines of their homes in order to learn the latest trendy steps. The new dances were there for the taking in every home that contained a TV set, and a willing partner was as near as the refrigerator door and its handle (ideal for practicing the Lindy Hop's pushes, pulls, and twirls). Little did they suspect that partners were soon to become things of the past.

The 1960s ushered in the era of solo, or open, dancing in which partners never touched as they gyrated in dances such as the mashed potatoes, the watusi, the swim, the monkey, and the pony. It began with the twist, a craze spawned by the combined forces of Dick Clark, *American Bandstand*, and a South Philly singer who went by the name of Chubby Checker, which cut across generational, racial, and class barriers to forever change how the world danced. As Checker pointed out, before he came along to launch the twist mania, "no one danced apart, except for those line dances like the stroll."[10]

Because of his extensive exposure on Clark's TV shows, Checker is commonly thought of as the originator of the twist, but by the time 1960 rolled around there was really nothing new about the dance—including its name. According to Marshall and Jean Stearns, authors of *Jazz Dance*, a pelvic dance motion called the "twist" was transported from Africa to America during the slave era. Likewise, the use of the word "twist" in popular song titles dates back to at least the 1840s ("Grape Vine Twist"). The song "Messin' Around," written in 1912 by black composer Perry Bradford, described a new dance in which the participants were instructed to place their hands on their hips, bend their backs, and "stand in one spot nice and tight, and twist around, twist around with all your might." Within a year's time another black-composed song, "Ballin' the Jack," which made the same "twist around with all of your might" reference, instigated a national dance craze.[11] (Chubby Checker recorded his own version of "Ballin' the Jack" in 1962.) Although "Ballin' the Jack" was not the first instance in which white Americans appropriated black dance steps, it was the first time such usurpation reached national proportions. In the 1920s, song titles with "twist" in them began to occur on a regular basis.

Rhythm and blues veteran Hank Ballard claims to have written "The Twist," but what he actually did was modify and embellish a song that had been given to him by the Sensational Nightingales, a gospel group who had no use for the secular number. Ballard then set the reworked lyrics of "The Twist" to the melody of "What'cha Gonna Do?" a hit for Clyde McPhatter and the Drifters in 1955, and had himself listed as the song's sole author. Ballard and the Midnighters recorded "The Twist" for King Records in November 1958, and the song was subsequently issued as the B-side of "Teardrops on Your Letter." Then, as "Teardrops on Your Letter" proceded to check in at a disappointing number eighty-seven on *Billboard*'s Hot 100 (as the chart was renamed in 1958) in the spring of 1959, black teenagers began to conjure up torso-twisting, hip-thrusting movements as they danced to the flip side. "The Twist" proved so popular at black record hops that it became an underground phenomenon and briefly appeared on *Billboard*'s rhythm and blues chart. How Dick Clark learned of the dance remains in dispute, but one thing is certain—his long arm was involved in determining the well-known outcome of the "twist" saga.

Clark claimed in his autobiography that it was during a *Bandstand* show in the summer of 1960 that he noticed a black couple doing a dance, "revolving their hips in quick, half-circle jerks, so their pelvic regions were heaving in time to the music." As the white teens watched in fascination, a few tried to imitate the dance. "Tony! For God's sake, keep the cameras off that couple!" Clark said he exclaimed to Tony Mammarella, his show's producer. He then asked the couple what they were doing and they told him it was the twist.

Clark said he then called Bernie Lowe at Cameo Records and told him that a dance being done to an old Hank Ballard record "looks like it'll catch on," and asked Lowe to record a new version of "The Twist" that could be used to promote the dance craze on *American Bandstand*.

There are two problems with this scenario. First, Tony Mammarella had already been disassociated from *American Bandstand* for over half a year by the summer of 1960. Second, by that time, Cameo's version of "The Twist" had already been released on Parkway, a subsidiary label.[12]

When questioned in 1994 about how he came upon the twist, Clark stuck to his guns, essentially repeating the aforementioned story, this time without a mention of Mammarella. It was "very simple," he said. "Kids were doing the twist in the studio—black kids, then white kids. I asked them what it was. They said it was the twist."

Clark's self-serving account aside, most likely it was fellow TV disc jockey Buddy Deane and singer Freddy Cannon who were responsible for sending the landmark dance Clark's way. According to musicologist Jim Dawson, the twist, after surfacing at a Hank Ballard performance at Baltimore's Royal Theatre in 1959, then made its way onto Deane's Baltimore TV show, where the host was quick to notice the enthusiasm it generated among the dancers.

Shortly thereafter, in November, Swan Records' Bernie Binnick accompanied Freddy Cannon to Baltimore to promote his latest release, "Way Down Yonder in New Orleans," on Deane's TV show. After Cannon lip-synched his record, Deane asked Binnick to observe how the teenagers in the studio danced to a certain record. He then played "The Twist."

Bernie Binnick was so intrigued he brought Hank Ballard's record back to Philadelphia with him and played "The Twist" for Clark. "I can't play that, it's too black," Clark allegedly replied, according to Cannon, who maintains he was present when Clark spoke those words. "Give it to Freddy here [to record] and we'll play it."[13]

Clark claimed in 1994 that he did not have "any recollection" of originally wanting Cannon to record "The Twist," and insisted it was not true. Kal Mann, however, maintained that Binnick and Swan were indeed given the first opportunity to re-record Ballard's song. Binnick purportedly declined Clark's suggestion to have Cannon record "The Twist" because "Way Down Yonder in New Orleans" (which was to become one of Cannon's biggest hits) was just beginning to break across the country and Swan—as did most other record companies of that era when they realized they had a hot record—intended to devote all of its resources to promoting it. One week later, the payola scandal erupted, and any talk of re-recording Ballard's song temporarily ceased. But "The Twist" would not go away.

The new dance craze continued to spread, and finally emerged on *American Bandstand* early in 1960, which is most likely when Clark first saw it performed. As author Jim Dawson wrote in *The Twist*, his history of that dance, Clark "saw a chance to promote 'The Twist' into a hit record, and he wanted control over its presentation."[14]

But while Clark envisioned the commercial possibilities in promoting "The Twist" on a national basis, he also recognized that to do so might incur major problems. Upon observing the suggestive hip movements of the twisters, Clark's initial thought was, "Oh boy, this is a little dangerous." He wondered if the dancers "were gonna be able to get away with this."

Most likely, Clark also wondered if *he* was going to be able to get away with it. He was able, of course, and then some. But only after eliminating the salacious Hank Ballard and the Midnighters from the picture. According to Ballard, the Midnighters' initial live act consisted of "Doing dirty shit on stage," including some members dropping their pants (which Ballard claims he did not do).[15] Not only had the group been arrested for giving lewd performances, several of their early recordings had been banned from the radio because of their double entendre lyrics.

Still mired in the payola scandal and fighting for his professional life, Clark, who was yet to testify in Washington, was in the midst of attempting to salvage the wholesome image he had labored so long and hard to cultivate and project. The last thing he was about to do was place himself in a position whereby he could be accused of promoting a dance as controversial as the twist, sung by a group with as bawdy a reputation as the Midnighters.

Sometime in the spring of 1960 Clark called Bernie Lowe and asked the Cameo-Parkway owner if he remembered Ballard's song. Lowe did, and Clark, knowing that the ex-musician "could turn [the song] sideways, or do whatever" to it, said to him, "I need another [version of 'The Twist']. . . . Come up with something." Lowe, however, expressed no interest in recording a song that another record company already had out on the market (King had recently re-released Ballard's record), particularly a song from which Lowe would receive no writing or publishing royalties.

But, unlike his boss, Kal Mann was interested. To keep a pulse on the teenage market, and to perhaps come up with an idea or two for a song in the process, Mann made it a practice to frequent local record hops. While doing so he observed blacks doing the twist, but it was not until Mann noticed whites beginning to pick up on the dance that he thought the time might be right for its exploitation. So it was that when Kal Mann learned that Dick Clark wanted a new version of "The Twist" for *American Bandstand*, Cameo's premier tunesmith was ready to oblige.

Eighteen-year-old Ernest Evans, a black Cameo-Parkway recording artist whose career was on the rocks at the time, was chosen to make the recording. Evans, who, as a young boy had moved to Philadelphia from his native South Carolina, yearned to be a singer like his South Philadelphia High classmates Frankie Avalon and Fabian. He took a part-time job in a South Philadelphia poultry market owned by Henry Colt (Caltabiano), who subsequently introduced Evans to Bernie Lowe at Cameo Records. Cameo's Dave Appell recalled that, beginning in early 1959, Evans began to hang around the studio each day, begging for a recording contract, "until we finally gave him a shot." Bernie Lowe finally signed the would-be singer and proceeded to get lucky.

Evans, who liked to do impersonations of other singers, happened to be at the piano in the Cameo studio working on his Fats Domino imitation the evening Clark and his wife Barbara stopped by to finalize the arrangements for a musical Christmas card containing imitations of famous singers doing "Jingle Bells" that the couple planned to send to their friends. Although, in retrospect, it sounds like a callous remark—not to mention an opening unlikely to be directed to someone on a first meeting—all parties agree that Barbara Clark said to the rotund singer, "You're Chubby Checker, like Fats Domino," and the name stuck. The Clarks then recruited the would-be singer to record their musical greeting, after which, said Checker, Cameo "got interested" in him. According to the singer, his first record, "The Class," a novelty on which he did impersonations of Elvis Presley, Fats Domino, and David Seville's "Chipmunks," "was a clone" of the singing Christmas card he did for the Clarks.[16]

"The Class" became a good-sized hit that summer, but things did not go well for Checker after that. His next two releases flopped, and as 1960 began, the ever-sparing Lowe—who had been reluctant to sign Checker in the first place—was reportedly ready to drop the singer from his label.

It appears all the more curious then, that Cameo-Parkway selected an artist who had fallen from grace with his record company to record a song that the company's owner did not want to record in the first place. Checker was tabbed to make "The Twist" "because we liked the sound," said Dave Appell. "He came pretty close to the original record. We figured we'd do [Ballard's] record with a kid, and then we would at least be on the Clark show."

Jim Dawson called Cameo's choice of Checker to record "The Twist" "a stroke of genius," noting that Ballard, who looked even older than he was, projected the impression that "behind his infectious laugh, lurked danger," while the teenage Checker was "as cuddly and telegenic as a Teddy bear." [17] Dick Clark had his singer.

Kal Mann and Dave Appell recorded Checker's version of "The Twist," but Bernie Lowe still considered the song a throwaway, telling Clark, "I got it, but I think its the B-side." Lowe was more interested in pushing the flip side of the record, a double entendre novelty called "Toot," that, for obvious reasons, did not interest Clark in the least. "I don't care [about 'Toot']," he told Lowe. "I need 'The Twist.'"

Clark got what he needed. Checker's "The Twist," a virtual copy of Hank Ballard's rendition, was released on Cameo's subsidiary Parkway label in May 1960. Ballard was swimming in a Miami hotel pool when he heard the song on a local radio station that played popular records. "I said, 'Wow, I'm finally gettin' some white airplay, I'm gonna be a superstar!'" he recalled with a laugh as he related the incident. "And it was Chubby Checker." [18]

But before any *Bandstand* appearance was arranged for Checker, one remaining problem had to be overcome. The original dance done to Ballard's "The Twist" entailed a very suggestive horizontal hip movement, "and that was nasty in 1959, 1960," recalled Checker. [19] Clark not only needed a new version of "The Twist," he needed a simpler (and safer) dance step to offer America's teenagers.

Although Ballard claimed to have written the song after watching the Midnighters improvise a dance step onstage, group member Cal Green said their twist move was "just a wiggle" with both feet on the ground. . . . All that other stuff came later, with Chubby." [20] Checker claims to have originated the twist moves—which he likened to extinguishing a cigarette with both feet while drying off one's derriere with a towel—but such motions can be traced back to pelvic dance moves that were brought to America from the African Congo by slaves, and approximations of Checker's now-familiar moves had appeared in several films since the 1930s. [21] In fact, there was a time when Checker confessed: "I truly don't know who came up with it. . . ."

Wherever those famous moves came from, Checker was on the money when he stated, "That little formula literally changed this planet." [22] The secret was in the dance's simplicity—almost anyone could do it—and in its open dancing format, which was a godsend to a pop music industry still reeling from the payola scandal. Dancing close, body-to-body and chest-to-chest, was still looked upon with disfavor by many critics of rock 'n' roll. "If you were a parent at home watching your daughter, watching a guy all over a girl, you figure, 'Is this what my daughter does at the record hops?'" said disc jockey Hy Lit. "We needed open dancing."

Heavily promoted by Dick Clark on *American Bandstand*, Checker's record caught fire. Ironically, Ballard's version of "The Twist" had recently been reissued by his record company and beat Checker to *Billboard*'s Hot 100 chart by two weeks, but once Checker's version was released, there was no contest between the two. Sporting a jacket and tie, the "cuddly and telegenic" Checker introduced his "twist" dance steps to America on Clark's Saturday night show in August, just days after the song appeared on the *Billboard* chart. Kal Mann cited Cameo's "pipeline with Clark," as one reason why Checker's version of the song headed straight to the top of the charts while Ballard's original recording stalled at number twenty-eight.

By the time Checker performed "The Twist" on *American Bandstand* in late September, Clark had taken to describing the latest dance sensation as "a pretty frightening thing. . . sweeping the country." It suddenly became socially acceptable for dancers to move their hips in public, and, noted one of *Bandstand*'s regular dancers from that era, "The Twist" "changed the way that we danced from that point on."[23]

As popular as "The Twist" was in 1960, however, the dance craze did not reach worldwide proportions for another year. After the song ran its course, Checker scored big with songs about two other dances—"The Hucklebuck" and "Pony Time." With three hits to his credit, the singer believed his streak was at an end. "How lucky can you get?" he thought. Luckier, still, he was to discover.

In an effort to rekindle America's "twist" fires (and sell more records), Kal Mann wrote "Let's Twist Again (Like We Did Last Summer)" in the spring of 1961, after which the song became a huge hit and sparked a twist revival that dwarfed the previous year's craze. At the height of the renewed twist mania, Checker was scheduled to appear on *American Bandstand* for an entire week.

Since the twist phenomenon of 1961 was not confined to America, the ensuing worldwide interest in the dance prompted Bernie Lowe to reissue Checker's "The Twist" that fall. In doing so, the parsimonious Lowe—who was not adverse to saving money by using the same instrumental track to record more than one song—outdid himself. The song Lowe had not wanted to record in the first place became the first non-Christmas record to reach number one on the charts twice. By 1962, the entire world was caught up in twist mania, all because Dick Clark needed a twist record to play on *American Bandstand*!

For every famous performer, such as Chubby Checker, who has been helped by Clark's promotion, there are scores of lesser-known acts who have been given an assist by the *American Bandstand* host. A typical example is the Dreamlovers (Donald Hogan, Morris Gardner, James Dunn, Clifford Dunn, Tommy Ricks, and Cleveland Hammock, Jr.), a group out of Philadelphia's Northeast High who had backed Checker on "The Twist" and on "Let's Twist Again" but were not acknowledged on the record label. The Dreamlovers asked Checker to "at least squeeze our name in there on one of those days" he appeared on *American Bandstand*. But Checker never did mention them.

After "The Twist," the Dreamlovers became Cameo-Parkway's resident back-up group and recorded hits with Dee Dee Sharp, the Dovells, and other singers. But despite their considerable session work, the group did not see much money for their efforts. "You got a [royalty] check," recalled James Dunn, but "by the time they finished [deducting 'expenses'], you didn't have very much." As they continued to churn out background vocals for Checker and other Cameo artists the Dreamlovers remained anonymous, until they finally scored a hit of their own with "When We Get Married." "When We Get Married" and "Let's Twist Again" rode the charts simultaneously that summer, and when the Dreamlovers appeared on *American Bandstand* to perform their hit they finally received their due. Dick Clark told the nation: "This is the group that backed up Chubby Checker."[24]

Although Cameo and Swan Records had been run virtually as one and the same company, the payola investigations forced them to separate their activities. That is not to say the fraternizing between Clark and his music business friends and cronies ceased. Frank Slay, who became Swan's A&R director in 1961, recalled how he, Clark, Lowe, Bernie Binnick, Tony Mammarella, and Harry Finfer formed a group known as the "Mothers Club" (Music Operator's Talent Hunting Educational Research Society), which met monthly in South Philadelphia. Slay claimed that of all the "mothers" besides Clark, it was Lowe who fared the best, "picking up all the marbles" in town by "catering exclusively" to *American Bandstand*'s need for hot dance records.

The hits of Bobby Rydell served to put Cameo-Parkway on an even keel, after which Lowe's stunning success with Chubby Checker's dance records dictated the new direction the company would take in becoming the dominant label in Philadelphia, as well as one of the most successful independent record labels of the early 1960s. But not every Cameo artist who appeared on

Clark's show to promote his or her latest dance record enjoyed the experience. Rydell had a hit with a song called "The Fish" during the summer of 1961, and, despite the fact that he vehemently disliked the song, a *Bandstand* appearance during which the singer was supposed to demonstrate the dance to America was arranged. Rydell recalled with a laugh that although he did sing the song on Clark's show he did not demonstrate the dance, "because I didn't know what the hell 'The Fish' was all about!"

· · ·

As Clark promoted "The Fish" and other Cameo dance records, three events took place that affected his personal life as well as the future of *American Bandstand*. First of all, his storybook marriage came to an end. In May 1961, Barbara and Dick announced "with deep regret" that after trying to resolve their differences they had decided that it was best to seek a divorce.[25] Not only was his marital break-up painful for Clark on a personal level, it was also a blow to his professional image, following as it did his adept comeback from the payola scandal. A vital part of the image Clark projected to America included having as a conjugal partner a faithful and devoted homemaker who was content to subjugate her needs and desires to the lifestyle of the family breadwinner.

Atypical of most women of that era, Barbara Clark had initially forged her own career as a schoolteacher, but once she became pregnant and abandoned teaching to become the doting mother of America's model family, her life changed drastically. Barbara's new role was regularly attested to by press photographs of her at home, smiling broadly as she cared for young Dickie. When her famous husband found the time, he, too, appeared in such photographs, but aside from those publicity pictures, Barbara and Dick did not share much of a life together.

By the time *American Bandstand* originated, Clark was routinely putting in eighteen-hour days, six days a week. He became even busier after he undertook his Saturday night TV show, and often did not return home to Philadelphia from his weekly jaunt to New York until Sunday morning, thus forgoing a good portion of the only day available to spend with his family.

To hear Clark tell it, his work kept him so busy that the split came as a surprise. But rumors of disharmony in the Clark household—including an affair on Barbara's part—actually began to circulate prior to the Washington payola hearings. As late as 1992, Clark told Ralph Emery he had been "devastated" to learn that Barbara wanted out of their marriage, yet he could not have been totally surprised.[26] The rumoured romance was apparently not Barbara's first.

Clark referred to it in his 1976 autobiography as her "latest relationship," and revealed that he had known in late 1959 or early 1960 that his wife was seeing another man.[27]

If, indeed, Clark was devastated, so were his legion of fans. One-time *Bandstand* regular Kenny Rossi, who viewed Clark and his wife as the ideal couple (as did most of America), "was really shocked" by the impending divorce.[28] The press had a field day with the celebrated break-up, reporting that while Clark was "shattered" and "shocked," Barbara "already had her next husband picked out."[29]

Clark, it seems, had every right to be shattered, particularly after Barbara informed him that she was uncertain she loved him when they got married, that they probably never should have done so in the first place, and that she was in love with another man. Their friends steadfastly maintaining to the public that no third party was involved in the breakup, a divorce was granted in November 1961. That December, Barbara was wed to a cousin of Clark.[30]

Devastated as Clark may have been, it did not take him long to become active in the romance department. It was announced in April 1962 that he planned to marry twenty-five year-old Loretta Martin, a secretary for General Artists Corporation, whom he had met through that booking agency's handling of Clark's "Caravan" tours. Clark and Martin were wed later that month.

Shortly after he and Barbara separated, Clark had made it known that he planned to expand the video capabilities of his Philadelphia-based Dick Clark Productions, and ABC announced that the network intended to reduce *American Bandstand*'s daily airtime from ninety to sixty minutes. That the two moves came almost simultaneously was no coincidence.

Although ABC had taken great strides to become a full-time operation, it was not yet on a par with its rivals. The network's 120 affiliated stations were still no match for NBC or CBS, each of whom had over 200 affiliates. Furthermore, there existed a number of two-station markets in which NBC and CBS could guarantee a sponsor delivery of a show in prime time, while ABC often had to settle for a late-afternoon spot—if it could get the sponsor's message on the air at all. Finally, because ABC could not deliver as many markets as its competitors, it could not charge its advertisers as much as the other networks charged theirs.

Under intense pressure to deliver large audiences for its sponsors, ABC was thus forced to spend millions of dollars to outbid its rivals for sure attractions. Adding insult to injury, years after NBC and CBS had phased in color broadcasting, ABC continued to broadcast in black-and-white. ABC still regarded *American Bandstand* as a valuable property, but the network no longer believed it could devote ninety minutes each day to the ever-popular show.

ABC's slashing of *American Bandstand*'s air time did not set well with Clark, who, particularly after the demise of his Saturday evening program, regarded *Bandstand* as much more than a successful TV show. By that time, *American Bandstand* had become nothing less than the corporate flagship of Clark's vast business empire, and any reduction of the show's stature was inconsistent with his competitive nature and sharp business instincts.

Just how dearly Clark regarded his long-running TV show became evident after he appeared in his second movie, *The Young Doctors*, which premiered in September 1961. Clark, who more than held his own in the film with veteran actors Fredric March, Eddie Albert, and Ben Gazzara, received rave reviews. Praising his "terse, standout performance," the UPI noted that, if he chose, Clark could "just about write his own ticket in movies."

No way, said the *Bandstand* host. "I'll stick with the kids who watch my show. They are my prime source. They make possible everything else."[31] (Clark revealed in 1994 that although "everybody has that fantasy they're gonna be an actor, or be in a movie someday. . . . [I] had no eyes to become a full-time actor.")

Ironically, as ABC sought to reduce *American Bandstand*'s air time, the show reached its peak as a purveyor of dance and dance music. As such, Clark's program was instrumental in turning America into a true land of a thousand dances. Once Chubby Checker legitimized the open dancing gyrations of the twist, it became acceptable to take the style even further. After that, "people made up anything, as long as they were dancing apart and having a good time," recalled the singer.[32]

The dances were named for animals—the pony, the fly, the duck, the monkey—and they were named for specific motions—the mashed potatoes, the loco-motion, the hitch-hike, the limbo, the swim. As was the case with "The Twist," they sometimes evolved from specific songs, but often a dance step would evolve for which there was no particular tune. "When that happened," said Clark, "I immediately called to tell my friends in the record business."[33]

Frequently the call went to Kal Mann and Dave Appell at Cameo-Parkway. Clark recalled in 1994 that Mann and Appell, along with "a handful of studio musicians, would go in and create these little broom closet masterpieces, and . . . could whip up a song in a given moment. They just manufactured songs for Bernie [Lowe]." Appell said he and his songwriting partner recognized the widespread appeal catchy dance records held for Clark's audience and they "wrote with that in mind." Mann thought *American Bandstand* "was a good thing" as far as Cameo-Parkway's dance records went, but he pointed out that the songs he and Appell composed still had to be of hit caliber. "You can't shine up shit! Dick Clark could take a song that didn't have it and play it to death and it wouldn't sell." On the other hand, Mann conceded that *Bandstand* was a big plus because "you could have a great record, and if it never gets played it's not gonna sell."

On one occasion word got back to Cameo that some of the teens on *American Bandstand* had been spotted doing a dance called the mashed potatoes. Mann and Appell promptly knocked out a song called "Mashed Potato Time" and had it recorded by a young singer named Dee Dee Sharp.

Born in Philadelphia in 1945, Dione LaRue (who was dubbed Dee Dee Sharp by Mann and Appell) grew up steeped in gospel music and felt uncomfortable recording such a banal, secular song as "Mashed Potato Time." Listening to the playback of herself, she thought it was "the funniest-sounding song I have ever heard in my entire life." A song about mashed potatoes, mused Sharp. "Are you kidding me?"

No one, least of all Bernie Lowe, was kidding. As "Mashed Potato Time" gathered momentum locally, he arranged for his latest discovery to promote the song on *American Bandstand*. But as Sharp prepped for her national television debut she faced one small problem. She did not know how to do the mashed potatoes dance.

In his promotion of any new dance, Clark selected *American Bandstand*'s best dancers, who then danced along with whatever artist made an appearance that particular day. It may have appeared to the viewers at home that Miss Sharp knew what she was doing, but the singer later revealed that during her performance she was "afraid of falling on [her] face. I'd do just enough to jump back out of the way, and then go back and do a little more, and then I'd jump back out of the way again."[34]

Despite her rudimentary dance lesson, Sharp's *Bandstand* appearance gave "Mashed Potato Time" a solid national kickoff. The next day the song skyrocketed onto *Billboard*'s Hot 100, where it reached the number two spot early in 1962 and precipitated a run of success for Sharp, during which she was cast as the first black female teen idol.

From 1961 through 1963 Cameo-Parkway sizzled. Bobby Rydell, Chubby Checker, the Dovells, the Orlons, and Dee Dee Sharp all turned out major hits with clocklike precision as the label averaged better than one hit single every month, tying for third in the United States in 1963 among companies producing hit single 45 rpm records.[35] *Bandstand*'s exposure of Cameo-Parkway records was a "tremendous" help, recalled Dave Appell. If a record "had it," then an airing on *Bandstand* "would bust it wide open."

Swan Records did not fare as well in the post-payola investigation era.

Frank Slay literally kept Swan afloat for Bernie Binnick and Tony Mammarella by producing Freddy Cannon records and leasing them to the label, but, ironically, one of Cannon's biggest hits for Swan proved to be a major embarrassment for ABC. The song was written by Chuck Barris, the network's designated payola watchdog, whose primary function, said Ted Fetter, had been to make certain "there was no criticism of the Dick Clark show."

Unknown to the powers at ABC, Barris was a would-be songwriter who had high hopes of selling a number he had written about, of all things, an amusement park. "But there was one small problem," explained Fetter, laughing as he recalled the incident. Following the payola investigations, ABC instituted a policy whereby any creative property (such as a song) developed by an employee of the network became the property of the network unless the writer obtained permission from ABC to peddle it elsewhere. In compliance with the edict, Barris brought the song to Fetter and told his boss he had "a chance to have it published."

Thinking the odds of Barris's amusement park song becoming a hit "were one in a million," Fetter told him he could take it wherever he thought he could sell it. With that, Barris took the tune straight to Bernie Binnick at Swan, who passed it on to Frank Slay. Slay thought the song needed some reworking before he deemed it ready for the marketplace, however. "We all kinda held our heads, wondering what the hell we were going to do with it," he recalled, "but we worked it up and changed the title and spruced it up."

Much to ABC's chagrin, "Palisades Park" became a huge hit in 1962, with Cannon performing the popular number on *American Bandstand* that summer. In fact, "Palisades Park" became Swan's biggest-selling record to that time and enabled Barris to reap a considerable writer's royalty bonanza from it. "Here was the guy we sent to watch Dick Clark, and he was really playing the same game!" said Fetter. Fortunately, Barris had in writing ABC's clearance to sell the song on his own, which, said Fetter, "saved his neck!"

As *American Bandstand* prepared to celebrate its fifth anniversary, ABC announced that, beginning in October 1962, the show's network air time would be reduced to thirty minutes daily in order to create room on its schedule for a new program called *Discovery*. Clark, who during the past year had watched helplessly while *American Bandstand*'s network time was slashed by one-third, was said to be "resigned. . . , but not happy" about this latest cutback.[36] "Obviously I didn't accept it lying down," he recalled in 1994, "but I don't remember that I could do anything substantially that would change the picture."

Mollified somewhat by a new contract given to him by ABC—one which permitted him to participate in more outside activities than ever before—

Clark announced that he was "at peace with the network." He did his best to defend ABC's action, calling *Bandstand*'s cutback "a difficult decision" for the network, which "had to take the highest rated daytime show, and the highest money maker and chop it nearly in half." But Clark was unable to mask his true feelings. After initially stating he would "do the same thing" if he were running the network, he paused briefly. "No, I wouldn't," he continued. "I'd try very hard to find some other solution."

At the time of *American Bandstand*'s fifth anniversary, Clark made a stunning prediction about the future of what was still ABC-TV's top-rated daytime television show: "I think it can run for 30 years if people at the network think enough of it to handle it properly. Nothing really changes, except, like people, it adds lines in the face, gains weight, loses hair. It's a program that can adjust itself to the times, the music of the day and the tastes of the teens."[37]

Clark's prediction was outrageous for its time—for *any* time—but three decades later he chuckled as he recalled the occasion. "How many thousand years ago was that?" he wondered. "I was almost right!" (*American Bandstand* was televised for thirty-two years.) Clark could not recall ("It's been too long!") whether his brash words had been a reaction to the slashing of *American Bandstand*'s airtime. "Probably it was the little jab at the [ABC] bosses, saying 'Hey, you're not making the right move!'"

Clark's outlandish, yet prophetic, words aside, the reduction of *Bandstand*'s air time marked the beginning of the show's inexorable decline as the nation's paramount shaper of teenage music, dance, and mores. Another significant change in that direction took place early in 1963, when, in order to free himself for other business activities, Clark began taping all five afternoon shows for the upcoming week on the preceding Saturday. Having already lost one-third of its daily air time, *American Bandstand* now lost much of its immediacy and spontaneity.

But as the show's status and influence began to wane, Clark's entertainment empire continued to expand. *Variety* dubbed him "the busy bee of the broadcasting biz" and noted that he had bounced back from the payola scandal, "with sundry other business ventures."[38] One thing in Clark's favor was that his new ABC contract freed him from the exclusivity in nighttime television that the network had previously commanded. Now able to expand his evening activities, Clark planned several nighttime TV specials and another daytime TV show that targeted the large and ever-expanding body of ex-*Bandstand* viewers who had outgrown that show. ABC also granted Clark permission to tape a radio show for national syndication, which he began to do in 1963.

Clark also cranked his acting career up another notch, starring in a TV pilot called *Kincaid*, in which he played the tailor-made role of a social work-er assigned to work with youngsters. It was said that if ABC accepted *Kincaid* (which was spun off of the network's new *Stoney Burke* show) as a series, Clark planned to move his base of operations to California. This was perhaps the first mention of the possible departure of one of Philadelphia's most famous citizens, and a somewhat surprising revelation at that. As recently as the sum-mer of 1961, Clark had made clear that *American Bandstand* owner WFIL "had no intention of letting [the show] go."[39]

The announcement of Clark's projected *Kincaid* series, along with talk of a possible move to California, gave rise to speculation regarding *American Bandstand*'s future. In an attestation to Clark's ironclad association with the show it was reported in *Variety* that no matter where *American Bandstand* originated, "there's no question about him continuing this series for as long as Triangle wants."[40]

Any move to California apparently became moot when, after *Stoney Burke* lasted only one season, ABC scrapped plans for the *Kincaid* series. Still and all, *American Bandstand* was about to undergo another drastic change. Six years after it began, the show's run as a daily TV outing came to an end. In August 1963, ABC moved *Bandstand* from weekdays to Saturday afternoons —ostensibly because five shows a week "seemed too demanding to its star, who wanted to devote more time to other phases of show business."[41] It was the network's contention that the taping of all five of Clark's weekly *Band-stands* on Saturday was a backbreaking assignment to everyone involved.

In obvious disagreement with ABC's assessment of the situation, Clark said he was willing to attempt the grueling schedule, and that *Bandstand*'s consignment to Saturday afternoon "was ABC's decision, certainly not mine. My guess is that the station managers wearied of the format and thought that they could put something else on that would prosper. The truth of it is that they lost the time period."[42]

In 1990, reassessing ABC's decision to broadcast *Bandstand* on a weekly basis, Clark attributed the cutback to affiliated stations that "got greedy and took the time back to put their own material on where they got 100 percent of the revenue. . . . As two or three stations grab it off, you get less clearance, therefore you get less ratings, and it's an endless cycle. You eventually get cancelled."[43]

Although Clark was troubled over *Bandstand*'s new status as a weekly show, ABC was clearly comfortable with the change. The network's daytime advertising sales were running 13 per cent ahead of 1962, and Clark's now weekly show continued to pick up new sponsorship.[44] (To fill *American Band-stand*'s vacant 3:30–4:30 afternoon time period, WFIL-TV broadcast *Major*

Adams — Trailmaster, re-runs of the long-running *Wagon Train* series that continued to be broadcast in prime-time by ABC.)

Saturday *Bandstand* retained the proven format of the now defunct weekday show, but sustained a crucial loss of spontaneity as a result of being taped instead of shown live. *American Bandstand's* relegation to a weekly schedule stripped it of much of its power as a potential hit song exposer. One-time Cameo-Parkway promo man Steve Harris pointed out that in the past, when he took a new release to a radio station and told the program director that Dick Clark would be playing the record every day, the program director would pay heed, giving that particular record "a little bit of an edge." But with *Bandstand* now seen only once a week, the opportunity to gain that edge no longer existed.

A striking example of how much of an edge was lost occurred not long after *American Bandstand* was consigned to Saturdays. One day, as Tony Mammarella and Bernie Binnick struggled to keep Swan Records competitive during the summer of 1963, Binnick approached Clark with a record whose American rights he had recently acquired while on vacation in England. "What do you think?" he asked.

Clark thought it sounded like "Buddy Holly and the Crickets and Chuck Berry and a lot of other early American songs sort of mixed together." He told Binnick he "didn't think a great deal of it."

"Well," said Binnick, "they have this different look."

Glancing at a picture of the group, Clark noticed their unusually long hair. "You're absolutely insane," he told Binnick. "It'll never fly.'" [45]

The group was the Beatles, and the song was "She Loves You," a huge hit in England that was on the verge of becoming the largest-selling record ever in that country. But a stateside indifference to the Beatles caused Capitol Records, the American arm of EMI, the group's English record label, to forego releasing any Beatles records. Instead, EMI leased the rights to the group's recordings to several small American labels, which is how Bernie Binnick came to secure the American rights to "She Loves You." Frank Slay surmised that Binnick was able to do so because EMI "probably saw the Dick Clark connection . . . [although they] didn't realize it was coming to an end."

As America and Dick Clark remained unmoved by English rock 'n' roll, Binnick pleaded with his friend and former business associate to at least play "She Loves You" on *Bandstand's* "Rate-A-Record." [46] Clark obliged, but said the song "didn't fare that well. It got in the low seventies (seventy-one out of a possible ninety-eight), which is passing." "She Loves You" promptly met the same fate as other Beatles' records issued in the States earlier that year. Disc jockeys would not even play it on the air.

Months passed. In December 1963, Binnick received a call from Beatles' manager Brian Epstein—in New York to arrange an American television appearance for his group—who wanted to know about the American status of "She Loves You." Stuck with most of the copies of "She Loves You" that he originally had pressed, Binnick told Epstein, "It was a stiff."

Epstein admonished him that "She Loves You" was on the brink of becoming a huge hit in the States. "I just signed a deal, the Beatles are coming to America."

Harkening back to *American Bandstand*'s glory years as the country's premier hitbreaker, Binnick asked Epstein if the Beatles were going to appear on Clark's show. No, Epstein told him, they were booked on the *Ed Sullivan Show*. "Oh my God, you blew it," exclaimed the Swan executive. "Ed Sullivan is shit! Dick Clark is the game!"[47]

But Clark's was no longer the only game in town—nor the most important one. Having just returned from England that December, Jack Paar, who hosted a Friday evening variety program on NBC, marveled to his TV audience over the unbelievable Beatlemania phenomenon he had observed overseas. Paar then showed a film clip of the Beatles performing "She Loves You" as the English teens went hysterical. According to Binnick, "the record exploded the following Monday." Dead in the water half a year after its release on Swan, "She Loves You" rocketed to number one in America, eventually displacing "I Want To Hold Your Hand" at the top of the charts on March 21, 1964, and creating a windfall profit for Binnick and Tony Mammarella's struggling record company. In what proved to be a portentous change for Clark, *American Bandstand* had nothing to do with the song's success.

• • •

After Clark was named the host of a California-based television panel show called *The Object Is* in December 1963, rumors of his impending move from Philadelphia increased. The fact that Clark was ready to transplant *American Bandstand* to the West Coast—ostensibly because of his obligations to a third-rate TV game show—was indicative of *American Bandstand*'s decreasing importance in Clark's general scheme of things. Once the show was reduced to one day a week, Clark realized he "had to pursue a life in television, and Philadelphia was not the television center of the world."[48] The choice was simple; either New York or California.

In retrospect, Clark explained in 1994 that California was "where the action was. Everything was going on there. The surfing craze was high on everybody's list of things to do, whether you lived near water or not. Everybody wanted to have bleached-blonde straight hair, even if you were living in downtown Detroit. It was the thing to do, so I figured I'd better get out here."

WFIL-TV's Jack Steck said Clark's move was "inevitable" and had long been "suspected" by the station, since *Bandstand* was "far outgrowing" the TV facilities in Philadelphia. Steck likened WFIL's aging and cramped studio to "a pair of shoes that get too tight; you get bigger ones."

Although the decision to head west was Clark's, ABC was more than willing to go along with it. Ted Fetter said as far as the network was concerned, Clark could "do whatever he wanted to do" with *Bandstand.* "They agreed that he'd get more stars out there than he was getting in Philadelphia," said Steck. "He had to wait until they came to New York to get 'em to come over here to Philadelphia, where, if he was out on the coast, he'd have everything he needed. I think Dick was right in making the move."

As it was, Clark was no stranger to California's siren song. Bob Marcucci, who after the payola investigations struck out for Hollywood to make movie stars of Frankie Avalon and Fabian, tried to convince Clark that he, too, should be there. "Dick, this is the place, everything's gonna happen here!" he exclaimed to his friend in 1960. But Clark had chosen to remain in Philadelphia for the time being.

It was not until 1963 that Clark called Marcucci and told him he had decided to make the move. Since the house Clark had already contracted to have built near Los Angeles was not yet completed, Marcucci had the *Bandstand* host, his wife Loretta, and their son Duane move into the producer's sprawling home for the duration.

Once in California, Clark settled into a routine of hosting *The Object Is* five days a week and taping five *Bandstands* each Saturday. But just as he could not make a hit record out of a flop, Clark could not make a hit TV show out of a dog. Lambasted by critics as "a sparkless word-association contest," within a matter of months ABC replaced *The Object Is* with a new game show called *Missing Links*, of which Clark became the emcee.[49] ABC's programming move resulted in some ironic twists for Clark, who was put into the position of bumping his old friend and one-time Philadelphia neighbor Ed McMahon from the show's emcee chair (*Missing Links*, hosted by McMahon, had originated on NBC-TV). And having moved to California—ostensibly to host *The Object Is*—Clark was now forced to fly cross-country each week to tape five episodes of a New York-based show. But more important, for the first time since its inception, *American Bandstand* no longer served as Clark's primary video pulpit. That distinction now went to the popular daily *Missing Links*, which enabled Clark to establish himself as a credible TV game show host to the extent that in the 1970s he would enjoy an extended run as such.

. . .

On February 9, 1964, less than three months after the country was shaken to its core by the assassination of President John F. Kennedy, the Beatles were introduced to America on the *Ed Sullivan Show*. In one fell swoop the U.S. succumbed to Beatlemania, and the epicenter of the pop music business was wrenched from America's shores and planted firmly in England. During those cataclysmic times Clark's abandonment of Philadelphia for Hollywood went virtually unnoticed, a sure sign that people had begun to look elsewhere for the latest trends in music, fashion, and hipness. Clark and *American Bandstand* (which, coincidentally, made its initial California broadcast one day before the Beatles' landmark appearance on the Sullivan show) were never completely able to come to grips with the change. Nineteen sixty-four, in fact, would be the year in which Clark's epic production began its steady diminution on the way to becoming—save for its longevity—just another television show.

CHAPTER 12

Where the Action Is

By 1964, a watershed year distinguished by racial conflict, social unrest and an increasingly unpopular war in southeast Asia, America had already embarked upon an era of civil strife and cultural upheaval that was to have a profound effect on the country's society, including its popular music. *American Bandstand* lay directly in that path of change.

Vietnam was not yet a factor in the lives of most Americans, but U.S. troop strength in southeast Asia, as well as casualties, began to rise dramatically as the country's role in that conflict changed from an advisory capacity to one of direct combat.

The smoldering issue of civil rights had flared into crisis with increasing frequency ever since Rosa Parks was jailed for refusing to give up her seat to a white bus rider in Montgomery, Alabama in 1955. The movement had reached new heights in 1963 in Birmingham, Alabama, when protests against segregation and discrimination were carried out in the face of harsh police measures. The violence there touched off a chain of protests across the country that culminated in a march of two hundred thousand whites and blacks upon Washington, D.C., during which the Reverand Martin Luther King, Jr. gave his now legendary "I have a dream" speech.

The civil rights protests and marches led to landmark gains in 1964, when Congress passed the most sweeping civil rights act since the Civil War, legislation designed to protect voter rights and prohibit discrimination in public places. In addition, Congress enacted the Equal Opportunity Act, which created domestic programs for the poor and the disadvantaged, and it ratified the Twenty-Fourth Amendment to the Constitution, which outlawed the poll tax in federal elections.

Despite these significant gains for blacks, resistance to the federal legislation persisted, particularly in the Deep South, where new levels of violence and disorder were reached. In Mississippi, civil rights activists engaged in a summer long program of voter registration and education among the state's black population, during which three civil rights workers — two white and one black — were murdered. But by no means was domestic violence peculiar to the South. Riots and vandalism in the North — most sparked by resentment of police brutality — rocked black areas of several major cities, including New York and Philadelphia.

The civil rights struggle extended into virtually all facets of life, including television, where activists continued to push for the integration of Buddy Deane's Baltimore-based TV dance show. Television, in particular, was an area in which black progress remained tightly in check by America's white power structure. Ever since 1957, when popular singer Nat (King) Cole lost his weekly NBC network television show because of a limited audience and the reluctance of advertising agencies to obtain national sponsorship for it, no black entertainer had been chosen to headline a network TV program or to star in a regularly televised dramatic series.[1] (The first black to star in a regular dramatic series was comedian Bill Cosby, who, in a serious role, was teamed with Robert Culp in NBC's *I Spy* series in 1965. In 1966, versatile entertainer Sammy Davis, Jr. became the first black since Nat Cole to head-line a network TV program, NBC's *The Sammy Davis, Jr. Show*.)

Despite the protests of civil rights activists, management at the TV station that broadcast Deane's dance show would not yield to demands to integrate the program, offering instead to give blacks three or four days of their own with Deane each month. The protests continued into 1964, at which time the station cancelled Deane's program rather than allow blacks and whites to dance side by side.[2]

While the number of blacks in *American Bandstand*'s studio audience remained inconsequential during the show's days in Philadelphia, more blacks begin to appear on the show once it moved to California. And, unlike Deane's televised dance program, *American Bandstand* was quietly, albeit belatedly, integrated. But as of 1964, Clark's program still lacked a regular black dance couple.

It had not taken Clark long to sever his umbilical cord to Philadelphia. Although he took some of the veteran *Bandstand* crew with him when he went to California, including Jack Steck's son-in-law, who became the show's director, the elder Steck recalled that after six months on the West Coast, a "Hollywood manager" fired all the transplanted Philadelphians and "built their own organization."

It was also after Clark moved to California that he achieved ownership of

American Bandstand. His first step was to assume physical production of the show, after which he cut a deal with WFIL to lease the rights to it. That arrangement continued for years, until WFIL, no longer directly involved with the show, "sort of gave up" on it, said Clark in 1994. When WFIL did that, Clark was there to assume the rights.

By that time, *American Bandstand* bore little resemblance to the homespun dance show it had been in Philadelphia. For one, ABC's modern Hollywood TV facility (Studio 55), in which the show was taped, was a far cry from the prosaic Philadelphia facility that had spawned *Bandstand.* (Ironically, at the time Clark left Philadelphia, WFIL was in the process of constructing a modern radio and television communications center on the northern outskirts of that city.)

Gone from the show were the proverbial Philadelphia "regulars," who, from the beginning, had combined an air of innocence with their urban, ethnic mystique to become *Bandstand*'s surprise celebrities. The transplanted show's new breed of California regulars, who were never featured as prominently as were their predecessors and who were visible to the nation for only one hour each week, never developed the continuity of identity or the intimate bond that their predecessors in Philadelphia had forged with *Bandstand*'s home viewers. "You weren't seeing them five days a week," recalled Clark in 1994, so "the fan mail dropped off, the following changed."[3]

In addition, many of the jaded newcomers aspired to become professionals and thus viewed *American Bandstand* not as a form of enjoyment, but as a stepping stone to their own stardom. For his part, Clark thought California audiences were "hams . . . [who brandished a] "hey look at me' quality."[4] Lou Christie, who made guest appearances on *Bandstand* in Philadelphia and in California, characterized Clark's new audience as "slick . . . Hollywood. It was more impersonal."

Clark's show may have become more impersonal, but from a performer's standpoint it remained a top-notch venue on which to appear. Philadelphian Eddie Holman, who, in the mid-sixties, had a hit record at age nineteen with "This Can't Be True Girl" and journeyed to California to plug the song on *American Bandstand*, was impressed that when he arrived there, Clark was at the singer's dressing room to greet him. "The first thing you saw when you went in was a door with a big star on it, and your name in the middle of the star." Once inside the clean and tidy dressing room, Holman was treated to a lavish spread of food and drink, after which his make-up session and performance went off with clockwork precision. "It was just the way [Clark] did things," said Holman. "He did things first class."

ABC-TV's glitzy Hollywood studio symbolized the abandonment of

Bandstand's somber, urban northeast setting for California's sunny destiny, but the show was never to equal its previous level of glory. Most likely, Clark sensed as much, for while he later boasted that *Bandstand* achieved "its highest rating ever" in 1964, he also conceded that that mark might have been achieved simply because there were "just more young people around" by then. Clark also saw fit to take a shot at ABC, deriding *American Bandstand*'s new Saturday afternoon hour on that network as a "class Z" time slot.[5]

The changes in Clark's show were affirmed by its host when he made a return visit to Philadelphia during the summer of 1964. Stating that he liked California well enough, the transplanted Easterner added: "I miss my Philadelphia friends, neighbors and business associates."[6] Not as much as they missed him.

Left high and dry when Clark abandoned Philadelphia, the once-robust record companies located there felt the sting of his absence. When *Bandstand* originated from that city, the pop music world focused its eyes on 46th and Market Street, and the careers of many local recording artists and disc jockeys — as well as the fortunes of those local record labels — benefitted from the proximity of Clark's show. *Bandstand*'s presence in Philadelphia "made a lot of people very wealthy," said Hy Lit. "A lot of record companies very wealthy, too."

Once the show moved west, however, even Clark had to admit that Philadelphia had gone from being "the hub" of a rapidly developing industry to just "one of the spokes of a very big big big business."[7] Writer/musician Artie Singer, who tasted the big time after he recorded Danny and the Juniors' "At the Hop," was more succinct. "Once *Bandstand* left, it was all over," he declared.

It had been all over for Chancellor Records for some time. Frankie Avalon experienced his final chart hits for the label in 1962, the same year Fabian moved from Chancellor to Dot Records. In 1963, when Bob Marcucci realized that Chancellor "wasn't doing what it should do," he shut it down. Beginning in 1964, Avalon recorded for a string of labels, including United Artists and Reprise, but he did not return to the charts until 1976, when his disco version of "Venus" became a moderate hit. After leaving Chancellor, Fabian never had another hit record.

Despite issuing the Beatles' million-selling "She Loves You," Swan Records had fallen upon hard times and was being run on a shoestring budget by Bernie Binnick and Tony Mammarella. Frank Slay recalled that Swan stayed in business by issuing records "they got for twenty cents" or — even better — free of charge.

Binnick's original agreement to release "She Loves You" stateside stipulated that if Swan sold fifty thousand copies of the song the label would have the option on future Beatles' releases in America. But Swan lost that option when "She Loves You" failed to sell in 1963. "It was a terrible loss," said Dick Clark with a chuckle of irony in 1994, recalling how he asked Binnick years after the song's belated success why the label owner had not simply bought fifty thousand copies of the record himself, thus guaranteeing his option on future Beatles' releases.

"Because the record stiffed," Binnick replied in all sincerity. "It was a bomb!"

Slay, who had long recognized that Swan's bread had been buttered by the label's connection to Dick Clark, "knew it was all over" when *Bandstand* announced it was about to leave Philadelphia. Slay warned Binnick that Swan was "a small little store operating outside of a very big factory, and the factory's closing." Instilled with a false sense of confidence by the belated success of "She Loves You," Binnick downplayed the loss of *Bandstand* as a promotional venue. "I'm a record man," he told Slay. "I can do it!" But Slay, who knew "She Loves You"'s belated burst of popularity had merely given Swan a "reprieve" from its ultimate fate, opted to leave the company for Warner Brothers Records. With him went Swan's opportunity to issue future records by Freddy Cannon, the label's most successful artist, and by 1967 Swan was in the throes of bankruptcy.

Despite the unprosperous fates of Chancellor and Swan, the Philadelphia label that suffered greatest from *Bandstand*'s move to California was Cameo-Parkway. As hot as that record company was from 1961 to 1963 (Chubby Checker, Bobby Rydell, Dee Dee Sharp, the Dovells, the Orlons, and the Tymes had combined for eighteen top forty hits in 1963 alone), Cameo-Parkway turned just as cold in 1964, when only Checker mustered a top forty hit. The Beatles and their British compatriots certainly had a hand in Bernie Lowe's undoing, but there were factors peculiar to Cameo-Parkway that contributed greatly to the company's demise.

Foremost was the complacency borne of Lowe's vaunted pipeline to *American Bandstand*. It had simply become too easy for Lowe to take unproven local talent, have them record songs written by Kal Mann and Dave Appell (songs whose copyrights were owned by Mann, Appell, and Lowe), and then use *Bandstand* as an in-house publicity arm with which to promote the label's artists. This short-term exploitive approach resulted in hit records, but it did not allow for artistic development. Other recording companies, such as Berry Gordy's Motown, adopted a more farsighted tack. Producer Jerry Ross thought Motown was successful because Gordy "would surround himself with other producers and writers, and grow," whereas Lowe "did not allow himself to grow."

Bobby Rydell, one of Cameo-Parkway's most successful artists, thought the company "got a little too greedy," to the extent that if someone brought Cameo a very promising record, "if the publishing company did not say Lowe, Mann, and Appell they didn't want to have anything to do with it because it wasn't dollars in their pocket." It was precisely for that reason that Lowe reportedly turned down Little Eva's "Loco-Motion," which became a number one hit on another label in 1962. Nevertheless, while Rydell admitted he "may not have gotten the exact amount as far as record sales were concerned," he certainly made a good deal of money with Cameo.

After Bernie Lowe sold Cameo, Rydell was lured to Capitol Records by what he termed "a hell of a deal." But Capitol was also the home of the Beatles and the Beach Boys, and after having been treated as a favorite son by the tiny Cameo label, Rydell was regarded as less than a top priority by Capitol. They "had me R&B, they had me country and western, I [even] did one thing big band," said the singer, recalling how he was mishandled by the giant label.

Kal Mann was more philosophical about Cameo-Parkway's demise. "Nothin' lasts forever," he said. And besides, Lowe "didn't want to go the rest of his life" owning the firm. After losing almost a half-million dollars in 1964 on the company he had started in his basement some eight years earlier, the following year Lowe sold his controlling interest to a former *American Bandstand* production executive and a group of investors from Texas.[8] Neil Bogart was hired to run Cameo-Parkway, which was subsequently purchased by Allen Klein in 1967. (Klein, a ruthless and predatory figure, first made his mark in the early 1960s as an accountant for show business personalities. He managed Sam Cooke from 1963 until the singer's untimely death in 1964. In 1965, Klein became business adviser to the Rolling Stones. At the time he acquired Cameo-Parkway, Klein had his sights set on the Beatles. He became their business adviser in 1969. After reissuing many of Cameo-Parkway's hits on vinyl in the early 1980s, Klein, as of this writing, has steadfastly refused to reissue any of those tracks in the compact disc era.)

Not that Cameo-Parkway's new owners did not attempt to exploit the pipeline Bernie Lowe established to *American Bandstand*. When Eddie Holman plugged "This Can't Be True Girl" on Clark's show, the record had already been out for over half a year and sales had long since peaked. Determined not to miss out on the national promotion of Holman's follow-up record, "Don't Stop Now," which was already recorded but was not yet pressed up for distribution, Cameo-Parkway had Holman take a dub (a copy of the master recording) of the song with him to lip-synch on *American Bandstand*. By the time Holman returned to Philadelphia the company was shipping the record, but, due in part to the diminished impact of *American Bandstand* as a promotional vehicle, "Don't Stop Now" never caught on. (The best was yet to come for Holman, who had a million-selling hit with "Hey There Lonely Girl" in 1970.)

There were various reasons for the decline of *American Bandstand* as a forum on which recording artists sought to introduce their latest releases. In usurping the spotlight from Clark's show, Beatlemania had served as a wake-up call, not only for Clark, but for the entire pop music business. Something was taking place within the industry that none of its vaunted movers and shakers—Clark included—had predicted. Even though change was now at hand, few of them understood the magnitude of it, but once Beatlemania reared its head in the States, Clark wasted no time in hopping aboard the bandwagon. He orchestrated *Bandstand* salutes to the Fab Four in the form of transcribed interviews, a filmed appearance, and a postcard-writing contest with prizes of four Beatle hairbrushes autographed by each member of the group.

Still, Clark remained unable to develop a correct take on the Beatles, who had quickly become the most popular rock 'n' roll band in the world. After his initial failure to detect early signs of the British onslaught, followed by his rush to exploit the group, Clark attempted to jump one step ahead of the phenomenon, proclaiming in July 1964 (when five of the top ten U.S. singles were by British acts) that interest in the Beatles was "tapering off," that "the hip kids" were already calling Beatlemania "kid stuff." Clark did concede that the Beatles' success was unparalleled, but he believed "all that overexposure will shorten their existence."[9] True to that belief, Clark eschewed booking any English acts on his live "Caravan" tours in 1964. But even he could not hold back the British floodgates for long.

One particular problem Beatlemania posed for *American Bandstand* was that, after enjoying years as the only nationally televised rock 'n' roll pulpit, the show now faced stiff competition on the home screen, with Clark thrust into the unfamiliar role of playing catch-up to the nation's new crop of trendy, prime-time rock 'n' roll shows.

Because of Beatlemania, children of ages ten to thirteen, who had not previously figured importantly as record buyers, joined their fourteen to twenty-year-old counterparts who had traditionally sustained the pop music business. Furthermore, the musical tastes of a healthy percentage of adults were rekindled by the British Invasion; this attested to by the rash of *discothèques* that replaced what once were dignified supper clubs throughout America. This new widespread acceptance of rock 'n' roll caused the broadcasting networks to seek additional viewers by making available new televised rock 'n' roll programs.

Shindig was the first of them. The youthful, fast-paced show featured scads of professional dancers and was hosted by Jimmy O'Neill, who, ironically, had watched *American Bandstand* when he was a teenager and fantasized about someday playing rock 'n' roll records for others to dance to. After making its premier in September 1964 as a half-hour prime-time show, *Shindig* was soon expanded to one hour. (In its second season the show appeared two nights a week for thirty minutes each evening.) The fact that *Shindig* was touted to ABC by ex-*Bandstand* watchdog Chuck Barris and was broadcast by the same network Clark helped come of age only added insult to injury for him. (Not that Clark suffered financially. It was reported that he earned a million dollars in 1964.[10])

Rival NBC-TV did not miss a beat in meeting the competition head-on. *Hullabaloo* premiered in prime time in January 1965. Like "Shindig," NBC's new show featured its own professional go-go dancers and showcased current pop recording stars. In addition, it included a weekly segment featuring British acts taped in London.

Reacting to the public's embrace of *Shindig* and *Hullabaloo*—both of which quickly developed into television's preeminent rock 'n' roll shows— Clark, in an attempt to recapture some of *Bandstand*'s old viewers, announced plans for a new music show of his own called *Where the Action Is*, aimed at teenagers and people in their early twenties.

Where the Action Is debuted on WABC-TV in June 1965, and was thenceforth seen each weekday afternoon. Although the show starred American pop rockers Paul Revere and the Raiders, Clark proclaimed *Where The Action Is* to be "a wonderful vehicle for a lot of the English artists."[11] (He had recently dispatched Jack Hooke to London to film British acts for broadcast on *Action*.) Even so, assuming the title of *Where the Action Is* unintentionally implied that *American Bandstand* was no longer the premier scene of pop music activity, that most certainly was the case.

The explosion of televised pop music shows such as *Shindig* and *Hullaballoo* served to further dilute *Bandstand*'s power and prestige. When Lou Christie had the number one song in America early in 1966 with "Lightnin' Strikes," he did not, as he had done in prior years, head straight for *American Bandstand*. Instead, Christie took a day out of his schedule to tape multiple performances of "Lightnin' Strikes," which were then shown on nine different

TV programs. "By the summer I was being replayed on every bloody show!" exclaimed the singer. So were many other recording artists, who now viewed *American Bandstand* as just another TV appearance.

Beatlemania, meanwhile, reigned supreme. All but the very youngest of the more than forty-three million American youths born between 1947 and 1957 were smitten by anything even remotely British, and English recording artists alone sold more than $76 million worth of records in the U.S. in 1964. The Beatles alone put an astounding thirty songs on *Billboard*'s Hot 100 chart that year.

Despite the continued English juggernaut, black musical alternatives hastened by the spirit and energy of the civil rights movement and fired by two independent record companies—Motown of Detroit and Stax of Memphis—began to take shape.

American Bandstand and Motown's pre-Beatle relationship, and the manner in which that association changed during the British Invasion, offer telling evidence of how Clark's show began to lose its status as a pop music showcase. Time and again during Motown's early years the company used the show to project its black artists to a massive white audience. But once Beatlemania struck, that situation changed.

It was no coincidence that Motown, the creation of Detroit-born Berry Gordy, Jr. and the first label to successfully groom, package, and market the music of black artists to white America, became a major force in popular music in 1964, the year of major civil rights legislative victories. From the start, the growth of Motown, reflected the progress of that movement.

In 1958, Gordy, a follower of Martin Luther King, Jr.'s program of peaceful integration and a part-time songwriter who had already written several numbers for Jackie Wilson, cast an eye towards the pop music Mecca of Philadelphia and produced and recorded an "answer" record to the Silhouettes' *Bandstand*-driven hit, "Get a Job." Gordy leased "I Found a Job," sung by a group from Detroit called the Miracles, to George Goldner, but not even Goldner's considerable clout within the industry could get it played on *American Bandstand*—or anywhere else, for that matter.

Gordy, a former prizefighter who worked on Detroit's auto assembly line, took matters into his own hands, borrowing $700 and founding Motown Records in 1959. One of his early productions, Marv Johnson's "Come to Me," became a surprise top forty hit early that year, but after Johnson's next record flopped, Gordy—"an ambitious, hustling dude," in the eyes of rhythm and blues writer and critic Nelson George—arranged for Johnson to make his national TV debut on *American Bandstand*.[12] Just days after the singer introduced "You Got What It Takes" to America on Clark's show that fall, the song appeared on *Billboard*'s Hot 100, on its way to becoming a top ten hit.

Later in 1959, Gordy recorded the Miracles' "Bad Girl," which he leased to Chess Records. But when the song barely scratched *Billboard*'s Hot 100, Miracle member and friend Smokey Robinson prodded Gordy to issue future productions on Gordy's own Tamla label. Gordy did just that, but by December 1960, Tamla had nothing to show for itself but a dozen or so flops—including "Way Over There," the Miracles' first recording for the fledgling label.

Later that December, Gordy released the Miracles' "Shop Around"—whose lyrics consisted of a mother's words of warning to her son about choosing a mate wisely—which began to sell around Detroit and in other markets across the country. Perhaps recalling the boost Marv Johnson received from his appearance on *American Bandstand*, Gordy arranged for the Miracles to make their nationwide TV debut on Clark's show some three weeks after "Shop Around" appeared on *Billboard*'s Hot 100. The song went on to become a number two hit nationally and put Motown on the map as an important independent record company, but the Miracles subsided to the lower echelons of the sales charts as the undercapitalized Gordy struggled to keep his record company afloat.

Gordy released seventeen-year-old Mary Wells's gritty "Bye Bye Baby" on a new label he named Motown, but it took almost a year for the song to develop into a small hit. Focusing on his goal of reaching the massive white audience, when Gordy issued Wells's follow-up, "I Don't Want to Take a Chance," he heeded the advice of the song title and arranged for Wells to make her national television debut on *American Bandstand*. Lo and behold, "I Don't Want to Take a Chance" sold better than "Bye Bye Baby." Wells's third Motown release, "The One Who Really Loves You," lip-synched on Clark's show in the spring of 1962, became the first of her handful of top ten hits for Motown. Due in part to the young singer's performances on *American Bandstand* (each of her three top ten hits in 1962 was kicked off by an appearance on the show), Mary Wells became Motown's first recording star.

The national exposure that Mary Wells, Marv Johnson, and the Miracles received from Dick Clark enabled Gordy to secure a creative and a financial foothold in the pop music business. Having done so, however, Gordy began to look beyond *American Bandstand* to sustain Motown's success. It was with an unheralded black female vocal trio called the Primettes that the Motown mogul would soon reach the pop music pinnacle—and demonstrate *Bandstand*'s reduced role in Gordy's grand design.

After a name change from the Primettes to the Supremes, followed by two unheralded releases on Tamla in 1961, the group languished in the nether world of failed recording artists. Gordy moved the Supremes to his Motown label, but the group's next two releases barely scratched *Billboard*'s Hot 100 and their third failed to make that chart altogether. Then, late in 1963—on the eve of Beatlemania, of all times—the Supremes, who were now under the tutelage of Motown's crack songwriting/production team of Brian Holland, Lamont Dozier, and Eddie Holland, came up with their first top forty hit, "When the Lovelight Starts Shining Through His Eyes," driven by an infectuous Bo Diddley-like beat.

But Motown continued to run hot and cold. Gordy recorded another local group, the Temptations, on his eponymic Gordy label, but they proved to be a disappointment. He fared better with Martha Reeves (a former Motown secretary) and the Vandellas, who, in 1963, recorded the top ten hits "Heat Wave" and "Quicksand." Other than that, there was little cause for optimism. The Marvelettes were unable to match their early hits, Marvin Gaye had not yet attained a significant breakthrough, and the Miracles' records continued to be unpredictable. Motown's biggest chart success in 1963 was provided by a twelve year old blind harmonica player named Steveland Morris, who, as Little Stevie Wonder, provided Gordy with the chart-topping "Fingertips—Pt. 2."

There were those who believed Berry Gordy had taken his all-black record company as far as he could within the framework of America's resistant racial barriers. Although Gordy's Motortown Revue of recording artists (featuring the Supremes as the opening act) played to integrated audiences in the South, Gordy (who, wrote Nelson George, "used his blackness as a weapon as shrewdly as any civil rights leader,"[13]) was hip enough to keep the photographs of his black artists off of their own album covers, lest the records not be displayed in record shops in that section of the country.

In addition to the racial problem, Gordy had to overcome the one-two punch of the arrival of Beatlemania upon America's shores and the departure of Mary Wells to a rival record company. In an attempt to secure the mass market he so desperately sought, Gordy set out to polish the image of his Motown recording artists. He hired the former operator of a finishing and modeling school to instruct his performers on grooming and manners, and he employed choreographer Cholly Atkins, a well-known dancer in the 1930s and 1940s, to teach Motown's artists how to move gracefully on and off the stage. Gordy modified Motown's sound so that it gave prominence to echo-enhanced vocals that drew upon the call-and-response pattern of gospel music, and he anchored the finished product—intentionally devoid of any traditional blues and the trappings of negative drug and liquor connotations that came with that genre—with a pounding rhythm section. Uniting his recently-polished artists with his new musical sound, and employing a merchandising slogan that would have done Dick Clark proud, Gordy called his revamped Motown "The Sound of Young America."

From the start, it had been evident to Gordy that the quickest way to America's white record buyers was through Clark, and prior to 1964, the label owner used *American Bandstand* propitiously as a promotional venue for his artists. But, as evinced by his subsequent handling of the Supremes, Gordy was also hip enough to observe that the country's rush to embrace Beatlemania marked the beginning of a diminished *American Bandstand*.

In the spring of 1964, with Brenda Holloway's soulful Tamla ballad "Every Little Bit Hurts" a fast-rising hit, Gordy booked the singer on Dick Clark's "Caravan" stage tour. Since the new-look Supremes' latest record, "Where Did Our Love Go," had just been released, Gordy, eager to get the group in front of Clark's massive white audience, wanted them to appear on the "Caravan" along with Holloway. But Clark showed no interest in a group whose previous release, "Run, Run, Run," had only reached number ninety-three on *Billboard*'s Hot 100. It took a hard sell by Gordy to convince Clark to add the Supremes to the bottom of the "Caravan's" seventeen-act bill. And then a surprising thing occurred. As the tour commenced, "Where Did Our Love Go" began to move up the sales charts. In response, Clark began to move the Supremes higher on his "Caravan" billing (the original posters for the show, which gave the Supremes bottom billing, were torn up and new ones printed). By the end of the tour "Where Did Out Love Go" was the number one song in America.

The Supremes had undertaken Clark's "Caravan" as virtual unknowns and had come off the tour as stars. Berry Gordy was now ready to introduce the group to America via national television, but this time he did not look to *American Bandstand*. Instead, as Brian Epstein had done with the Beatles, Gordy headed for *The Ed Sullivan Show*. One reason for doing so was that Clark's show, which was now taped up to a month or more in advance of its broadcast date, had lost its immediacy, and thus its ability to instantly project hits in the mercurial world of pop music. Although Gordy did employ *American Bandstand* for the national TV debut of the Four Tops vocal group, 1964 was the year that Motown, as well as other record companies, began to rely increasingly on alternative network television shows and specials to promote their recording artists.

When *American Bandstand* lost its status as television's number one plug among recording artists and their record companies, Clark's show ceased to be the instant trendsetter it had been during its heyday. The sixties spawned a myriad of fashion trends, including go-go boots, tie-dyed shirts, Nehru jackets, bouffant hairdos, and wire-rimmed granny glasses, and five years earlier those fads most likely would have been instigated by *American Bandstand*. But when the Byrds' Roger McGuinn donned his trend-setting granny glasses for the group's national television debut in 1965, he did so on *The Ed Sullivan Show.*

Despite its diminished status, *American Bandstand*, as it had done for Motown, had a hand in putting Stax Records on the musical map—not so much by providing a performing venue for the label's recording artists, but by advocating the Stax sound, which came to be known as soul music. But while Clark's dance show became a mainstay for the soul music produced by Stax (and a myriad of other labels), for the first time in *American Bandstand*'s venerable history, the motives for its exposure of recorded music were transposed. Whereas, prior to the British Invasion, record companies more or less depended on Clark's show to publicize their artists and records, during the rapidly changing era of Beatlemania it was *American Bandstand* that came to rely on popular music as a drawing card to retain its audience.

While Motown proclaimed itself "Hitsville, U.S.A." and strove to capture the American mainstream, Stax—which was formed in Memphis in 1960 by two white owners whose building sign read "Soulville, U.S.A."—set its sights distinctly on the R&B market. Employing a mix of black and white musicians that resulted in a musical miscegenation with great appeal to blacks, Stax's music, much like Motown's, utilized gospel-like vocal lines that drew heavily on a call and response structure and featured a persistent rhythm section. But what came to be known as the "Memphis Sound" was characterized by spoken passages, repetitive phrases and a "down-home" style devoid of Motown's slickness.

Soul music was an outgrowth of rhythm and blues, but it also combined musical, political, and capitalistic measures to mirror the increasingly militant struggle of America's blacks to find their own identity. Due in part to the high tide of integrationist sentiment during that particular era, soul was able to withstand the British invasion and become as effective a marketing device during the sixties as rock 'n' roll was in the Fifties.

The social forces that precipitated the rise of soul also created a complex situation for *American Bandstand*. Since its inception, Clark's show had been produced in a homogeneous manner, catering to an audience that happened to be overwhelmingly white. But as blacks gained a new sense of pride, dignity, and individuality they became more interested in their own culture. Thus, halfway through the 1960s, *Bandstand* not only faced the loss of a significant portion of its mainstream audience to Beatlemania, it also confronted the challenge of catering to two distinct audiences—one black and one white.

Ironically, as President Lyndon Johnson's Great Society moved to bring blacks into the America's mainstream, more and more blacks did just the opposite. By 1965, heightened tensions, not only between blacks and whites, but among blacks who were at odds over how to deal with white racism, were obvious. Resistance to civil rights legislation persisted, especially in the South, while a pattern of escalating violence continued in the North. That summer thirty-four people died during rioting by blacks in the Watts section of Los Angeles—the highest total in almost fifty years—and a wary America heard the first ominous strains of "Get Whitey!" and "Burn, baby, burn!" As whites in America grew increasingly uneasy over black violence, the broad, substantial support previously enjoyed by the civil rights movement began to dissipate.

Nowhere was this growing division of black and white reflected more than in the country's pop music. The British Invasion, the emergence of Motown as a dominant record company, and the rise of soul music engendered the divergence of American popular music to a degree not seen since before the rock 'n' roll era had begun a decade earlier. Nineteen sixty-five was the year in which rock 'n' roll became for the most part music made by whites, while blacks saw it "as white boys' music that didn't reflect their musical taste or cultural experience," wrote Nelson George. "The ties between the music known as rock 'n' roll and its original black audience were being severed, and black America didn't seem to care." [14]

Confronted by this musical dichotomy, Dick Clark tried to be all things to all people. In an effort to attract a wider audience *American Bandstand* increasingly programmed soul music in 1965. And—perhaps not coincidentally—the show introduced its first black regular dance couple, Famous Hooks and June Strode, to home viewers.

Clark also moved to placate his white audience. With recordings by British artists holding nine of the top ten chart places in America that spring, the *Bandstand* host succumbed to the inevitable and booked the English group Herman's Hermits to appear on his "Caravan." It was not surprising that the group was led by the cuddly and innocuous teen idol-type Peter Noone, and even less astonishing that Clark assumed the stateside management of the Hermits, whose recording of "Mrs. Brown You've Got a Lovely Daughter" had recently been the number one song in America.

When Americans danced in 1965, they did so to British Invasion tunes and to the sound of Berry Gordy's Motown, as exemplified by the incredibly hot Temptations, Supremes, and Four Tops. Soul music joined Motown in the pop mainstream when Wilson Pickett's "In the Midnight Hour" and James Brown's "Papa's Got a Brand New Bag" hit the pop charts almost simultaneously that summer.

Reflecting the growing popularity of black pop, 35 percent of the guest artists appearing on *American Bandstand* in 1965 were soul or rhythm and blues singers—including Jackie Wilson, Marvin Gaye, Smokey Robinson and the Miracles, Gene Chandler, Jr. Walker and the All-Stars, the Four Tops, Jewel Akens, and Fontella Bass.[15] But the increasing exploitation of pop music elsewhere on television began to take its toll on the show's guest list. Along with the paucity of British stars appearing on *Bandstand* that year, conspicuously absent were the top-echelon acts Jay and the Americans, the Supremes, the Temptations, the Beach Boys, and the Four Seasons, all of whom, in an increasingly competitive business, chose to do their business elsewhere.

By 1966, the American concensus on civil rights had disappeared. Race relations continued to deteriorate. The movement, fired by younger, more militant leaders, entered a new phase punctuated by the slogans "Black Power" and "White Backlash." Martin Luther King, Jr. and his marchers were jeered and assaulted during a demonstration in Chicago, and the latest civil rights act, which would have banned discrimination in private housing, met defeat in Congress. Summer riots continued to escalate, as Atlanta and other cities fell victim to the conflagrations.

The problems of race and of war continued to preoccupy the U.S. in 1967, as Detroit became the scene of the worst rioting in the nation's history, which resulted in thirty-eight deaths there. The rate of black progress—too slow for blacks and too fast for whites—satisfied almost no one. Through it all, *American Bandstand* faced new challenges of its own, including the onset of the psychedelic era and the birth of "free-form" FM radio, both of which would help relegate Clark's show, once a proud creator of fads and fashion, to being an artifact of pop culture.

Not long after Clark relocated *Bandstand* to the Los Angeles area, music and fashion trend-setting also shifted to California. Not to Los Angeles, however, but north to San Francisco, where America's hippies dwelled. Predominantly white middle-class children who rejected the values and rewards of their parents and of society in general (ironically, the same values and rewards that blacks were struggling to obtain), the hippies strove for fun and enjoyment as they repudiated the affluent way of life in which making money was the object of life and work. Most hippies lived in Haight-Ashbury, a racially integrated neighborhood with a permissive atmosphere, which became a favorite haunt of college students, writers, and folk and jazz musicians.

In 1965, advocating the mind-altering drug LSD, Harvard's Dr. Timothy Leary implored the disenchanted younger generation to "tune in, turn on, and drop out." Which is exactly what many of them did. They also joined rock bands and lived in communal houses where they could jam loudly night and day while remaining relatively free of drug busts by the police. The age of psychedelia was under way.

The first Human Be-In, a free festival headlined by the Grateful Dead and the Jefferson Airplane, attracted twenty thousand "flower people" to San Francisco in 1967. That was followed by the Monteray Pop Festival in June, featuring the Buffalo Springfield, Eric Burdon and the Animals, the Byrds, Canned Heat, Country Joe and the Fish, Jimi Hendrix, the Jefferson Airplane (who, only weeks earlier, made their national TV debut on *Bandstand*), Janis Joplin, the Mamas and the Papas, Scott McKenzie, Otis Redding, and the Who. Monteray served as a prelude to San Francisco's fabled "Summer of Love," which was celebrated in song by McKenzie's "San Francisco (Be Sure To Wear Flowers In Your Hair)," the Beatles' "All You Need Is Love" (taken from their memorable "Sgt. Pepper's Lonely Hearts Club Band" album), and the Doors' "Light My Fire," as flower children from coast to coast packed up and took off to the hippie havens of California where they proceded to blow their minds on LSD.

As detrimental as the musical changes wrought by the psychedelic drug era were to *American Bandstand*, the decline of stylized dancing proved just as harmful. Whereas, during *Bandstand*'s early years, the particular coupling of certain dance partners had taken on soap opera proportions, partners now became irrelevant. Dancers shunned conformity and challenged acceptable social behavior as popular dance became rebellious, risky, and free-form. *Bandstand*'s dancers, some appearing high on drugs, simply moved to the music in any manner they felt. "It wasn't a dance era particularly," recalled Dick Clark in 1994. "Psychedelic music was all the rage . . . [and] it was real hard to dance to."

While Clark encountered psychedelia and the decline of stylized dancing, another development occurred that pushed *American Bandstand* further away from rock 'n' roll's cutting edge. From the start, *Bandstand* catered to the singles-buying, AM-oriented rock 'n' roll audience, but the Top Forty format adhered to by an increasing number of AM radio stations had proven to be a stifling influence on the spectrum of music to which audiences were exposed. During the mid-1960s, approximately 11,000 single records were released annually, but AM radio programmed from a list of only thirty singles each week.[16] To exacerbate the matter, most FM broadcasts simply duplicated the broadcasts of their AM sister stations. But in 1965, the FCC ruled that jointly-owned AM/FM stations in large markets had to program non-dupli-cated music for at least half of their airtime, and to comply, the more prof-itable AM broadcasters put their FM operations on a non-commercial basis, employing a stereo rock 'n' roll format.

At first hardly anyone listened. But there were those—chief among them Tom "Big Daddy" Donahue, the Philadelphia disc jockey fired by WIBG during the payola scandal, who had since taken refuge with San Francisco's KYA radio—who believed radio's future did not lie in the Top Forty. Don-ahue joined San Francisco's KMPX-FM in April 1967, and began to experi-ment with a myriad of musical forms, ultimately giving rise to what became known as alternative, free-form radio. (In recognition of this feat, Donahue was inducted into the Rock 'n' Roll Hall Of Fame in 1996.)

In creating the free-form FM radio format, which quickly gained favor with listeners everywhere, Donahue unwittingly drove another nail into the coffin of *Bandstand*'s hype and hipness. Alternative FM radio relied on stereo album tracks, whereas AM radio could not broadcast in stereo and would not alter its commercial-oriented, under-three-minute song selection. Donahue's format thus boosted album sales to new heights and put a significant dent in the sales of single records, thereby reducing the music industry clout of the singles-driven *Bandstand*. As the cutting edge of pop music shifted to coun-terculture album fare, *American Bandstand* appeared more "establishment" than ever, and an appearance on Clark's show was no longer automatically courted by the hottest white rock artists.

Furthermore, as record companies sought to sign artists with album sales potential, in a bid to render the music more relevant (and profitable), the industry shed the appellation "rock 'n' roll" in favor of the sobriquet "rock." Adding insult to *Bandstand*'s injuries, much of rock 'n' roll—or rock—began to focus upon social issues, topics theretofore anathema to Clark's inoffensive AM format.

Not that Clark sat idly by as the market shifted away from him. In order to make *American Bandstand* appear hip as possible he sometimes relied on his old Philadelphia connections to help recruit fashionable new talent. One such contact was producer Jerry Ross, who, in the mid-sixties, produced hits for Mercury Records by Bobby Hebb ("Sunny") and Philadelphia's James Barry Keefer, known to the public as "Keith" ("98.6").

In 1967, Mercury sent Ross to Chicago to audition a band called Mother Blues that the producer characterized as "flower people." Ross liked what he heard and signed them. With a style modeled after the Mamas and the Papas and a song (given to them by Ross) called "Sunday Will Never Be the Same," the group—now called Spanky and Our Gang—was an instantaneous smash. "And, of course, I brought 'em to *American Bandstand* and everybody loved 'em," said Ross, who was also instrumental in placing Jay and the Techniques on Clark's show. "If you had Dick's attention and his respect as a promotion man he would listen to new artists and give 'em exposure. So [getting artists on *American Bandstand*] was never a problem. All I had to do was make a phone call."

Clark also sought other ways in which to appeal to the singles-dominated AM radio audience, one result being *American Bandstand*'s embracement of sixties punk, or garage band, music. Punk rock, in which middle-American garage bands combined cheap instruments and odious attitudes to turn out brief but loud retro-sounding songs perfectly suited to slip between the commercials on AM radio, came about largely as a reaction to the British Invasion. Most of the Sixties punk bands were of the one-hit-wonder variety—if they were that lucky. *American Bandstand* welcomed them all, including the Blues Magoos, the Count Five, the Gentrys, the Kingsmen, the Knickerbockers, the Leaves, the Music Explosion, the Music Machine, ? and the Mysterians, the Syndicate of Sound, and the Shadows of Knight.

But as *Bandstand* tried desperately to remain in the pop music vanguard, rock's hippest bands came to regard it as being too square to be taken seriously. After the Jefferson Airplane, the first of the San Francisco groups to get national distribution and whose psychedelic impact was enormous, appeared on Clark's show to lip-synch their drug paen "White Rabbit," singer Grace Slick, who most likely performed in a chemically-induced state, professed to have no memory of the performance. Steve Harris, who worked as a promo man for Elektra Records after leaving Cameo-Parkway, said that when the Doors made their national TV debut on *Bandstand,* Clark wanted leather-clad "Lizard King" Jim Morrison to wear a tie. And when England's Pink Floyd lip-synched their latest release on *Bandstand*, Syd Barrett, the group's quirky leader, stood close-mouthed, refusing to move his lips when the cameras focused on him.

Like a protective parent, Clark personally took the hit for *Bandstand*'s growing irrelevance. Although one of network television's few remaining black-and-white programs (ABC did not colorize it until the "Summer of Love" of 1967), *American Bandstand* did not suffer greatly in the broadcast ratings, but Clark did admit in 1994 that the psychedelic era "just wasn't a rip-roaring party time for us." Too old to understand the drug culture, *Bandstand*'s host revealed that those years comprised "a difficult period" for him, "and it baffled [him] as to why people would do this to themselves."

Clark had "pretty well understood the music" up until then. But events beyond his control began to occur so quickly that he confessed to a reporter in

1967 that, "now I'm scared." Clark, who perceived the hippie scene as "a very thin minority [but] terribly influential," replaced *Where the Action Is* with *Happening '67* (which was to be updated as *Happening '68* and *Happening '69*) during the "Summer of Love." As difficult as conditions were for Clark, who now openly admitted he was "the fastest follower in the business," things were about to grow worse.[17]

If there was one particular year in which American society threatened to disintegrate, that year was 1968. Mired in the increasingly unpopular war in Vietnam, with any signs of a negotiated settlement dashed by the Communist-led Tet Offensive in January, President Johnson told the nation he would not seek reelection that fall. Weeks later, a white gunman assassinated Martin Luther King, Jr. in Memphis, igniting black rioting and violence in some 125 cities and causing more than thirty deaths and thousands of injuries and arrests.

Then Robert F. Kennedy—perhaps the only white politician with an enthusiastic black following—was murdered in Los Angeles in June. Over one hundred thousand blacks and whites marched together in Kennedy's processional, but many wondered if nonviolence itself was at an end as subsequent rioting left forty-six dead. More than fifty-five thousand troops were needed to quell the violence.

The Democratic Convention held in Chicago that summer symbolized the country's internal bleeding, as antiwar demonstrators in full view of the mass media were beaten mercilessly by police. That fall, Republican Richard Nixon, running on a "law and order" theme and boasting of a "secret plan" to end the Vietnam war, eked out a narrow victory over his Democratic opponent, Hubert H. Humphrey. Although it was the second-smallest margin of the popular vote in seventy-six years, to many blacks—90 percent of whom had voted for Humphry—Nixon's victory signaled the perpetuation of institutional racism. America had not been so racially and politically divided for over a century.

This divisive mood extended to popular music, where even Berry Gordy's Motown, the most successful black-owned record company, developed critics—both black and white—who viewed the label's aggressive upward mobility as an unnecessary attempt to escape blackness and sell out to the Establishment.

Black music itself grew more ethnic as the percussive polyrhythmic dance music called funk emerged as a more urgent counterpart to soul. Attempting to focus on any kind of danceable music, *American Bandstand* had a hand in funk's inception by affording frequent appearances to soul singer James Brown. Brown, who made his national TV debut on *American Bandstand* in

1957, introduced "Cold Sweat" (believed by many to be the first "funk" record) on Clark's show just before the song became a hit during the summer of 1967. As *Bandstand* clung to funk's danceability, James Brown came as close as one could to becoming a regular guest on the show. "For a long time, our shows were the only ones giving him any television exposure at all," Clark noted in 1969.[18]

Despite frequent *American Bandstand* appearances by Brown and other black recording artists, the emerging combination of black power and black music presented Dick Clark with new problems. Especially for his touring stage shows, and particularly in the South. In order to generate ticket sales, it had been the longstanding practice of Clark and other promoters about to play a southern city to seek local radio airplay there for the artists who were to perform on the upcoming show. Black radio stations were often employed to publicize black artists, but then when it came time to stage the concert, a local booker—inevitably a white person—was utilized.

That situation was altered by the civil rights gains of the sixties. Jack Hooke, who handled much of the advance work for Clark's road shows during that era, discovered that blacks were no longer willing to allow a "lilly white promoter with a black act" to come to the South, and threatened to boycott such shows.

Seasoned in booking and producing rock 'n' roll road shows, Hooke was friendly with many black disc jockeys in key southern cities. Fearing possible trouble with a forthcoming show he had scheduled for Montgomery, Alabama, he met with a record spinner in that city who went by the sobriquet the Bellboy. "Man, you got trouble," the Bellboy told him. "We play [the artist's] records and then when it comes to make a buck on the promotion you give it to a white promoter. Don't we deserve? Ain't more than right, Jack." The Bellboy advised Hooke to "give a piece of your end to the local black promoter" in order to avoid any trouble. Hooke, in turn, suggested to Clark, who stood to make about $18,000 from the Montgomery concert, that he "give four or five thousand to the black promoter."

"If that's what you have to do," replied Clark, "do it."[19]

But the emerging black forces did not see things strictly in terms of black and white. There was also the color green with which to contend. Since his initial conversation with Hooke, the Bellboy had been told by a rising black figure in the civil rights movement (whom Hooke requested remain anonymous) that the movement leader would also have to be included in any deal cut between Clark's company and the local concert promoter. "You're gonna have to give up a piece of the show," the Bellboy advised Hooke.

Expecting the civil rights leader to "squeeze me and protect the black promoter," Hooke met with him. But to his surprise, Hooke claims, he was able to "buy off" the black leader relatively inexpensively. "Four-hundred fuckin' dollars and he was a partner. It was [an] awful goddamned cheap [price] to sell his people down the road."

With a monetary ceiling apparently established, Hooke offered the Bell-boy the same amount to emcee the upcoming show. "Man, I'm gonna spend more than that on a suit to wear at the occasion!" cried the disc jockey, who realized Hooke had gotten away easy in his deal with the civil rights leader. "So I gave him a thousand bucks," recalled Hooke, and Clark's show went on.

Dick Clark's operation may have adapted to the changes of life on the road, but as *American Bandstand* continued to court its traditional AM radio audience by focusing on the singles-driven fare of soul, funk, pop and punk, it reached its nadir as a showcase for new artists. In 1968, the percentage of *Bandstand*'s guest artists appearing for the first time on network television — after a steady decrease from 61 percent in 1965 — reached an all-time low of 31 percent.[20]

It was a sign of the times. Recording artists now had the opportunity to book more attractive venues on which to introduce themselves to the American public, and that is exactly what they did. The few acts who did choose to make their national TV debuts on Clark's show comprised a mixed bag that encompassed heavy metal precursors Blue Cheer and Iron Butterfly; "bubble gum" rock proponents 1910 Fruitgum Co. and the Ohio Express; the Jerry Ross-produced groups Spanky and Our Gang and Jay and the Techniques; the hard rocking Steppenwolf; and the poppish Andy Kim and Merilee Rush.

And yet, despite the adverse conditions encountered by *American Bandstand* during the Sixties, it was during this era that Clark's show came to be recognized as "the foundation upon which [he] has built a company."[21] Indeed, *Bandstand* may have been the most discernible of Clark's multitudinous enterprises by that time, but it was hardly his most profitable. Clark's ever-expanding video production activities were now a main source of income. Besides owning and producing *American Bandstand*, Dick Clark Productions (described in 1966 by the *Philadelphia Inquirer* as "a powerhouse of stars, shows, tours and packages"[22]) produced and promoted some three hundred teenage concerts annually. DCP, involved with motion picture production and the owner of the rights to about seventy television properties and a nationally syndicated radio show, then grossed in excess of five million dollars annually.[23]

In addition, Clark's business empire included a controlling interest in a group of newspapers which catered to teenage interests; his positions as a youth consultant for the Dr. Pepper soft drink and for Vox, a musical equipment manufacturer; his ownership and operation of two Arby's fast-food restaurants; his part ownership of several California oil wells; and his ownership of several radio stations.[24]

Despite this vast array of resources, Clark was discomforted that *American Bandstand* continued to grow more irrelevant to the country's youth, and soon found a scapegoat for the woes of his dance show. "Let's face it," he said, "kids have turned to the movies."[25] With that, Clark forged what appeared to be an improbable alliance with American International Pictures (AIP), an outfit that specialized in low-budget gore and violence-laden exploitation flicks (one of the most notorious being 1957's *I Was a Teenage Werewolf,* which combined horror with juvenile delinquency). In response to an early 1960s outcry over film violence, AIP had acted to clean up its image in Clark-like fashion, turning out a string of financially successful beach movies starring Annette Funicello and Frankie Avalon. But as the decade grew more turbulent, AIP reverted to the time-honored triumverate of sex (*The Wild Angels* in 1966), drugs (*The Trip* in 1967), and rock 'n' roll (*Wild in the Streets* in 1968) in order to turn a buck. Dick Clark was about to do likewise.

If Clark's alliance with AIP seemed out of step with his clean-cut image, it also belied the notion that his image was anything but a fantasy to begin with. His sanctimonious public persona served both him and *American Bandstand* well, but when it came to doing hard-nosed business, Clark—within the boundaries of propriety—followed the dollar wherever it took him.

Cloaked in his benign image, he proceeded to employ not only rock 'n' roll, but the very un-Clark-like topics of sex and drugs to produce three pictures for AIP. 1968's *Psych-Out,* which dealt with San Francisco's hippies and starred a young Jack Nicholson as the ponytailed leader of a rock band, adhered to what writer Digby Diehl referred to in 1970 as director Cecil B. Demille's classic formula of "nine reels of blood, horror, violence and sex; one reel of redemption."[26] Taken to task because the film's cast of "teenagers" looked more like "thirty-somethings," Clark pleaded "artistic license. I can't defend it," he told Diehl. "There are a lot of goofs in it, you could correct if you had more time." Which was something that Clark, who owed AIP two more films that year, did not have.

Clark's next film was a motorcycle melodrama called *The Savage Seven,* which he described as a "Contemporary Western."[27] Seeking a musical tie-in for the film that could be promoted by the nation's disc jockeys ("We want them to convince their listeners of a 'must see' attitude"), Clark selected the rock group Cream's latest release, "Anyone for Tennis," as the movie's theme (he reportedly flew into a rage when Atco Records initially failed to place the film's title on the record label).[28]

Sporting a Teddy Roosevelt-style moustache for an uncharacteristic role as a mobster, Clark also starred in the third movie he made for AIP. *The Killers Three* was a knockoff of the recent stylized gangster hit, *Bonnie and Clyde*, to which film critic Leonard Maltin opined, it "doesn't offer much by the way of comparison, unless you find the idea of Dick Clark in wirerims a gas."[29] *The Killers Three* was so violence-laden that even Clark had to admit, "much of it" was left on the cutting room floor.[30]

If nothing else, Clark's AIP deal displayed his penchant for exploiting America's youth market. "Sixty percent of the population is under 35, and 50 percent of it is under 25," he noted in 1968. "It is the most powerful economic group in the country."[31]

Clark had recently undergone hard times in attempting to cater to the under-twenty-fives, but as the sixties drew to a close he professed to make sense of it all, claiming that popular music was "becoming musical once again." Whereas, Clark had initially underestimated the Beatles impact, he now looked to the Fab Four as a bellwether in the restoration of some semblance of reason and order to the pop music scene. "The roll is going back into rock 'n' roll, and the Beatles had a lot to do with it," he declared. "We went to the brink of disaster with psychedelic music, then beyond to what can only be described as 'un-understandable' music.

"There was no excuse for it. The challenge was to see how far out they could go, and in the process they lost a lot of people." Ultimately, Clark proclaimed that the Beatles—who scored big that year with the retro-sounding "Get Back," a departure from their recent drug-influenced style—had started "a rebirth of honest rock 'n' roll."[32] Ironically, while the *Bandstand* host hailed the Beatles as a stabilizing influence on pop music, they had almost ceased to exist as a functioning band.

Clark was on the money when he spoke of pop music as being "cyclical . . . moving backward (or forward) to another era," a point driven home by one of his own employees, no less.[33] When Richard Nader had aproached Clark with the idea of staging a rock 'n' roll concert of 1950s artists who were no longer recording, Clark told him he thought it was "a dreadful idea."[34] Nader, who believed strongly in the concept, left Clark and set out on his own as a promoter. In 1969, he staged the first major rock 'n' roll revival, at New York's Madison Square Garden. The event was such an overwhelming success that it paved the way for a regular series of such concerts and caused many defunct groups of the fifties and sixties to reunite and resume performing. (One such group was the Elegants. "I never would have believed it," mused lead singer Vito Piccone, whose group had a number one hit in 1958 with "Little Star."

"We had a better career the second time than we did the first time!") Clark took notice and filed Nader's idea for future use.

American Bandstand may have lost the mainstream white rock audience, but as black music grew more popular Clark intended to be there every step of the way. "Soul music is hot," he proclaimed in 1969.[35]

So it was. And so it was that *American Bandstand*'s increased dependence on black music provided one of the great ironies of the show's history. The latest development in soul had its genesis in the fertile black music scene of Philadelphia. The process had been overshadowed by *American Bandstand*'s pop hoopla while Clark's show remained in that city, but it began to flourish in the vacuum created by *Bandstand*'s departure to California. The genre was known as Philadelphia soul, and its breakthrough record, sung by the Delfonics, out of Overbrook High School there, was, "La La Means I Love You," which reached number four on the national charts early in 1968.

The smoldering embers of Philadelphia soul, a style that was to reestablish the City of Brotherly Love as an integral part of the pop music scene, were couched in the ashes of Swan and Cameo Records. Its principal protagonists were three black men—Kenny Gamble, Leon Huff, and Thom Bell. In 1963, Jerry Ross, who was then producing a local female group called the Sapphires for Swan Records, crossed paths with the teenaged Gamble, who, besides leading a band called the Romeos, was interested in learning song production. During 1963 and 1964 Gamble and Ross worked side-by-side, producing records for Swan and Cameo, coauthoring the Sapphires' biggest hit, "Who Do You Love," and cutting some sides with Chubby Checker and Dee Dee Sharp (who Gamble would marry in 1970, and later divorce). After seeing teenagers dance to the latest Motown sounds at a Hy Lit record hop, Gamble and Ross wrote and produced the Motown-ish "The 81," recorded for Cameo by Candy and the Kisses in 1964. The piano player on that session was Leon Huff, who had made a name for himself as a session pianist in New York. When the classically trained keyboardist Thom Bell left the Romeos in order to try his hand at production ("Mixed-Up, Shook-Up Girl" for Patty and the Emblems in 1964), Gamble asked Huff to take Bell's place.

Recruiting a young, racially mixed group of Philadelphia musicians—including some former members of Gamble's band—to help them, Gamble and Huff began to write and produce records together. Their trademark style featured lush orchestrations, distinctive instrumental parts, and a driving rhythm section that resulted in a big band dance beat with black overtones. Gamble and Huff's sound had its genesis with the Intruders, Philadelphia's quintessential soul group. Beginning with 1966's "(We'll Be) United," the

Intruders enjoyed a two-year string of modest hits written, produced, and recorded by the talented duo.

Meanwhile, Thom Bell, who was doing production work at Cameo when the label folded, began to produce and arrange for the Delfonics. "La La Means I Love You" became a top five national hit for them early in 1968. That song was followed almost immediately by the Intruder's "Cowboys To Girls," which reached number six nationally in 1968 and became Gamble and Huff's first million-seller. With a steady stream of hits throughout the late 1960s, the Intruders and the Delfonics established the medium tempo, high-pitched harmony style emblematic of the Philadelphia soul sound, and set the standards for the elegant black pop that was to emerge as a musical force during the 1970s.

Soul music was hot, and *American Bandstand* once again embraced a form of music generic to Philadelphia. But unlike a decade earlier, when the music industry depended on *Bandstand* for the promotion of its product, Clark's show now relied more on the industry's music to generate an audience for itself.

American Bandstand had been buffetted mercilessly by the winds of change in the 1960s. The once-vaunted show was reduced from a daily live offering to a weekly pre-recorded venue, its renowned dancing tradition had been trashed during the psychedelic drug era, and the rise of free-form FM radio, with its emphasis on stereo album tracks and social relevancy, stripped it of its hipness and hitmaker status. If no one else held hopes for the revival of ABC's long-running dance show, Dick Clark certainly did. "Everyone, and the music field is no exception, has become sub-teen oriented," he observed in 1969. "These younger kids have quickly become a very influential force. . . . That's where the money is."[36]

But as Clark set his sights squarely on the next generation of America's youth, the underlying question remained: What, if anything, could save *American Bandstand* from its slide into unhipness and irrelevance?

CHAPTER 13

America's Oldest
Living Teenager

The Age of Aquarius may have taken hold in the world of popular music by the time the 1970s began, but the new decade was otherwise permeated by a mood of darkness and divisiveness. As the war in southeast Asia continued to drag on, so did domestic unrest, particularly on college campusus. President Nixon and his administration, now virtually at war with the demonstrators, invoked the support of "the great silent majority" to counterbalance the protesters, but an antiwar demonstration that spring at Kent State University in Ohio ended with National Guardsmen firing their rifles into a crowd of student demonstrators, killing four of them and serving to further fan the flames of the antiwar effort. Moreover, as unemployment increased almost twofold from 1969 to 1970, and the buying power of the dollar continued to decline, a sense of hopelessness and apathy overcame much of America's youth. The deaths of rockers Jimi Hendrix, Janis Joplin, and Jim Morrison within a year's time only served to deepen this languid mood.

If America's outlook appeared solemn, the same held true for *American Bandstand*. *TV Guide*, once the show's most ardent promoter (but no longer corporately linked to it), now referred to Clark's show as "one of the dinosaurs of television." Indeed, *Bandstand* had outlasted its flashy sixties competitors (*Shindig* went off the air in January 1966, after having existed for a little over a year, while *Hullaballoo* disappeared in August 1966), but as the TV magazine pointed out, Clark's show no longer commanded its "former influence as a make-or-break record outlet."[1]

There were other reasons for *American Bandstand*'s diminished status aside from the rock mainstream's continued disinterest in the show. The seventies marked the beginning of America's solitary society, in which three of every five marriages ended in divorce and 40 percent of the children born during that decade were to spend at least some of their childhood in a one-parent home. As the new crop of college students comprising the last of the baby boomers focused their energies on immediate, material concerns, the seventies came to be known as the Me Decade, in which the search for one's *self*, whether it was self-mastery, self-knowledge, or self-actualization of one's human potential, took precedence over most everything else. With this quest for self-actualization came the pursuit of the singles lifestyle—singles' bars, singles' pads, swinging singles, and single recording stars. Reflecting the listlessness of the era, many young people turned away from the heavy percussion of hard rock to the softer sounds of introspective singer-songwriters such as Carole King, Don McLean, Melanie, Joni Mitchell, Laura Nyro, Carly Simon, Paul Simon, James Taylor, and Neil Young. These singers not only performed their own material and often produced their own records, but could, on their own, hold audiences of several hundred through lengthy concerts.

Not everyone flocked to the soft, introspective sound, however. At the opposite end of the rock mainstream were supergroups such as Led Zeppelin, Deep Purple, and Crosby , Stills, Nash and Young, all of whom performed mega concerts in giant arenas. Although disparate in style, the singer-songwriters and the supergroups had one thing in common—both were anathema to the dance-oriented *American Bandstand.*

Bandstand also suffered from fundamental changes within the pop music business itself, which, at that time, was undergoing a period of corporate consolidation. Unlike the show's halcyon days, when independent record companies wheeled and dealed for airplay and Dick Clark sometimes spun records on *Bandstand* the very day they were released (or, as he had done with some of his own records in the 1950s, even before they were released), now five major record manufacturers—Columbia, Warner-Seven Arts, RCA Victor, Capitol-EMI, and MGM—controlled more than half the market. And no single record was important enough for any of those large corporations to create a fuss.

To import a sense of freshness to Clark's show it was billed as *American Bandstand–'70* and the set was redesigned, adding more neon and glitz. "I'm the only constant on the show," its long-time host remarked. "I act 20 years older than the kids because I *am.*"[2]

But Clark was not the only constant on the show. Musicwise, *Bandstand* continued to rely heavily on the singles-driven markets of soul and pop, with almost a third of the acts making their national TV debut on *American Band-stand* during the early seventies soul oriented, and almost half of them AM pop fare. Few true rock groups chose to make their network television debut there. And while *Bandstand* was seen on nearly two hundred stations and its advertising time was nearly bought out by youth-oriented sponsors such as Noxema, Cover Girl, Clearasil, Coppertone, and Maybelline, the show remained in need of an energizer.

"Right now is comparable to the period just before the Beatles invasion," said Clark in the summer of 1972. "American popular music is in the doldrums now awaiting the arrival of the next messiah."[3] But in his assessment of the current state of pop, Clark again demonstrated that when it came to judging new talent he could be as fallible as the next person. He had been off the mark with the Everly Brothers in the 1950s and with the Beatles in the 1960s, and now, as he proclaimed the absence of a pop messiah, one was developing virtually under his nose. Clark's words appeared in the press just weeks after thirteen-year-old Michael Jackson appeared on *Bandstand* to lip-synch three of his hits, including "Ben," which would soon become his first number one song. The fact that the black pop created by Jackson and his compatriots was to propel Clark's show throughout the seventies made all the more egregious his disregard for the budding superstar. (When it came to predicting pop saviors, *Rolling Stone's* Jon Landau, for one, was more lucid than Clark, proclaiming in 1974: "I have seen rock 'n' roll's future, and his name is Bruce Springsteen.")

While *Bandstand* floundered, a new era of black awareness and pride borne of the civil rights movement of the sixties began to take shape, resulting in a black renaissance that was to touch virtually all aspects of American popular culture. This revival was reflected in the proliferation of action-filled "blaxploitation" films such as *Shaft* in 1971 and *Superfly* (not to mention *Blacula*) in 1972, but nowhere was it more evident than within the nation's bastion of whiteness, network television.

Having witnessed the systematic appropriation of their music by whites, and having been treated as second class citizens on America's televised dance shows—either in their consignment to a segregated program such as Mitch Thomas's *Delaware Bandstand* or by their allotment of a certain number of "blacks only" days, as in the case of Buddy Deane's program—in the 1970s, blacks finally attained their own first-rate televised dance show.

A vestige from the days of the black entertainer-as-buffoon stereotype, the initial roles of blacks in American pop culture were comedic in nature. The black ingress into network TV followed that tradition, on a trail blazed by comedians Flip Wilson and Bill Cosby. Beginning in 1969, Cosby (who, despite his groundbreaking network dramatic role in *I Spy* in 1965, remained primarily a comedian) starred in his own situation comedy. The following year Wilson became the first black performer to achieve major popularity as host of his own variety hour. But it was the ground-breaking *All In the Family*, beginning in 1971, that changed the course of television comedy by bringing a sense of harsh reality to the TV world inhabited by homogenized, inoffensive characters and stories. *All In the Family* centered around the bigoted Archie Bunker (played by Carroll O'Connor) and the sharp-tongued George Jefferson (played by Sherman Hemsley), who minced no words in displaying his disdain towards whites. Jefferson's widespread acceptance by American television viewers (the character was subsequently spun off to his own highly rated series) not only reflected a growing self-esteem among blacks, it indicated that whites and blacks were at least willing to admit that fundamental problems existed between the races.

The black renaissance also gave rise to network television's first black dance show. *Soul Train*, replete with young dancers and lip-synching guest recording artists, was created by Don Cornelius because "there is an inner craving among us all, within us all, for television that we can personally connect to."[4] Within a year after it debuted on a tiny UHF station in Chicago in 1970, the weekly *Soul Train* was syndicated on a nationwide basis and drew particularly well in urban markets like New York and Philadelphia where large black communities existed. Cornelius, *Soul Train*'s creator, producer, and original host, said that although his show presented black personalities and style, "It was really the same show [as *American Bandstand*]. A dance show is a dance show, is a dance show. We've always realized that we were doing *American Bandstand* or whoever did this [type of production] before us."[5]

Unlike in earlier times when black youths were forced to settle for "separate but equal" televised dance fare, *Soul Train* became *the* choice of many blacks. *American Bandstand*, which now programmed black music heavily and encouraged blacks into its studio, was faced with a competing show on which some black recording artists, out of loyalty to their race, preferred to be seen.

Soul Train was a natural outgrowth of an era in which black music diversified and produced some of the most exciting, innovative sounds of the day and gained even broader acceptance among the white masses. Witness the fact that in May 1972, for the first time in the annals of pop music, the top eight singles on the U.S. charts were all by black artists (Roberta Flack's "The First Time Ever I Saw Your Face" was followed in order by Michael Jackson, Al Green, the Chi-Lites, Joe Tex, Aretha Franklin, the Staples Singers, and the Stylistics), and three out of every ten records on Top forty radio that year were R&B. Leading the way in this trend was the rejuvenated sound of Philadelphia soul.

Working with a wide range of recording artists both black and white, producers Kenny Gamble, Leon Huff, and Thom Bell successfully shepherded Philly soul into the seventies, to the point where the dance music proferred by *American Bandstand* and *Soul Train* came to be dominated by the likes of the Stylistics, the O'Jays, Harold Melvin and the Bluenotes, MFSB, and the Three Degrees. The essence of the style was provided by Gamble and Huff's own Philadelphia International record label, which was bolstered by a national distribution deal with CBS Records. In 1974 Gamble and Huff produced the Three Degrees' million-selling, number one "TSOP (The Sound of Philadelphia)," which became the theme for *Soul Train*.

Philadelphia International's Motown-like success was achieved by appealing to whites as well as to blacks. As R&B critic Nelson George observed, the label's "musical influence and crossover sales confirmed the historic truth that good, innovative black music, made by blacks, will naturally sell to whites once they get to hear it."[6] In scenes reminiscent of *Bandstand*'s 1950s heyday, Archie Bell and the Drells, Wilson Pickett, Double Exposure, First Choice, the Trampps, the Salsoul Orchestra, and numerous other artists from across the country flocked to Philadelphia to record for Gamble and Huff, and hit songs once again emerged from that city like clockwork. Irv Nahan recalled that "at one time you couldn't get in [to Sigma Sound, where Philadelphia International recorded] because Gamble and Huff tied the studios up all the time."

In addition to riding this wave of spirited black dance music, *American Bandstand* reached out in other directions to increase its audience. As an entirely new "teenybopper" generation of early teens and pre-teens entered the rock marketplace, Clark's show reverted to the familiar teen idol-mania it had so deftly proferred in days gone by. David Cassidy, whose appearances on *The Partridge Family* TV series prompted the launching of his singing career (as was the case for Ricky Nelson in *The Adventures of Ozzie and Harriet* in the 1950s), became a teenybopper favorite and was mobbed wherever he went. Fourteen-year-old Donnie Osmond, the youngest of the Osmonds singing group, became the darling of the subteens, but one no longer had to be a teenager to cash in on the phenomenon. Despite the fact that he was approaching his thirties, *Shindig* refugee Bobby Sherman was marketed as a teen heartthrob, while, at the other end of the spectrum, Jimmy Osmond made his singing debut on *American Bandstand* when he was just nine years old.

Clark, who boasted that he commanded "one of the best organizations in the country for reaching the youth market," nurtured this teenybopper phenomenon by heavily promoting the aforementioned recording stars and other AM teen idols, including the Jackson Five, Leif Garrett, the Bay City Rollers, John Travolta, and former Monkees Mike Nesmith and Davey Jones (although Nesmith and Jones were in the same age bracket as Bobby Sherman).[7]

Meanwhile, America's mood of uncertainty continued. Nineteen seventy-three saw the end of U.S. involvement in the Vietnam War, as well as the end of the military draft, but the country was fraught by other setbacks. More and more involved in trying to distance himself from the previous year's break-in at the Democratic Party headquarters in Washington, President Nixon told an increasingly skeptical nation that he was "not a crook," and vowed never to resign from office. But his vice president, Spiro Agnew, did resign, after pleading no contest to a charge of receiving a kickback when he was governor of Maryland. What affected America most severely in 1973, however, was an Arab oil embargo that wrought havoc on gasoline supplies across the country and spurred a domestic energy crisis featuring long lines at gas stations. The oil embargo also had a dire effect on the pop music recording industry in that it created a polyvinyl chloride shortage that drove many small labels out of business and curtailed the activities of the major recording companies.

American Bandstand suffered along with the rest of the depressed music industry, and the show's diminished impact caused Dick Clark to more or less place it on automatic pilot while he shifted his high profile image to the one facet of the pop music business that made gains during that otherwise stagnant time. As the "good old days" became increasingly attractive to millions of baby boomers about to become thirty-somethings, a nostalgia movement began to coalesce. Eying this demographic change in the marketplace, the music industry began to exploit its back catalog, which came to represent a relatively expense-free source of revenue to the hard-pressed recording business.

Richard Nader's earlier rock 'n' roll revival concerts had shed some light on the coming nostalgia craze, which reached full bloom in 1973. That year the film *American Graffiti* became a surprise hit and boosted the sales of records from the fifties and early sixties; the musical *Grease* opened on Broadway; and some of the British stars who got their start in the 1960s toured the U.S. in a recreation of the British Invasion. In 1974, *Happy Days*, a TV show about teenage life in the 1950s, with Ron Howard playing Richie Cunningham and Henry Winkler as the Fonz (and scores of *American Bandstand*'s Hollywood regulars utilized as extras each week) appeared. Within two years, *Happy Days* was the number one program in all of television.

Brandishing the music of *Bandstand*'s first decade, Dick Clark moved to become the chief exponent of the budding nostalgia trend. In an effort to maintain (or regain) contact with *Bandstand*'s original viewers, Clark plunged into the nostalgia trip with a vengeance. (One report had him considering opening an "oldies nightclub" in New York "to cash in on the revival of interest in rock 'n' roll of the '50s."[8])

Not one to miss an opportunity to capitalize on his properties, the forty-three-year-old Clark celebrated the twentieth anniversary of *American Bandstand* with a televised special in June 1973, despite the fact that his show passed that particular milestone a year earlier. (The first *Bandstand* reunion, which commemorated the show's first decade on ABC, was produced in 1966.) Broadcast at 11:30 P.M. on a weekday evening, *Bandstand*'s belated anniversary bash garnered ABC's highest late-night rating ever—which is not to say the show met with universal approval.

Offering one striking example of why, to this day, Clark harbors intense disdain for critics of any kind, veteran Philadelphia TV reporter Rex Polier, commenting on *Bandstand*'s ersatz birthday celebration, wrote that Clark "has never been anything more than a slick shill for himself and the recording industry." Polier went on to say that Clark's anniversary special, replete with jitterbugging period garb such as black leather jackets (which had been expressly prohibited on the actual show during the Fifties) "reflected the put-on that *Bandstand* has always been: A coldly commercial proposition camouflaged in such a manner that the teenagers used for 'window dressing' in the studio are hypnotized into believing they are enjoying themselves."[9]

Meanwhile, in what was to develop into an annual event, a true reunion of *Bandstand*'s early regulars took place in Philadelphia that fall. The event was organized by Andrea Kamens and attended by Anne Polidere Altieri, Billy Cook, Tommy DeNoble, Mickey Duffey, Jack Keller, Carol McColly Kirkbride, Joanne Montecarlo, Barbara Morrison, and Adam Valleriano, among others, all of whom were then in their early and mid-thirties. Most were married with children and held blue collar jobs. Some were divorced, and one was widowed. Many described themselves as "old fashioned by contemporary standards." The *Philadelphia Bulletin* reported that "almost all disapprove strongly of drugs, most voted for Nixon and Agnew, and a few said they'd do the same today. Current sexual mores make them quite uncomfortable."

To a one, each of the former *Bandstand* stars looked back fondly upon that bygone era when they were unexpectedly transformed from ordinary sons and daughters of first and second-generation immigrant families to teenage celebrities. *Bandstand* made Polidere Altiere feel "important then," she said. "People would recognize me, and we all got so much fan mail." "It was just so much fun," agreed Kamens. "You never have that kind of fun now." McColly-Kirkbride recalled her *Bandstand* tenure as "definitely the greatest time of my life," and Valleriano lamented how the music from the Fifties "was much better" than the music of the Seventies. He then caught himself, exclaiming, "Geez, I sound like I'm ancient, don't I?"

There is a certain poignancy about any gathering of adults—former *Bandstand* dancers or not—who consider a few brief teenage years to be the zenith of their lives. Perhaps the mood was best summed up by Jack Keller, who, unlike most of his high school peers, transcended the blue collar lifestyle to become a concert pianist. "You could never replace that experience unless you did something spectacular later on in your life," he observed. "Most of them didn't." [10]

Ironically, although once they left the show the vast majority of *Bandstand*'s chosen few reverted to living ordinary lives, in the eyes and minds of millions of TV viewers they remained teenaged celebrities frozen in time. The ninety-minute *Bandstand* anniversary was watched by so many people that ABC rebroadcast it on New Years' Eve, which placed Clark, who simultaneously appeared on George Carlin's comedy special on another network that evening, in the peculiar position of competing with himself for a share of the TV audience.

Along with his series of televised *Bandstand* reunions, Clark sought other ways to incorporate the nostalgic element of pop music into network television. He had previously attempted to inject current music into the medium by producing what he characterized as "middle-of-the-road rock" specials for the likes of Three Dog Night, Roberta Flack, and Chicago.[11] But after experiencing a difficult time selling them to ABC, he abandoned the concept in 1972, proclaiming that "TV hasn't learned how to deal with rock music fans."[12]

Clark fared somewhat better with older rock 'n' roll. Following *Bandstand*'s anniversary special, ABC broadcast *Dick Clark Presents the Rock 'n' Roll Years*, which starred Bobby Rydell, Fabian, Chubby Checker, Bobby Vee, James Brown, and the Platters. That, in turn, led to *The Rock 'n' Roll Years*, a prime-time "replacement" series for the network's ill-fated *Bob and Carol and Ted and Alice* comedy series. Although limited to a five-week run, *The Rock 'n' Roll Years* was regarded by Clark as "a chance to establish rock 'n' roll on prime-time TV and earn another time slot."[13]

He obtained that coveted time slot in 1974, producing ABC's short-lived *Action '74* series. Then, during the summer of 1976, Clark sold CBS-TV a package of four weekly thirty-minute prime-time shows headlined by Frankie Avalon and featuring guest appearances by Annette Funicello and other stars of *Bandstand*'s early years. "People grew up with them and like to remember them and see the way they are now," rationalized Clark.[14] And the viewers did —but apparently not on a regular basis.

Clark ultimately failed to establish rock 'n' roll in prime time television, but he was successful in adapting the musical nostalgia concept to the stage. Taking a page from Richard Nader, Clark proceeded to develop his "Good Ol' Rock 'n' Roll" stage revue, which, featuring Jackie Wilson, Freddy Cannon, and the Coasters, played to record-breaking crowds during a month-long summer gig in Las Vegas in 1974.

When Clark revived the show in September, 1975 (with Dion replacing Freddy Cannon) he unwittingly became linked with rock 'n' roll tragedy. Near the end of the opening show of a week-long run at the Latin Casino in Cherry Hill, New Jersey, Jackie Wilson collapsed on stage and lapsed into a coma. The revue went on, with Chuck Jackson brought in to replace Wilson, and one year later a benefit hosted by Clark, Georgie Woods, and *Soul Train*'s Don Cornelius was held for the stricken singer. A highlight of that event was a 1959 film clip provided by Clark, which showed Wilson's striking national debut, lip-synching "Lonely Teardrops" on *American Bandstand*. (At the time of the benefit, hope for Wilson's improvement remained, but he died 1984, having never emerged from his comatose state.)

Despite this misfortune, Clark's "Good Ol' Rock 'n' Roll" revue developed into a first-rate pageant for "oldies" performers, many of whom experienced renewed popularity during the 1970s. The Angels, for one, had disbanded during the psychedelic drug era of the sixties before reuniting and appearing on Clark's revue. Peggy Santiglia-Davison characterized Clark's live shows as "a cut above the competition. You knew that if you did a Dick Clark show it was going to look good and sound good. You have to appreciate that as a performer. It was such a good feeling to think that he put together such a quality oldies show . . . [and] made it so special and so much fun because he respected the integrity of the artists." Santiglia-Davison should know. "We've been revived so many times it's not even funny," she quipped in 1993.

The esteemed reputation generated by the "Good Ol' Rock 'n' Roll" revue embodied Clark's strident work ethic. By the early seventies he was being characterized in the press as "something of a mini-conglomerate with most of his interests somehow linked to the youth market."[15] But along with this desire to maintain his grip on the youth market, there dwelled within Clark an urge to relate to an older audience, all the better to keep in touch with the nation's aging baby boomers. This he deftly accomplished with a triumphant return as a TV game show host.

In 1973, Clark debuted as emcee of CBS-TV's new daytime game show,

The $10,000 Pyramid, prompting *Variety* to note that the "smoothly hosted" program (on which celebrity guests teamed up with contestants to answer a series of questions) "moved remarkably well for a new entry."[16] Bowing to a combination of inflation and sensation, *Pyramid*, which moved to ABC from 1974 to 1980, was upgraded to the $20,000 mark in 1976. By the time it reached the $25,000 level in 1982, Clark was better known to TV audiences as that show's emcee than for hosting *American Bandstand*.

Despite the high visibility generated from Clark's regular appearances on *Pyramid* and *Bandstand* (where, from 1974 to 1980, he adroitly cross-promoted himself by way of his "We'll see you next week" on the *Pyramid* signoff), 99 percent of his activities were carried out away from the television cameras.[17] As part of Clark's weekly routine during the mid-seventies he flew to New York once a week, arriving there at 1:00 A.M., just hours before a scheduled 8:30 breakfast meeting. After breakfast he taped two *Pyramid* shows, conducted a working lunch, and then taped two additional *Pyramids* before returning to the airport in time to catch a 4:30 flight back to Los Angeles.

But even as Clark toiled virtually nonstop, he could not avoid the lingering problem of a languishing *American Bandstand*. Although he put on a brave front and boasted how the show had more than twice the audience it enjoyed during its heyday, Clark was forced to concede that that increase in viewers was due mostly to the growth of the total television audience and not to any renewed interest in *Bandstand*. "I grant you that," he defiantly told *Rolling Stone* in 1973. "But it still reaches an average of ten million record buyers a week."[18]

Maybe so, but in order to revive *Bandstand*'s fortunes, something new was desperately needed. That something arrived none too soon in the form of disco. Like soul before it, disco was more than just music. It was a complete lifestyle centered around dancing. Flashy, grandiloquent dancing, which, for Clark, proved to be heaven-sent. "Once the drug [era subsided] everything was fine," he told *Goldmine's* Jeff Tamarkin in 1990. "I had no trouble understanding disco music. It's dance music."

A reaction to the dance-resistant FM album rock of the early part of the decade, disco emerged from the black, Latin, and gay all-night clubs of New York City to provide a more potent elixir for *Bandstand* than even Clark himself could have conjured. Discomania began to gather momentum in 1974, when dance hits by George McCrae, the Hues Corporation, Barry White, and Gloria Gaynor appeared on the charts, and touch-dancing, replete with all the vigorous movements reminiscent of the jitterbug and the fox trot of the thirties and forties came into vogue once again. By the end of the year the biggest dance revival in ten years was underway.

Amidst the explosion of discomania, *Bandstand* continued to give prominence to soul music. During 1974, 60 percent of the show's guest artists were black. (Perhaps it was mere coincidence that the act making the most appearances on *Bandstand* that year—three—was the funk group Kool and the Gang, who were managed by Clark's former Philadelphia-based business partner and promotional whiz, Harry Finfer.)

Welcome as it was, disco's arrival proved to be a double-edged sword for *American Bandstand*. Although the music caused a resurgence in *Bandstand*'s popularity, the manner in which disco hits were generated belied the show's loss of hitmaking status (as well as that loss throughout the entire broadcasting structure). Radio and television did not determine which disco songs became popular. That privilege reverted to the dancers themselves, who heard obscure danceable black pop records in the clubs they frequented and, by word of mouth, caused the most popular of them to make their way to the radio, thereby bypassing the industry's traditional promotional channels.

No matter how records now made their way to *Bandstand*, Clark reveled in the disco scene. "Everybody but everybody is dancing in every nook and cranny of the world, every area of society," he exclaimed to the show's home viewers as the *American Bandstand* logo blinked alternatingly red and blue on the rear wall and a giant mirrorball rotated as strobe lights flashed from the ceiling.[19] But while disco afforded *Bandstand* a rebirth as a national dance forum, Clark's show still lacked focus and a core audience. Anyone tuning in during that era could expect to see a gamut of performers ranging from rock and soul artists such as the Electric Light Orchestra, Michael Jackson, Smokey Robinson, Johnny Rivers, and Grace Jones, to the dreary likes of pop singers Jimmy Osmond, Bobbi Martin, Mac Davis, and Helen Reddy. Moreover, *Bandstand* continued its decline as a platform for new talent. No soul, funk, or disco artist of significance debuted there in 1975, and only 29 percent of all the show's guest artists that year—an all-time low—relied on *Bandstand* for their initial network TV appearance.[20]

Sales of records and tapes rose to $2.74 billion in 1976, thanks in part to disco, whose rhythms now crossed over to rock and jazz. But *Bandstand*'s percentage of guest artists making their network television debut slipped again to a new low of 27 percent that year, proof that recording artists had other TV opportunities at their disposal and were taking advantage of them.[21]

Nineteen seventy-six was also the year in which Clark's autobiography (written by Richard Robinson with Clark's assistance), *Rock, Roll & Remember*, was published. In preparing the book Clark returned to Philadelphia for the recollections of former *Bandstand* producer Tony Mammarella. True to his generous character, Mammarella openly shared his memories with his old associate, despite the lingering hurt caused by the payola scandal. (Shortly thereafter, on November 29, 1977, Mammarella, who since 1968 had done public relations work for various organizations before opening his own firm in the 1970s, died of brain cancer at the age of fifty-three.)

With the full force of Clark's publicity machine behind it, including a nationally syndicated six-hour radio special of the same title on which Clark reminisced about his *Bandstand* days in Philadelphia, *Rock, Roll & Remember* generated myriad press reviews, most of which treated the work as a light-hearted nostalgia romp. But the most telling critique may have come from the *Philadelphia Inquirer's* Abe Peck, who wrote that Clark portrayed himself "as a regular guy who went on living in a garden apartment after making his first million."[22]

Clark's "regular guy" facade was yet another instance in his lasting portrayal of himself as something less than he actually was. Since his audition at WFIL in 1952, if not before, there was always more to Clark than met the eye —which is precisely how he preferred it. In 1976, when *Bandstand* guest John Travolta asked him how he was, Clark replied: "I'm surviving, I guess. That's about all you can do."[23] By then, Clark was anything but a regular guy, and he was far removed from garden apartment status and concerns about "survival." This had been demonstrated by the latest upheaval in his personal life.

Following an acrimonious and protracted proceding, Clark and his second wife, Loretta, were divorced in January 1975. The couple had originally separated in February 1972, and Clark was sued for divorce the following year on grounds of "irreconcilable differences." Unlike his first marital split, this time it was Clark, claiming he had been "quite unhappy for a long while," who wanted out.[24] "Technically, I think, she divorced me," he told Ralph Emery in 1992, "and that was fine." (Clark later maintained that the procedings took so long because he had to sort through some sixty companies before reaching a settlement, but insiders claimed he simply did not want to pay what he eventually did pay—a reported million dollars.[25])

If nothing else, Clark's latest domestic difficulties drove home the fact that the surest way to successfully meld the personal and business aspects of his life was to take up with someone as hard-working as himself. By the time his second divorce was granted, Clark was already living with Kari Wigton, his executive assistant since 1971.

It was a perfect match. Clark described Wigton as "the first woman I've known who lives my life, understands it, puts up with it—and works with me!" She characterized Clark as a "perfectionist" who was "very difficult to work with. . . . You know you're doing okay only if you don't get fired."

Despite doubts that, as a "two-time loser," he would ever marry again, Clark and Wigton were wed in July 1977, and proceded to take up residence in a spanking-new, self-designed, half-million-dollar beach home near Malibu.[26] So much for the garden apartment.

Considering the success of *American Bandstand*'s highly-rated twentieth anniversary TV special, it would be logical to assume that ABC was eager to broadcast another such outing. But when Clark informed the network that he wanted to do a twenty-fifth anniversary show during the winter of 1977, ABC president Fred Silverman (who had not been with the network when *Bandstand*'s twentieth anniversary was broadcast) demanded that Clark make a "presentation" before the project was okayed. Such common treatment did not sit well with the show's host. "It was like going into cardiac arrest," a miffed Clark told the *Philadelphia Inquirer*'s Harry Harris in 1977. "It was like saying my children were ugly!" Then, as a determined Clark had done twenty years earlier, he conducted what he characterized as "a whale of an educational procedure" on ABC. "I swallowed my pride, sent [Silverman] 400 names of vocalists who had performed on *Bandstand*, and I said, 'Pick any 75.'"[27] Clark had originally sought one hour for *Bandstand*'s anniversary special (which eventually starred Chuck Berry, Johnny Rivers, Seals and Crofts, Junior Walker, and the Pointer Sisters), but after his "presentation" to Silverman the show was expanded to two hours.

Clark then discovered that the show's publicity material slated to appear in *TV Guide* had arrived too late to be included in the magazine's weekly listings, which sent him into a rage. "Listen, that m.f. had six months to get it there!" he exclaimed to an aide. "I'll try to extend the deadline [with *TV Guide*]. You call the bastard's boss and get him off his kiester! The article *has* to be in!"[28]

And it was. "I fought like a wildcat to get this show on the air," Clark told writer Brad Darrach. "Get in my way when I want to accomplish something, I can be a mean mother."[29]

At that point in his career, the "mean mother" was being hailed in print as a "shrewd businessman with a self-confessed 'work fetish.'"[30] Dick Clark Productions was now an umbrella for eight separate corporations, and was one of Hollywood's most active middle-sized production companies (by the end of the seventies it was to net him a reported $25 million.[31]) One particularly successful project Clark developed in conjunction with ABC was the American Music Awards, concocted by him in 1974, after the network expressed interest in televising a Grammy-like music awards ceremony. The American Music Awards, which Clark unabashedly shilled on *American Bandstand* without ever acknowledging that he produced the show, eventually ranked second in prestige only to the Grammy Awards. (Clark also produces Hollywood's Golden Globe Awards and the Academy of Country Music Awards.)

Clark used some of his other corporations to produce his ninety-minute "Good Ol' Rock 'n' Roll" stage show; to arrange pop music concerts for the likes of Led Zeppelin, Chicago, Alice Cooper, Sonny and Cher, and the Osmonds; to produce record albums; to own and operate Los Angeles radio station KPRO; and to produce his syndicated radio broadcasts. As for *American Bandstand*, that was but a cog in the mechanism of Clark's revenue-generating operation. Other than a source of pride, *Bandstand*'s primary role in the scheme of things was to keep its host in the limelight, all the better to drive the vast Dick Clark entertainment complex.

"The truth is I've been going in 80 different directions all my life and nothing has changed," Clark told reporter Rex Polier in 1978. "Ostensibly, the objective is money. But that is only because long ago I found out that money is the only way they measure you [in Hollywood]. It's the only way you can command any respect. . . . Money is the yardstick for everything."[32]

But Clark was fired by more than money. He also thrived on a challenge and did not hesitate to undertake production assignments that counterparts in the industry thought too risky to attempt, if not impossible to accomplish. And Clark delivered. Not for nothing was he characterized as "one of the most astute people in show business . . . [who] knows perfectly well what he can and cannot do." In 1978, for example, Clark produced the highly successful three-hour TV movie biography of Elvis Presley (starring Kurt Russell) without ever receiving permission from any living person portrayed in the film. He did so by carefully adhering to widely known facts in order to avoid any lawsuit. Later that year he did the same with *The Birth of the Beatles*, a two-hour unauthorized re-creation of the group's early years in which Clark employed four unknown actors to portray the Beatles and utilized music prerecorded by a studio group. Apple, which represented the Beatles' corporate enterprises, unsuccessfully sued Clark and ABC-TV to keep the project on the drawing boards, and was also unsuccessful in obtaining a court injunction to keep the movie from being sold.

That is not to say everything touched by Dick Clark Productions turned to gold. One of his more spectacular failures was his own short-lived prime-time television variety show. Clark originally told the *New York Post*'s Bob Williams back in 1974, three years after Ed Sullivan's long-running (twenty-three years) variety show ended, that since he, Clark, was finally considered "an adult performer" his goal was to become "the new Ed Sullivan of TV."

What Clark envisioned for himself was "a straight variety show — 'live from Hollywood-in-prime-time.'"[33]

He finally got his wish in the fall of 1978, when the self-produced *Dick Clark's Live Wednesday*, a musical variety blend of "oldies" artists, Clark's film clips, and current singers, was broadcast by NBC. But *Variety* found the show's host "looking back more than he was looking forward — and it suggested the wrong direction for the long pull."[34] The viewers apparently agreed, as *Dick Clark's Live Wednesday* was cancelled after three months.

Meanwhile, *American Bandstand* continued to be imbued with the disco craze. "Do you realize there are 15,000 discothèques this year," Clark told *Bandstand*'s viewers in 1978. "There were 10,000 last year; 3,000 the year before. "Do you agree it's gonna get bigger?"[35] he asked a female guest in the studio audience. She did, and she was right.

As U.S. record and tape sales topped $4 billion for the first time, three out of every five records in the country were disco that year. The movie *Saturday Night Fever*, which starred *Bandstand* favorite John Travolta, then took the music (as well as the craze) to record heights. The double album soundtrack was shipped gold and went on to top the sales charts for six months, and when all was said and done, it sold eleven million copies in the U.S.and twenty-five million worldwide, and won a Grammy for Album of the Year. (In 1996, "Saturday Night Fever" remained the top-selling soundtrack album of all time.)

Bandstand staged an "All Disco Day" in 1978, emceed by Donna Summer (who thus became the show's first guest host). Also appearing on *Bandstand* that day was the white vocal group Brooklyn Dreams, of which Bruce Sudano, Miss Summer's husband, was a member. During the course of the program — and in front of a completely integrated studio audience — the couple freely and matter-of-factly alluded to their interracial marriage. If nothing else, this seemingly innocuous exchange demonstrated just how far the racial disposition of network TV had come in the two decades since Alan Freed's rock 'n' roll show was brought down by the mere sight of a black and a white dancing together.

Disco continued to breathe new life into *American Bandstand*, but as the decade of the seventies drew to a close, the craze was about to turn cold. In fact, the bottom was about to fall out of the entire pop music industry. With the country on the verge of another economic recession in 1979, total record and tape sales dropped 11 percent to $3.7 billion, with the drop largely attributed to a decrease in disco sales and an increase in home taping. Thus began an industrywide shakeout of epic proportion.

As superstars failed to meet the expectations of over-optimistic record executives, the major companies struggled to overcome the collapse of the disco boom. They closed pressing plants, regional offices, and warehouses, and — for a fourth consecutive year — they raised their prices. The record manufacturers also ended their unlimited return policy for retailers and imposed merchandise quotas on them, forcing many of the small independent stores out of business.

Thanks to a musical genre dubbed New Wave, *American Bandstand* remained immune to this general downtrend in the pop music industry. New Wave was a polymorphous style that arose following the development of the mid-seventies punk scene responsible for dissonant-sounding bands such as the Sex Pistols, the Heartbreakers, and the Ramones. In *From the Velvets to the Voidoids: A Pre-Punk History for a Post-Punk World*, Clinton Heylin wrote that once punk was deemed unmarketable, "musicianship improved," and the music's sources and influences began to expand until the New Wave "ragbag . . . included powerpop merchants . . . British guitar/synth bands . . . ska revivalists . . . thrash exponents . . . and a million other splinters of inspiration."[36]

New Wave's nebulousness suited *American Bandstand*'s needs to a tee, enabling Clark's show to introduce a wide-ranging array of pop-punk artists under one all-encompassing blanket without breaking stride with the upbeat disco pace *Bandstand* had acquired in recent years. The first New Wavers to be featured on Clark's show were New York City-based Talking Heads, who made their network TV debut there early in 1979. Later that year, *Bandstand* introduced Blondie to America (at which time lead singer Debbie Harry lip-synched the AM radio-deleted "pain in the ass" lyric of "Heart Of Glass"), and then did the same for Englishman Joe Jackson.

As the decade of the seventies and discomania faded into history, things could not have fallen in place more fortuitously for *American Bandstand*. Clark's show hung its hat on the highly danceable fare of the New Wavers and — without missing a beat — began to attract a hip, if somewhat narrow, audience.

• • •

If the seventies came to represent the "me" decade, the eighties symbolized the decade of greed. Newly elected president Ronald Reagan wasted no time instituting the age of Reaganomics, when individuals were encouraged to grab as much as possible for themselves, secure in the thought that some of their wealth would eventually "trickle down" to the less fortunate, thus improving everyone's lot. (That was the idea, but after eighteen months of Reagan, the U.S. poverty level reached its highest mark since 1967, 14 percent.) Wall Street's high-risk, short-term-yield philosophy, exemplified by hostile takeovers, leveraged buyouts, and mega-mergers, was mirrored by the country in general as consumption rose faster than incomes. As recession and inflation continued, people saved less, borrowed more, and "shopped till they dropped." Image took precedence over substance, and the world of pop music —the New Wave *American Bandstand* included—fell servile to affectation.

With image now the Holy Grail, *American Bandstand* strove to match the tenor of the times, and as the show headed into the eighties, it became more orchestrated than ever before. The once-again overhauled studio set eliminated the strobe lights and revolving mirrorball—throwbacks to the suddenly-passé disco era—and, as if to proclaim the program's New Wave epiphany, the railinged low risers at the rear of the studio dance floor were replaced by two gleaming, silver-railed, translucent-floored circular towers that enabled some of *Bandstand*'s dancers to rise above the multitudes.

The age limit for *Bandstand*'s studio dancers, many of whom could have passed for professionals—if, indeed, they were not already so—was raised, with many of the latest group of regulars now in their early twenties. Dress code? Not on anyone's life. Disowning the loose-fit look of the disco era, form-fitting was now chic, particularly for the show's females, who were allowed to appear in tight-fitting T-shirts (with messages such as "Packaged in America" emblazoned across prominent female breasts), Spandex-tight pants, high-cut tights, and leotards. As dresses and skirts worn by some of the dancers swirled, their showy undergarments were visible to the camera's eye.

In order to one-up their peers in attracting the attention of the TV cameras, many of the dancers went out of their way to dress cleverly. There was the obvious, such as T-shirts that advertised "Dick Clark's *American Bandstand*" in large block letters, and matching male-female cheerleader uniforms adorned with giant block "B's" (presumably signifying *Bandstand*). And there was the absurd; from Boy Scout uniforms to ballerina outfits. Shorts, worn by girls and guys alike, were also quite popular.

Harkening back to the sixties, almost everybody danced apart, and at times the dance floor was so crowded that the only way partners could be distinguished was by their matching costumes (not an altogether rare occurrence). But unlike *Bandstand*'s early years, when the show's dancers were admonished to not so much as make eye contact with the TV cameras, mugging for the home viewers was now condoned, if not encouraged.

The show's weekly Top Ten board, Rate-A-Record segment, spotlight dances, and dance contests still prevailed, only now, viewers at home phoned in their ballots while the couples danced. And as Clark had done for almost a quarter of a century, he still sat in the bleachers, trademark pencil microphone in hand, and bantered with the studio guests. But although he was now surrounded by the hippest, most mature audience in *Bandstand*'s history, Clark still occasionally experienced difficulty eliciting intelligible responses from the younger generation. In one particular instance he asked a girl in the audience who had visited Vancouver to offer her impression of that city.

> GIRL: It was very nice.
> CLARK: That's sort of a "nyah" answer. Would you like to elaborate?
> GIRL: Yes.
> CLARK: What? What else did you see there. Did you see a lot of people?
> GIRL: Yeah.
> CLARK: It's a big place.
> GIRL: Yeah.
> CLARK: What about the natural beauties. . . . This is like, did you ever get an answer, "Yeah, right, no?" You know, Merv Griffin would cut his throat and throw himself out of a window if he got an interview like you. What, were you vacationing there?
> GIRL: Yeah.
> CLARK: I'll tell you . . . [does a double-take, laughs and buries his face in one of his hands as he gives up].[37]

Clark fared better when he focused on the music. As a bastion of New Wave, *Bandstand* featured a wider range of pop music than it had in over a decade. Bryan Adams, Bananarama, Pat Benatar, the Boomtown Rats, Kim Carnes, A Flock of Seagulls, the Go-Go's, Billy Idol, Loverboy, John Cougar Mellencamp, Men At Work, the Motels, Public Image Ltd., the Romantics, the Stray Cats, and Wham! were some of the recording artists who made their network TV debut there in the early part of the decade. As a result, *Bandstand*'s musical relevancy actually increased to some degree.

The percentage of acts making their network debut on Clark's show rose to 38 percent in 1980, the highest total since 1974, with the number of white rock acts (which had accounted for only 15 percent of *Bandstand*'s guest artists in 1979) actually doubling.[38] That was great news for the dashing, white New Wavers, but their good fortune came at the expense of the black pop artists who had sustained Clark's dance show throughout the seventies. As it was, no black artists made their national TV debut on Clark's show during 1980 or 1981, and of all *Bandstand*'s guest performers during those two years, only 28 percent were black.[39] Fortunately for them, *Soul Train* was still going strong. (As it was at the time this book was written.)

Bandstand was even responsible for the creation of two dances in the early eighties—the Smurf and the bird. Smurfers tilted their head to one shoulder and sidestepped with their heels together, then tilted to the other shoulder and repeated the movement in the opposite direction, all the while swinging their arms up and down. Those doing the bird flapped their arms up and down like wings, but displayed more exaggerated hip movement than did the Smurfers. Although these dances were never mistaken for the twist—or the frug or the hully gully, for that matter—dancing propelled *Bandstand* into the eighties.

In the end, however, that was not enough. Clark's show was about to experience the initial throes of its death rattle. With the pop music business about to undergo its most significant change in the way music was promoted since the advent of *American Bandstand*, the latest advances in technology threatened to change the character of how, when, and where Americans amused themselves. Although more Americans than ever before (99 percent) owned TVs, a 1980 *Washington Post* poll indicated that 54 percent watched less television than they did in 1975, the year the Sony Corporation introduced videocassette recorders to America. A thriving videocassette rental market had emerged, and sales of arcade and video games mushroomed (during 1977–82 the home video game market developed into a $7 billion industry). Clearly, *American Bandstand* faced new, stiff competition for the minds, wallets, and purse strings of its shrinking audience.

American Bandstand's unofficial death knell sounded on August 1, 1981, the day the Warner Ammex Satellite Entertainment cable channel instituted 24-hours-per-day broadcasting of music videos on what it called the Music Television Network (MTV). Showing the most popular music videos four and five times a day, MTV not only targeted the under-twenty-five audience, but also twelve and thirteen-year olds. Which did not leave much room for *American Bandstand*.

Music videos, of course, were not new to the industry. Bob Horn used Snader films on his *Bandstand* back in 1952; some two hundred TV disc jockeys were provided a variety of three-minute "tele-records" during the mid-1950s, and a French musical video jukebox called Scopitone (and a similar machine called Colorsonics) went on the market during the sixties. What was new, was the massive young audience eager to flock to TV's first all-music video channel. MTV's music videos mesmerized teens around the clock (the average viewer watched an hour of the music channel a day on weekdays and ninety minutes on weekends) and boosted the sales of records and tapes much as *American Bandstand* had done a quarter-century earlier.

Broadcast to 2.5 million households, MTV showed a pretax loss of $15 million its first year on the air, yet the upstart cable channel managed to sign 125 sponsors who had faith in the concept. It did not take long for that faith to be rewarded handsomely. By 1983, America was wired for cable. As network television suffered a steady loss of viewers to the new cable channels, MTV reached more than 17 million homes on 2,000 affiliates, and music videos—with some $40 million in sales—became the fastest growing record-business product that year.[40] MTV showed revenues of $73 million in 1984, and *Billboard* found that new acts making their bow on the music channel enjoyed an immediate 10 to 15 percent increase in sales. (Reminiscent of the performance fee kickbacks artists were sometimes required to make to *American Bandstand* in the show's early days, now recording artists were often obliged to pay up to half their video production costs out of their royalties.) "MTV is very attractive," stated an executive from one important Madison Avenue advertising agency. "It allows you to target very discreetly to a particular segment of the population. For youth-oriented companies that's terrific."[41]

But it was not so terrific for *American Bandstand*. In 1985, MTV was sold to Viacom International and underwent organizational changes that served to exacerbate the woes experienced by Clark's show. Viacom added a new cable channel called Video Hits One (VH-1) that employed a softer, less aggressive format than MTV and targeted an older demographic audience of twenty-five-to-forty-nine-year-olds—encompassing virtually all of those who had grown up with *American Bandstand* since the show's inception to the 1970s.

Furthermore, MTV's wild success (coupled with charges of racism lodged against the music channel for initially ignoring black artists) triggered a spate of music video shows on conventional television. ABC-TV introduced its black-oriented, after-prime-time *New York Hot Tracks* and NBC-TV instituted the weekly, integrated *Friday Night Videos*. Cable TV's Black Entertainment Channel stepped up its *Video Soul* segment to 15 hours a week.

Although MTV's nonstop programming of the hottest and hippest music videos rendered *American Bandstand* an anachronism within the music industry, Clark, who had futilely held out against the British Invasion two decades earlier, stubbornly refused to bend with the video trend. He resolutely told *Bandstand*'s viewers that although *Bandstand* would occasionally show "those musical video tapes they have on television . . . you can see them all night all the time everywhere, and it just isn't something we do."[42]

Clark was loath to admit as much, but *American Bandstand* had reached the point in its storied history where it could do little more than receive homage for its past accomplishments. Like a champion prizefighter long past his prime but still on his feet, the once estimable show entered its period of canonization. (Clark began to receive individual kudos in 1976, when he was enshrined on Hollywood's Walk of Fame. In May 1980, Clark was honored as "Man of the Year" by the Philadelphia Broadcast Pioneers, and he was inducted into the Emerson Radio Hall of Fame in New York in June 1990.)

In October 1981, with MTV as yet a two-month-old infant, Philadelphia's Market Street was declared "American Bandstand Boulevard" in honor of the show's thirtieth anniversary, and a street sign bearing that name was erected at Market and 15th Streets. The following year Clark presented the original *American Bandstand* TV podium to the Smithsonian Institutions—and, although it smacked more of a grudging admission of *Bandstand*'s fabled past than a reflection of the show's then-diminished status—Clark won an "Outstanding Daytime Series" Emmy as its producer in 1982–83.

About the same time that the aggrandizing coffee table *History of American Bandstand*, packed with photographs, record charts, and anecdotes about the show, was published in 1985, Clark revealed that his "secret fantasy" was for *Bandstand* to return to the air five days a week. But he also proffered the first hint that he did not plan to emcee the show indefinitely. After predicting that *Bandstand* would be on "as long as there's television," Clark added that long after he stopped hosting the show, "someone will be doing it." [43] Not surprisingly, the remark went almost unnoticed. *American Bandstand* without Dick Clark? The thought bordered on the unimaginable.

During the summer of 1986 Clark released his *Dick Clark's Best of Bandstand* videocassette, which contained performances by Paul Anka, Edd Byrnes, Chubby Checker, Mark Dinning, Fabian, the Fleetwoods, Bill Haley and the Comets, Buddy Holly and the Crickets, Jerry Lee Lewis, and Connie Stevens (despite the title of the package, most of the performances were taken from Clark's old Saturday night show, not from *Bandstand*). In making these complete performances available to the public for the first time, Clark challenged the abiding knock on him that he only showed tantalizing fragments of the wealth of vintage music clips he possessed, lest they fall into the sinful (and royalty-free) hands of some video bootlegger. Jeff Tamarkin, editor of the music collectors' publication *Goldmine*, noted that Clark's narration on the videotape was "less self-congratulatory than usual, making this the historical document collectors hoped it would be and cementing into place this still-running TV program's rock-solid place in rock 'n' roll history." [44]

Also that year, the Pennsylvania Historical and Museum Commission placed the former WFIL-TV studio in which *Bandstand* had been spawned on the National Register of Historic Places. "Every good thing that ever happened to me in my business life started happening in that building," remarked Clark on the occasion, likening the historical designation to "having one of your children graduate with honors." [45]

Clark also continued to utilize his treasure trove of vintage music video clips to adroitly foster *Bandstand*'s immortality (as well as his own) through periodic televised reunion specials. But the more history the show has put behind itself, the more frustrating such reunion shows have become for Clark's aging legion of home viewers. Because of *Bandstand*'s record longevity, Clark now has so much ground to cover that his multi-generational audience, each age group interested primarily in its own particular era at the expense of all the others, is left unsatisfied by the fleeting glimpses of the artists that are shown—as well as by the omission of others. *Bandstand*'s 1985 "33 1/3" reunion was little more than a series of ten-second film clip collages, broken up by a handful of guest artist appearances.

Reunions aside, in the overall scheme of things, *American Bandstand* provided an ongoing sense of stability and familiarity for Clark's audience, facilitating Dick Clark Productions—from which he netted approximately $12 million a year by the late eighties—to continue to fare well. Although Clark (whose income from DCP was augmented by an estimated $3 million a year he derived from personal television and radio appearances[46]) professed to not know his worth, he nevertheless appeared on the "*Forbes* 400" list of wealthiest Americans for 1986.[47] His estimated worth of $180 million was said to have been generated from "rock 'n' roll and television."[48] (Coincidentally, Motown's Berry Gordy, Jr. appeared on that same listing, with aproximately the same net worth as Clark.)

By 1987, it was time for the ultimate corporate move. Anticipating the generation of up to $15 million in working capital from investors. Clark offered 15 percent of DCP stock to the public and put himself on the company payroll as CEO at almost a million dollars a year plus a percentage of the company's pre-tax profits if they exceed $7 million annually. But after what *Forbes* magazine characterized as a "dismal public offering" of DCP, coupled with "setbacks" at Clark's radio stations, he fell off *Forbes*'s list in 1987. That year, the financial magazine estimated his worth to be "far below [that year's] cutoff" of $225 million.[49]

Nineteen eighty-seven was also the year in which *American Bandstand* entered the *Guinness Book of World Records* as television's longest-running variety program. Ironically, this achievement occurred during a time when *Bandstand*'s status at ABC (which, in a startling move, had recently been sold to new owners) reached its nadir.

The handwriting on the wall had appeared back in 1984 for ABC. Although profits actually increased that year, the network nevertheless ended on a dismal note after its programmers rejected "The Cosby Show" family comedy for its fall line-up. While Cosby's show was picked up by rival NBC and went on to become the biggest new hit of the television season, ABC went into a tailspin. The network's afternoon soap operas fell to a second place rating, its nightly news show dropped to third, and—worst of all—with only a couple of highly rated programs on its schedule, ABC dropped to third place in the prime-time rating race. The network lost money with its cable TV operations (it had recently invested a quarter-billion dollars in the ESPN channel) and was plagued by the steady loss of viewers to independent stations, cable TV outlets, and to VCR use. After laying out astronomical sums for the broadcast rights to the 1986 Olympic Games, its *War and Remembrance* mini-series, and various other projects, the cash-poor network began to cut back on its staff.

Ted Fetter, the only person at the network who originally had faith in *American Bandstand*, thought one of ABC's problems was that it missed the boat in not utilizing Dick Clark's entrepreneurship to a greater degree. "I think if we had set up a company called 'The Dick Clark Company,' a subsidiary of ABC, and said, 'Dick, here's a half-million dollars a year, go!' he would have done his thing, and we would have done better." (When told of Fetter's remark in 1994, Clark laughed heartily. "That's very insightful," he responded. "I agree!")

But by then it was far too late for Clark to be of any help to the ailing network. Certain investors skilled at engineering corporate takeovers were already accumulating ABC stock, causing network president Leonard Goldenson to become alarmed. Goldenson said he simply "could not allow the company [he] had watched over for more than thirty years to be dismembered by profit-hungry raiders."[50] If he had been a younger man, the ABC president would have fought them, but Goldenson was approaching eighty years of age. Rather than risk a hostile takeover in which ABC might be broken up and sold piecemeal, Goldenson decided to sell the network. His first choice as a buyer, IBM, turned him down.

Enter the much smaller Capital Cities Communication Corporation, a media conglomorate consisting of seven TV stations, twelve radio stations, and assorted newspapers and magazines. In 1985, FCC regulations were altered to henceforth allow one company to own up to twelve broadcasting stations—a change made in the hopes of encouraging smaller companies like Cap Cities to acquire more stations and thus compete with the giant networks. But Cap Cities, citing the mutual benefit of joining its resources and facilities with ABC (and with Leonard Goldenson's blessing), took advantage of the relaxed FCC regulations and acquired the entire network. The acquisition cost Cap Cities the then-hefty sum of $3.5 billion, a 60 percent premium over the network's market value before the deal was announced, and nearly $3 billion more than Ed Noble originally paid for it in 1943.

This marked the first time that a major television network had ever been sold, and, at the time, was the largest corporate acquisition not involving an oil company. The blockbuster transaction (which Goldenson said "stunned [his] friends and colleagues at ABC") may have benefitted Cap Cities and ABC, but it was a blow to *American Bandstand*.[51] Dick Clark now became one step removed from Goldenson, his network godfather, who had stuck by him through thick and through thin, and who regarded Clark more like the son he never had than as a hired hand. Goldenson became chairman of Cap Cities' executive committee and was replaced as ABC's chief executive by Frederick Pierce, to whom *American Bandstand* was nothing more than a miniscule component in the factoring of the network's bottom line.

Intent on improving ABC's standing, the new ownership eyed *American Bandstand*'s sagging ratings and informed Clark that it would no longer guarantee a spot for his show on its Saturday-morning schedule unless *Bandstand* was reduced to thirty minutes from its then current hour length. Clark, who had set a standard of his own in 1984 as the first TV personality to simultaneously host regular series on all three major networks (NBC-TV's weekly *Bloopers, Commercials and Practical Jokes*, ABC's *American Bandstand*, and CBS's *The New $25,000 Pyramid*), refused. In October 1987, after some five thousand *Bandstand* telecasts, the show's unprecedented three-decade affiliation with ABC came to an end.

Clark syndicated *The New American Bandstand* to independent television stations for the 1987–88 season, a move he admitted in 1994, "was probably a mistake" on his part. Clark explained how, had he agreed to let ABC cut the show to thirty minutes, it would probably still be on the air, "because we would have speeded it up. We would have gone to shortened versions of the records . . . [and] modernized it to the point where it would be as contemporary as it always was through its lifetime.

"But I thought, 'The heck with this. Syndication is on the rise. We can do it.' I made the disastrous mistake of probably giving it to a distributor who wasn't equipped to handle that kind of show. They were very prosperous, very well-known, reputable, did good work in other things, but once-a-week daytime things were not their strong suit at that moment in time, and we ended up on a lot of independent stations, which in that day was not the thing to do, and we lost the audience."

Clark's assessment of *American Bandstand*'s problem was delusive, if, indeed, he believed it himself. To blame the show's demise on its syndication process is to ignore the fact that a good portion of its audience was lost simply because the show no longer held the interest of enough viewers.

Nevertheless, as part of a move to extricate *Bandstand* from his ill-fated decision to put it into syndication, Clark announced in March 1989, that he was about to step down as host of the show with which he had become synonymous, that he had "finally decided it was time to give someone else a chance." The move reportedly prompted Federal Reserve Board Chairman Alan Greenspan to somberly remark: "I can't conceive of any news I can give the American people that would offset that."[52]

Along with removing himself from the forefront of his long-running show, Clark decided to hitch *Bandstand*'s falling star to the booming cable TV industry (which, ironically, had contributed considerably to the program's downfall). For its debut on cable's USA Network in April 1989, the *American Bandstand* set was relocated—sans its proverbial podium—to an outdoor location on the Universal Studios lot tour, just outside of Los Angeles. The first song of the opening show was introduced by Clark, who, after reminding the audience he had "spent the better part of [his] adult life on this dance floor," announced that it was now time for him "to pass the microphone over to the next man."

The next man was David Hirsch, who, at twenty-six, was the same age as Clark was when Clark inherited *Bandstand* from Bob Horn in 1956. As Clark, now fifty-nine, bowed out, Hirsch, a former USA Network producer who was recruited by *American Bandstand* producer Larry Klein, acknowledged the pressure he felt as the one chosen to succeed such a formidible personality. It was one thing to come to Hollywood as an unknown and secure a television show of his own, said Hirsch, but it was "much different to say, 'Here's a kid from Detroit who is expected to fill the shoes of Dick Clark. That gets to you.'"

Hirsch could be forgiven if he felt more like the first mate taking command of a sinking ship rather than the new emcee of a venerable television show. "Maybe this change might help to gain some new viewers," he wistfully proposed. "I would love it if people would watch again. . . . I know a hell of a lot of people do watch it. But for those who don't, I'd say, 'Give it a look again. It's not as dated as people may think.'"[53]

But Hirsch was whistling in the dark. Since the advent of MTV, *American Bandstand* had ceased to be regarded as a significant stage on which to expose new music, and the show remained an enticing venue for artists on the "Adult Contemporary" playlist only because there were few other ways to reach that particular audience. *Bandstand*'s glory years, when the show exposed countless hit records to America, made stars of aspiring young singers, sparked the latest dance crazes, set the latest trends in fashion, and made a television studio crammed with otherwise ordinary teenagers celebrities in their own right, were long gone. "It's just another cable outlet now," said one record company executive. "It *helps*, but I wouldn't spend any money to fly a band in to do it unless they were doing fifteen other things at the same time."[54]

It was time for the man responsible for *American Bandstand*'s unprecedented television run to assess the situation. Perhaps the latest popular dance craze, the Brazilian lambada, which featured a "thigh straddle" in which the male's crotch gripped the female's thigh as they remained locked together while gyrating their hips in an up-and-down-motion, played a part in his decision. In any event, as Clark recalled in 1994: "I looked at [*Bandstand*] one day and it was being done in a parking lot at Universal and it had no lighting and it had no production quality, and it really hurt! I said, 'Let's just not do this anymore. It isn't something that anybody's terribly proud of, and I don't want it to be remembered that way.'"

In September 1989, a mere six months after he stepped down as the show's host, Clark yanked the plug, and after thirty-seven consecutive years on local and network television, *Bandstand* disappeared from the home screen.

Epilogue

D ick Clark turned sixty just weeks after *American Bandstand* disappeared from television. It had been thirty-four years since he last celebrated a birthday while not acting as the host of the landmark show. Vacationing in Brazil with his wife Kari for the occasion, Clark turned down interview requests, choosing to celebrate the milestone quietly, and to reflect on the demise of the show he once acknowledged had made "everything else possible."[1] He later confessed to missing *American Bandstand* "very much. You don't hang around something for that many years and not miss it."[2]

Five years later, in 1994, Clark insisted he harbored no regrets over not staying on as *Bandstand*'s host until the show left the air. He insisted it was "the appropriate thing to do. I had turned sixty and I thought that was a good time to bring a new guy in." But Clark did second guess his decision to move *American Bandstand* to cable TV, and he admitted to "one other mistake. For historic purposes I should have asked [USA Network] to agree to leave [the show] on another three months so it would have lived into the nineties. I didn't think that out at the time." (At the time Clark spoke those words, *Soul Train* was drawing closer to *Bandstand*'s record thirty-one-year run as a national show. In 1996, Don Cornelius's program entered its twenty-sixth consecutive year on the air, making it the longest-lasting program in first-run syndication.)

The demise of *American Bandstand* gnawed at Clark even though he accepted the fact that his show could never come back "in its original form." Given today's fragmented, multicultural society of sound bites, quick cuts, shortened attention spans, remote control buttons, and one-hundred-plus cable channels, it is inconceivable that a particular television program could ever again capture an entire generation for ninety minutes a day, five days a week, the way *American Bandstand* once did. "I kind of doubt whether you'll ever see the day when, for an hour, people will sit down and watch kids dance to records on over-the-air television," said Clark in 1994. "It certainly can't return to the days of the impact it had when it was first on." Yet clearly, Clark had no intentions of letting his show fade into oblivion. His acute entrepreneurial streak flashed brightly as he pointed out the "many things that the [*Bandstand*] imprint can be put upon."

Not that Clark has had difficulty remaining before the public forefront in the absence of his record-breaking dance show. He has endorsed an array of commercial products, and as spokesman for the American Family Publishers sweepstakes, his picture goes into tens of millions of homes annually. He regularly hosts a string of self-produced TV specials, and judging from the title of his *All-New All-Star TV Censored Bloopers: Unplugged!* broadcast in November 1995, he could prolong that series indefinitely. In 1994, Clark again competed with himself on national television when NBC's *American Bandstand*'s No. 1 Hits" special and ABC's "The Television Academy Hall Of Fame Special"—Clark was one of the inductees—were aired simultaneously. In addition, Clark's annual *New Year's Rockin' Eve* TV show, which he has hosted live from New York's Times Square for the past twenty-four years, has developed a tradition in its own right. (Former bandleader and radio and television New Year's Eve staple Guy Lombardo, who once jokingly quipped that when he died he planned to take the holiday with him, did not reckon with Clark.)

Then there are Clark's televised *American Bandstand* reunion specials, which offer proof that some things do not change. Just as critics lambasted the program when it was first broadcast in 1957, *New York Times* TV critic John J. O'Connor derisively characterized *Bandstand*'s fortieth anniversary show in 1992 as crass exploitation, "clipsville, a fearful barrage of excerpts, most lasting no longer than ten seconds."[3]

Clark's televised reunions, his other high-profile interests, and his behind-the-scene responsibilities for Dick Clark Productions afford him more than enough activity. So what, then, makes Clark run? Why does a man of his wealth and accomplishment—who admits he stopped working for money more than thirty years ago—continue to recycle video bloopers and hawk magazine subscriptions, flashlight batteries, and vitamins?

Part of the answer can be found in the genetic make-up of thoroughbred race horses, which continue to run on their own, even after being retired from competition—it is simply what they do. Clark himself has stated it is "the nature of the beast" within him that causes him to do what he does, whether it entails shining shoes or selling peanut butter sandwiches for pennies as a young boy, selling hit records to teenagers in mid-life, or negotiating multi-million dollar production deals in his later years.

In 1981, Clark told *Us* magazine he believes in "the accumulation of worldly goods" and wants "as much as the good Lord will let [him] get."[4] Uttered during the decade of greed and excess, Clark's words seem appropriate enough, yet it would be a mistake to interpret them solely in that manner. His long-time friend Duane Eddy pointed out that while some people enjoy "hunting, fishing, or bowling . . . [Clark] liked to make money . . . not so much for greed, as it's his hobby." Given his health then, Clark (who has given up alcohol and tobacco and adheres to á low-sugar, low-fat diet) will never retire. "Boy, I hope this carcass of mine keeps going," he remarked shortly after reaching the sixty-six-year mark. "So far, so good."[5]

But he no longer professes to be a "workaholic."[6] The *Saturday Evening Post* reported in 1995 that Clark, who now schedules frequent vacations, prides himself in "dropping out at a moment's notice" to nap, read a book, garden, paint, or listen to music. Perhaps that is why, since his singular appearance on *Forbes's* list of the 400 wealthiest Americans in 1986, Clark has not approached that vaunted status again. (If anything, he has apparently fallen further from *Forbes's* list. Assuming his net worth to be slightly over the $200 million mark, that is still a far cry from the $350 million it took to crack the "*Forbes* 400" in 1995.[7]) Do not count Clark out just yet, however. His entrepreneurial drive, now stoked by a paternalistic streak (in 1995, he told the *New York Daily News'* Cathy Slewinski there are five hundred DCP employees to "feed and house."), still burns fiercely.[8] Clark still earns plenty of money, just not as quickly as some others do.

As for *American Bandstand*, Clark continues to dutifully embellish the show's already-impressive legend. Most recently, he told the *Saturday Evening Post* he was "proud" that *Bandstand* "was *the* place where young people turned to see what was hot and *who* was hot."[9] Granted, Clark's show earned landmark status as it forged the country's first teenage constituency, influenced popular music and culture on a worldwide scope, and helped the ABC network come of age as a major broadcaster. But all that was accomplished during *American Bandstand*'s first six years on the air, when Clark's program stood virtually alone as the most important factor in the pop music business —to say nothing of its influence on society itself. Although *Bandstand*'s golden era ended in 1963, its unprecedented power during those early years resulted in an inordinate share of the *Bandstand* legend spilling over to the show's later years.

This spillover effect has worked to Clark's advantage. His latter-day self-promotion of the *American Bandstand* legend has, for the most part, been embraced by the media. Such as when the *Saturday Evening Post* misleadingly portrayed Clark as having been the force who integrated *Bandstand* immediately upon taking over as emcee in 1956, when, in fact, the show was not truly integrated until almost a decade later. The *Post* also stated that Clark "stays on top of the competition by . . . [among other things] keeping two jumps ahead of the trends."[10] In fact, once Clark became the self-confessed "fastest follower in the business" in the mid-sixties, neither he nor *American Bandstand* has been much of a trendsetter.

Still, Clark's *American Bandstand* odyssey has not been a complete cakewalk. In the days when the show did generate enough interest to merit critical analysis, critics flayed it mercilessly. And much the same can be said of Clark, who readily admits he has "been criticized for dealing in froth and light entertainment, like game shows and music" all his life.[11] There are several reasons why Clark has been (and continues to be) castigated so. Foremost may be that he had the temerity to offer the American people the television programming that they desired—a rewarding idea for short-term advancement, but risky over the long haul. As the French writer Voltaire observed, "The public is a ferocious beast: One must either chain it up or flee from it." Having done neither, Clark has paid the price by being saddled with a reputation as a production *schlockmeister*.

In addition, the fact that Clark achieved overwhelming success in such an external manner has aroused scorn and resentment in many people. Had Clark's life turned out to be tragic, in the manner of, say, Alan Freed, who died drunk and penniless, chances are the *Bandstand* host would be exalted, if not deified, by now. But Clark continues to be successful in a most public manner, while those with even larger fortunes discreetly go about their business without stirring the resentment he does. Oprah Winfrey, for one, has amassed assets greater than Clark's (a reported $340 million), yet she is cited as the paradigm of the successful woman while he, in the eyes of some, remains a villain.[12]

Clark's underlying problem is the rock 'n' roll purist's image of him as "the Great Satan," who softened and whitened rock 'n' roll while lining his pockets in the process. The truth is otherwise. Just as Alan Freed (or someone equally wreckless and aggressive) was needed to serve as a lightning rod to diffuse the animosity engendered by anyone who dared to champion black music to mainstream white America in the 1950s, Clark (or someone else with his inoffensive, WASPish charm and wholesome, reassuring appearance) was necessary to facilitate rock 'n' roll's next step; its development into something greater than fringe music. The pocket-lining Clark indulged in as he made rock 'n' roll respectable was not essential to the music's dissemination, yet it was fundamental in generating the negative feelings many rock 'n' roll preci-sionists still feel towards him.

As 1995 drew to a close—some six years after *American Bandstand* went off the air—it was announced that reruns of the show from 1976 to 1984 would be broadcast on Viacom's VH-1 cable music channel beginning in Jan-uary 1996. Which begs the question: Did *American Bandstand* cease to exist from 1990 to 1995 simply because it stopped taping and no longer apeared on the air? Apparently not, to Clark's way of thinking. When the rebroadcasts began he claimed to have hosted the show for a period of "almost forty years," a time span that could only be derived by including those missing years.[13] (Further evidence of Clark's synonymousness with his legendary show occurred in October 1996, when he produced a "fortieth Anniversary of *American Bandstand*" special for the Family cable channel. No matter that *American Bandstand* was thirty-nine years old at the time, not forty. Or that Clark already produced a "fortieth Anniversary Special of *American Band-stand*" in 1992. He reached the four decade figure this time by appropriating the year he hosted WFIL's local *Bandstand* during 1956–57.)

Thus did Viacom, the parent company of MTV, the music channel that played a decisive roll in *American Bandstand*'s demise (and shortly thereafter contracted Dick Clark to overhaul MTV's rambling and lackluster annual awards show) provide an ironic twist to *Bandstand*'s long history by putting the program back on the air.

The *Best of American Bandstand* rebroadcasts include a minute or two of a newly recorded introduction (in which Clark, the quintessential cross-pro-moter, takes the liberty to shill for his restaurant chain of "*American Band-stand* Grills"). For the new introductions, taped in ABC's Hollywood studio where the original show was long staged, Clark trundled out an assortment of *Bandstand* memorabilia, including several podiums that were used over the years, the giant cut-out map of the United States on which *American Band-stand* was emblazoned from coast to coast, a weekly Top Ten board, and an old television camera bearing the ABC logo.

Clark has stated that his numerous TV appearances are "a blessing and a curse" in that the camera accentuates every physical deterioration; yet he con-tinues to age remarkably well.[14] On the *Bandstand* reruns from the 1970s disco era, the only thing that does not appear hopelessly dated is Clark him-self (although at times he does appear unhip and out of his element). When the newly taped *Bandstand* introductions are juxtaposed with Clark's original *Bandstand* appearances, especially those from the eighties, the viewer is some-times hard-pressed not to wonder, "Is that him now, or then?"

Hindsight lends an air of quaintness to the resurrected *Bandstand* shows,

rendering some of them more compelling now than when they were originally broadcast (they are also heavily edited; from sixty minutes down to thirty,
with about one-quarter of that time allotted to commercials). Clark can be
seen in 1981, talking with guest Sheena Easton about how Prince Charles's
new girl has made "Diana" a hit all over again in England.[15] In 1976, he
evokes derisive laughter from the studio audience by asking Cleveland-born
Eric Carmen if the singer's much-maligned (pre-Rock 'n' Roll Hall of Fame)
home town was considered a "music center."[16] That same year, prior to the
filming of *Saturday Night Fever*, 22-year-old John Travolta, hair stylishly
down to his shoulders, prophetically tells Clark about his as-yet-untitled
movie, in which the singer is "gonna get to dance . . . and it's gonna be hot! I'll
be like, the king of the discos."[17] During another *Bandstand* rerun, a twenty-
five-year-old Madonna, clad in off-the-shoulder black, tells Clark of her
dream "to rule the world." (At the time, most viewers probably thought she
was kidding.)

     Witnessing Clark confer glibly with a wide array of guest artists reveals his
endless aplomb. When Travolta, greeted warmly by *Bandstand*'s studio audience after he made his singing debut there in 1976, remarks that it is "nice to
sing when there's a lot of affinity goin' on in the air," Clark does not miss a
beat. "Affinity? Is it still here?" he asks as he looks searchingly around the studio.[18] (It is also amusing to those who recall the payola scandal to see Clark in
the 1970s hold up a record album cover of a guest-artist, mention the album
jacket photo of a popular local disco, but not divulge the disco's name lest he
"get into trouble" for doing so, and then observe him freely tout his own
American Music Awards and *Pyramid* game shows on other *Bandstand*
broadcasts.)[19]

     By including *Best of American Bandstand* in its 1970s retro-programming,
VH-1 sought to appeal to the seventy-six million baby boomers born
between 1946 and 1964. If preliminary viewer ratings for 1996 are to be
believed, the cable channel handily met its goal. And in doing so, Viacom
unwittingly accomplished something else.

     At one suburban Long Island (N.Y.) elementary school early in 1996, the
sixth grade students were preparing for a physical education demonstration
they were to conduct for their parents. Part of the program included a group
dance, for which the students were to choose the music and choreograph the
steps. As expected, there was much debate over the selection of the music.
One favorite, familiar to them from its inclusion in the film *Dirty Dancing*,
was the Contours' "Do You Love Me (Now That I Can Dance)." Other popular choices included the Beatles' version of "Twist and Shout" and James
Brown's "I Feel Good." There was also one other possibility. A group of

eleven-year-old girls made a pitch for a "really cool" song they had captured on tape and brought in for their peers to hear. It was called "Bandstand Boogie," and they had discovered it while watching VH-1's *Best of American Bandstand.*

"Bandstand Boogie" was not selected by the students for the dance, but it did put a smile on the face of one of their teachers old enough to remember Bob Horn. Dick Clark, it seems, is well prepared for the twenty-first century.

Appendices

Appendix I. American Bandstand *Timeline*

November 30, 1929: Dick Clark born.

Summer 1947: Clark's first broadcasting position is as a summer replacement announcer at WRUN radio in Utica, New York.

—1950s—

November 1951: While Clark works as a television newscaster at Utica-Rome's WKTV, the East and West Coasts are linked by coaxiable cable, making coast-to-coast television transmission a reality.

May 13, 1952: Clark hired as a radio announcer by WFIL in Philadelphia.

October 6, 1952: WFIL-TV institutes its daily Philadelphia *Bandstand* show, hosted by Bob Horn and Lee Stewart.

Spring 1953: Although *Bandstand* is primarily a mainstream pop music venue, Bill Haley and the Comets, from nearby Chester, Pa., perform their hit, "Crazy, Man, Crazy, on the show. The song is regarded as one of the first rock 'n' roll records.

Summer 1954: Horn begins to program black rhythm and blues on *Bandstand*, starting with the Chords' "Sh-Boom."

1955: Stewart is removed from *Bandstand*, leaving Horn as the show's sole host.

January 1956: Elvis Presley makes his national television debut, promoting his first hit record, "Heartbreak Hotel," on the Dorsey Brothers' NBC-TV variety show.

June 1956: Horn fired as *Bandstand* host.

July 9, 1956: Dick Clark becomes new *Bandstand* host.

August 5, 1957: American Bandstand debuts on WABC-TV.

February 15, 1958: The Dick Clark Show, originating in New York City on Saturday nights, debuts on WABC-TV.

November 1959: The broadcasting payola scandal breaks, and ABC insists Clark sell his music-related companies in order to remain on *American Bandstand*.

1950s: Paul Anka, Frankie Avalon, Chuck Berry, Freddy Cannon, Johnny Cash, the Chantels, Chubby Checker, the Coasters, Eddie Cochran, Sam Cooke, Bobby Darin, Dion and the Belmonts, the Drifters, the Everly Brothers, Fabian, the Flamingos, Connie Francis, Annette Funicello, Buddy Holly and the Crickets, Jerry Lee Lewis, Little Anthony and the Imperials, Johnny Mathis, Bobby Rydell, Neil Sedaka, Simon and

Garfunkel (as Tom and Jerry), and Jackie Wilson are among the recording artists making their network television debut on *American Bandstand*.

—1960s—

April 1960: Clark testifies before a Washington subcommittee investigating payola.

Summer 1960: With a big boost from *American Bandstand*, Chubby Checker's "The Twist" revolutionizes popular dancing.

September 1960: Clark's Saturday night TV show is discontinued by ABC-TV.

Summer 1961: ABC reduces *American Bandstand*'s daily airtime from ninety to sixty minutes.

October 1962: ABC reduces *American Bandstand*'s daily airtime from sixty to thirty minutes. Clark predicts his show can run for thirty years.

Early 1963: American Bandstand ends live broadcasts as Clark opts to tape all five upcoming weekday shows on the preceding Saturday.

August 1963: American Bandstand's daily status is ended as ABC begins to broadcast a sixty-minute version of the show on Saturdays only.

February 8, 1964: American Bandstand leaves Philadelphia for California.

February 9, 1964: The Beatles make their American television debut on CBS-TV's *Ed Sullivan Show*.

1960s: The Beach Boys, James Brown, Creedence Clearwater Revival, Neil Diamond, the Doors, the Four Tops, Aretha Franklin, Marvin Gaye, Lesley Gore, Jay and the Americans, the Jefferson Airplane, the Lovin' Spoonful, the Mamas and the Papas, Van Morrison, Pink Floyd, Otis Redding, Johnny Rivers, Linda Ronstadt, Smokey Robinson and the Miracles, Del Shannon, the Shirelles, Nancy Sinatra, Sonny and Cher, the Temptations, Ike and Tina Turner, Conway Twitty, Bobby Vinton, Mary Wells, Stevie Wonder, and the Young Rascals are among the recording artists making their network television debuts on *American Bandstand*.

—1970s—

November 1979: Clark turns fifty.

1970s: ABBA, Aerosmith, Blondie, the Captain and Tennille, the Carpenters, the Chi-Lites, Jim Croce, the Electric Light Orchestra, the J. Geils Band, Andy Gibb, Al Green, Joe Jackson, the Jackson Five, Eddie Kendricks, Gladys Knight and the Pips, Barry Manilow, Harold Melvin and the Blue Notes, Tony Orlando and Dawn, Helen Reddy, the Spinners, Rick Springfield, the Staples Singers, Steely Dan, Talking Heads, and the Village People are among the recording artists making their network television debuts on *American Bandstand*.

—1980s—

August 1, 1981: The all-music video cable channel MTV debuts.

1987: American Bandstand enters *Guinness Book of World Records* as television's longest-running variety program.

October 1987: Rather than agree to ABC's proposal to cut *American Bandstand*'s weekly airtime to thirty minutes, Clark syndicates the show to independent TV stations.

April 1989: Clark steps down as host of *American Bandstand* at age fifty-nine. David

Hirsch becomes the new host as the show is moved to the USA cable network.
September 1989: American Bandstand ceases to be broadcast.
1980s: Adam Ant, Bryan Adams, Pat Benatar, Bon Jovi, Kim Carnes, the Go-Go's, Billy
Idol, Janet Jackson, Cyndi Lauper, Huey Lewis and the News, Madonna, John Cougar
Mellencamp, Men At Work, George Michael and Wham!, Prince, the Romantics, and
the Stray Cats are among those recording artists making their network television
debuts on *American Bandstand.*

—1990s—

January 1996: The Best of American Bandstand rebroadcasts begin on Viacom's VH-1 cable
channel.

Appendix II. Dick Clark's Top Ten

These are the ten biggest chart hits in which Dick Clark held some sort of financial interest during the 1950s, along with the number of times he played each song on *American
Bandstand.* Key: P-owned publishing of song; RC-owned all or part of the record company
on which song was issued; M-owned part of the company that managed the artist; PP-had
all or a portion of the records pressed at Mallard Pressing. (All chart positions taken from
Billboard. Additional information from U.S. House of Representatives, *Responsibilities. . . ,*
pp. 1457–1541.)

1. "At The Hop." Hit version by Danny and the Juniors (ABC-Paramount 9871).
   Reached No. 1 in 1958. 51 plays. P (Sea-Lark).
2. "Butterfly." Hit versions by Charlie Gracie (Cameo 105) and Andy Williams (Cadence
   1308). Reached No. 1 in 1957. Although "Butterfly" became a hit prior to the advent of
   American Bandstand, and Clark had no direct business tie to the song at its release,
   Bernie Lowe did later give Clark a substantial portion of "Butterfly"'s publishing rights
   for the promotion that Clark gave to the song.
3. "Diana." Hit version by Paul Anka (ABC-Paramount 9831). Reached No. 1 in 1957.
   24 plays on *AB*, more prior to that on the local Philadelphia *Bandstand.* Although
   Clark had no direct business link to "Diana," Am-Par did give him (through Sea-Lark)
   the copyright to the song on the B-side of the record ("Don't Gamble With Love"),
   enabling Clark to collect a royalty for each copy of "Diana" that was sold.
4. "Sixteen Candles." Hit version by the Crests (Coed 506). Reached No. 2 in 1958–59.
   35 plays. P (January), PP.
5. "Guitar Boogie Shuffle." Hit version by the Virtues (Hunt 324). Reached No. 5 in
   1959. 43 plays. RC, PP.
6. "Tallahassee Lassie." Hit version by Freddy Cannon (Swan 4031). Reached No. 6 in
   1959. 46 plays. RC, PP.
7. "Rebel-'Rouser." Hit version by Duane Eddy (Jamie 1104). Reached No. 6 in 1958. 42
   plays. RC, M.

8. "Forty Miles of Bad Road." Hit version by Duane Eddy (Jamie 1126). Reached No. 9 in 1959. 35 plays, including 2 of flip side. RC, M, PP.
9. "Don't You Just Know It." Hit version by Huey Smith and the Clowns (Ace 545). Reached No. 9 in 1958. 33 plays, with 31 of them occurring before the song appeared on *Billboard's* Top 100. P (Kincord), PP.
10.   "La De Dah." Hit version by Billy and Lillie (Swan 4002). Reached No. 9 in 1958. 55 plays. RC.

Appendix III. The Bottom Ten

Although popular notion has it that Clark could create a hit simply by playing it on *American Bandstand*," that was not always the case. These are the most-played songs on *American Bandstand* in which Clark had a financial interest, that failed to appear on *Billboard's* Top 100. Key: **RC**-record company; **P**-song publishing. (All information from U.S. House of Representatives, *Responsibilities...*, pp. 1457–1541.)

1. Mary Swan: "My Heart Belongs to Only You" (Swan 4016). 40 plays over 9 weeks. RC.
2. Echoes: "Scratch My Back" (Swan 4013). 30 plays over 10 weeks. P (Request), RC.
3. Diamonds: "Young in Years" (Mercury). 28 plays over 9 weeks. P (Arch).
4. Little Anthony and the Imperials: "So Much" (End 1036). 27 plays over 7 weeks. P (January).
5. Billy and Lillie: "Smoky Grey Eyes" (Swan 4029). 27 plays over 8 weeks. RC.
6. Quaker City Boys: "Everywhere You Go" (Swan 4026). 20 plays over 9 weeks. RC.
7. Chris Kevin: "Here He Comes, There He Goes" (Colt). 19 plays over 5 weeks. Master recording leased by Swan under an arrangement whereby Swan stood to reap up to 90 percent of the profits.
8. Malcolm Dodds: "Unspoken Love" (End). 18 plays over 7 weeks. P.
9. Steve Gibson: "Bless You (For Being An Angel)" (Hunt 326). 16 plays over 5 weeks. RC.
10. Patty Saturday: "Ladies' Choice" (Swan 4022). 16 plays over 6 weeks. P (Kincord), RC.

Notes

Magazine and newspaper abbreviations

BB:	*Billboard*
CC-P:	*Camden (New Jersey) Courier-Post*
GM:	*Goldmine*
NYDN:	*New York Daily News*
NYHT:	*New York Herald Tribune*
NYJA:	*New York Journal-American*
NYP:	*New York Post*
NYT:	*New York Times*
PB:	*Philadelphia Bulletin*
PDN:	*Philadelphia Daily News*
PI:	*Philadelphia Inquirer*
PJ:	*Philadelphia Journal*
RS:	*Rolling Stone*
VAR:	*Variety*

Preface

1. "The Forbes Four Hundred," *Forbes*, October 27, 1986, p. 231.
2. Ralph Emery interview with Clark, The Nashville Network, June 22, 1992.
3. Lloyd Sachs, "'You're Jealous,' Dick Clark Tells His Detractors," *PB*, June 28, 1978.

Chapter 1. Genesis

1. This anecdote is recalled by Steck.
2. When commercial radio came into prominence in the 1920s Steck, who was born in 1897 in West Philadelphia, was at the forefront. He sang with the Fox Fur Trappers trio for fifteen dollars a show on the fledgling CBS network. In 1931 he became a radio announcer on Philadelphia's WPEN. Steck moved to WFIL in 1936, where he remained for four decades, working his way up the managerial ladder. (He died in 1994, one year after being interviewed for this book.)
3. Clark's "everything I wasn't" is from the Emery Interview. Katherine Murray's

"sassiest baby" is from Helen Bolstad, "The Real Dick Clark," original manuscript for *Pine Publications*, June 20, 1958, p. 3. Billy Rose Collection, Lincoln Center, New York Public Library. Julia Clark's "lugged Dick around" is from Gael Greene, "Dick Clark: The Early Days," *NYP*, September 23, 1958.

4. Stephen Kahn, "Philadelphia's Pied Piper: Dick Clark—New Idol of Millions," *PDN*, April 14, 1958.

5. Dick Clark & Richard Robinson, *Rock, Roll & Remember*, p.15.

6. Emery interview with Clark.

7. Clark & Robinson, p. 20.

8. Greene, September 23, 1958.

9. Clark & Robinson, p. 21.

10. "Dick Clark's 'Formula' for Teen Appeal," *NYHT/JA*, April 5, 1958.

11. Michael Barrier, "American Handstand," *Nation's Business*, October, 1987, p. 90.

12. Clark & Robinson, p. 26.

13. Greene, September 23, 1958.

14. Emery interview with Clark.

15. Greene, September 23, 1958.

16. Interview with Steck.

17. Barbara's "only boy for me" and Clark's "sure of ourselves" are from Bolstad, "The Real Dick Clark," p.6. Her "missing half my life" is from Bolstad, "Why Do Teens Trust Dick Clark?," manuscript written for *Photoplay*, March 16, 1958. Lincoln Center, New York Public Library.

18. Kahn, April 14, 1958.

19. David P. Szatmary, *Rockin' In Time: A Social History of Rock & Roll*, p. 60.

20. Clark & Robinson, p. 37.

21. Julia Clark's quotes and the reporter's "eminently hirable" are from Greene, September 23, 1958.

22. "For Teenagers It's a Heaven and Haven," *TV Digest*, March 29, 1952, p. 9.

Chapter 2. Bob Horn's *Bandstand*

1. Author's interview with Steck.

2. U.S. House of Representatives, *Responsibilities of Broadcasting Licensees and Station Personnel: Hearings Before a Subcommittee of the Committee on Interstate and Foreign Commerce*. 86th Congress, 2nd Session on Payola and Other Deceptive Practices in the Broadcasting Field, Washington, D.C. Government Printing Office, 1960. Testimony of Mammarella, p. 737.

3. Ben Fong-Torres, "Dick Clark: Twenty Years of Clearasil Rock," *Rolling Stone*, August 16, 1973, p. 16.

4. WPEN allowed Grady and Hurst to do weekend television so long as they continued to do their daily radio program on WPEN.

5. Harry Harris, "Around The Dials: Bandstand—Disc Jockey Formula for TV," *PB*, January 16, 1953.

It is generally accepted that the first network TV disc jockey was Jack Kilty, who, on his *Disc Magic* show that originated on NBC-TV in 1947, played popular records of the day on the air.

6. Harry Harris, "Bandstand Celebrates First Birthday," *PB*, October 12, 1953.

7. Walt Gollander, "The Three Chuckles," *Record Exchanger*, February 1973, p. 19.

8. Harris, January 16, 1953.

9. Rex Polier, "Town's Teenagers Go for Jitterbug on TV," *PB*, March 29, 1953.

10. Thomas Clavin, "Riding the High Waves of the Rock-and-Roll Crest," *NYT*, Long Island Section, December 12, 1993, p. 2

11. John A. Jackson, *Big Beat Heat*, pp. 85–87.

Freed's "Rock and Roll Jubilee Ball" was held in Manhattan's St. Nicholas Arena in January 1955. The all-black talent featured Clyde McPhatter and the Drifters, Fats Domino, Joe Turner, the Moonglows, the Clovers, the Harptones, and Ruth Brown, among others. It was after this historic event that the music business began to use the phrase "rock and roll" to describe what had heretofore been referred to as rhythm and blues.

12. "Two Down and Eons To Go," *TV Guide* (Philadelphia edition), October 9, 1954, p. A–2.

13. Interview with Steck.

14. Rex Polier, "Teen-Agers Outpull Name Guests on 'Bandstand,'" *PB*, July 17, 1955.

15. Michael Shore with Dick Clark, *The History of American Bandstand*, p. 40.

16. Harris, October 12, 1953.

17. Thayer's show, which originated on WTCN-TV, Minneapolis, in September 1952, was a daily afternoon show featuring popular music of the day, appearances by guest artists, and a studio audience comprised of local teenagers. Born in 1922, Thayer, who enjoyed a distinguished career in broadcasting that culminated with his being named president of NBC radio in 1974, said he chose the drug store setting for his show because when he was growing up, "that's where we hung around." On *Jack's Corner Drug*, Thayer, who died in 1995, shortly after being interviewed for this book, employed public relations stunts, promotions for local advertisers, and celebrity guest interviews. "I was really trying to make it a disc jockey show on television," he commented.

18. Jeff Tamarkin, "The Beat Goes On" (Interview with Clark), *GM*, December 28, 1990, p. 11.

19. Unlike other American cities where blacks were commonly consigned to the most undesireable locations, a great portion of the blacks who migrated north to Philadelphia after the Civil War and during World War I originally congregated in the most desirable areas of the heart of the city, drawn there by their occupations as domestics and menial workers for Philadelphia's wealthiest families. This migration intensified racial tensions between blacks and whites, however, and caused many of the whites to flee to the suburbs. Excluded from this exodus were the Italian immigrants, who comprised the largest ethnic group to arrive in Philadelphia in the early 1900s. Because of their extreme poverty, their inability to read or write English, and a perceived allegiance to the Roman Catholic Pope as well as to secret societies such as the Mafia, these immigrants were met with suspicion and distrust as well as prejudice, causing them to huddle together in cultural enclaves and to stay within their communities and not rise beyond them. Consequently, they were one of the few white groups who remained in Philadelphia, living just several blocks south of the heart of the city's black ghetto. As both ethnic groups were afforded greater opportunities to co-mingle in the city's schools and on its streets, competition for low-skilled jobs and inferior housing resulted in a degree of tension and animosity between them. Still, the fact that there was any co-mingling at all allowed for both groups to influence each other, especially musically.

20. Clark and Robinson, p. 43.

21. Polier, July 17, 1955.

22. Fong-Torres, p. 18.

In 1958 Horn pleaded "no defense" to the U.S. government's charge that he had failed to report income "paid by record distributing firms for plugging certain records," amounting to $1,715 for 1953, $8,255 for 1954, and $12, 890 for 1955 ("U.S. Indicts Bob Horn," *PB*, April 17, 1958, and "Horn Admits Tax Evasion," *PB*, September 22, 1958).

23. Clark and Robinson, p. 45.

24. Ibid. p. 46.

25. Frank Brookhouser, "Man About Town" column, *PB*, October 3, 1956.

Realizing they had to do television to keep up with the competition, Grady and Hurst bought out their WPEN radio contract in 1955, thus enabling them do their daily television show on WPFH-TV. (In 1958 WPFH-TV moved to Philadelphia and changed its call letters to WVUE-TV.)

Chapter 3. Dick Clark's *Bandstand*

1. Although the newspapers in 1956 identified the young girl by her real name, her name has been changed in this book to Dolores Farmer to protect her identity. Farmer's employer in 1994/95 indicated that she was not interested in being interviewed for this book.

2. Robert Goodwin, "Horn's Wife, Son Testify for Him," *PDN*, January 31, 1957.

3. "Dated Horn At 13, Girl Says," *PB*, January 28, 1957.

4. "Horn Denies Girl's Story," *PB*, January 29, 1957.

5. Lee Stewart, "Horn Denies Girl's Charge in Phila. Trial," *CC-P*, January 30, 1957.

6. "Bob did go with other women," revealed Agnes Mammarella. "There was never any question about that. That's what kind of man he was." Irv Nahan described Horn as a "party guy."

7. "Bandstand's Bob Horn Held For Driving While Drunk," *PB*, June 21, 1956.

8. Author's interview with Steck.

9. The conversation with the reporter was recalled by Steck.

10. *PB*, June 21, 1956.

11. "Philly Disk Jock Falls Victim to His Sheet's Drive," *VAR*, August 15, 1956.

12. Henry Schipper, "Dick Clark" (Interview), *RS*, April 19, 1990, p.68.

13. Interview with Steck.

14. Although anti-Italian sentiment largely abated after World War II, nativistic and racist American mentality had nevertheless imposed upon Italian-Americans a set of stereotypes remarkably similar to those foisted on blacks. While the latter were portrayed as either childlike Uncle Toms or sullen, incorrigible felons, the latter were cast as "spaghetti-twirling, opera-bellowing buffoons in undershirts . . . or swarthy, sinister hoods." (Richard Gambino, *Blood of My Blood: The Dilemma of the Italian-Americans*, p. 98.)

15. This exchange was recalled by Steck.

16. After being told in 1994 of Steck's account of Clipp's luncheon meeting, Clark, who professed to know nothing about it ("That's the first I've heard of it. I, of course, was not privy to that."), replied: "Boy, then I owe [Rogers] a great deal of gratitude."

17. Schipper, p. 68.

18. Clark and Robinson, p. 48.

19. Wallace Terry, "Am I Embarrassed?" *Parade*, September 22, 1991, p. 5.

20. Stephen Kahn, "Philadelphia's Pied Piper: Part Three," *PDN*, April 16, 1958.

21. Clark and Robinson, p. 50.

22. Ibid., p. 49.

23. Shore with Clark, p. 9.

24. "Remember Bob Horn?" *PB*, October 30, 1973.

25. "Probe Accuses Steve Allison And Bob Horn," *PB*, October 24, 1956.

26. Schipper, p. 70.

27. "Vice Ring Depravities Bared by Wiretapping," *PI*, December 13, 1956.

28. Clark and Robinson, pp. 48, 49.

29. Ibid., p. 50.

30. Ibid., p. 51.

31. Schipper, p. 68.

32. Clark's "150 percent deliberate" is from Schipper, p. 68. His "smoked and drank" is from Fong-Torres, p. 19.

33. Schipper, p. 70.

34. Ibid.

35. Szatmary, p. 54.

36. Arnold Shaw, *Dictionary of American Pop/Rock*, p. 278.

37. This conversation with Lowe is recalled by Mann.

38. Author's interview with Mann.

39. When Lowe formed Cameo he kept a controlling share of the publicly owned company. "I got most of the publishing," said Mann, Cameo's second-largest stockholder, "so it turned out alright.... I still own the copyrights."

40. Lowe's quotes are from U.S. House, *Responsibilities . . .* , pp. 1116, 1117.

41. U.S. House, *Responsibilities . . .* , p. 1177.

When I asked Clark to elaborate on this incident in 1994 and informed him that I had carefully studied the extensive House subcommittee payola hearings transcripts, he replied, "You're more current than I."

42. Ibid., p. 1186.

43. Ibid., p. 1120.

Had a writer not been designated for "Butterfly," the song would have entered public domain, enabling any future arranger of the song to claim writing credit for his or her version and receive writing royalties for it.

44. The quotes of Lowe and Clark are from U.S. House, *Responsibilities . . .* , pp. 1117, 1120, 1122, 1188.

45. Clark and Robinson, p. 151.

46. U.S. House, *Responsibilities . . .* , p. 1187.

47. Ibid., p. 1132.

48. The four dates were: November 25, 1954 (Thanksgiving Day); sometime around January 15, 1955; February 17, 1955; and March 10, 1955. Farmer swore she partook in a two-day trip on Horn's yacht on August 26th and 27th, 1955.

49. "Dated Horn At 13 . . . ."

50. "Bob Horn Calls Witness 'Liar,'" *PB*, January 30, 1957.

51. Ibid.

52. "Horn and Girl Both Cry Lie," *PB*, January 31, 1957.

53. "Horn Accuser Called False," *PB*, January 29, 1957.

54. "Four-Day Trial Of Horn Ends In Hung Jury," *PB*, February 1, 1957.

55. Fong-Torres, p. 19.

56. Bob Rolontz, "The Philadelphia Story: Part II," *BB*, March 24, 1958, p.4.

57. "Disk Jockey Move to Video Is Still a Long Hard Trip," *BB*, November 13, 1954, p. 21.

58. Huntington Williams, *Beyond Control: ABC and the Fate of the Networks*, p. 47.

59. Leonard Goldenson, *Beating the Odds: The Untold Story Behind the Rise of ABC*, p. 137.

60. Ibid., p. 143.

61. Robert Sobel, *The Manipulators: America in the Media Age*, pp. 265, 266.

The baby boom increased the number of births in the United States from two-and-three-quarter million in 1945 to an all-time high of almost four-and-one-half million in 1956.

62. "The New ABC of It," *Newsweek*, December 10, 1956, p. 108.

63. Interview with Steck.

64. Author's interview with Fetter.

Fetter stayed with ABC for twelve years—an inordinate amount of time in the impermanent world of broadcasting executives—and eventually became the network's national director of programming.

65. Fong-Torres, p. 19.

66. Clark and Robinson, p. 88.

67. The "people watch . . . nationally" quote is from the interview with Fetter. The rest of the paragraph is from the author's interview with Clark.

68. Interview with Fetter.

69. This conversation was recalled by Fetter.

70. Clark and Robinson, p. 88.

71. This conversation was recalled by Steck.

72. Interview with Steck.

73. "Horn Acquitted In Morals Case," *PB*, June 26, 1957.

74. "The New ABC of It," p. 108.

75. Schipper, April 19, 1990, p. 126.

76. William G. Weart, "Crowds Banned In Levittown, PA," *NYT*, August 22, 1957, p. 16.

77. "3 Schools Integrate: Districts Near Philadelphia End Segregation," *NYT*, September 10, 1957, p. 10.

78. David Nasaw, *Going Out: The Rise and Fall of Public Amusements*, p. 246.

79. The *Variety* quote appeared in the news item: "Toughest Season in Ten Years," *NYT*, July 25, 1957.

80. Goldenson, p. 168.

81. Val Adams, "Top TV Time Sales Seen for Autumn," *NYT*, July 29, 1957.

82. "Great Break for Young Dick Clark" (TV column), *PDN*, July 23, 1957.

83. Ibid.

84. Harvey Rachlin, *The Encyclopedia of the Music Business*, p. 316.

Chapter 4. Philadelphia, U.S.A.

1. Szatmary, p. 54.

2. Formed in 1956, Jamie Records was named for the daughter of Allen Sussel, who ran Universal Record Distributors for its owner, Harold Lipsius. Universal owned and distributed the Jamie and Guyden labels.

3. Harry Harris, "Bandstand Bows Today on Network," *PI*, August 5, 1957.

4. Rex Polier, "Dick Clark and His 'Kids' Go Bigtime," *PB*, August 4, 1957.

5. Clark and Robinson, p. 9.

6. Harry Harris, "WFIL's 'Bandstand' Goes National—Not Without Some Strain," *PI*, August 6, 1957.

7. J.P. Shanley, "TV Teen-Agers Only," *NYT*, August 6, 1957.

8. Vance Packard, *The Hidden Persuaders*, pp. 132, 140.

9. Harris, "Bandstand Bows...."

10. In those days independent stations and stations affiliated with one network could broadcast specific shows originating on another network.

11. Clark and Robinson, p. 12.

12. Ibid., p. 55.

13. Barrier, p. 90.

Clark maintained that the best business decision he ever made was "to become a producer when I was a performer." (Pat Hackett, "Dick Clark" (interview), *Interview* magazine, February 1986, p. 128.)

14. Joe Smith, *Off the Record*, p. 104. Clark's estimate of $50,000 is from Fong-Torres, p. 19.

15. "They're Having a Ball," *TV Guide*, September 28, 1957, p. 13.

16. "American Bandstand" (review), *TV Guide*, October 19, 1957, p. 23.

TV Guide erred in its claim that Clark was the nation's first disc jockey to have a TV show. That distinction goes to Cincinnati's Paul Dixon (a radio deejay who was paired with Dotty Mack for a TV program). Other successful radio jocks who predated Clark on network TV included Peter Potter (*Juke Box Jury*) and Martin Block, who were both seen on ABC-TV.

17. Ibid., p. 23.

18. Michael Matza, "The 'Bandstand' Beat Goes On," *PI Magazine*, May 26, 1989.

19. Leslie Bennetts, "And Not a Pair of Bobby Sox in Sight, *PB*, October 30, 1973.

20. Shore with Clark, p. 53.

21. Ibid., p. 45.

22. Marilyn Marter, "Whatever Happened to All Those Kids on 'Bandstand?'" *PI*, November 20, 1972.

23. Shore with Clark, p. 36.

24. Ibid., p. 39.

25. Ibid.

26. Edward Hershey, "An Ex-Bopper Looks Back at 20 Years of Apple Pie," *Newsday*, July 12, 1973.

27. Shore with Clark, p. 67.

28. Ibid., p. 41.

29. Ibid., p. 36.

30. Ibid., pp. 43, 46, 70.

31. Ibid., pp. 45, 50.

32. Bennetts.

33. Shore with Clark, p. 51.

34. Ibid., p. 46.

35. June Bundy, "TV Spinners as Strong on Network as on Local Air," *Variety*, November 11, 1957.

36. Daniel Wolf, *You Send Me: The Life and Times of Sam Cooke*, p. 161.

37. Cases of mistaken racial identity occurred as late as 1961, when a black vocal group called the Pentagons scored a national hit with the white pop-sounding "To Be Loved (Forever)." Pentagons producer Lee Silver recalled that before the group performed their

hit on *American Bandstand*, everybody assumed lead singer Joe Jones was white, "and then they saw him" for the first time.

38. Clark did not have any recollection of the Rays incident in 1994, but said, "I'm sure it's right. It sounds like the sort of thing that would happen. The people who made records in those days didn't have an aura of stardom, they didn't have an entourage, they didn't have limousines. There probably wouldn't have been anything that would have caused the door-man to believe this was a recording star."

Miller recalled that Clark was so embarrassed by the incident that he ushered the Rays into his office and helped them regain their composure by previewing the latest record by Sam Cooke ("You Send Me"), that Clark was very high on.

39. The recognition of adolescents as a distinct group was brought about in large part when most males eighteen and over were removed from American society by the military effort during World War II. In their absence, younger boys stepped in to assume more adult roles that their elders had traditionally taken.

Teenage boys and girls had little trouble earning spare cash in the labor-scarce work force made so by the war. Ironically, it was Walter Annenberg's Triangle Publications, the future owner of *Bandstand*, that created *Seventeen* magazine in 1944, in an attempt to cater to the bobby soxer market.

40. *American Bandstand* (review), *TV Guide*, p. 22.

41. Joe Smith, p. 103.

42. "TV Jock Finally Comes Into Own," *Variety*, October 7, 1957.

43. Clark and Robinson, p. 63.

44. Tamarkin, "The Beat Goes On," p. 12.

45. Donald Clarke, ed., *The Penguin Encyclopedia of Popular Music*, p. 1074.

46. Clark's quote was recalled in Marcucci's interview with author.

Clark did not remember the incident. He said Marcucci had been his friend for so long "I've forgotten we ever had any bad times."

Chapter 5. At the Hop

1. A look at the other black vocal groups that appeared on "American Bandstand" in 1957—the Tune Weavers, the Bobettes, and the Rays, each of whom had a white pop-style hit on the charts—supports Andrews' contention.

2. Smith, p. 103.

3. U.S. House, *Responsibilities . . .* , p. 1180.

4. Bob Bosco, "Joey/Flips from Bandstand to Obscurity," *Record Collector's Monthly*, November/December, 1991, p. 6.

5. Nelson George, *The Death of Rhythm and Blues*, p. 9.

6. Steve Roeser, "I'm Tired of Being Called a Rip-Off Artist!" *Sh-Boom*, March, 1990, p. 25.

7. "Turkish Tycoons: The Erteguns," *Time*, July 28, 1967, p. 43.

8. Szatmary (2nd edition), p. 28.

9. Edwin Howard, "He's Made $2 Million on Discs—Without a Desk," *Memphis Press-Scimitar*, April 29, 1959.

10. Clark and Robinson, p. 174.

11. Ibid., pp. 174, 175.

12. "Challenging the Giants," *Newsweek*, December 23, 1957, p. 70.

13. There was no official industry sales count in those days, a fact that enabled many a

record company to deny an artist such as Charlie Gracie his due royalties. The Record Industry Association of America (RIAA) did not begin to certify gold (million-selling) records until 1958.

14. Sam Clark's words were recalled by Silver.

15. When Tony Mammarella reluctantly testified before the congressional subcommittee investigating payola he said Sam Clark had called and told him "of certain records that he has that look good, and things like that." Asked if Sam Clark ever arranged to have those records programmed on "American Bandstand," Mammarella equivocally replied, "I can't remember a specific instance, but there might be a time, yes; and there might be a time, no; I don't know." (U.S. House, *Responsibilities* . . . , p. 823.)

Jack Hooke, who later worked for Dick Clark, said the "Bandstand" host had a "very strong connection with Larry Newton," who ran Am-Par under the tutelage of Sam Clark. Hooke added that Sam Clark liked Dick Clark "very much."

16. U.S. House of Representatives, Special Subcommittee on Legislative Oversight of the Committee on Interstate and Foreign commerce, Washington, D.C., *"Payola" and Related Deceptive Methods in the Broadcast Field*, Executive Session — Confidential Testimony of Alan Freed, April 25, 1960, unpublished, pp. 8, 43.

This alleged incident was denied by Leonard Goldenson in his testimony at the same payola hearings. (U.S. House of Representatives, *Responsibilities* . . . , p. 1372.)

17. Todd Everett, "Lloyd Price," liner notes to compact disc, "Lloyd Price Greatest Hits," p. 11.

18. Ibid.

19. Musicologist/author Russell Sanjek wrote that "Clark was onto the wrong version of 'Tequila' for several weeks before the studio audience let him know his error." (Russell Sanjek, *American Popular Music and Its Business: The First Four Hundred Years: Vol. III From 1900 to 1984*, p. 445.)

20. U.S. House, *Responsibilities* . . . ," p. 1170.

21. Ibid., pp. 1096, 1097.

22. Clark's "All of a sudden . . . I could get into" is from Smith, p. 103. His "no decision of any importance . . . approval and advice" is from U.S. House, *Responsibilities* . . . , p. 1173.

During the late 1950s, Clark's career was guided by personal manager Marvin Josephson, an attorney who owned Broadcast Management Inc. In addition to Clark, Broadcast Management had as its clients Captain Kangaroo and newscaster Chet Huntley. Josephson later founded International Creative Management (ICM), the literary and talent agency that today represents a multitude of show business luminaries. Clark said he also had the advice of an additional attorney in setting up his various businesses, "and we had an accounting firm, of course."

23. Russell and David Sanjek, *American Popular Music Business in the 20th Century*, p. 132.

24. Hackett, p. 129.

25. According to the 1960 House payola investigation transcripts, the song was first played on Clark's show weeks before Swan Records began operations. Swan was formed in December 1957. "Did You Cry" was first played on "American Bandstand" on November 19, 1957. (See: U.S. House, *Responsibilities* . . . , p. 1505.)

26. Granahan recalled that his original $150 investment in "Click Clack" "got us a million-seller." His quotes are from Wayne Jancik, "Gerry Granahan," *GM* , December 28, 1990, p. 42.

27. "La De Dah" was first played on "American Bandstand" on November 22, 1957, three days after Clark began to play "Did You Cry" on that show. (See: U.S. House, *Responsibilities . . .*, p. 1505.)

28. Kay Gardella, "Bandstand Emcee Tries Out Nighttime Spot," *NYDN*, February 11, 1958.

Chapter 6. Saturday Night

1. "ABC May Use 'Bandstand' As Opposition to Como," *PB*, September 20, 1957.
2. Clark and Robinson, p. 115.
3. "New TV Seg For Clark," *Variety*, November 25, 1957.
4. "Challenging the Giants," p. 70.
5. Ibid.
6. Mammarella's quotes are from U.S. House, *Responsibilities . . .*, p. 737. Clark's quote is from Clark and Robinson, p. 117.
7. Clark and Robinson, p. 124.
8. Greene, "Dick Clark: Part Six," *NYP*, September 28, 1958.
9. Shore with Clark, p. 49.
10. "Whatever it is . . . He's Got It," *TV Guide*, October 4–10, 1958, p. 14.
11. Also appearing with the Royal Teens—who had plugged "Short Shorts" on *American Bandstand* less than two weeks ago—were turban-topped Chuck Willis, whose "C.C. Rider" had inspired the "stroll" dance craze a year earlier, and Pat Boone, the "Mr. Clean" of rock and roll who already hosted his own ABC-TV series.
12. Lewis's "I ain't no puppet" is from Myra Lewis with Murray Silver, *Great Balls of Fire!* p. 162. "Stood the teenage pewsters" is from *The Dick Clark Show* (review),*Variety*, February 19, 1958.
13. Connie Francis's quotes are from Jerry Osborne, "Connie Francis" (interview), *DIS-Coveries*, September, 1991, p. 31.
14. The "sort of sit-down version . . . hideous efforts by no-talent performers" is from the *Philadelphia Bulletin* TV column, March 3, 1958. "Young, wholesome type . . . pleasantly and informatively" is from *The Dick Clark Show* (review), *Variety*. O'Brian's "past the blue-jeans age . . . just past the Mousketeer age" is from Jack O'Brian, "Clark Show: Teen Age Mess," *NYJA*, February 17, 1958.
15. John P. Shanley, "Dick Clark—New Rage of the Teenage Set," *NYT*, March 16, 1958.
16. "Dick Clark Gets a Good Rating," *NYHT*, February 18, 1958.
Trendex's overnight survey for Clark's first show gave him a 16 rating and a 26.3 share of the total TV audience for that particular time slot. CBS's *Perry Mason* drew a 22.3 and 36.7, while NBC's *People Are Funny* garnered a 19.4 and 31.9 share.
17. "IFIC" buttons were worn proudly, not only during Clark's show, but long after, as a badge of recognition (or boast) to friends that the wearer was one of the chosen few to have been there.
18. Greene, September 28, 1958.
19. Clark and Robinson, p. 128.
20. Goldenson, p. 101.
21. All the conversations involving Judd Phillips are taken from Lewis with Silver. Clark's quote appears on p. 162.
22. Lewis with Silver, p. 163.

23. William H.A. Carr, "Disc Maker Says He Cut Clark In," *NYP*, November 30, 1959.

24. Clark's "never forget what you and Jerry have done for me" and Lewis's "married to Myra" are from Lewis with Silver, pp. 163 and 179.

25. The account of Phillips's conversations with Beechnut's ad agency and with Clark, as well as the "Judas" quote, are from Lewis with Silver, pp. 180, 206. Clark's "very coward-ly act" is from Clark and Robinson, p. 141.

Although Clark revealed that his decision to disassociate himself from Lewis was one that he, Clark, has remained sorry for "ever since" (Clark and Robinson, p. 141), he said in 1994 that his dispute with Lewis "was long gone and we've put it behind us many times."

26. Clark has managed to successfully incorporate his Saturday night show into the *American Bandstand* legend. Although the package notes to *Dick Clark's Best of Bandstand* videocassette (Vestron Music Video, 1986) invite the consumer to "share all the excitement and enthusiasm of *American Bandstand*," the tape's fourteen performances (except for that of Buddy Holly and the Crickets, who performed on NBC-TV's *The Arthur Murray Party*) are taken from Clark's Saturday night show, not from *American Bandstand*.

27. Silver's quotes are from Ed Ward, *Rock of Ages; The Rolling Stone History of Rock and Roll.*, p. 167.

28. Smith, p. 104.

29. Greene, September 25, 1958.

30. To give Clark's show a truly national feeling, ABC decided to occasionally stage it in cities other than New York. This particular show, from the Miami Beach Auditorium, occurred on July 19, 1958.

31. Clark's "Do you want me to introduce you" quote is from the author's Eddy inter-view. SRO was formed by Clark and Wilde in the spring of 1958, ostensibly to book Clark's personal appearances.

32. Lipsius, owner of Universal Distributors, was a kingpin of the Philadelphia music business and, according to Rick Lewis, "one of the guys who helped" Clark piece together his music empire.

33. Eddy's 1959 releases were: "The Lonely One" (which reached No. 23); "Yep!" (No. 30); "Forty Miles of Bad Road" (No. 9); "Some Kind-A Earthquake" (No. 37); and "Bon-nie Came Back" (No. 26).

34. In the pre-videotape era, "you didn't just stop the tape and continue," explained Maestro, who said Clark's show had to be started again from the beginning.

35. U.S. House, *Responsibilities . . . ,* pp. 1278, 1281.

After the first year of the agreement, Clark was permitted a limited number of TV guest appearances on rival networks, subject to ABC's prior consent.

Chapter 7. A Television Personality

1. "Pied Piper of Teen-Age Set," *TV Guide*, May 24–30, 1958, p. 10.

The magazines in which articles on Clark appeared were: *Photoplay* (March, 1958); *Time* (April 14, 1958), and *TV Radio Mirror* (April 22, 1958). Clark appeared on Mur-row's show in April 1958. Two complete location crews with massive cameras and heavy cables virtually took over his suburban Drexel Hill residence days in advance in order to prepare and choreograph every moment of the live broadcast. Clark's first cover appear-ance on *TV Guide* occurred with the May 24–30th, 1958 edition.

2. The "television personality" quote is taken from *TV Guide*'s program listings for

April 25, 1958. Clark's "It's all a little frightening" is from "Tall, That's All," *Time*, April 14, 1958, p. 64. His "It's a wonderful thing . . . so much influence" is from "Pied Piper of Teen-Age Set," p. 11.

3. Gardner's "personality with a 'great sell'" is from "Hy Gardner's Typewriter X-Rays Dick Clark," *NYHT TV Magazine*, October 5, 1958, p. 7. The "as perfect as . . . three days to film it" quote is from Bolstad, "The Real Dick Clark," p. 10.

4. "Most valuable properties" is from John P. Shanley, March 16, 1958. "Out to get as much mileage as possible" is from "Dick Clark's 'Eve' Show And 'Pop' for 'Bandstand,'" *Variety*, November 19, 1958. Clark's "It'll be a cold day in Hades" is from Kahn, Part 5, April 18, 1958.

5. Bob Williams, "Dick Clark's Bandstand Turns City Into Teeners' Mecca," *PB*, July 20, 1958.

6. Ren Grevatt, "On the Beat" (column), *BB*, March 3, 1958.

7. Ibid.

8. Smith, p. 104.

9. "Pickin' On the Wrong Chicken" was assigned to Clark by Am-Par in April 1958, some days after Clark began playing the song on "Bandstand." Am-Par simultaneously released the song on ABC Paramount #9911.

To mounting criticism that Clark gave an "extra ride" to songs in which he had an interest (see Appendices II and III), one Philadelphia reporter wrote that "Dick vigorously denies this; he notes that his company has had only one smash hit—'At the Hop'—and a lot of flops." (Bob Williams, July 20, 1958.)

10. Wayne Jancik, "Down The Aisle With The Quin-Tones," *GM,* December 28, 1990, p. 48. The quote was attributed to Landersman by Quin-Tones member Phyllis Carr.

11. Jancik, "Down The Aisle. . . ," p. 48.

The fact that Clark received 95 percent of the publishing rights for "Down the Aisle" was reported by Jancik in this article.

12. Ibid., p. 27.

13. U.S. House, *Responsibilities. . .* , p. 1231.

14. Ibid., p. 1232.

15. Ibid., p. 887.

16. "Pied Piper of Teen-Age Set," p. 9.

17. "Dick Clark's 'Eve' Show. . . ," November 19, 1958.

18. Gail Shister, "The Ageless Prince of Frivolity," *PI Magazine*, November 18, 1984, p. 42.

19. According to a listing of artists in *The History of American Bandstand* by Shore with Clark, during the show's first year 75 percent of its guest performers were white.

20. Jon Pareles, "Thanks, Reminiscenses And Tunes, Lots of Tunes," *NYT*, March 2, 1996.

21. Jim Dawson, *The Twist*, p. 95.

22. U.S. House, *Responsibilities. . .* , p. 849.

23. Ibid., pp. 878, 882.

24. Wayne Jancik, "Fabian: The Teen Idol at 47," GM, December 28, 1990, p. 24.

25. The quotes of Fabian and his mother are from the John Palmieri interview.

26. Jancik, "Fabian. . . ," p. 24.

27. This conversation was recalled in the author's Marcucci interview.

28. Bill Davidson, *Redbook*, March 1960.

29. Marcucci claimed Chancellor earned over $7 million for Am-Par during the first year of their distribution deal.

30. Clark's quote was recalled by Marcucci.

31. Clark and Robinson, p. 135.

32. Ibid., p. 136.

33. Clark's "owed their existences to black music" is from Clark and Robinson, p. 82. His "terrified . . . didn't know what the reaction was going to be . . . it just happened" is from Schipper, p. 126.

34. Greene, "Dick Clark: Part 3," September 24, 1958.

35. This was attested to by the Crests' Johnny Maestro, who pointed out that because the group was integrated, "we couldn't get any of the national TV shows except Dick Clark."

36. Greene, September 24, 1958.

37. "Mr. Clark and Colored Payola," *New York Age*, December 5, 1959.

38. Holly G. Miller, "Dick Clark's Role After Rock, " *The Saturday Evening Post*, July/August, 1995, p. 34.

39. The "document on incipient idiocy" quote is from Bill Ladd, "Teen-Agers' Understanding Big Brother—That's Key to Dick Clark's Success," *Louisville* (KY) *Courier-Journal*, April 12, 1959. "Egocentric incompetents, entirely lacking in talent" is from J.P. Shanley, "Television" (column), *America*, February 14, 1959, p. 587. "No musical gifts . . . hit records" is from Harriet Van Horne, "R 'n' R Apostle a Proper Fellow," *NYWT*, June 14, 1959.

40. "Horn Admits Tax Evasion."

41. "The 'Payola' Rock" (editorial), *PB*, April 19, 1958.

42. Greene, "Dick Clark: Part 4," September 25, 1958.

43. Clark interview with Ralph Emery. Clark had previously stated that "With all the companies I had, we had a budget for paying guys to play records." (Smith, p. 105.)

Chapter 8. Rubicon

1. Jancik, "Fabian. . . ," p. 24.

2. By that time, Avalon and Fabian had open access to Clark's TV shows. Marcucci said he had "proven" to Clark "that they were both big stars. We had gotten unbelievably big and we just kept on going back and doing anything he would want us to do."

3. Donald J. Mabry, "The Rise and Fall of Ace Records: A Case Study in the Independent Record Business," *Business History Review*, p. 446.

4. U.S. House, *Responsibilities. . . ,* p. 1299.

5. Jason Berry, Jonathan Foose, and Tad Jones, *Up from the Cradle of Jazz: New Orleans Music Since World War II*, p. 111.

6. "Sea Cruise" was one of the biggest hits of 1959, and also became one of the classic rock and roll tunes of all time. Ford claimed that whenever he or Clanton was booked on Clark's Saturday show, Ace Records' New York distributor "ordered a hundred thousand" copies of whatever song was to be performed that evening.

7. Wayne Jones, "Freddie Cannon . . . Still Where The Action Is," *GM*, November, 1979, p. 14. Cannon declined to be interviewed for this book.

8. "We went everywhere and we got turned down everywhere" (including Chancellor Records), said Rydell. Bob Marcucci did not reject the young singer for any lack of talent, he simply had all he could do to properly record and manage Frankie Avalon and Fabian.

9. Arnold Shaw, *The Rockin' '50s*, p. 247.

10. Carol Gelber, "8,000 Fans Greet Fabian at Theatre for Premiere," *PB*, November 12, 1959.

11. Joseph Stone and Tim Yohn, *Prime Time and Misdemeanors*, p. 247.

12. Jeff Tamarkin, "The Beat Goes On," p. 13.

13. "Wider TV Inquiry to Study Bribery and Paid Plugs," *NYT*, November 7, 1959.

14. In 1960 the subcommittee consisted of Rep. Oren Harris (D-ARK); John J. Bennett (R-MI); Steven Derounian (R-NY); Samuel Devine (R-OH); John J. Flynt (D-GA); Peter F. Mack (D-IL); John E. Moss (D-CA); Walter Rogers (D-TX); and William Springer (R-IL). Chief counsel for the subcommittee was Robert W. Lishman.

15. Goldenson, p. 163.

Goldenson, who regarded "American Bandstand" as nothing less than "an anchor for the whole daytime lineup [that] . . . drew people to the network who weren't there before" (Goldenson, p. 163), estimated that Clark's TV shows were responsible for some $11 million in annual gross revenue for ABC. (U.S. House, *Responsibilities...*, p. 1401).

16. Goldenson's "any other information" to "taking you off the air" are from U.S. House, *Responsibilities. . .*, pp. 1388, 1389, 1439.

17. Clark's words were recalled by Fetter.

18. This exchange between Goldenson and Clark is from Goldenson's testimony, U.S. House, *Responsibilities. . .*, pp. 1389, 1401.

19. Schipper, p. 70.

20. Clark's "seemed strangely reluctant . . . he would bring his lawyer" and "some things . . . difficult to explain" are from Clark and Robinson, pp. 187, 188. His "right arm" is from the liner notes to the *Dance With Dick Clark-Volume 1* album. His "I don't want to know at this point" is from U.S. House, *Responsibilities. . .*, p. 1300.

21. Matt Damsker, "Dick Clark Is Still Active, Visible," *PB*, June 6, 1976.

22. Patricia O'Haire, "Mr. Bandstand," *NYDN*, May 21, 1989.

23. U.S. House, *Responsibilities. . .*, p.1389.

24. Ibid., p. 1401.

25. Ibid., p. 1303.

26. Kelly's "caught with our pants down," and all of Mammarella's quotes, are from U.S. House, *Responsibilities. . .*, pp. 1238, 815.

27. Mammarella's "advice . . . on overcoming deficiencies . . . in the selection of the recordings," and "to the best of" are from U.S. House, *Responsibilities. . .*, pp. 774, 816. Clark's "from that point on" is from U.S. House, *Responsibilities. . .*, p. 1300.

28. Goldenson, pp. 163, 164.

29. Clark's words were recalled by Goldenson. (U.S. House, *Responsibilities. . .*, p. 1390).

30. Clark's "felt warmly about him . . . harsh language" and "Early yesterday morning . . . resignation has been accepted" quotes are from U.S. House, *Responsibilities. . .*, pp.1301, 815. Goldenson's "Dick was clean" is from Goldenson, p. 164.

31. Goldenson, p. 164.

32. "Dick Clark Bows to ABC, to Drop Side Businesses, *PB*, November 17, 1959.

33. Josephson's "never any secret" is from "Dick Clark Bows To ABC. . . ." The *Variety* quote is from "Dick Clark's Music Ties First Casualty of ABC-TV's Sensitivity to 'Payola,'" *Variety*, November 18, 1959. Clark's "confidence in the integrity" is from U.S. House, *Responsibilities. . .*, p. 1216.

34. ABC's statement in support of Clark is from U.S. House, *Responsibilities. . .*, p. 809.

35. "Clark Grateful to Friends and Network for Support," *PB*, November 18, 1959.

36. U.S. House, *Responsibilities. . .* , p. 1244.

37. Ibid., p. 1238.

38. Ibid., pp. 1238, 1239.

39. Clark and Robinson, p. 188.

40. Smith, p. 103.

41. *PB*, November 19, 1959.

42. Clark's "reign of terror" is from Clark and Robinson, p. 183. "Amassed a wealth of information" and "bad case of the jitters" are from "House Group Amassing File On TV, Radio 'Payola' Here," *PB*, November 19, 1959. "Running into thousands of dollars" is from David Wise, "Charge Big Payoffs to Disc Jockeys," *NYHT*, November 21, 1959.

43. Wise, *NYHT*.

44. Earl Wilson, "Alan Freed's Story," *NYP*, November 23, 1959.

45. "Clark's 'World of Talent' Will Be Dropped by ABC," *PB*, November 26, 1959.

46. Clark's millionaire status is referred to in Noah James, "We Do What the Networks Want," *NYT*, July 14, 1985, and in Barrier, p. 90.

Chapter 9. Clarkola

1. U.S. House, *Responsibilities. . .* , p. 1259.

2. The F.B.I. report, from "Duke Mon" to "Schaef," dated December 7, 1959, is on file in the Urban Archives of the Temple University Library in Philadelphia.

3. Abe Peck, "The Oldest Living Teenager: Dick Clark Recalls the '50s," *PI*, December 26, 1976.

4. *Laws of the General Assembly of the Commonwealth of Pennsylvania Passed at the Session Of 1939, Harrisburg;* Section 667, "Bribery, etc. of Servants and Employes," p. 941.

5. All quotes, from "widespread interests in almost every phase" to "I always heard it was ten per cent," are from Alfred T. Hendricks and William H.A. Carr, "Check of Record Firm Indicates Dick Clark Still Has Holdings," *NYP*, December 16, 1959.

6. All quotes, from "potential links" to "I'm damned if I know. . . . I doubt if anyone [at the network] knows" are from Hendricks and Carr, "Check of Record Firm. . . ."

7. Barris's "hated my guts" is from Chuck Barris, *The Game Show King: A Confession*, pp. 27, 28. His "not quite sure myself" quote is from Hendricks and Carr, "Check of Record Firm. . . ."

8. Clark and Robinson, p. 186.

9. Jackson, pp. 244, 245.

10. "$172,469,000 Peak for ABC in 1959," *Variety*, April 6, 1960.

11. "ABC-TV 80% Sold For '60–'61 Season; $125,000,000 Gross," *Variety*, April 20, 1960.

12. "Vote of confidence" is from "Not Beached," *Variety*, January 27, 1960. Moore's quote is from Marie Torre, "Dick Clark Gets Raise In 'Vote of Confidence,'" *NYHT*, March 28, 1960. Clark's contract still had five years to run at the time.

13. "Unbothered by all that payola-probing" is from "UA Extends Dick Clark," *Variety*, April 13, 1960. "Might very well find" is from Ernie Schier, "*Because They're Young* Stars 'Teacher' Dick Clark," *PB*, April 18, 1960.

14. U.S. House, *Responsibilities. . .* , testimony of Goldenson, pp. 1406–1410; testimony of Clark, pp. 1217, 1323–1328, 1347–1353.

15. U.S. House, *Responsibilities. . .* , testimony of Kelly, p. 1244.

16. Ibid., pp 1216–1218.

17. "House Probers, FTC in Hot Race For Clark's Data," *Variety*, January 27, 1960.

18. Ibid., pp. 761 and 765.

19. U.S. House, *Responsibilities...*, pp. 732–828.

20. Ibid., p. 776.

21. "Obviously quite seriously involved" is from "Dick Clark Had Interest In 17 Music Companies," *PB*, March 4, 1960. "Casual and superficial" is from "Prober Says Dick Clark Admits Gifts of Jewelry," *Camden (NJ) Post*, March 10, 1960.

22. Lishman's quotes are from "Dick Clark Whitewashed? Just Wait and See, Say Mack and Moss; Committee 'Won't Be Stampeded,'" *Variety*, March 23, 1960. Clark's "No comment and goodbye" is from "Dick Clark Had Interest...." Moore's "a sincere and honest young man" is from Marie Torre, "Dick Clark Gets Raise...."

23. Fong-Torres, p. 19.

24. U.S. House, *Responsibilities...*, pp. 1179, 1180.

25. Abe Peck.

26. Freed testimony, p. 8.

27. "A Closed Hearing Is Held on Clark; Payola Inquiry Goes Into Disc Jockey's Business Ties—Alan Freed Testifies," *NYT*, April 26, 1960.

28. Freed testimony, pp. 28–31

29. "Music Business Goes Round and Round: It Comes Out Clarkola," *Life*, May 16, 1960, p. 122.

30. U.S. House, *Responsibilities...*, pp 961–967.

31. The "certainly does not support" quote was made by Dr. Joseph F. Daly, Chief Mathematical Statistician, U.S. Bureau of the Census. The "no firm conclusion" quote was made by Joseph L. Tryon, Teacher of Economics and Statistics, Georgetown University. The "far more interested" quote was made by Rep. Moss. (U.S. House, *Responsibilities...*, pp. 1001, 1009, 986, respectively) The "300 pounds" is from Mary McGrory, "Weighty Evidence," *NYP*, April 27, 1960.

32. Clark and Robinson, p. 204.

33. "Was neatly lacquered in place ... the same air of proper respectibility" is from "Music Business Goes Round...," p. 118. Clark's "prejudgement ... convicted, condemned, and denounced" is from U.S. House, *Responsibilities...*, p. 1168. "Frankly we're listening and watching" is from William H.A. Carr, "Probers Asking: Why Wasn't Clark Fired?" *NYP*, May 1, 1960.

34. Clark's "I want to make it clear, immediately" to "with honesty and integrity," are from his subcommittee testimony (U.S. House, *Responsibilities...*, pp. 1168–1185). "Even more self-possessed" is from Anthony Lewis, "Dick Clark Denies Receiving Payola; Panel Skeptical," *NYT*, April 30, 1960.

35. Clark's "are not guilty of payola" is from U.S. House, *Responsibilities...*, pp. 1307, 1308. Derounian's "awful lot of royola" is from "Nobody Blew the Whistle," *Newsweek*, May 9, 1960, p. 30.

36. U.S. House, *Responsibilities...*, pp. 1240, 1241.

37. Jackson, pp. 269, 270.

38. The exchange between Clark and Bennett is from U.S. House, *Responsibilities...*, pp. 1214, 1215. Clark's "late knowledge" and "it never occurred to me" are from U.S. House, *Responsibilities...*, pp 1189–1197.

39. Ibid., pp. 1334, 1335.

40. Ibid., p. 1215.

41. Derounian's "Christian Dior" is from U.S. House, *Responsibilities...*, p. 1201. His "golden egg" is from William H. A. Carr, "Probers Asking: Why...."

42. U.S. House, *Responsibilities...*, p. 1243.

43. Ibid., pp. 1219, 1221.

44. "Nobody Blew the Whistle," p. 30.

45. U.S. House, *Responsibilities...*, p. 1350.

46. Marie Torre, "Dick Clark Wants to Put Payola Furor to Rest," *NYHT*, June 7, 1960.

47. Clark's "allowed his kid to skip school" is from Schipper, p. 70. His "The kid had cut school" is from Hal Humphrey, "Do Viewers Benefit From the TV Probes?," *PB*, August 29, 1961.

48. William H. A. Carr, "Probers Asking...."

49. Moss's "giving a plug" and "I can call it 'Clarkola'" are from U.S. House, *Responsibilities...*, pp. 1319, 1320,1323. Clark's "made a great deal of money" is from Anthony Lewis, "Dick Clark Denies...."

50. U.S. House, *Responsibilities...*, p. 1351.

51. Mack's "top dog in the payola field" and Goldenson's quotes are from Bob Williams, "Prober Brands Clark 'Top Dog In Payola Field,'" *PB*, May 3, 1960.

52. Schipper, p. 126.

Chapter 10. The Past as Prologue

1. "Blanc's Hope: Injunction to Ban Payola," *Philadelphia Sunday Bulletin*, August 14, 1960.

2. Marie Torre, "Dick Clark Wants to Put...."

3. This figure was Clark's estimate. U.S. House, *Responsibilities...*, p. 1194.

4. Damsker.

5. Sanjek, p. 186.

6. The conversation with Clark was recalled by Zacherle.

7. "Dick Clark," ABC Television biography sheet, June, 1960. New York Public Library.

8. Clark's quotes are from "Guilty Only of Success," *TV Guide*, September 10–16, 1960, pp. 10, 11.

9. Bennetts.

10. Shore with Clark, pp. 51–53.

11. Ibid., p. 45.

12. Marter.

13. "Dick Clark Troupe Pulls 29G In H'wood," *Variety*, September 3, 1958.

14. "Folds In Mpls.," *Variety*, September 3, 1958.

15. "Clark Takes Promoter Off Hook In Mpls. Flop," *Variety*, September 10, 1958.

16. "Youth Stabbed in Teenage Fight After Dick Clark's Sunnybrook Hop," *Philadelphia Sunday Bulletin*, December 28, 1958.

17. "75 Teen-Agers Jailed For Rock 'n' Roll Riot," *Louisville Courier-Journal*, October 19, 1959.

18. Ibid.

19. Clark's "very unfortunate" is from "Dick Clark Says Juvenile Adults Caused Riot at His Show in K.C.," *NYP*, October 21, 1959. "Peace and well-being" is from "Lesson for Youth," *PB*, October 20, 1959.

20. Schipper, p. 126.

21. The conversation between Hooke and Ross was recalled by Hooke.

22. Schipper, p. 126.

23. Clark's "The shocking part" is from Schipper, p. 126. His "weren't welcomed in hotels" is from his 1994 interview with the author.

Chapter 11. From Chubby Checker to the Beatles

1. Shore with Clark, p. 121.

2. "Nationwide dance revival" and "one of the greatest things" are from Kahn, Part 4, April 17, 1958.

3. "Dancing; Part 3; New Worlds."

4. The quotes by Fusco, Peatross, and Kiene are from "Dancing."

5. Shore, with Clark, p. 116.

6. Grevatt.

7. Smith, p. 104.

8. Bolstad, "Why Do Teens Trust Dick Clark?"

9. Smith, p. 104.

10. Wayne Jancik, "Chubby Checker: Twistin' Time Is (Still) Here," *GM*, December 28, 1990, p. 20.

11. Dawson, *The Twist*, p. 2.

12. Clark's version is taken from Clark and Robinson, p. 100.

13. Dawson, *The Twist*, p. 27.

14. Ibid, p. 25.

15. Bruce Pollock, *When Rock Was Young*, pp. 108, 109.

16. The quotes of Barbara Clark and Checker are from Jancik, "Chubby Checker. . . , pp. 18, 20.

17. Jim Dawson, "The Twist by Hank Ballard and the Midnighters," *DISCoveries*, June, 1994, p. 40.

18. Ron Mann, *Twist*.

19. Ibid.

20. Dawson, "The Twist by Hank Ballard. . . ," p. 40.

21. Dawson, *The Twist*, pp. 1–4.

22. Checker's "I truly don't know" and "changed the planet" are from Smith, p. 196.

23. Clark's "pretty frightening" and Betty Romantini Begg's "changed the way that we danced" are from Mann.

24. Clifford Dunn interview.

25. "Dick Clark and Wife Are Getting a Divorce," *PB*, May 17, 1961.

26. Emery interview.

27. Clark and Robinson, p. 227.

28. "Dick Clark's Fans Shocked By News of Divorce Plans," *PB*, May 18, 1961.

29. John Harris, "Clark Breakup Stirs Rumors and Mystery," *NYHT*, May 19, 1961.

30. *The Philadelphia Daily News* noted in its "Tank Town Talk" column of January 9, 1962, that Barbara's new husband was "a former in-law." In interviews with the author, Agnes Mammarella and others identified Barbara's new husband as Clark's cousin.

31. Rick Du Brow, "Dick Clark, Film Star, Prefers Philadelphia," *PB*, August 27, 1961.

32. Jancik, "Chubby Checker. . . ," p. 20.

33. Clark and Robinson, p. 97.

34. Sharp's quotes are from Mann.

35. Harry J. LaCroix, "Cameo Grows Rapidly By Setting Its Sights on Teen-Age Market," *PI*, November 11, 1963.

36. Joan Crosby, "Meet Dick Clark: He Thinks His Show Can Run 30 Years," *PDN*, August 17, 1962.

37. Clark's "at peace with the network" to "the tastes of the teens" are from Joan Crosby.

38. Herm Schoenfeld, "Biz Ventures (Show and Otherwise) Put Dick Clark Right Back on Top," *Variety*, February 6, 1963.

39. Du Brow.

40. Schoenfeld, "Biz Ventures. . . ."

41. "Dick Clark Ends 10-Yr. Cross-the-Board Run; Doing Sat. Hour Only," *Variety*, June 12, 1963.

42. Tamarkin, "The Beat Goes On," pp. 13, 16.

43. "Dick Clark Recalls *Where the Action Is*," *GM*, April 20, 1990, p. 22.

44. "ABC-TV Daytime Rides June Boom; Sales Hit $15 Mil., *Variety*, July 3, 1963.

45. This conversation with Binnick is from the Clark interview of 1994, except for "this different look" to "It'll never fly," which are from Smith, p. 105.

46. In early 1962 Chicago's Vee Jay Records issued the Beatles' first two English hits, "Please Please Me" and "From Me to You," but the records went virtually unnoticed.

47. The Binnick-Epstein conversation was recalled by Shively.

48. Steven Rea, "Dick Clark's own story of *American Bandstand*," *PI*, November 7, 1985.

49. John Horn, "New Game Shows, Worse Than Most," *NYHT*, December 31, 1963.

Chapter 12. Where the Action Is

1. Oscar Godbout, "Nat Cole Scores Ad Men On Ouster," *NYT*, November 22, 1957.

2. Quotations relating to *The Buddy Deane Show* are from "Dancing; Part 3."

3. Clark with Shore, p. 92.

4. "Clark Blames Game Show Lemon On Calif. Where 'Everybody's a Hambone,'" *Variety*, June 3, 1964.

5. "Beatles Craze 'Tapering Off,' Dick Clark Says," *PI*, July 10, 1964.

6. Ibid.

7. Damsker.

8. "Cameo Records Shows $499, 319 Loss for '64," *PB*, March 12, 1965.

9. "Beatles Craze 'Tapering Off. . . .'"

10. "Born. To Dick Clark, 35, Pied Piper. . . ," *Time*, January 22, 1965.

11. Tamarkin, "The Beat Goes On," p. 16.

12. George, p. 87.

13. Ibid.

14. Ibid., pp. 92, 93.

15. Shore with Clark, pp. 134, 135.

16. Russell and David Sanjek, p. 207.

17. "Teen-Age Music Due to Go Farther Out, Predicts Dick Clark," *Louisville Courier-Journal*, October 8, 1967.

18. Walter F. Naedele, "Two J. Browns In Movies? Clark Says There's Room," *PB*, June 15, 1969.

19. Clark's and the bellboy's quotes are from the interview with Hooke.

20. Shore with Clark, pp. 134–139.

21. "TV Show Helped Found an Empire," *Newark Evening News*, August 6, 1967.

22. Mimi Mead, "Clark Building Vast Empire," *PI*, June 2, 1966.

23. "Dick Clark Strikes It Rich on Coast," *Variety*, January 12, 1966.

24. "TV Show Helped Found an Empire."

25. Digby Diehl, "The Oldest Living Teen-Ager," *TV Guide*, February 14, 1970, p. 46.

26. Ibid.

27. Ibid.

28. Tom Gray, "A Producer Who Promotes His Pictures in Advance," *Motion Picture Herald*, October 9, 1968, p. 7.

29. Leonard Maltin, *TV Movies 1985–86* (Revised), p. 466.

30. Gray, p. 7.

31. Nelson, Nels, "King of the Teenagers Goes After Pre-Geriatric Set," *PDN*, May 22, 1968.

32 "Good News For Eardrums: Dick Clark Says Music Is Coming Back," ABC *Feature*, March 5, 1969. New York Public Library.

33. Ibid.

34. Clark and Robinson, p. 264.

35. "Good News For Eardrums. . . ."

36. Ibid.

Chapter 13. America's Oldest Living Teenager

1. Diehl, p. 44.

2. Ibid., p. 46.

3. Untitled *NYT* article, July 17, 1972.

4. Andy Meisler, "For 'Soul Train's' Conductor, Beat Goes On," *NYT*, August 7, 1995.

5. Ibid.

6. George, p. 146.

7. Diehl, p. 44.

8. "Dick Clark Plans Oldies Club," PJ, July 21, 1972.

9. Joe Adcock, "Dick Clark: Old-timer to the under 25s," *PB*, June 29, 1980.

10. All reunion quotes are from Bennetts.

11. "'American Bandstand's' 20th Anni," *Variety*, May 30, 1973.

12. "Dick Clark, who's been an impresario of rock music shows. . . ," *NYP* television column, July 20, 1972.

13. "Dick (Bandstand) Clark moves into the prime-time. . . ," *NYP*, television column, November 27, 1973.

14. Bob Williams, "Dick Clark, Avalon, Annette," *NYP*, June 28, 1976.

15. Jim Forkan, "Dick Clark Superstar," *Our Town* (NY), p. 6.

16. *The $10,000 Pyramid* (review), *Variety*, April 11, 1973, p. 52.
There also was a nighttime version of *Pyramid*, hosted by Bill Cullen.

17. Ian Dove, "Yes, Rock Has Lasted; So Has Dick Clark," *NYT*, June 1, 1973.

18. Clark's "But it still . . . buyers in a week" is from Fong-Torres, p. 19. His "I had no trouble understanding" is from Tamarkin, "The Beat Goes On," p. 16.

19. *Best of American Bandstand*, December 3, 1977.

20. Shore with Clark, pp. 170, 171.

21. Ibid., pp. 172, 173.

22. Peck.

23. *Best of American Bandstand*, September 11, 1976.

24. Toni Holt, "Dick Clark Pays $1 Million for Divorce, *The National Tattler*, January 19, 1975.

25. Ibid.

26. Clark's "first woman I've known" and Wigton's "perfectionist . . . very difficult to work with . . . don't get fired" are from Brad Darrach, "It's Not Just Another Pretty Face, It's Showbiz Conglomerate King Dick Clark," *People*, February 14, 1977, p. 74. Clark's "two-time loser" is from the Emery interview.

27. Harry Harris, "'Bandstand' special tops all, Clark says," *PI*, February 2, 1977.

28. Darrach, p. 73.

29. Ibid., pp. 73, 74.

30. Forkan, p. 6.

31. Rex Polier, "If I Fail I Get the Gong," *PB*, September 3, 1978.

32. Ibid.

33. Bob Williams, "Dick Clark, who dates back on TV . . ." (television column), *NYP*, August 19, 1974.

34. "Dick Clark's Live Wednesday," *Variety*, September 27, 1978.

35. *Best of American Bandstand*, May 13, 1978.

36. Clinton Heylin, *From The Velvets to the Voidoids. . .*, p. xiii.

37. *Best of American Bandstand*, February 21, 1981.

38. Shore with Clark, pp. 175, 207.

39. Ibid., pp. 207, 208.

40. Russell and David Sanjek, p. 247.

41. Szatmary (Second Edition), pp. 257, 258.

42. *Best of American Bandstand*, July 24, 1982.

43. Rae.

44. "Dick Clark's Best Of Bandstand" (review), *Goldmine*, August 15, 1986.

45. David Morris, "A Historic Designation for Home of 'Bandstand,'" *PI*, August 30, 1986.

46. Nikki Finke Greenberg and Eric Gelman, "Clark Around the Clock," *Newsweek*, August 18, 1986, p. 27.

47. Hackett, p. 128.

48. "The Forbes Four Hundred," *Forbes*, October 27, 1986, pp. 229, 231.

49. "Who's Gone This Year, *Forbes*, October 26, 1987, p. 306.

50. Goldenson, p. 461.

51. Goldenson, p. 466.

52. Clark's "finally decided" is from "Dick Clark Leaving 'Bandstand,'" *PDN*, March 22, 1989. Greenspan's quote is from Jeff Greenfield, "Dick Clark, a constant in changing world," *Chicago Sun-Times*, March 27, 1989.

53. Clark's "spent the better part . . . to the next man" and Hirsch's "much different. . . . That gets to you" and "I would love it . . . not as dated" are from Steve Pond, "Dick Clark's Last Stand," *RS*, May 18, 1989, pp. 47, 48.

54. Ibid., p. 48.

Epilogue

1. Rex Polier, "In Sentiment, At Least, a Native Philadelphian," *PB*, October 29, 1981.

2. Tamarkin, "The Beat Goes On," p. 16.

3. John J. O'Connor, TV column, *NYT*, May 12, 1992.

4. Clark's "accumulation of worldly goods . . . as much as the good Lord" is from Alan W. Petrucelli, "Author-Ized," *Us*, March 3, 1981, p. 63. His "nature of the beast" is from Shister, p. 40.

5. Christy Slewinsky, "Dick Clark Is Having a Ball for the 24th Year," *St. Petersburg Times*, December 31, 1995.

6. Petrucelli.

7. "The Forbes 400 Richest People in America," *Forbes*, October 16, 1995.

8. Slewinski.

9. Newly taped *Best of American Bandstand* introduction for the program of March 3, 1979.

10. Holly G. Miller, "Dick Clark's Role After Rock," *The Saturday Evening Post*, August, 1995, p. 34.

11. Slewinski.

12. All figures are from *Forbes*, October 16, 1995.

13. This was stated in *Best of American Bandstand*'s newly recorded introduction for the show of July 28, 1984.

14. Miller, p. 88.

15. *Best of American Bandstand*, March 7, 1981.

16. Ibid., January 31, 1976.

17. Ibid., September 11, 1976.

18. Ibid., January 31, 1976.

19. Ibid., May 12, 1979.

Bibliography

Government Documents

Commonwealth of Pennsylvania, Harrisburg, PA. *Laws of the General Assembly*. Section 667, p. 941: Bribery, etc. of Servants and Employes. Passed at the Session of 1939.

Internal memo, To: "Schaef," From "Duke Mon," Federal Bureau of Investigation, regarding Dick Clark's involvement, if any, in Chips Distributing, Jamie Records, and Bernard Lowe Enterprises, December 7, 1959.

U.S. House of Representatives, *Responsibilities of Broadcasting Licensees and Station Personnel: Hearings Before a Subcommittee of the Committee on Interstate and Foreign Commerce*. 86th Congress, 2nd Session on Payola and Other Deceptive Practices in the Broadcasting Field. Part I: February 8, 9, 10, 15, 17, 18, 19, March 4, 1960. Part II: April 27, 28, 29, May 2, 3, August 30, 31, 1960, Washington, D.C. Government Printing Office, 1960.

U.S. House of Representatives, Special Subcommittee on Legislative Oversight of the Committee on Interstate and Foreign Commerce, Washington, D.C., *"Payola" and Related Deceptive Methods in the Broadcast Field*, Executive Session—Confidential Testimony of Alan Freed, Accompanied by Counsel Warren Troob, April 25, 1960, unpublished.

Books

Amfitheatrof, Erik, *The Children Of Columbus: An Informal History of the Italians in the New World*. Boston: Little, Brown and Company, 1973.

Barnouw, Erik, *The Sponsor: Notes On a Modern Potentate*. New York: Oxford University Press, 1978.

Barris, Chuck, *The Game Show King: A Confession*. New York: Carroll & Graf, 1993.

Berry, Jason; Foos, Jonathan, and Jones, Tad, *Up From the Cradle of Jazz: New Orleans Music Since World War II*. Athens, Ga.: University of Georgia, 1986.

Clark, Dick, and Robinson, Richard, *Rock, Roll & Remember*. New York: Thomas Y. Crowell, 1976.

Clarke, Donald, ed., *The Penguin Encyclpaedia of Popular Music*. New York: Viking Penguin (paperback), 1989.

Dawson, Jim, *The Twist*. Boston: Faber & Faber, 1995.

Gambino, Richard, *Blood of My Blood: The Dilemma of the Italian-Americans*. Garden City, N.Y.: Doubleday, 1974.

Gelatt, Roland, *The Fabulous Phonograph: 1877–1977*. New York: Macmillan, 1977.

George, Nelson, *The Death of Rhythm & Blues*. New York: Plume/Penguin, 1988.

Goldenson, Leonard, *Beating the Odds: The Untold Story Behind the Rise of ABC*. New York: Macmillan, 1991.

Guralnick, Peter, *Last Train to Memphis: The Rise of Elvis Presley*. Boston: Little, Brown and Company, 1994.

Heylin, Clinton, *From the Velvets to the Voidoids: A Pre-Punk History for a Post-Punk World*. New York: Penguin (paperback), 1993.

Jackson, John A., *Big Beat Heat: Alan Freed and the Early Years of Rock & Roll*. New York: Schirmer/Macmillan, 1991.

Jancik, Wayne, *One Hit Wonders*. New York: Billboard Books, 1990.

Lewis, Myra, with Silver, Murray, *Great Balls of Fire: The Uncensored Story of Jerry Lee Lewis*. New York: St. Martin's Press (Paperback), 1982, 1989.

Lukacs, John, *Philadelphia Patricians and Philistines 1900–1950*. New York: Farrar, Straus, Giroux, 1980.

McLuhan, Marshall, *Understanding Media*. New York: New American Library Paperback, 1964.

McLuhan, Marshall, and Fiore, Quentin, *The Medium Is the Massage*. New York: Random House, 1967.

Mayer, Martin, *Madison Avenue, U.S.A.*. New York: Pocket Books (paperback), 1959.

Maltin, Leonard, *TV Movies 1985–86* (Revised). New York: Signet (paperback), 1984.

Moquin, Wayne, ed., *A Documentary History of the Italian Americans*. New York: Praeger, 1974.

Nasaw, David, *Going Out: The Rise and Fall of Public Amusements*. New York: Basic Books, 1993.

Packard, Vance, *The Hidden Persuaders*. New York: Pocket Books (Paperback), 1957.

Passman, Arnold, *The Deejays*. New York: Macmillan, 1971.

Pollock, Bruce, *When Rock Was Young*. New York: Holt, Rinehart and Winston, 1981.

———. *When the Music Mattered: Rock in the 1960s*. New York: Holt, Rinehart and Winston, 1983.

Postman, Neil, *Amusing Ourselves to Death: Public Discourse in the Age of Show Business*. New York: Viking, 1985.

Rachlin, Harvey, *The Encyclopedia of the Music Business*. New York, 1981.

Sanjek, Russell, *American Popular Music and Its Business: The First Four Hundred Years: Volume III From 1900 to 1984*. New York: Oxford University Press, 1988.

Sanjek, Russell & Sanjek, David, *American Popular Music Business in the 20th Century*. New York: Oxford University Press, 1991.

Shaw, Arnold, *Dictionary of American Pop/Rock*. New York: Schirmer, 1982.

———. *The Rockin' '50s*. New York: DaCapo Press (paperback), 1987.

Shore, Michael, with Clark, Dick, *The History of American Bandstand*. New York: Balantine, 1985.

Smith, Joe, *Off the Record: An Oral History of Popular Music*. New York: Warner Books, 1988.

Sobel, Robert, *The Manipulators: America in the Media Age*. Garden City, N.Y.: Doubleday, 1976.

Sterling, Christopher H. and Kittross, John M., *Stay Tuned: A Concise History of American Broadcasting*, Belmont, California: Wadsworth, 1978.

Stone, Joseph & Yohn, Tim, *Prime Time and Misdemeanors*. New Brunswick, N.J.: Rutgers University Press, 1992.

Szatmary, David P., *Rockin' in Time: A Social History of Rock and Roll*. Englewood Cliffs, N.J.: Prentice-Hall, 1987.

Ward, Ed; Stokes, Geoffrey; & Tucker, Ken, *Rock of Ages: The Rolling Stone History of Rock & Roll*. New York: Rolling Stone Press, 1986.

Weaver, Pat & Coffey, Thomas M., *The Best Seat in the House: The Golden Years of Radio and Television*. New York: Alfred A. Knopf, 1993.

Weigley, Russell F., ed., *Philadelphia: A 300-Year History*. New York: W.W. Norton, 1982.

Whitburn, Joel, *Pop Memories 1890–1954*. Menomonee Falls, Wisc.: Record Research Inc., 1986.

———. *Top Pop Singles 1955–1986*. Menomonee Falls, Wisc.: Record Research Inc., 1987.

Williams, Huntington, *Beyond Control: ABC and the Fate of the Networks*. New York: Atheneum, 1989.

Wolff, Daniel; with Crain, S.R.; White, Clifton; and Tenenbaum, G. David, *You Send Me: The Life and Times of Sam Cooke*. New York: William Morrow, 1995.

Articles and Documents

"ABC May Use *Bandstand* As Opposition to Como," *Philadelphia Bulletin*, September 20, 1957.

"ABC-TV Daytime Rides June Boom; Sales Hit $15-Mil.," *Variety*, July 3, 1963.

"ABC-TV 80% Sold For '60–'61 Season; $125,000,000 Gross," *Variety*, April 20, 1960.

Adams, Val, "A.B.C. Will Audition 8 Negroes to Select a Network Reporter," *New York Times*, August 8, 1962.

Adams, Val, "Top TV Time Sales Seen for Autumn," *New York Times*, July 29, 1957.

Adcock, Joe, "Dick Clark: Old-timer to the under 25s," *Philadelphia Bulletin*, June 29, 1980.

American Bandstand (review), *TV Guide*, October 19, 1957.

"*American Bandstand*'s 20th Anni," *Variety*, May 30, 1973.

Anderson, John, "Round and Around With 'The Twist' Man," *Newsday* (Long Island), August, 1993.

"*Bandstand*'s Bob Horn Held for Driving While Drunk," *Philadelphia Bulletin*, June 21, 1956.

Barrier, Michael, "American Handstand," *Nation's Business*, October 1987.

"Beatles Craze 'Tapering Off,' Dick Clark Says," *Philadelphia Inquirer*, July 10, 1964.

Bennetts, Leslie, "And Not a Pair of Bobby Sox in Sight," *Philadelphia Bulletin*, October 30, 1973.

"Blanc's Hope: Injunction to Ban Payola," *Philadelphia Sunday Bulletin*, August 14, 1960.

"Bob Horn Calls Witness 'Liar,'" *Philadelphia Bulletin*, January 30, 1957.

Bolstad, Helen, "Why Do Teens Trust Dick Clark?" *Photoplay*, March 16, 1958.

"Born. To Dick Clark, 35, Pied Piper (at $100,000 a year) to the country's rock 'n' rollers," *Time*, January 22, 1965.

Bosco, Bob, "Joey/Flips from *Bandstand* to Obscurity," *Record Collector's Monthly*, November/December, 1991.

———. "The Real Fabulous 4," *DISCcoveries*, January, 1996.

Brookhouser, Frank, "Man About Town," *Philadelphia Bulletin*, October 3, 1956.

Bundy, June, "TV Spinners as Strong on Network as on Local Air," *Variety*, November 11, 1957.

"Cameo Records Shows $499, 319 Loss for '64," *Philadelphia Bulletin*, March 12, 1965.

Carr, William, H.A., "Disc Maker Says He Cut Clark In," *New York Post*, November 30, 1959.

———. "Probers Asking: Why Wasn't Clark Fired?" *New York Post*, May 1, 1960.

"Challenging the Giants," *Newsweek*, December 23, 1957.

"Channel Chat," *Philadelphia Bulletin*, March 3, 1958.

"Charge Big Payoffs to Disc Jockeys," *New York Herald-Tribune*, November 21, 1959.

"Clark Blames Game Show Lemon On Calif. Where 'Everybody's a Hambone," *Variety*, June 3, 1964.

"Clark Grateful to Friends And Network for Support," *Philadelphia Bulletin*, November 13, 1959.

"Clark Takes Promoter off Hook in Mpls. Flop," *Variety*, September 10, 1958.

"Clark's *World of Talent* Will Be Dropped by ABC," *Philadelphia Bulletin*, November 26, 1959.

Clavin, Thomas, "Riding the High Waves of the Rock-and-Roll Crest," *New York Times*, Long Island Section, December 12, 1993.

"A Closed Hearing Is Held on Clark; Payola Inquiry Goes Into Disc Jockeys Business Ties —Alan Freed Testifies," *New York Times*, April 26, 1960.

Crosby, Joan, "Meet Dick Clark: He Thinks His Show Can Run 30 Years," *Philadelphia Daily News*, August 17, 1962.

Damsker, Matt, "Dick Clark Is Still Alive, Visible," *Philadelphia Bulletin*, June 16, 1976.

Darrach, Brad, "It's Not Just Another Pretty Face, It's Showbiz Conglomorate King Dick Clark," *People*, February 14, 1977.

"Dated Horn At 13, Girl Says," *Philadelphia Bulletin*, January 28, 1957.

Davidson, Bill, "Fabian," *Redbook*, March 1960.

Dawson, Jim, "The Twist by Hank Ballard and the Midnighters," *DISCoveries*, June, 1994.

"Dick (*Bandstand*) Clark moves into the prime time . . . " (TV column), *New York Post*, November 27, 1973.

"Dick Clark a Constant in Changing World," *Chicago Sun-Times*, March 27, 1989.

"Dick Clark and Wife Are Getting a Divorce," *Philadelphia Bulletin*, May 17, 1961.

"Dick Clark Bows To ABC, to Drop Side Businesses," *Philadelphia Bulletin*, November 17, 1959.

"Dick Clark Ends 10-Yr. Cross-the-Board Run; Doing Sat. Hour Only," *Variety*, June 12, 1963.

"Dick Clark Gets a Good Rating," *New York Herald-Tribune*, February 18, 1958.

"Dick Clark Had Interest in 17 Music Companies," *Philadelphia Bulletin*, March 4, 1960.

"Dick Clark Leaving *Bandstand*," *Philadelphia Daily News*, March 22, 1989.

"Dick Clark letting public in on his act," *NYP*, November 14, 1986.

"Dick Clark Pays $1 Million for Divorce," *The National Tattler*, January 19, 1975.

"Dick Clark Plans Offering," *NYT*, November 6, 1986.

"Dick Clark Plans Oldies Club," *Philadelphia Journal*, July 21, 1972.

"Dick Clark Recalls *Where the Action Is*," *Goldmine*, April 20, 1990.

"Dick Clark Says Juvenile Adults Caused Riot at His Show in K.C.," *New York Post*, October 21, 1959.

"The Dick Clark Show," *Variety*, February 19, 1958.

"Dick Clark Strikes It Rich on Coast," *Variety*, January 12, 1966.

"Dick Clark Troupe Pulls 29G in H'wood," *Variety*, September 3, 1958.

"Dick Clark Whitewashed? Just Wait & See, Say Mack and Moss; Committee 'Won't Be Stampeded,'" *Variety*, March 23, 1960.

"Dick Clark, who's been an impresario of rock music shows. . . ," *New York Post* television column, July 20, 1972.

"Dick Clark's 'Eve' Show And 'Pop' for *Bandstand*," *Variety*, November 11, 1958.

"Dick Clark's Fans Shocked By News of Divorce Plans," *Philadelphia Bulletin*, May 18, 1961.

"Dick Clark's 'Formula' for Teen Appeal," *New York Herald-Tribune/Journal-American*, April 5, 1958.

"Dick Clark's Live Wednesday," *Variety*, September 27, 1978.

"Dick Clark's Music Ties First Casualty of ABC-TV's Sensitivity to 'Payola,'" *Variety*, November 18, 1959.

"Dick Clark's Philly Production Centre," *Variety*, August 16, 1961.

Diehl, Digby, "The Oldest Living Teen-Ager," *TV Guide*, February 14, 1970.

"Disc Jockey Move to Video Is Still a Long Hard Trip," *Billboard*, November 13, 1954.

Dove, Ian, "Yes, Rock Has Lasted; So Has Dick Clark," *New York Times*, June 1, 1973.

DuBrow, Rick, "Dick Clark, Film Star, Prefers Philadelphia," *Philadelphia Bulletin*, August 27, 1961.

"Folds In Mpls.," *Variety*, September 3, 1958.

Fong-Torres, Ben, "Dick Clark: Twenty Years of Clearasil Rock," *Rolling Stone*, August 16, 1973.

"For Teenagers It's a Heaven and Haven," *TV Digest*, March 29, 1952.

"*Forbes 400* Richest People in America," *Forbes*, October 16, 1995.

Forkan, Jim, "Dick Clark Superstar," *Our Town* (N.Y.), September 8, 1972.

"Four-Day Trial of Horn Ends in Hung Jury," *Philadelphia Bulletin*, February 1, 1957.

Gardella, Kay, "*Bandstand* Emcee Tries Out Nighttime Spot," *New York Daily News*, February 11, 1958.

Gardner, Hy, "Hy Gardner's Typewriter X-Rays Dick Clark," *New York Herald-Tribune Magazine*, October 5, 1958.

Gelber, Carol, "8,000 Fans Greet Fabian at Theatre for Premiere," *Philadelphia Bulletin*, November 12, 1959.

Godbout, Oscar, "Nat Cole Scores Ad Men on Ouster," *New York Times*, November 22, 1957.

Gollander, Walt, "The Three Chuckles," *Record Exchanger*, February 1973.

Goodwin, Robert, "Horn's Wife, Son Testify for Him," *Philadelphia Daily News*, January 31, 1957.

Gray, Tom, "A Producer Who Promotes His Pictures in Advance," *Motion Picture Herald*, October 9, 1968.

"Great Break for Young Dick Clark" (TV column), *Philadelphia Daily News*, July 23, 1957.

Greenberg, Nikki Finke & Gelman, Eric, "Clark Around the Clock," *Newsweek*, August 18, 1986.

Greene, Gael, "Dick Clark" (six-part series), *New York Post*, September 22–26, 28, 1958.

Grevatt, Ren, "On the Beat" (column), *Billboard*, March 3, 1958.

"Guilty Only of Success," *TV Guide*, September 10–16, 1960.

Hackett, Pat, "Dick Clark" (Interview), *Interview*, February, 1986.

Harris, Harry, "Around the Dials: *Bandstand*—Disc Jockey Formula for TV," *Philadelphia Bulletin*, January 16, 1953.

———. "*Bandstand* Bows Today on Network," *Philadelphia Inquirer*, August 5, 1957.

———. "*Bandstand* Celebrates First Birthday," *Philadelphia Bulletin*, October 12, 1953.

———. "*Bandstand* Special Tops All, Clark Says," *Philadelphia Inquirer*, February 2, 1977.

———. "WFIL's *Bandstand* Goes National—Not Without Some Strain," *Philadelphia Inquirer*, August 6, 1957.

Harris, John, "Clark Breakup Stirs Rumors and Mystery," *New York Herald-Tribune*, May 19, 1961.

Hendricks, Alfred T. & Carr, William H.A. "Check of Record Firm Indicates Dick Clark Still Has Holdings," *New York Post*, December 16, 1959.

Hershey, Edward, "An Ex-Bopper Looks Back At 20 Years of Apple Pie," *Newsday* (Long Island), July 12, 1973.

Horn, John, "New Game Shows, Worse Than Most," *New York Herald-Tribune*, December 31, 1963.

"Horn Accuser Called False," *Philadelphia Bulletin*, January 29, 1957.

"Horn Acquitted In Morals Case," *Philadelphia Bulletin*, June 26, 1957.

"Horn Admits Tax Evasion," *Philadelphia Bulletin*, September 22, 1958.

"Horn and Girl Both Cry Lie," *Philadelphia Bulletin*, January 31, 1957.

"Horn Denies Girl's Charges," *Philadelphia Bulletin*, June 25, 1957.

"Horn Denies Girl's Story," *Philadelphia Bulletin*, January 29, 1957.

"House Group Amassing File On TV, Radio 'Payola' Here," *Philadelphia Bulletin*, November 19, 1959.

"House Probers, FTC in Hot Race for Clark's Data," *Variety*, January 27, 1960.

Howard, Edwin, "He's Made $2 Million on Discs — Without a Desk," *Memphis Press-Scimitar*, April 29, 1959.

Humphrey, Hal, "Do Viewers Benefit From the TV Probes?," *Philadelphia Bulletin*, August 29, 1961.

James, Noah, "We Do What the Networks Want," *New York Times*, July 14, 1985.

Jancik, Wayne, "Down the Aisle With the Quin-Tones," *Goldmine*, December 28, 1990.

———. "Fabian: The Teen Idol at 47," *Goldmine*, December 28, 1990.

———. "Chubby Checker: Twistin' Time Is [Still] Here," *Goldmine*, December 28, 1990.

———. "Gerry Granahan," *Goldmine* No. 272, December 28, 1990.

Jones, Wayne, "Freddie Cannon . . . Still Where The Action Is," *Goldmine* No. 42, November 1979.

Kahn, Stephen, "Philadelphia's Pied Piper" (five-part series), *Philadelphia Daily News*, April 14–18, 1958.

La Croix, Harry, J., "Cameo Grows Rapidly By Setting It's Sights On Teen-Age Market," *Philadelphia Inquirer*, November 11, 1963.

Ladd, Bill, "Teen-Agers' Understanding Big Brother — That's Key to Dick Clark's Success," *Louisville (Ky.) Courier-Journal*, April 12, 1959.

Lenzner, Robert & Matzer, Marla, "Late Bloomer," *Forbes*, October 17, 1994.

"Lesson for Youth," *Philadelphia Bulletin*, October 20, 1959.

Lewis, Anthony, "Dick Clark Denies Receiving Payola; Panel Skeptical," *New York Times*, April 30, 1960.

Mabry, Donald J., "The Rise and Fall of Ace Records: A Case Study in the Independent Record Business," *Business History Review*. Boston: Harvard Business School, Autumn 1990.

Marter, Marilyn, "Whatever Happened to All Those Kids on *Bandstand*?" *Philadelphia Inquirer*, November 20, 1972.

Matza, Michael, "The *Bandstand* Beat Goes On," *Philadelphia Inquirer Magazine*, May 26, 1989.

McGrory, Mary, "Weighty Evidence," *New York Post*, April 27, 1960.

Mead, Mimi, "Clark Building Vast Empire," *Philadelphia Inquirer*, June 2, 1966.

Meisler, Andy, "For *Soul Train*'s Conductor, Beat Goes On," *New York Times*, August 7, 1995.

Miller, Holly, G, "Dick Clark's Role After Rock, " *The Saturday Evening Post*, August 1995.

"Mr. Clark and Colored Payola," *New York Age*, December 5, 1959.

Morris, David, "A Historic Designation for Home of *Bandstand*," *Philadelphia Inquirer*, August 30, 1986.

"Music Business Goes Round and Round: It Comes Out Clarkola," *Life*, May 16, 1960.

Naedele, Walter F., "Two J. Browns in Movies? Clark Says There's Room," *Philadelphia Bulletin*, June 15, 1969.

Nelson, Nels, "King of the Teenagers Goes After Pre-Geriatric Set," *Philadelphia Daily News*, May 22, 1968.

"New TV Seg For Clark," *Variety*, November 25, 1957.

"Nobody Blew the Whistle," *Newsweek*, May 9, 1960.

"Not Beached," *Variety*, January 27, 1960.

O'Brian, Jack, "Clark Show: Teen Age Mess," *New York Journal-American*, February 17, 1958.

O'Connor, John J, TV column, *New York Times*, May 12, 1992.

———. "TV: Dick Clark's Originality Enhances Pop Music," *New York Times*, July 17, 1973.

O'Haire, Patricia, "Mr. *Bandstand*," *New York Daily News*, May 21, 1989.

"$172,469,000 Peak for ABC in 1959," *Variety*, April 6, 1960.

Osborne, Jerry, "Connie Francis" (interview), *DISCoveries*, September 1991.

Pareles, Jon, "Thanks, Reminiscenses And Tunes, Lots of Tunes," *New York Times*, March 2, 1996.

Pauly, David, "Big Media, Big Money," *Newsweek*, April 1, 1985.

"The Payola Rock" (editorial), *Philadelphia Bulletin*, April 19, 1958.

Peck, Abe, "The Oldest Living Teenager: Dick Clark Recalls the '50s," *Philadelphia Inquirer*, December 26, 1976.

Petrucelli, Alan W., "Author-Ized," *Us*, March 3, 1981.

"Philly Disk Jock Falls Victim to His Sheet's Drive," *Variety*, August 15, 1956.

"Pied Piper of Teen-Age Set," *TV Guide*, May 24–30, 1958.

Polier, Rex, "Apple Couldn't Cancel 'Beatles' Special," *Philadelphia Bulletin*, November 23, 1979.

———. "Dick Clark and His 'Kids' Go Bigtime," *Philadelphia Bulletin*, August 4, 1957.

———. "If I Fail I Get the Gong," *Philadelphia Bulletin*, September 3, 1978.

———. "In Sentiment, at Least, a Native Philadelphian," *Philadelphia Bulletin*, October 29, 1981.

———. "Teen-Agers Outpull Name Guests on *Bandstand*," *Philadelphia Bulletin*, July 17, 1955.

———. "Town's Teenagers Go for Jitterbug on TV," *Philadelphia Bulletin*, March 29, 1953.

Pond, Steve, "Dick Clark's Last Stand," *Rolling Stone*, May 18, 1989.

"Probe Accuses Steve Allison And Bob Horn," *Philadelphia Bulletin*, October 24, 1956.

"Prober Says Dick Clark Admits Gifts of Jewelry," *Camden* [N.J.] *Post*, March 10, 1960.

Rea, Steven, "Dick Clark's Own Story of *American Bandstand*," *Philadelphia Inquirer*, November 7, 1985.

"Remember Bob Horn?," *Philadelphia Bulletin*, October 30, 1973.

Rolontz, Bob, "The Philadelphia Story: Part II," *Billboard*, March 24, 1958.

Sachs, Lloyd, "'You're Jealous,' Dick Clark Tells His Detractors," *Philadelphia Bulletin*, June 28, 1978.

Schier, Ernie, "'Because They're Young' Stars 'Teacher' Dick Clark," *Philadelphia Bulletin*, April 18, 1960.

Schipper, Henry, "Dick Clark" (interview), *Rolling Stone*, April 19, 1990.

Schoenfeld, Herm, "Biz Ventures (Show & Otherwise) Put Dick Clark Right Back on Top," *Variety*, February 6, 1963.

"75 Teen-Agers Jailed For Rock 'n' Roll Riot," *Louisville Courier-Journal*, October 19, 1959.

Shanley, J.P., "Television" (column), *America*, February 14, 1959.

———. "TV Teen-Agers Only," *New York Times*, August 6, 1957.

Shanley, John P., "Dick Clark—New Rage of the Teenage Set," *New York Times*, March 16, 1958.

Shister, Gail, "The Ageless Prince of Frivolity," *Philadelphia Inquirer Magazine*, November 18, 1984.

Slewinski, Christy, "Dick Clark Is Having a Ball for the 24th Year," *St. Petersburg Times*, December 31, 1995.

Stewart, Lee, "Horn Denies Girl's Charges In Phila. Trial," *Camden* [N.J.] *Courier Post*, January 30, 1957.

"Tall, That's All," *Time*, April 14, 1958.

Tamarkin, Jeff, "Dick Clark's Best of *Bandstand*" (review), *Goldmine*, August 15, 1986.

———. "The Beat Goes On" (Dick Clark interview), *Goldmine*, December 28, 1990.

"Tank Town Talk," *Philadelphia Daily News*, January 9, 1962.

"Teen-Age Music Due To Go Farther Out, Predicts Clark," *Louisville Courier-Journal*, October 8, 1967.

"The $10,000 Pyramid" (review), *Variety*, April 11, 1973.

Terry, Wallace, "Am I Embarrassed?" *Parade*, September 22, 1991.

"The New ABC of It," *Newsweek*, December 10, 1956.

"They're Having a Ball," *TV Guide*, September 28, 1957.

"3 Schools Integrate: Districts Near Philadelphia End Segregation," *New York Times*, September 10, 1957.

Torre, Marie, "Dick Clark Gets Raise in 'Vote of Confidence,'" *New York Herald-Tribune*, March 28, 1960.

———. "Dick Clark Wants to Put Payola Furor to Rest," *New York Herald-Tribune*, June 7, 1960.

"Toughest Season in Ten Years," *New York Times*, July 25, 1957.

"Turkish Tycoons: The Erteguns," *Time*, July 28, 1967.

"TV Jock Finally Comes Into Own," *Variety*, October 7, 1957.

"TV Show Helped Found an Empire," *Newark* [N.J.] *Evening News*, August 6, 1967.

"Two Down and Eons To Go," *TV Guide* (Philadelphia edition), October 9, 1954.

"UA Extends Dick Clark," *Variety*, April 13, 1960.

"U.S. Indicts Bob Horn," *Philadelphia Bulletin*, April 17, 1958.

Van Horne, Harriet, "R 'n' R Apostle a Proper Fellow," *New York World-Telegram*, June 14, 1959.

Weart, William G., "Crowds Banned in Levittown, PA.," *New York Times*, August 22, 1957.

"Whatever it is . . . He's got it," *TV Guide*, October 4–10, 1958.

"Wider TV Inquiry to Study Bribery & Paid Plugs," *New York Times*, November 7, 1959.

Williams, Bob, "Dick Clark, who dates back on TV. . . ." (TV column), *New York Post*, August 19, 1974.

———. "Dick Clark's *Bandstand* Turns City Into Teeners' Mecca," *Philadelphia Bulletin*, July 20, 1958.

———. "Prober Brands Dick Clark 'Top Dog In Payola Field,'" *Philadelphia Bulletin*, May 3, 1960.
Williams, Edgar, "New Home for WFIL," *Philadelphia Inquirer Sunday Magazine*, December 15, 1963.
Wilson, Earl, "Alan Freed's Story," *New York Post*, November 23, 1959.
Wise, David, "Charge Big Payoffs to Disc Jockeys," *New York Herald-Tribune*, November 21, 1959.
"Vice Ring Depravities Bared by Wiretapping," *Philadelphia Inquirer*, December 13, 1956.
"Youth Stabbed in Teenage Fight After Dick Clark's Sunnybrook Hop," *Philadelphia Sunday Bulletin*, December 28, 1958.

Television and Radio Programs; Documentary Films

The Best of American Bandstand, Dick Clark & Paul Brownstein, co-executive producers; Jeffrey Panzer, producer, Dick Clark Productions, Inc., Viacom VH-1, 1996.
Dancing; Part 3: New Worlds, Rhoda Graver, executive producer. A production of Channel Thirteen/WNET (New York) in association with RM Arts and BBC-TV, 1993.
"Dick Clark's Best of *Bandstand*" (videocassette), Dick Clark Television Productions/Vestron Music Video, 1986.
Ralph Emery interview with Dick Clark, The Nashville Network, June 22, 1992.
Al Roker interview with Dick Clark, *The Al Roker Show*, CNBC, October 29, 1995.
Twist, a Triton Pictures release, produced and directed by Ron Mann, 1993.

Interviews (All conducted by John A. Jackson.)

Andrews, Lee [Lee Andrews & the Hearts]. July 7, 1993.
Appell, Dave. January 20, 1994.
Baker, Lavern. June 27, 1992.
Beaumont, Jimmy [Skyliners]. June 27, 1992.
Blavat, Jerry. September 2, 1992.
Boyd, "Little Eva." June 27, 1992.
Bucceroni, Emil. October 1993.
Chalfin, Paul M. October 15, 1993.
Christie, Lou. July 19, 1993.
Clark, Dick. September 22, 1994.
Collins, Clarence [Little Anthony & the Imperials]. February 12, 1993.
Davison, Peggy Santiglia [Delicates/Angels]. July 18, 1993.
Dunn, James [Dreamlovers]. February 23, 1994.
Dunn, Clifford [Dreamlovers]. February 23, 1994.
Eddy, Duane. March 19, 1994.
Fetter, Theodore (Ted). April 26, 1994.
Ford, Frankie. August 15, 1992.
Frazier, Joe "Speedo" [Impalas]. June 27, 1992.
Gourdine, Anthony [Little Anthony & the Imperials]. February 12, 1993.
Gracie, Charlie. November 10, 1992.
Harris, Steve. September 28, 1993.
Holman, Eddie. September 15, 1994.
Hooke, Jack. July 8, 1993.
Hurst, Ed. November 17, 1994.

Lewis, Rick [Silhouettes]. June 28, 1993.

Lit, Hy. September 1, 1992.

McDermott, Thomas. October 15, 1993.

MacDougal, Weldon [Larks]. July 27, 28, 1993.

Maestro, Johnny [Crests/Brooklyn Bridge]. February 23, 1994.

Mammarella, Agnes. November 18, 1992.

Mann, Kal. January 30, 1993.

Marcucci, Bob. February 25, 1994.

Martinelli, Ernie. March 30, 1993.

Miller, Hal [Rays]. January 24, 1994.

Nahan, Irv. July 13, 1993.

Palmieri, John. February 25, 1994.

Paris, Fred [Five Satins]. June 27, 1992.

Peterson, Ray. August 15, 1992.

Picone, Vito [Elegants]. August 4, 1993.

Randazzo, Teddy [Three Chuckles]. January 25, 1994.

Ross, Irv. September 28, 1993.

Ross, Jerry. December 11, 1993.

Rydell, Bobby. April 22, 1993.

Shively, Val. July 13, 1993.

Silver, Lee. February 25 & 26, 1994.

Singer, Artie. July 13, 1993.

Sirico, Jiggs [Angels]. September 29, 1993.

Slay, Frank. December 14, 1992.

Steck, Jack. January 27, 1993.

Stone, Joseph. September 25 & 29, 1979, March 8, 1980.

Terranova, Joe [Danny & the Juniors]. November 23, 1992.

Testa, Jim [Four J's/Fabulous Four]. March 1, 1994.

Thayer, Jack. November 12, 1994.

Wright, Ernest [Little Anthony & the Imperials]. February 12, 1993.

Zacherle, John. March 29, 1993.

Miscellaneous Items

"Age No Barrier to *Bandstand* Beat," ABC-TV *Feature* release, October 17, 1957. Billy Rose Collection, Lincoln Center, New York Public Library.

Bolstad, Helen, "The Real Dick Clark," manuscript written for *Pines Publications*, June 20, 1958. Billy Rose Collection, Lincoln Center, New York Public Library.

———. "Why Do Teens Trust Dick Clark?," manuscript written for *Photoplay*, March 16, 1958. Billy Rose Collection, Lincoln Center, New York Public Library.

"Dick Clark," ABC-TV news release biography sheet, June, 1960. Billy Rose Collection, Lincoln Center, New York Public Library.

Everett, Todd, "Lloyd Price," Liner notes to MCA compact disc, *Lloyd Price: Greatest Hits* (MCAD–11184), 1994.

"Good News For Eardrums: Dick Clark Says Music is Coming Back," ABC news release *Feature*, March 5, 1969. Billy Rose Collection, Lincoln Center, New York Public Library.

The Jamie/Guyden Story (Liner notes to compact disc), Bear Family BCD 15874–BH, 1995.

Index

ABC. *See* American Broadcasting Company
ABC-Paramount Records. *See* American
    Broadcasting Company, Am-Par Records
ABC-TV. *See* American Broadcasting Company,
    ABC-TV
Academy of Country Music Awards (TV program).
    See Clark, Dick, and video production
Ace Records, 146–48, 305n.6
Action '74 (TV program). *See* Clark, Dick, video
    production
All-New All-Star TV Censored Bloopers: Unplugged
    (TV program). See Clark, Dick, and video
    production
Altieri, Anne Polidere, 261
American Bandstand (TV program), x, 9, 125, 152,
    153, 159, 164, 165, 189, 277, 301n.15,
    303n.26, 305n.2. *See also* American
    Broadcasting Company, creates *American*
    Bandstand; *American Bandstand* timeline,
    Appendix I; *Best of American Bandstand*;
    Clark, Dick, as *American Bandstand* host;
    Teenagers: on *American Bandstand*, as
    American Bandstand viewers
    airtime, 65, 104, 223, 225, 278
    anniversary specials, reunions, 261, 262, 267,
        275, 276, 282, 285
    and artist performance fee kickbacks, xi, 85, 86,
        151, 274
    awards received, 274–76
    as benefit to ABC, x, 59, 67–69, 73, 74, 103,
        131, 142, 143, 306n.15
    and blacks, xii, 56–58, 83, 84, 140–43, 208–10,
        212, 213, 231, 242–44, 248, 249, 253, 257,
        258, 265, 269, 272, 284, 300n.1, 304n.19
    created by ABC, x, xii, 51–56, 60, 61, 63–68,
        73, 74, 85, 97
    and dance, ix, 19, 26, 55, 65, 66, 69, 71, 73, 99,
        103, 126, 151, 207–19, 221, 222, 224, 231,

    243, 245, 248, 249, 254, 256, 258, 259, 264,
    265, 269–73, 282
    decline of, xi, xii, 207, 220, 221, 223–29, 232,
        233, 236–38, 241, 242, 244–47, 250, 251,
        254–57, 260, 264, 265, 273–81, 283, 285
    dress code, 261, 271
    as flagship of Clark's business empire, 221, 250,
        268, 276
    influences fads, fashion and trends, 71, 72, 241,
        242, 283, 284
    and Italian-Americans, 26, 71
    media criticism of, 59, 66, 107, 108, 261, 282,
        284
    Monday night edition, 103, 104, 108
    jeopardized by payola, 55, 156–58, 161–63,
        168, 171, 172, 174, 176–78, 180–88
    popularity of, 66–69, 73, 74, 103, 104, 126, 131,
        142, 146, 147, 173, 194, 196, 198, 199,
        206–8, 233, 247, 261, 264, 269, 279,
        302n.16
    and "regulars," 69–73, 197, 220, 261, 262
    rights acquired by Dick Clark, 231, 232, 250
    as rock 'n' roll promotional venue, xi, 43, 63, 64,
        74–84, 89, 91–102, 106–8, 111–21,
        128–36, 138, 139, 142–52, 193, 198, 199,
        210–19, 221–23, 226, 232, 235, 238–49,
        259, 263, 265, 266, 272, 279, 280, 283,
        300n.37, 301n.15, 301n.25, 302n.11,
        302n.27, 304n.9, 305n.2
    sponsors, 66, 74, 195
American Bandstand Grills. *See* Clark, Dick, and
    businesses, other
American Bandstand '70 (TV program). *See* Clark,
    Dick, and video production
American Bandstand's No. One Hits (TV program).
    See Clark, Dick, and video production
American Broadcasting Company (ABC), 4, 48,
    76, 91, 140, 141, 143, 195, 200, 208, 221,

CPSIA information can be obtained at www.ICGtesting.com
Printed in the USA
LVOW071514190412

278337LV00003B/56/P